Postmodern Urbanism

To Tad

Postmodern Urbanism

revised edition

Nan Ellin

PRINCETON ARCHITECTURAL PRESS · NEW YORK

Princeton Architectural Press
37 East 7th Street
New York, NY 10003
212.995.9620

For a free catalog of other books published by Princeton Architectural Press,
call toll free 1.800.722.6657 or visit our web site at www.papress.com

First published in 1996 by Blackwell Publishers Inc., Cambridge, Massachusetts,
a division of Blackwell Publishers Ltd, Oxford, UK

03 02 01 00 99   5 4 3 2 1   Revised edition

Editing: Jan Cigliano
Cover design: Therese Kelly
Book design: Therese Kelly and Brian Noyes
Special thanks: Eugenia Bell, Jane Garvie, Caroline Green, Clare Jacobson,
Mark Lamster, Anne Nitschke, and Sara E. Stemen of Princeton Architectural Press
—Kevin C. Lippert, *publisher*

Library of Congress Cataloging-in-Publication Data
Ellin, Nan, 1959–
        Postmodern urbanism / by Nan Ellin.
            p. cm.
        Includes bibliographical references and index.
        ISBN 1-56898-135-X (alk. paper)
    1. City planning—History—20th century—Themes, motives.
    2. Architecture and society—History—20th century.
    3. Architecture, Postmodern.   I. Title.
NA 9095.E45   1999
711'. 4'09045—dc21   95-867
                                                            CIP

Photo Credits
Cover: Nancy Wolf, "Implosion," 1994; gouache and colored pencil on paper. Collection of
Sallie Mae, Student Loan Marketing Association. Photo by Tony Holmes
9: Deborah Berke
87: SWA Group
131: *Good Housekeeping*
150: P.C. Vey, by R. Bernstein, *New York Times*, April 8, 1990
All others: Nan Ellin

CONTENTS

Acknowledgments | vii
Foreword to the Revised Edition | 1

1 THE ROMANTIC RESURGENCE | 13

2 URBAN DESIGN THEORY ON THE EUROPEAN CONTINENT | 22
Neorationalism
Neoclassicism
Open Architecture
The French Version
Architectural Exhibitions

3 URBAN DESIGN THEORY: THE ANGLO-AMERICAN AXIS | 60
The Townscape Movement
Advocacy Planning, Community Participation,
    Environmentalism, and Feminism
Regionalism and Vernacular Design
Venturi and Contextualism
Historical Eclecticism
Historic Preservation and Gentrification
Critical Regionalism
Master-Planned Communities, Gated Communities, and
    Defensive Urbanism
Neotraditional Urbanism, or The New Urbanism
Edge Cities
Postmodern Architecture vis-à-vis Urban Design

4 THE POSTMODERN REFLEX | 124
The Challenge to Modernity and the Growth in Privatism
The Postmodern Temper
The Ironic Response
The New Sensibility

5 THEMES OF POSTMODERN URBANISM | 154
Form Follows Fiction
Form Follows Fear
Form Follows Finesse
Form Follows Finance
The Result
On Balance

6 THE MODERN PROJECT: CONTINUED OR ABANDONED? | 205
Supporters and Detractors
Significance for Urban Design
Prescriptions

7 CRISIS IN THE ARCHITECTURAL PROFESSION | 234
Contours of the Crisis
Manifestation of the Crisis: The Gap
Postmodern Urbanism as Response to the Crisis
Opportunities for the Architectural Profession

8 RECONCEIVING THE CITY AND CULTURE | 267
Metaphors for the City and Culture
Reconceiving the City
Reconceiving Culture
Studying the City and Culture
New Metaphors: Text and Collage
Conclusion: Beyond Irony and Artifice

Appendix A   The Pendular Swing | 297
Appendix B   Timeline of Postmodern Urbanism | 308

References | 335

Index | 380

ACKNOWLEDGMENTS

FOR FUNDING THIS PROJECT, I gratefully acknowledge the Fulbright Commission, the French Cultural Embassy (Bourse Chateaubriand), the Alliance Française, and the French Ministère de l'Equipment, du Logement, de l'Aménagement du Territoire et des Transports (MELATT). Much of the research for this book was undertaken in France. For graciously hosting me there, I thank Nicole and Antoine Haumont, Françoise Choay, Pierre Guinchat, Philippe Robert, Yves Bories, Dominique Ducamp, Bertrand Warnier, Ruth Marquèz, Danièlle Valabrègue, Mai Huynh, the Klein family of Vauréal, and the St Léger family of Jouy-le-Moutier.

I also wish to thank my professors and colleagues at Bryn Mawr College, Columbia University, New York University, the University of Southern California, the Southern California Institute of Architecture, the University of Cincinnati, and Arizona State University, especially Judith Shapiro, Daniel Walkowitz, Madeleine Holzer, Magali Sarfatti Larson, Barbara Danish, Richard Sennett, Peter Marcuse, Saskia Sassen, Richard Plunz, Mary McLeod, Barry Bergdoll, Kenneth T. Jackson, Zeynep Celik, Kevin Starr, Elyse Grinstein, Margaret Crawford, Michael Rotondi, Brenda Scheer, Udo Greinacher, Lucille Schultz, Jay Chatterjee, Mary B. Reilly, Ron McCoy, John Meunier, Mary Kihl, Leslie Van Duzer, Renata Hejduk, Darren Petrucci, Catherine Spellman, Ellen Soroka, Fritz Steiner, Charles Dellheim, and the late George Collins. For sharing personal insights into this historical moment with me, I am very grateful to Anthony Vidler, David Harvey, and Charles Jencks. And for technical assistance, I would like to express my appreciation to Lester Cohen of Baltimore, Bill Kasson of the Herberger Center for Design Excellence (ASU), and Sebnem Yucel.

Nancy Wolf, whose artwork graces the cover of this new edition, provides a rare synthesis of art and urban/social commentary. I am grateful to her for this inspired work and to Karen Franck for bringing it to a larger public in her monograph on Wolf entitled *Hidden Cities, Hidden Longings* (Academy Editions).

I am indebted to the editor of the first edition, John Davey at Blackwell Publishers, for his encouragement of this undertaking from its inception and for his always thoughtful and constructive commentary. At Princeton Architectural Press, I extend my gratitude to Kevin Lippert for his vision and conviction; to Clare Jacobson for her expertise, humor, and good grace; and to Therese Kelly and Jan Cigliano for applying their fine eyes to detail without ever losing sight of the big picture.

I have been blessed with the love and support of my parents Carole and Morton Ellin as well as Jean and Ed Ballew, without whom this book would not have been possible. To Tad, I still dedicate this book from the bottom of my heart. And I remain ever so thankful for our precious daughter Theodora, whose soulful smile and zest for life continue to light up each day.

FOREWORD TO THE REVISED EDITION:
BEYOND POSTMODERN URBANISM

THIS REVISED EDITION is newly designed with more illustrations and an updated Timeline and References. I have otherwise retained the original text, allowing it to remain a document of its particular time and place, and resisting the temptation to continue chronicling urban design theory or to adjust or buttress my arguments.

I write this foreword to the new edition with a renewed sense of optimism, albeit guarded. It is guarded because most of the sub-optimal trends I describe in the book still abide. It is optimistic, however, because a very dim ray of hope has begun to pierce the cloud cover, thanks to a broadly based exploration of alternatives.

The end of the period covered in this book, about 1990, marked a threshold into a territory that, while vaguely familiar, has never been occupied in quite the same way before. The predominant urban design reflexes of the 1970s and 1980s, including historicism, regionalism, theme-ing, and defensive urbanism, attempted to satisfy longings for community and security on the one hand, and for intrigue and adventure on the other, all of which were found sorely lacking in modern urbanism. Although postmodern urbanism offered certain correctives in this regard, it failed to satisfy these persistent longings sufficiently, and in many instances, deeply intensified them (see end of chapter 5).

The failure of postmodern urbanism has led to a reconsideration of design values, goals, and the means for achieving these goals. Instead of responding reactively to rapid change through escapist and distilling strategies, there have been efforts to embrace, steward, or partner (rather than control or manage) it.

More is not necessarily more we have come to realize, because the bombardment of our senses produces a natural defense mechanism which Georg Simmel described as the blasé attitude in his classic 1902 article on urban life in Berlin. As urbanization has proceeded apace over the last century, so has the extent to which we are "rendered indifferent due to the abuse that we sustain" (the definition of blasé) to the point where change is occurring at the expense of our psyches, our environment, and our communities. The pursuant challenges posed to the separation between body and soul, between people and nature, and amongst peoples have led to a search for restoring connections. While the actual goals of this search vary widely, the path followed can be characterized more uniformly as one of slowness, simplicity, sincerity, and spirituality.

In a recent discussion about the impact of rapid change entitled "Fast Forward," Mark Kingwell contends that the "sensory overload of speed leads necessarily to saturation, to senselessness." Rather than erect our defensive walls ever higher, however, Kingwell detects "an underground of . . . resistance in the culture, a theme of sundial slowness set against the overarching digital quickness of life" (44). Along with sundial slowness is an effort to simplify our lives, manifest in what has been dubbed the "simplicity movement" which crosses lines of ethnicity and social class.[i] If the sixties witnessed the "We generation" emphasizing peace and love, the seventies the "Me generation" emphasizing self-awareness and self-actualization, the eighties the "Whee generation" emphasizing materialism and escapism, then perhaps the nineties will be remembered as the "Whoa generation" placing a self-imposed brake upon the rapid changes which are wreaking havoc on our landscapes and our well-being.

Along with the appeals of slowness and simplicity, there has also been a return to sincerity. A similar shift occurred in Europe around the time of the French Revolution, when "a younger generation tired of the artificiality of the older and sought to substitute an authenticity for the artifice" (Nilsen).[ii] This pendulum swung back during the early part of this century when a new younger generation tired of directness and Victorian sentimentality. The result was modern forms of cultural expression that were self-referential (about their own processes of making) and explored multi-perspectival and defamiliarizing techniques. This was followed by postmodern forms of cultural expression where irony declined into mere cleverness and style overtook substance, prompting the current return to sincerity.[iii]

Bereft by supreme skepticism, and in search of something to believe in, we have also turned to angels, UFOs, paranormal phenomena, and cyberspace. Finally, we have been reconsidering our wisdom traditions, igniting an extraordinary resurgence in spirituality throughout the contemporary world.

This shift is apparent in the emerging metaphors for the city and culture (the subject of chapter 8). In retrospect, the postmodern metaphor of *collage* is a catch-all grab bag suggesting inclusivity and perhaps a certain unpredictable beauty, but also an element of hazard, confusion, disjuncture, and lack of sense. The other predominant metaphor for the city and culture during the same period—that of the *text*—allows for an infinite number of perspectives or "readings" of urban and cultural experiences. It may be understood as an effort to impose an order on apparent chaos, or alternatively, as an occupational hazard of scholars for whom the text is their stock in trade. The collage and text metaphors, which supplanted the predominant modern metaphor of the machine (beginning in the late nineteenth century), are now in turn being supplanted by other metaphors, indicative of current understandings of the city and culture.

Like the collage and text, these emerging metaphors also suggest an inclusivity. But this time, it is no longer for the sake of inclusivity itself. Rather, there is attention paid towards whole ness, a more calculated beauty, a smoothness, a lightness (lack of heaviness), and a strong sense of connectedness. In this spirit, these emerging metaphors are also more than metaphors, carrying literal and place-derived meanings as well.

The most overarching of the current metaphors is *ecology*. In the words of Sim Van der Ryn and Stuart Cowan, "It is time to stop designing in the image of the machine and start designing in a way that honors the complexity of life itself . . . we must mirror nature's deep interconnections in our own epistemology of design" (1996).[iv] Likewise, ecology has become a model for understanding culture, as anthropologists and cultural theorists are increasingly regarding culture as a part of nature rather than in opposition to it. Cultural theorist Catherine Roach, for example, argues "against the idea that nature and culture are

dualistic and opposing concepts," suggesting that this idea is "environmentally unsound and [needs] to be biodegraded, or rendered less
harmful to the environment" (1996, 53). While these understandings of
connected-ness have many precedents, there is something qualitatively
different this time around in the emphasis on change as a constant and
on the reconfiguration of space and time due to digitalization.

Other prevalent metaphors for city and culture are the *border* and the
edge. Current buzz-phrases among anthropologists, cultural theorists,
architects, and urban planners include border cultures, borderlands, edge
conditions, edge cities, and cities on the edge. In one respect, this fascination with borders and edges (which might be regarded as more jagged
than borders or as tears through borders) is a response to the dissolution
of traditional limits and lines of demarcation due to rapid urbanization
and globalizaton. Previously clear boundaries between countries, between
center and periphery, between city and countryside, and between "us" and
"them" have grown increasingly murky. Rather than being the locus of
activity and innovation, the traditional center (central city versus outskirts, as well as First World versus rest of the world) has imploded or
dissolved to produce multicentrality or a lack of centers.

As a result, we are all, in some sense, now living on the border or on
the edge. These borders or edges may be geographically situated
between neighborhoods divided by ethnicity, social class, or physical barriers; between functionally distinct zones; between city, suburb, and
countryside; or between built form and the natural landscape. They may
also be the conceptual membranes that separate academic disciplines,
professions, theory from practice, and designers from their constituents.
It is along these borders and edges that our greatest dilemmas reside as
well as our greatest opportunities for resolving them. It has grown
increasingly clear that our future depends on the ways in which we
negotiate the challenges posed by this condition.

Among architects and planners, a great deal of attention is being
paid towards the border and the edge in both their literal and figurative
manifestations. Theory and practice focus increasingly on places that are
betwixt and between, places that are perceived as somehow liminal in
space and/or time. This is apparent in the fascination with spaces considered interstitial, *"terrains vagues,"* "no man's lands," or "ghost wards"
(Schwarzer 1998). It is also apparent in the concern for designing along
national borders and between ecologically-differentiated areas such as

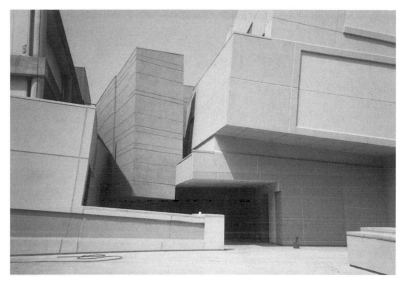

"Enfolding" of the existing building with the new College of Design, Architecture, Art and Planning, University of Cincinnati. Peter Eisenman, architect, 1997

along waterfronts and coastlines and for preserving or creating edges between city and countryside (e.g., Daniel Libeskind's 1987 City Edge project for Berlin, Steven Holl's 1991 proposal for creating edges on urban peripheries in an effort to counter sprawl, the Banlieues 1989 project in France). The notion that the talents and energies of architects and urban planners should contribute to mending seams, not tearing them asunder, to healing the world, not to salting its wounds, has grown much more widespread in acceptance.

Related to this interest in borders and edges is the obsession with the "fold" (via Gilles Deleuze) amongst the contemporary Eisenman School. "Unlike the space of classical vision," Peter Eisenman contends, "the idea of folded space denies framing in favor of a temporal modulation" (Eisenman 1992). Given "the exhaustion of collage as the prevailing paradigm of architectural heterogeneity," architectural theorist Jeffrey Kipnis suggests that "folding holds out the possibility of generating field organizations that negotiate between the infinite homogeneity of the grid and the hierarchical heterogeneity of finite geometric patterns" (Kipnis). In cooking, Greg Lynn explains, a "folded mixture is neither homogenous, like whipped cream, nor fragmented, like chopped nuts, but smooth and heterogeneous." Likewise, he sees "pliant systems" in architecture as an opportunity to "neither repress the complex relations of differences with fixed points of resolution nor arrest them in contradictions, but sustain them through flexible, unpredicted, local connections," practices which are "capable of bending rather than breaking" (Lynn). Charles Jencks (1995) describes this process as "enfolding," connecting that which is different by smooth transitions to reach a reconciliation, not a resolution.

In anthropology and cultural studies, the border has become significant as a place (again geographic as well as conceptual) where people engage in defining and re-defining themselves and others. As global flows have accelerated, there has been a perceived need to negotiate one's identity, on a virtually continual basis, and perhaps in a chameleon-like fashion, with different identities surfacing depending on the circumstances. While posing a potential threat to individual and group identity, this condition also presents an opportunity for less prescriptive groupings. The anthropologist Renato Rosaldo speaks of "border crossings" as the "sites of creative cultural production" where interconnections take place (Rosaldo 1989, 208). Anthropologist Anna Lowenhaupt Tsing in *The Diamond Queen* tells of the shaman with whom she studied in the Meratus Mountains of Indonesia who taught her that survival is "creative living on the edge" (Tsing, 37). In this study, she refutes the traditional division of the world into centers and peripheries, instead seeing "heterogeneity and transcultural dialogue in even the most out-of-the-way places" (Tsing, 10). Borrowing from cultural theorist Gloria Anzaldúa (*Borderlands/La Frontera: The New Mestiza*), Tsing proposes the analytic and geographic zone of the "borderlands," which are "the critical spaces created as contrasting discourses of dominance touch and compete in a contested hierarchy" (Tsing, 21, 225).

Part of the appeal of *ecology* and of *borders* and *edges* is their ability to adapt creatively to change, their inherent flexibility. As these new metaphors suggest, the celebration of diversity persists but no longer for its own sake. Rather, there is an emphasis on what happens when diverse regions, peoples, styles, technologies, and so forth, collide or merge. And on what should happen. The timidity characterizing much postmodern commentary is being gradually eclipsed by bolder personal positions and polemics which recognize that excessive striving for even-handedness and thoroughness ultimately allows the market to hold sway.

While the emphasis of ecology on whole-ness and of the border and edge on sectioning may appear contradictory at first glance, a closer look reveals their complementarity, perhaps even symbiosis. After centuries of increasingly dividing labor; cataloguing things and knowledge; segregating the landscape according to function as well as social class, age, and ethnicity; objectifying nature and people and fetishizing objects; we are now witnessing concerted efforts to de-alienate by bringing it all back together, albeit in a new way. This translates into valuing interdependence over independence and challenging other interrelated dualisms which characterize the western philosophical tradition such as mind/body, reason/emotion, spirit/flesh, masculine/feminine and, of course, culture/nature.[v] The question is no longer whether to grow or to apply new technologies but how best to accomplish these. Some of the manifold ways in which this re-integration is apparent are a shift back from monoculture to polyculture and from functional zoning to mixed use; massive restructurings of the labor force (initiated from above as well as below); re-envisioning the purpose and structure of museums, schools, libraries, and zoos; increased participation in local politics, in urban development, and in what we consume from food, to goods, advertising, and information; and in new collaborations among professions and between professions and academia.

The politics of universalism (or abstract rights) has yielded to a politics of difference or recognition (Charles Taylor cited by Jencks 1993, 10), whereby decision-making depends on context rather than on modernist binary logic. Mary Catherine Bateson describes this sensibility saying, "Instead of concentration on a transcendent ideal, sustained attention to diversity and interdependence may offer a different clarity of vision, one that is sensitive to ecological complexity, to the multiple rather than the singular" (Bateson 1990). In the design world specifically, this holistic approach has been described as "designing without boundaries" (Benzel 1997). The widely hailed Carnegie Foundation report on architectural education (Mitgang and Boyer 1996, see Appendix B) supports such an approach, calling for more interdisciplinary courses as well as a much improved relationship between the schools and the profession.

As these shifts have been underway, so were parallel developments in cosmology, astronomy, and physics that suggest new ways of conceiving centrality, order, and chaos. The desire for paradigms (or "meta-narratives") which express a whole-ness is perhaps epitomized by the contemporary search for a "theory of everything," a coherent cosmology, among scientists. In an effort to reconcile relativity theory with quantum physics, for instance, physicist Lee Smolin has proposed that our universe is part of an endless chain of self-reproducing universes that make their own laws, evolving as natural species evolve, according to processes of natural selection. This theory of "cosmological natural selection" proposes that there are laws but these are forever changing within certain parameters. Like chaos theory and complexity science, it suggests that beneath the apparent irregularity lies an order that is regular, unyielding, and complex.

Interestingly, this idea of self-organizing change through feedback is not new, but has only recently gained widespread acceptance, thanks to computer technologies that are capable of graphically portraying this process along with the emergent sensibility described above. With the assistance of computers, we can now represent fractals (geometry of the irregular), waves, folds, undulations, twists, warps, and more, providing a hyper-rational means of representing the "higher level order" that has long been integral to the worldviews of Buddhism, Taoism, and the Romantics, as well as to cosmologies proposed by Albert Einstein (quantum mechanics, 1905), Arthur Koestler (the holonic), Alfred North Whitehead, and others. After centuries of technological innovations serving as prosthetic devices which have combated the natural environment while alienating us from it, we have reached a point where our technology is corroborating and elaborating upon the holistic worldviews, a process which may itself illustrate the proposition that our universe is self-organizing on ever higher levels.

The crisis that scientists have been trying to resolve corresponds to the crisis in urban design in the concerted efforts to reconcile constant change and diversification on the one hand with some sense of order and predictability on the other. In architecture and urban planning, this debate has been articulated as critical regionalism, alternative or appropriate modernities, and ecological and sustainable design.[vi] Intimations of this shift are widespread and variously articulated.

Architect Steven Holl contends that "paradigm shifts comparable to those of the beginning of the twentieth century seem imminent" because of the electronic connection of "all places and cultures in a continuous time-place fusion" and the simultaneous "uprising of local cultures and expression of place." In these new paradigms, he says, "all material heaviness

Modica Market Building by architect Deborah Berke, and Hybrid Building by architect Steven Holl at Seaside, Florida, 1989

seems to disappear." Holl maintains, "Working with doubt allows an acceptance of the impermanence of technological change while opening up to metaphysical particularities of place." Such an architecture would fuse "the worlds of flow and difference" through hybridization which "would be a general consequence in seeking a new unity of dissociated elements in architecture." Holl calls for hybrid building programs, hybrid construction techniques, and hybrid detail explorations. He asserts: "A new architecture must be formed that is simultaneously aligned with transcultural continuity and with the poetic expression of individual situations and communities. Expanding toward an ultra-modern world of flow while condensed into a box of shadows on a particular site, this architecture attempts William Blake's, 'to see the universe in a grain of sand.' The poetic illumination of unique qualities, individual culture and individual spirit reciprocally connects the transcultural, transhistorical present" (http://www.walrus.com/~sha/loca_foc.htm).

Corollary to this search is that expressed by architect Tom Hahn as "finding the higher order in the simple." Believing "that there are no ugly materials, just ugly ways of using them," Hahn values "an aesthetics based on the discovery of inherent elegance," or an "architecture of the mundane" that does not rely on the pretense of arbitrary formalism, but rather seeks to "make the most with the least" (Hahn lecture, ASU 1998). Architects Deborah Berke and Steven Harris, as well as architectural theorist Margaret Crawford, have proposed an "architecture of the everyday" (inspired by the work of Henri Lefebvre and the Situationists from the 1950s to the 1970s) which Berke describes as "blunt, direct, and unselfconscious. It celebrates the potential for inventiveness within the ordinary and is thereby genuinely 'of its moment.' It may be influenced by market trends, but it resists being defined or consumed by them" (Berke, 226). Harris maintains that an architecture of the everyday objects to the "focus on authorship and the obsession with the display of heroic formal dexterity in both the fabrication of the architectural object and the representation of the architectural project"; it resists the commodification/consumption paradigm by focussing on "the quotidian, the repetitive, and the relentlessly ordinary" (Harris, 3).

While simplicity is sought, it is not the pared down "form follows function" of modernism. From less is more, the goal might now be described as "more from less,"[vii] after scenic detours through "less is a bore" and "more is more." The difference is in the inspiration (not platonic forms and geometry, but nature, the vernacular, the mundane, the "everyday") and the goal (not universality or nostalgia or theme-ing, but a critical regionalism or appropriate modernity). The resultant product is therefore also different, not a generic machine for living, nor an escape from the present into the past or from reality into fiction or virtual reality, nor a surrender to market forces. Rather, it is a place that sustains the environment including the people who use it. From the modern "form follows function" to the postmodern "form follows fiction, fear, finesse, and finance," perhaps now form does not follow. Neither does it lead. It walks hand in hand.

Rather than respond to specific problems with piecemeal solutions that only exacerbate the problems or push them elsewhere (reactive solutions), the emphasis on holism and seeing or forging connections at a higher and more complex level is leading to some more proactive responses. As our connections to the environment and other people grow increasingly tenuous—a condition commonly described as the breakdown in community and the family as well as the ecological crisis—efforts to re-think urban design have been seeking to resurrect such connections or to provide spaces which allow them to take root and thrive. Some examples include the emphasis on bioregions, the convening of world congresses to protect the environment (ecological crisis can be incentive for peace), the growth in metropolitan governments on a regional scale, increased consideration of culture in discussions about contextualism and (critical) regionalism, initiatives for "smart growth" and the creation of quality public spaces and transit systems, urban infill projects, the revitalization of housing projects, the building of transit-oriented developments, and the exponential growth of neighborhood associations and community gardens along with the important establishment of community land trusts.

Perhaps we have reached a place where the question of whether to continue or abandon the modern project (the subject of chapter 6) has become moot. Our hyper-rational embrace of computer technologies along with the simultaneous revalorization of simplicity, slowness, sincerity, and spirituality may be conspiring to eradicate the either/or proposition. This is because now we are doing both simultaneously, each providing feedback for and adjusting the other accordingly. We know we will never return to a pre-industrial integration, but the possibility of integration at another level now appears within our reach. With continued vision, diligence, and a bit of luck, we may adjust the way urban design is taught, theorized, and practiced so that what is still just a glimmer of possibility may expand into a veritable sunburst.

Nan Ellin
Tempe, Arizona
1998

NOTES

i   This is apparent in the re-release and popularity of Duane Elgin's *Voluntary Simplicity* in 1993 after originally appearing in 1981 to lackluster sales. Other books in this vein include *Downshifting* (1991) by Amy Saltzman, *Your Money or Your Life* (1993) by Joe Dominguez and Vicki Robin, *Simple Living* (1993) by Frank Levering and Wanda Urbanska, *The Simple Living Guide* (1997) by Janet Luhr, *Inner Simplicity* (1995), *Simplify Your Life: 100 Ways to Slow Down and Enjoy the Things that Really Matter* (1997), *Simplify with Kids* (1997), and *Living the Simple Life* (1998), all by Elaine St. James, and *The Circle of Simplicity: Return to the Good Life* (1997) by Cecile Andrews. A quarterly newsletter called *Simple Living* (edited by Luhrs) has been appearing since 1992 and there is an extensive website on the topic at www.simpleliving.com. I am grateful to television news producer Kevin Sites for alerting me to this trend.

ii   An example in poetry would be the shift from Alexander Pope's mock-heroic *The Rape of the Lock* (1704) in which he ridiculed fashionable life in England to William Wordsworth's *Lyrical Ballads* (1798) in which he produced poetry using ordinary speech (1798) (Nilsen).

iii   According to art critic Richard Nilsen, our "armor of irony . . . has begun to fall off" because irony "is essentially linguistic," "divorced from reality, but somehow accepted as its mirror," and we now "demand real experience" (Nilsen). My discussion of the shift to sincerity draws largely from Nilsen (1998).

iv   James Wines, John Todd, and others share this view which evolved from the earlier discussions of Aldo Leopold (1949), Ian McHarg (1968), Gregory Bateson (*Ecology of Mind*), Charles and Ray Eames (powers of 10), E.F. Schumacher (1973), Ivan Illich, Murray Bookchin, and others. It is also an extension of Jane Jacob's understanding of the city as a "problem of organized complexity" (Jacobs 1961) as well as Robert Venturi's discussion of complexity (1966).

v   Art critic Suzi Gablick, for instance, observes a "change in the general social mood toward a new pragmatic idealism and a more integrated value system that brings head and heart together in an ethic of care" (1993, 11).

vi   Among urban developers, this threat to previously clear boundaries has incited an anxious effort to obscure "an increasingly pervasive pattern of hierarchical relationships among people and orderings of city space" with "a cloak of calculated randomness," as demonstrated by the plan to revitalize New York City's Times Square (P. Marcuse 1995, 243). Among the public at large, a reflex has been the atavistic marking of one's turf with walls, gates, and prohibitions, lending a new and eerie resonance to Max Weber's "iron cage" metaphor. These are both unfortunate reactions discussed at length in the book, though not the focus here.

vii   Buckminister Fuller's call for "more from less" is now finding a much broader constituency. Recent advocates of "more from less" include Ian Ritchie *(Well) Connected Architecture* (London: Academy Editions, 1994), 70–73, excerpted in Jencks and Kropf. Also Tom Hahn above.

1

THE ROMANTIC RESURGENCE

OVER THE LAST SEVERAL DECADES, Western landscapes have undergone a sea change along with the ways we experience them and our visions for improving them. The importance of place has diminished as global flows of people, ideas, capital, mass media, and other products have accelerated. And the walking city has evolved into a less legible landscape where the erstwhile distinctions between city, suburb, and countryside no longer abide. The most common ways to describe this shift—both geographical and perceptual—are de-territorialization and placelessness. A by-product of this shift is a profound sense of loss and a corresponding deep nostalgia for the "world we have lost." To quell this sense of loss a search has been underway, the goal of which is variously articulated as urbanity, a center, a usable past, a sense of community, a neighborhood, a vernacular, diversity, meaning, innocence, origins, roots, certainties, leadership, and heroes.

These goals have been sought through the preservation or rehabilitation of old central cities, the building of new cities which resemble old ones, the cooperative movement and other grassroots social movements, as well as through a reassertion of traditional social values and institutions, particularly marriage, the family, and religion. As the global village grows smaller by the day, local efforts have been arising to assert, rediscover, or even invent traditions to combat homogenization or ideological colonialism. In reaction to globalization, then, we have been witnessing "re-tribalizations." This book examines the ways in which architects and urban planners have been responding to these transformations since the 1960s, efforts that may be grouped under the rubric "postmodern urbanism."

The pervasive sense of placelessness generated by the acceleration of global flows has been registered in many critiques of society and of the city. In sociology, titles appearing from the 1950s to the early 1970s promised to explore its repercussions, such as *The Lonely Crowd* (Riesman et al. 1950), *The Quest for Community* (Nisbet 1953), *The Quest for Identity* (Wheelis 1958), *The Eclipse of Community* (Stein 1960), *The End of Ideology* (Bell 1960), *The Secular City* (Cox 1965), *The Concept of Community* (Minar and Greer 1969), *The Pursuit of Loneliness* (Slater 1970), *The Social Construction of Community* (Suttles 1972), and *The Private Future: Causes and Consequences of Community Collapse in the West* (Pawley 1973). At the same time, critiques of the city were bemoaning the loss of a center. A sampling of these includes *The Heart of the City: Toward the Humanization of Urban Life* (Tyrwhitt et al 1952), *The Exploding Metropolis* (Fortune 1957), *The Death and Life of Great American Cities* (Jacobs 1961), *The Death of our Cities* (Doxiadis 1960), *Megalopolis* (Gottmann 1961), *The Twilight of Cities* (Gutkind 1962), *Sick Cities* (Mitchell 1963), *The Heart of our Cities: The Urban Crisis, Diagnosis and Cure* (Gruen 1964), and *Le Droit à la Ville* (Lefebvre 1967). While most of these analyses proposed means for recuperating the lost community and/or center, an acceptance of or resignation to this loss became apparent during the 1970s and 1980s in discussions both of society and of the city (an increasingly blurry distinction), as betrayed in titles such as *The Uses of Disorder* (Sennett 1970), *A Nation of Strangers* (Packard 1972), *The Fall of Public Man* (Sennett 1974), *Place and Placelessness* (Relph 1976), and *No Sense of Place* (Meyrowitz 1985).[1]

Alongside these publications were other expressions of discontent, couched mainly in terms of opposition to American involvement in the Vietnam War. American and European students rallied against the capitalist system generally and its implications for architectural education and practice in particular.[2] These critiques of society, of the city, and of architectural training and practice coincided with a larger assault on traditional academic disciplinary boundaries as scholarship relating to the built environment began to undergo a minor revolution. Architectural historians widened their purview from focusing on designer intentions and formal analyses of monuments to addressing issues such as patronage, legal codes, site planning, and community reactions (G. Wright 1988). Slightly further afield, the traditional disciplines of history, political science, economics, sociology, anthropology, geography, and psychology all began devoting more attention to the built environment, and new fields of study emerged focusing on the relationship between people and their surroundings, fields such as urban studies, urban sociology, urban anthropology, proxemics, ekistics, environmental studies, and environmental psychology.

There have always been pockets of resistance to Enlightenment ideals, but the acceleration of global flows after the Second World War and especially since the late 1960s lent an unprecedented vigor to this challenge. With earlier assaults on the modern project as heirs,[3] philosophers, social scientists, and literary critics began to speak of the dissolution of foundations, poststructuralism, and deconstructionism. The architectural metaphors here are particularly apt because of two concurrent developments: (1) The dissolution of the central city as a political, economic, social, and symbolic locus; and (2) The general dissatisfaction with the products of modern architecture and city planning, namely the destruction of existing urban fabrics and the building of (a) isolated structures surrounded by open space (in American central cities and European suburbs) and (b) mass-produced tract housing throughout the world. Following the war, many Western cities decentralized, buttressed by the implementation of new transportation technologies, real estate speculation, government subsidies, and modern planning theory which called for dispersion and the separation of functions. It is probably not without significance that this extensive decentralization followed the first use of the atomic bomb for humanly destructive purposes, in Hiroshima and Nagasaki. This atomic fission worked against the fusion of people into concentrated settlements because of the fear of attack and the invigorated challenge to the modern quest for mastery over nature on which dense cities rely.

The foundations indeed seemed to be crumbling. It was apparent to architects, planners, and the general public that something needed to be done to improve the physical landscape and the sense of desolation it aroused. This critique of modern architecture and urban design began mounting in the late 1950s mainly from "social planners" at the University of Pennsylvania (Scott Brown 1990a) and in the pages of the British

Architectural Review. A decade later this flicker had become a flame, as much of what was being built was consensually disparaged by its designers (architects and planners) and its users alike on aesthetic as well as social and political grounds. In numerous polemics and manifestos, critics proclaimed the death of the Modern movement and hailed the birth of new and better ways to design the environment.[4] In the words of David Ley, "A corporate urban landscape, the product of an increasingly corporate society, became the legacy of the modern movement, and through the 1960s and 1970s a critique emerged that the planning and design of the modern city was a blueprint for placelessness, of anonymous, impersonal spaces, massive structures and automobile throughways" (Ley 1987, 42–3). This criticism, he maintained, was "directed against a functionalist landscape, the placelessness which is the consequence in the advanced industrial city of centralized corporate decision-making, of standardization and the loss of human scale in mass society" (ibid.).

The lack of legibility of post-World War II landscapes incited a desire for the familiar and issued calls for designing "contextually" with regards to historical and local contexts. Sometimes this was couched in terms of designing "in the vernacular." In the United States, the vernacular was conceived primarily in terms of "ordinary" buildings, while in Europe—with its longer urban tradition—it was articulated largely in terms of a quest for urbanity. The French architect Bernard Reichen identified, in the early 1980s, a "desire for centrality" saying, "In this time of economic crisis, of the loss of models, of the feeling of insecurity, the city reassures and is still warm. Ultimately, it is the last space where freedom exists" (cited by Brière). This sentiment was epitomized by Henri Lefebvre's vindication of the "right to the city" (Lefebvre 1967) and it recalled the medieval saying "*Stadtlutft macht frei*" (city air makes one free). But although the late-twentieth-century quest for meaning and for a center has elicited nostalgia for cities of the past, it has not been accompanied by a desire to relinquish technological innovations which raise the standard of living, or that corresponding child of the Enlightenment, the pursuit of progress and modernity. Rather, that which appeals is the apocryphal simplicity, authenticity, intensity, and harmony of social relationships along with a built environment that expresses and facilitates these.

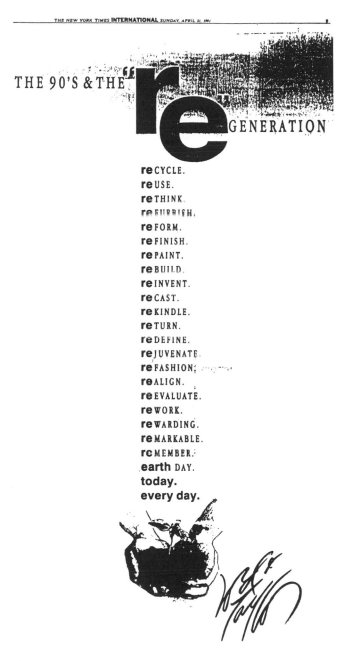

An advertisement for Lord & Taylor in honor of Earth Day dubs this the "re-generation." Courtesy Lord & Taylor (New York Times, April 21, 1991)

Remedies for the de-centeredness of the modern city have ranged from strict academic historicism, to a more ironic or parodic return that interprets the past, to drawing inspiration from the site, the social context, and/or from mass culture. The political intents sustaining these urban design attitudes range from the most conservative to the most radical, with only a loose correlation between these and the formal tendencies. As with other forms of postmodern expression, the conservative tendency clings to old "truths" as well as to the reigning power structure, manifest in the call to re-everything—rehabilitate, revitalize, restore, renew, redevelop, recycle, renaissance, and so forth. It has been apparent in the neotraditionalist vogue which expresses a desire to return to a time when life was simpler, saner, and generally more satisfactory. While this perspective tends to overlook change, the radical prospect sees change—including challenges posed to the canon and the status quo—as an opportunity for introducing ideas and practices which will bring about greater social equality. At this other end of the political continuum, we see an affirmation and insistence upon forging ahead rather than looking back. Architects and planners traverse the entire political spectrum, as does the general public, whose growing interest in urban design during this period can be understood as both symptom and symbol of the perceived loss of a center.

Despite the formal and political variation within postmodern urbanism, a common denominator is its romantic turn. Romanticism has been described as "the revulsion against uniformity, generality, calculated simplicity, and the reduction of living phenomena to common denominators; the aesthetic antipathy to standardization; the abhorrence of platitudinous mediocrity. More positive views of Romanticism describe: the attentiveness to the detailed, the concrete, the factual; the quest for local color; the endeavor to reconstruct in imagination the distinctive lives of peoples remote in space, time, or cultural condition; the cult of individuality, personality, and nationality; indulgence in the occult, the emotional, the original, the extraordinary.... Both the loosening of standards and the quest for a new 'community' are romantic in character" (Cahnman).[5]

The various strands of postmodern urbanism may be considered characteristic of mannerism, a romantic attitude which often follows the upset of a unified aesthetic and social vision, which focuses on the self and the past, and which values imitation, tradition, and roots. Romanticism both drives and is driven by nostalgia. The nostalgic paradigm, according to sociologists, presupposes "the idea of history as decline; the sense of a loss of wholeness; the feeling of the loss of expressivity and spontaneity; and the sense of loss of individual autonomy" (Robertson, 53). This particular wave of globalization since the 1960s has incited a nostalgia which "isn't what it used to be" (Robertson, 53)[6] in part because it is so deeply infused with cynicism. Twentieth-century social thought is a child and progenitor of positivist thinking which presupposes that we can never prove that something is true, only that it is false. Modeled after the physical sciences, the social sciences have been engaged in formulating hypotheses and trying to disprove them, a habit that leads inexorably to cynicism. As Herbert Marcuse pointed out in *One-Dimensional Man*, this kind of thinking only "criticizes within the societal framework and stigmatizes non positive notions as mere speculation, dreams or fantasies" (Marcuse, 178) and in doing so, "leaves the established reality untouched" (Marcuse, 179). To the extent that such thinking obtains in society generally, so does the ineffectuality as well as the cynicism and resultant search for meaning. There is a void and the search for something to fill it. By the 1960s, this cynicism had ushered in an assault on accepted notions of scientific progress, of morality, and of ethics, replacing these with an insistence upon cultural relativism and pluralism, offsetting debates concerning "political correctness" and "multiculturalism."

Often described as a loss of meta-narratives or organizing myths, this assault was not unrelated to the decline of meaningful public space and rapid suburbanization that were occurring throughout the United States and Western Europe. As the boundaries between city, suburb, and countryside were blurring, so were those between high culture, mass culture, and popular culture, those among the academic disciplines, and those between fiction and non-fiction. And functionalism was being simultaneously assaulted by the social sciences, architecture, and urban planning as a guiding theoretical framework.

In chapters 2 and 3, I survey the reactions to functionalism in Western urban design theory. After presenting the larger social context in which these reactions are inscribed, in chapter 4, I review and assess the underlying themes of postmodern urbanism in chapter 5. The relationship between postmodern urbanism and the Enlightenment or modern project is explored in chapter 6. Chapter 7 addresses the so-called "crisis" in the architectural profession, an outcome of the disjuncture between design education, theory, and practice on the one hand and transformations which have been taking place in the larger society and political economy on the other. Chapter 8 describes the contemporaneous reactions to functionalism in the social sciences and documents new ways of thinking about both the city and culture. Appendix A seeks to historicize this moment in urban design theory rather than regard it as somehow outside of history or "post-paradigmatic," an odd but not insignificant tendency of many discussions of postmodernism. And Appendix B provides a chronology of postmodern urbanism in the form of a timeline.

The scope of this interdisciplinary endeavor has entailed sacrifices of depth and exhaustiveness, rendering it guilty of omission, reductivism, and an over-reliance on secondary sources. But these sacrifices are made in pursuit of achieving a synthetic interpretation of urban design theory ultimately capable of revising it, to better channel the vast talent of architects and planners and to improve the quality of the built environment. The obvious hazard of writing about so timely an issue is the daily outpouring of relevant literature, indeed as this book goes to press. Nonetheless, the major foundations of postmodern urban design theory described in chapters 2 and 3 have by now been laid. And arising from this base, a new kind of skyline has been taking shape at this culmination of the millennium which signals changes not only in landscapes, but also in perception and lifestyles as well as political and social relations. At this critical juncture, it is important to assess the shortcomings as well as the enduring value of postmodern urbanism so as to avoid repeating its errors and to most fully reap its benefits.

NOTES

1. For example, Vance Packard (1972, begun in 1968) describes the period during which he is writing, saying, "A great many people are disturbed by the feeling that they are rootless or increasingly anonymous, that they are living in a continuously changing environment where there is little sense of community" (vii). Investigating "this rootlessness" in the US and abroad, he prescribes remedies for coping with and adjusting to it.

2. In the United States, Herbert Muschamp explained, the anti-war demonstrations of the late 1960s "were also protests against isolationism at home: against the divisive culture of the car and the suburb and their failure to supply the social cohesion advertised by the traditionalist forms of suburban buildings. For the children of the postwar mass-produced suburbs, it became a rite of passage to rebel against their parents' version of the American dream" (Muschamp 1993a). Andreas Huyssen contended that these "events of the 1960s"—as they came to be known—"sprang precisely from the success of modernism, from the fact that in the United States, as in West Germany and France, for that matter, modernism had been perverted into a form of affirmative [rather than critical] culture (Huyssen, 190).

3. The romantic rebellion against Enlightenment thought was expressed in Nietzsche's attack on Western philosophy, Heidegger's critique of metaphysics, W. James's radical empiricism, Dewey's pragmatism, and Polanyi's critique of positivism. Other reactions to Enlightenment thought—past and more recent—have been voiced by Kant, Hume, Leibniz, Goethe, Schiller, Schleiermacher, Levy-Bruhl, the later Wittgenstein, Whorf, Kuhn, Schneider, Sahlins, Feyerabend, and Geertz (Shweder).

4. See, for instance, the critiques of Blake, Brolin, Rainwater, Sennett, R. Goodman, W. H. Whyte, Gutkind, and Gruen.

5. Cahnman is drawing from Lovejoy's discussion of early-nineteenth-century romanticism. Richard Shweder explains that a "central tenet of the romanticist view holds that ideas and practices have their foundation in neither logic nor empirical science, that ideas and practices fall beyond the scope of deductive and inductive reason, that ideas and practices are neither rational nor irrational but rather nonrational. . . . For the romantic, the choice between alternative self-contained worlds must be an act of faith. Wary of any attempt to make the nonrational appear rational, wary of any ploy to make a genuine and unavoidable act of faith appear as though it were dictated by reason, the romantic views science (especially social science) as 90% ideology and views tradition, religion, and ritual as indispensable components of human thought and practice" (Shweder, 28). On romanticism in architecture and urbanism, see Geoffrey Scott (1914) and Peter Collins (1965).

6. As Jean Baudrillard points out, "when the real is no longer what it used to be, nostalgia assumes its full meaning" (Baudrillard 1983b, 12–13).

2

URBAN DESIGN THEORY
ON THE EUROPEAN CONTINENT

SINCE THE·1960S, and particularly since the international fiscal crisis of 1972, we have been witnessing a broad-based romantic reaction to modernism in the United States and Western Europe. In urban design, this was manifest as a reaction to modern urbanism, particularly as articulated by the modern movement's Athen's Charter (1933). Detractors from the modern movement were critical, in part, of the tenets themselves, but mainly of the products of such tenets that failed to realize their promises. Instead of applying the industrial mode of production and machine imagery toward producing universally satisfactory urban design which would house a more egalitarian society, these landscapes had, in the words of Liane Lefaivre, "become synonymous with inhumanity, desolation, and devastation" (Lefaivre, 17). The German architect Claude Schnaidt sadly reported that "Modern architecture, which wanted to play its part in the liberation of mankind by creating a new environment to live in, was transformed into a giant enterprise for the degradation of the human habitat" (1961; cited by Frampton 1980, 287). And Tom Wolfe, more sardonically, exclaimed that these landscapes represented "nothing but an eccentric sixty-year-old German student-socialist vision of Worker Housing blown up larger and larger" (Wolfe 1980, 3).

From the 1960s to the 1980s, then, a great transformation occurred in urban design theory, especially pronounced during the decade of 1965–1975. A number of different trends emerged, all contributing "to

a more general and now widely shared Manichean view of functionalism as a negative and regressive ideology" (Gandelsonas 1975). Against
the universalism of the Modern movement, these reactions featured a
renewed interest in the specificity of regional and historical styles along
with a respect for the diversity of urban subcultures ("pluralism" or
"multiculturalism") and a desire to distinguish public monuments and
civic institutions from domestic architecture. These reactions have also
tended to presuppose many meanings (multivalency) or many "readings," rather than only one "truth" and have sought to express this
through the symbolic dimension of built form.

This chapter examines urban design theory that sprouted primarily
from continental European soil, focusing on neo-rationalism, neo-classicism, and open architecture, before more thoroughly surveying the
urban design scene in France during this period. Whereas the North
American critique of Le Corbusier's urban vision initially tended to
focus on individual buildings or on suburbia, the European critique proceeded directly to formulate another urban vision. This might be attributed to the deeply engrained historical and cultural attachment to cities
among Europeans along with the continued desirability of and investment in central cities, as well as political economies that—in contrast to
the American one—subsidize large-scale plans. In reaction to the high
modernism which had informed most urban development after the
World War II and which mandated a clean break from the past (see chapter 6), European urban designers began turning to the pre-industrial
past for inspiration and legitimization. The closed book on ancient,
medieval, renaissance, baroque, and vernacular townscapes was
reopened and closely studied.

NEORATIONALISM

Beginning in the 1960s in Italy and Spain, a group who came to be
known as the neorationalists sought to achieve urbanity by reconceiving the architectural object. Influenced by the writing of G. C. Argan on
Quatremère de Quincy (1795–1825), these architects and theoreticians
expressed city building in terms of typology and morphology and
regarded buildings and cities as "theatres of memory." Like eighteenth-
century rationalist Marc-Antoine Laugier, the neorationalists were trying to find "the fundamental types of habitat: the street, the arcade, the
square, the yard, the quarter, the colonnade, the avenue, the boulevard;

the centre, the nucleus, the crown, the radius, the knot. . . . So that the city can be walked through. So that it becomes a text again. Clear. Legible" (Delevoy, 17). The tool for achieving this was the "type" which began to replace the "model" of the moderns. In contrast to the model, which is a universal product in a neutral space, the pre-industrial type is an architecture conceived in relationship to its historic, geographic, and economic context (Rodier 1981). As architectural historian Robert-Louis Delevoy contends, "Everything is precise and clearcut in the Model, while everything is more or less vague in the Type" (Delevoy, 16). Type, he explains, assembles the distinctive features of a certain category of objects and its application involves "an architecture in reverse, a craft architecture, an ecological architecture, a historicist architecture" (Delevoy, 21). According to Delevoy, "the new rationalists have opted, via culture, via history, for a slowdown," for a return to the "urban art" of late-nineteenth-century European capitals (Delevoy, 21).[1]

The turn to typology was influenced by structuralist thought (particularly that of Claude Lévi-Strauss), which posited the existence of archetypal/universal structures of the mind. Translated into urban design, these did not become the abstract platonic structures of modernist architecture, but actual built structures found repeatedly in pre-industrial cities. Typology was also influenced by deconstructionist thought—most significantly that of Jacques Derrida—which sanctioned the "deconstruction" of functionalism as a goal for architecture and urban planning and which condoned the "reading" of architecture as a text with many interpretations.[2] This recourse to "types" was made, in part, to legitimize architecture in the face of a perceived crisis in architectural production and in the architectural profession by referring to past forms. Though not explicit, the recourse to types probably also revealed a nostalgia for the time when architects did not design for mass society, but for a small elite with large coffers, a nostalgia for an apocryphal moment when architects did not need to worry about maintaining a livelihood or justifying their work.

The most influential of the early neorationalists was Aldo Rossi. In his book *Architecture of the City* (1966; English version 1982), one of the first critiques of the modern movement in Europe, he rejected functionalism as a primary determinant of form because of its denial of the complexity of the city and because of its inability to explain the persistence of certain forms once their function has changed or become obsolete.

Rossi rejected the principle that form follows function, asserting instead "the relative autonomy of architectural order" (Frampton 1985, 294).[3] As Mario Gandelsonas (1975) has pointed out, the neorationalists wished to create an "autonomous" architecture which would transcend culture and history and which would not communicate ideas other than its own. Rossi's desire to account for the irrational as well as the rational led him to seek inspiration from the "rational" architecture of the Enlightenment. In Frampton's words, "Rossi structured his work about historical architectonic elements that could recall and yet transcend the rational if arbitrary paradigms of the Enlightenment" (Frampton 1985, 294). After the architecture of the Enlightenment was described as an "architecture of *tendanza*" in the catalogue "Illuminism and Architecture in 18c. Venice" (1969), the group who formed around Rossi's ideas came to be known as "La Tendanza."

Adapting the ideas of urban geographers Maurice Halbwachs and Georges Chabot, Rossi described the city as a locus of collective memory and emphasized the consequent importance of monuments and a sense of place. Rossi aspired to the "analogous city," which, as Kenneth Frampton explains, is comprised of an "architecture whose referents and elements are to be abstracted from the vernacular, in the broadest possible sense" (Frampton 1985, 294). To design by analogy means borrowing past city forms (morphology) and building forms (typology)— the formal/aesthetic aspect of the past—without their meanings because the meanings of these forms have changed with time. These forms borrowed from the past, Rossi said, should be "collaged" as Piranesi collaged Roman monuments without reference to their past contexts. In contrast to Le Corbusier, for whom the architecture was supposed to provide the "spectacle," Rossi asserted that "places are stronger than people, the fixed scene stronger than the transitory succession of events" (Rossi 1968). The significance of a place, for Rossi, lay not in its function, or even in its form, but in the memories associated with it.[4] This understanding suggested that other fields of study should become important to the architect, especially anthropology, cultural geography, urban history, and economics.

As David Mangin suggests, Rossi's desire to build with memory recalls the Renaissance "theatres of memory" as well as the practice of antiquity whereby students of rhetoric used buildings as mnemonic devices. Mangin describes Rossi's references as his "architectural madeleines," "his architectural Summer of '42s" (Mangin). In Paul Goldberger's interpretation, "what Aldo Rossi has really made is an architecture of sentiment for the unsentimental, an architecture of nostalgia for those who resist easy emotions" (Goldberger 1990b). Not incidentally, Herbert Muschamp points out, Rossi's aesthetic was formed in postwar Italy where "the wreckage of war [joined] remnants of the Classical world" (Muschamp 1991).

Rossi's understanding of type is a highly personal one, relying on autobiography, memory, and fleeting impressions as opposed to the canonical view originally proposed by Quatremère de Quincy in 1825, which holds that types are to be sought in history (Francescato, 7). Although recognizing the importance of tradition and continuity, Rossi also saw the need for change due to transformations in the political economy. But since functions evolve with time, Rossi rejected the idea of context as a determinant of urban design, interested instead only in that which remains permanent, notably the monument (from the Latin *monumentum* meaning memory or remembrance). According to Rossi, cities need monumentalism in order to possess the dignity and tension necessary to express greater social ambitions (Lesnikowski 1982). Though rarely discussing actual building proposals, he claimed that we can and should design monuments which are expressive of collective memory, acknowledging at the same time that what constitutes a monument is a mystery (Harvey 1989, 85).

A Marxist, Rossi regards the city as the embodiment of existing power relations, claiming, "The history of architecture is always the history of the ruling classes" (Rossi 1966). But he disputes the equation made by the modern movement and Team X equating monumentalism with fascism and totalitarianism (Lesnikowski 1982). Like Manfredo Tafuri (1973), Rossi maintains that architecture alone cannot be democratic or fascist; only people can make it so.

The scope of Rossi's influence expanded when his work was translated into English—beginning with an article in *Oppositions* in 1975, originally published in the catalogue for the 1973 Triennale—and through his affiliation with the Institute for Architecture and Urban Studies in New York City from 1976 to 1979, where he established an office in 1986. According to Tzonis and Lefaivre, Rossi "became a hero to grateful architects who embraced him for having almost single-handedly restored their confidence in the profession" (cited by Boddy 1993,

96). Trevor Boddy reported that "powerful graphics, easily imitable 'toy-like forms,' and a fuzzy poetic combined to give Rossi an immense influence on global architecture through the 1970s, but now surprisingly little seems likely to endure" (ibid.).

The influential Venice Triennale of 1973 was organized by Rossi and entitled "Rational Architecture." It featured past and present practitioners of rationalism including Massimo Scolari, Enzo Bonfanti, and Rossi himself, among others.[5] The Triennale of Milan the following year codified the notion of an autonomous architecture, and in 1975, a larger version of the Venice exhibit took place in London. Other contributions to neorationalist thought include Vittorio Gregotti's *Il territorio dell'architettura* (1966), Giorgio Grassi's *La costruzione logica dell'architettura* (1967), the neorationalist journal *Contraspazio* edited by Bonfanti and Scolari during the 1960s, and the work of Manfredo Tafuri, Saverio Muratori, Carlo Aymonino, Rafael Moneo, and Paolo Portoghesi.

Portoghesi emphasizes the importance of rediscovering archetypes, which, he believes, can bring meaning back into architecture. These archetypes, he explains, "are elementary institutions of the language and practice of architecture that live on in the daily life and collective memory of man. These differ greatly depending on the places where we live and where our spatial experiences were formed" (Portoghesi 1983, 11).[6] A reintegration of archetypes, Portoghesi says, "would bring architecture back to the origin of its nature as a human institution based on conventions, participated in by everyone and transformable only through long collective processes" (Portoghesi 1983, 40). This architecture, he acknowledges, "may not have the characteristics prescribed by a certain populist participation. . . . But [it] is certainly closer to the majority of people than that technocratic architecture which arose from the crisis of the Modern Movement because it constantly borrows from a common patrimony" (Portoghesi 1983, 40–42).[7]

As neorationalism migrated to northern Europe, its urbanistic component evolved into the Movement for the Reconstruction of the European City. This movement hatched during the 1970s, after a period of gestation during which it was being formulated by a number of historians and architects working independently in various European locales. Along with the student and worker insurgencies of 1968, which signaled a widely perceived legitimacy crisis in the political economy, this movement was both symptom and symbol of widespread dissatisfaction with postwar urban development and with the consequent legitimacy crises in the urban design professions.

The most complete statement of neorational urbanistic thought is found in the bilingual French-English publication *Architecture rationelle: Témoignages en faveur de la réconstruction de la ville européenne Rational Architecture*, 1978 (Testimonies in favor of the reconstruction of the European city). Originally assembled for the 1975 London exhibition by Léon Krier, the collection also includes articles by Delevoy, Vidler, Scolari, and Huet. The perceived importance of this book was expressed by Delevoy, who said that it "acts as a guide, forms a corpus, develops as a method and has the distilled conciseness of a manifesto. It puts forward a theory, the absence of which has been cruelly felt since the decade 1930–40. It suggests a practice, which may well fill the gap created in 1960 by the setback of Brasilia: a masterly demonstration and striking failure of a 'way of town-planning thought'" (Delevoy, 15). In this book, Delevoy maintains, a "deconstruction of the functionalist system founded by Le Corbusier and institutionalized by the CIAM [International Congress of Modern Architecture], . . . seems imbued with the same inspiration that once surged through all the works of the true author of the Athens Charter" (Delevoy, 15).

Anthony Vidler's contribution to this collection asserts that the neorationalists were embracing "the third typology" which takes "the traditional city as the locus of its concern" (Vidler 1978, 29). This third typology, he explains, followed upon the heels of the second typology, inspired by the machine, which in turn succeeded the first typology, inspired by nature. Vidler claims that "This third typology, like the first two, is clearly based on reason, classification, and a sense of the public in architecture; unlike the first two, however, it proposes no panacea, no ultimate apotheosis of man in architecture, no positivistic eschatology" (ibid.). Whereas the first two sought to legitimize architecture as a "natural" phenomenon and hoped that architecture would (like nature or the machine) affect or control social life, this third typology was not, Vidler contends, attempting to validate itself.[8]

Vidler recalls Victor Hugo's admonition in the chapter of *Notre Dame de Paris* (1831) entitled *"Ceci tuera cela"* (This will kill that): "Architecture is becoming ever more tarnished, faded and dim. The printed word, that cankerworm of the edifice, sucks up and devours architecture, which casts off its raiment and visibly dwindles away. It is shabby, poor and bare. It no longer expresses anything, not even the memory of another age's art. Confined to itself, abandoned by the other arts because human thought abandons it, architecture recruits labourers for want of artists. Every trace of vitality, originality, life and intelligence is gone . . ." (cited by Delevoy, 14). Hugo realized in the early nineteenth century, Vidler notes, that "communication through the printed work, and lately through the mass media has apparently released architecture from the role of social book into its own autonomous and specialized domain" (Vidler 1978, 31). The result was that architecture was no longer "a realm that has to relate to a hypothesized society in order to be conceived and understood. . . . The need to speak of nature, of function, of social mores—of anything that is beyond the nature of architectural form itself —is removed" (ibid.). Contrary to the second typology, then, the third "denies all the social utopian and progressively positivistic definitions of architecture for the last 200 years" (ibid.). Neorationalism, Vidler says, thus "refuses any 'nostalgia' in its evocations of history, except to give its restorations sharper focus; it refuses all eclecticism, resolutely filtering its 'quotations' through the lens of a modernist aesthetic" (Vidler 1978, 32).[9]

According to Léon Krier, who was the most vociferous spokesperson for the Movement for the Reconstruction of the European City, the major themes of the movement included: the physical and social preservation of historical centers as desirable models of collective life; the conception of urban space as the primary organizing element of urban morphology; typological and morphological studies as bases for a new architectural discipline; the growing awareness that the history of the city delivers precise facts permitting immediate and precise action toward reconstructing the street, square, and quartier; the restructuring of dormitory cities into complex parts of the city, into cities within the city, and into *quartiers* which integrate all the functions of urban life; and the rediscovery of the primary elements of architecture such as the column, the wall, and the roof (Krier 1978b, 42). The planners and architects involved in this movement were proposing "a coherent alternative to the current system based on profit, on the destruction of a lived memory and culture of the city, on the alienation of the division of labor, on frenzied consumption, and on all forms of waste: energy and speculative, urbanistic and real estate, but also social waste" (Dethier, 70).

This movement diverged from the modern movement with regards to the architectural mode of production as well as the product. Its adherents called for a rediscovery and vindication of craftsmanship, traditional building techniques, and pre-industrial landscapes. Krier and Maurice Culot asserted that their "theses simply maintain that from now on we must go back and take up the work of imitation of the most beautiful pre-industrial examples in their proportions, dimensions, and morphological simplicity, as well as in their mode of production aiming at the usage of traditional materials and craftsmanship rather than industrialization" (Krier and Culot).[10] Culot admitted to "a malicious pleasure in wanting to take on the discussion of the city where it has been brutally interrupted by the second industrial revolution." He conceded, nonetheless, that it is impossible to pick up where modernism began saying, "it is useless to claim that we want to rely on a tradition, a popular culture which is no longer anything but a caricature of itself" (cited by Champenois, 4–5). For Culot, then, it is "necessary to recreate, artificially, the cultural foundations" (Champenois).[11] He is, not surprisingly, an ardent supporter of the work of François Spoerry of Port Grimaud fame.

Krier's manifesto for this movement declared: "Industrial production . . . has destroyed in less than two hundred years those cities and landscapes which had been the result of thousands of years of human labor and intelligence, of culture. We have now to recognize the absolute value of the pre-industrial cities, of the cities of stone" (Krier 1978b). Architects, Krier maintained, should once again value the role of memory, both by using their own memories of the past and by creating settings which might become "theatres of memory" (Krier 1980). What architects must do, Krier intoned, is to "go back and imitate the best pre-industrial examples in their proportions, their dimensions, and their morphologies, as well as in their mode of production using traditional materials and craftsmanship rather than the industrial mode of production" (ibid.). Understanding the reconstruction of the European city as one component of a global strategy of anti-industrial resistance, Krier's battle cry declared, "Forward comrades, we must go back" (Krier 1981).

The formula for Krier's reconstruction of the European city, then, was as follows:

A city can only be reconstructed in the forms of streets, squares, and quarters. These quarters must integrate all functions of urban life, in areas not to exceed 35 hectares and 15,000 inhabitants.
The streets and squares must present a familiar pattern.

Their dimensions and proportions must be those of the best and most beautiful
pre-industrial cities.

Simplicity must be the goal of urban topography, however complex.

The city must be articulated into public and domestic spaces, monuments and
urban fabric, squares and streets, classical architecture and vernacular building.
And in that hierarchy. (Krier, cited by Dutton 1986)

Krier and Culot explained their strategy as follows: "We have been
able to develop and formulate our excessively simple theses which are at
the basis of our work by simultaneously studying the best examples of
pre-industrial architectural construction and participating in urban
struggles in popular neighborhoods" (Krier and Culot 1980, 22). They
said that their participation in urban struggles "has demonstrated that
these theses are completely applicable and that a majority of the population can rally around a shared feeling that is not dictated by the industrial mass media but is still profoundly rooted in the landscape and
memory still present in ancient cities" (ibid.). According to Michèle
Champenois, "Culot and his friends refuse to engage in the aesthetic
debate. They want to 'address the problems of the city in terms of conflicts'" (Champenois, 4–5). In Bernard Huet's "*Petit Manifeste*," he asserts,
"Architecture can no longer be 'natural' nor universal. It must be 'his-
toricized' and inserted within the dialectic of social relations" (Huet
1978, 54). Similar to Tafuri and Rossi, Krier believes, "There exists neither authoritarian nor democratic Architecture. There exists only
authoritarian and democratic ways of producing and using architecture.
. . . Architecture is not political, it can only be used politically" (Krier
1980). Also like Rossi, Léon Krier along with his brother Rob Krier[12]
understand *type* in a personal fashion.

During the 1970s, the architectural school of La Cambre in Brussels contributed a great deal to this discussion. Visitors hosted by La
Cambre to participate in juries included Scolari, Huet, Devillers, Montès, Panerai, Castex, and L. Krier (Lucan 1989, 126). Robert Delevoy
served as Director of the school from 1965 to 1979 during which time
Maurice Culot served as Assistant Director. Culot founded the *Archives
de l'architecture moderne* (AAM) in 1968, which began publishing its journal in 1975. Culot was also a member of ARAU, *L'Atelier de Recherche et
d'Action Urbaines* (Studio for Urban Research and Action). Founded in
1968 by another professor at La Cambre, the urban sociologist René

Schoonbrodt,[13] the ARAU proposed "counterprojects" elaborated at La Cambre for fueling debate on urban issues.

The origins of this heightened activity at La Cambre might be traced to the "Battle of the Marolle," an urban struggle in 1969 which incited the inhabitants' movement in Brussels against the destruction of the city by speculation. Immediately following this battle, Culot and his colleagues developed the concepts of "anti-industrial resistance" and "the reconstruction of the European city." A decade hence, in April 1978, at the conference "*La ville dans la ville*" in Palermo, the "Declaration of Palermo" was drafted by Léon Krier, Pierluigi Nicolin (editor of *Lotus*), Angello Villa, Maurice Culot, and Antoine Grumbach. Printed as "A European 'Declaration': Reconstructing the City" (Dethier), it was the first articulation of the Movement for the Reconstruction of the European City. Then in November 1978, the "*Déclaration de Bruxelles*" was issued. In an article entitled "Testimony from a Combattant," Culot explained that this movement was inspired by the work of Christopher Alexander, Henri Lefebvre, the *Atelier de Recherche et d'Action Urbaines*, Bernard Huet, and Léon Krier.

In the Summer of 1979, the minister of National Education, Jacques Hoyaux, expelled 24 professors of the "Culot group" from their teaching posts, an event which came to be known as "*L'affaire de la Cambre.*" A poster was rapidly produced depicting a young man with shoulder-length hair and a cloth gagging his mouth. The caption read: "*Hoyaux exclut 24 enseignants. Hoyaux ferme l'école d'architecture. Hoyaux soutient la grosse promotion immobilière. Hoyaux empêche les étudiants et enseignants de travailler avec les habitants. La Cambre baillonnée. LA CAMBRE FERMÉE*" (Dethier) [Hoyaux expells 24 teachers. Hoyaux closes the school of architecture. Hoyaux supports the real estate industry. Hoyaux prevents students and teachers from working with inhabitants. La Cambre is silenced. LA CAMBRE IS CLOSED]. Soon after the closure, the French architect Jean Dethier assembled a special supplement for the French state journal on public housing, *La Revue 'h'*, in the form of a large poster describing the events occurring at La Cambre in Brussels and reprinting a number of articles written about it (Dethier). This event resonated throughout Western Europe and many letters in support of the expelled professors were sent to Minister Hoyaux.[14]

Commenting upon the closing of La Cambre, Dethier remarked: "We must look to Nazi Germany to find the only known precedent in Europe aiming to dismantle an architecture school and its teachers in order to put an end to the cultural politics being elaborated there: this was the case of the Bauhaus in 1933" (Dethier). Two reporters for *Le Monde Diplomatique* delared, "This evidence of the Belgian cultural misery is only foreshadowing the universal misery of a world incapable of responding by a radical politics to that which is only a stage—important, it is true—in the modification of an unchanged capitalist production" (Roland Lewet and Yannis Thanassekos in Dethier). An article in the Belgian newspaper *Quotidien* maintained that "La Cambre was attacked at the moment when the school was becoming legitimate, at the moment when it was demonstrating the validity of an alternative model to the urbanistic horrors, when it was proving that the destruction of the city was not inevitable. A veritable war operation has been launched before this movement becomes irreversible. . . . In Germany, in France, in Belgium, we are witnessing a return to the traditional architectural pedagogy. This is not a coincidence!" (G. Lefevre). An article in *La Revue Nouvelle* maintained, "A convergence has been established between certain architectural professionals who could no longer accept the growing reputation of these teachers who spoke about and practiced an alternative architecture; sectors of the construction and real estate industries were feeling their economic interests threatened; those who, in the petty political world of Brussells, were getting worried about the involvement of teachers at La Cambre in urban conflicts aligning themselves with the inhabitants" (Lambert).

On November 20, 1979, the expelled teachers formulated a statement: "Education should deepen the study of mechanisms by which inhabitants are excluded from the city by the structures of multinational capitalism, which exert their power by cornering the market for the profit of those who control the old central cities, thus dispossessing the workers and those with least access to the urban facilities to which they have a right" (in Dethier). Then, in 1980, this group founded a new private school called *La Nouvelle Cambre pour la Reconstruction de la Ville.* With Delevoy as President and Schoonbrodt as Director, the faculty included: Culot, Jean Dethier (Paris), Bernard Huet (Paris), Léon Krier (London), François Loyer (Rennes), Jacques Lucan (Paris), Fernando Montés (Paris), Pierluigi Nicolin (Milan), and Philippe Panerai (Versailles). Meanwhile, Hoyaux reopened La Cambre and appointed, in Dethier's words, *"des architectes affairistes cons sur la place"* ("some local idiotic businessmen-architects"). But the work of the ARAU, AAM, and related groups continued.

In an article entitled "Rot in the trenches? No thanks" (1980), Krier and Culot adopted a belligerent tone, asserting that they were in a "situation of war" and engaged in a "project of resistance." "To be committed to a global project of reconstructing the European city," they said, "is senseless unless at the same time one also becomes committed to reconstruct the philosophical bases of architecture." Otherwise, they continued, architects are collaborating "in this process of self-destruction of civilized society." Consequently, their objective became that of mobilizing people to reconstruct their cities, and of reconceptualizing the philosophical bases of architecture. They concluded, "This is the work in which we are engaged and we have no intention of dirtying our hands in the mud of industrial construction sites."

The professional directions taken by Culot and Krier derive from these beliefs. For Culot, one cannot both teach and build because "practice alienates and renders teaching inept" (cited by Champenois) and he has opted for teaching. Krier has asserted that architects should not compromise by building within a system they do not support. Maintaining that "a responsible architect cannot possibly build today" (Krier 1978b) and that "building can only mean a greater or smaller degree of collaboration in civilized society's process of self-destruction" (ibid.), Krier deliberately removed himself from architectural practice for a period of time.

Born in Luxembourg in 1946, Léon Krier lives in London and has taught at the Royal College of London and the Architectural Association. Although he greatly admired Le Corbusier at one time, and said that he was "the only one with whom I would have really liked to work" (Krier 1982, 101), Krier later came to regard Le Corbusier as a "destroying angel" (ibid.) because of his desire to rebuild old cities along modernist principles. Whereas Le Corbusier regarded the city as a machine, Krier saw it as a natural object or an "individual, possessing a body and a soul" (ibid.). They nonetheless shared the belief that the crisis of the city called for comprehensive and radical solutions.

Two intellectual debts of Krier are to Ferdinand Toennies's *Gemeinschaft and Gesellschaft* (1887) and Heinrich Tessenow's *Handwerk und Kleinstadt* (1919). From Toennies, he understood the impact of the loss of community and developed the idea of maintaining small-scale towns with a close-knit community. From Tessenow, he came to see architecture as a response to the demands of daily life, and the small town as the appropriate context for producing handicrafts and thus the highest manifestation of human values (Krier 1982). Krier was also influenced by Camillo Sitte's view that the city should be a "*Gesamtkunst-werk*," a comprehensively interwoven system rather than a functionally divided one (ibid.). But unlike Sitte, Krier wished to go beyond cosmetic changes to social and political ones (ibid.). His work is also inspired by that of eighteenth-century rationalists Boullée and Ledoux, particularly their rational seeking of beauty and universal truths, and by Fourier and the 1920s Expressionists. Krier has also examined the architecture of Albert Speer, the architect of the Third Reich, and has written with L. O. Larson, *Albert Speer: Architecture 1932–1942* (1986).

Krier worked for James Stirling in the late 1960s on a megastruc-tural design for Siemens headquarters in Munich. Marking a shift in his work from monumental symmetrical megastructures to a more conven-tional kind of monumental city design was Krier's Leinfelden City Center project of 1971, where the main and cross axes are lined with continu-ous large-scale buildings and the intersection houses a cluster of office towers (Barnett 1986, 37, 190). In the late 1970s, Krier proposed a reconstruction for central Warsaw, which did not attempt an academic restoration but a construction of his idea of a traditional city. For Roma Interotta in 1978, Krier placed different versions of the same structure in four locales, "a long-span hipped roof supported on columns that were actually individual buildings" (Barnett 1986, 37). Invited to redesign the historic center of Bremen in 1979, Krier proposed converting ware-houses into housing, narrowing streets that had been widened to accom-modate increased traffic, closing certain squares and constructing new ones, redesigning 1950s housing and 1960s public buildings to appear more traditional, and building new "monuments" (Krier 1982, 105).

In Krier's entry for the Amiens competition, he placed a church and bell-tower in the center of the town, saying that even if people don't go to church anymore, it is important to have such a public space, a landmark which is always open to all and fulfils mystical and symbolic functions. For a project on the periphery of Berlin (1980, IBA competition for Berlin-Tegel), Krier proposed a densely built fabric to mark the edge of the city, including public buildings which serve as points of reference and perime-ter buildings which define blocks. He explained, "The reconstruction of the old city with its social, typological and functional complexity ought to serve as a model for the transformation of suburbs into true and proper centres" (cited in Krier 1982, 105).[15]

Krier undertook a project for the completion of Washington, DC (Jencks 1987; Krier 1986), which called for dividing it into four independent towns, each no larger than Georgetown (one of the four). All residents would live within walking distance of their workplace. The Tidal Basin would be enlarged and would wash against tree-lined banks, while a Grand Canal would stretch from the Washington Memorial to a "Constitution Square" cut into the Hill on the west side of the Capitol. Development would be overseen by a Federal agency that would assure strict adherence to volumetric, stylistic, and functional guidelines. Revenues from sale of land would go toward public buildings and open spaces (Krier 1986).

In the early 1980s, Krier served as a consultant for the master planning of Seaside, Florida (see chapter 3), where he also built a house for himself. Then, in 1988, he became an advisor to Prince Charles, who not only commissioned Krier to design four new towns in England, but has also been adopting Krier's theories in recommended reforms for the entire European Community (see chapter 3).

As neorationalist ideas were diffused throughout Europe, they were variously elaborated upon, adapted, combined with other theories of urban design, and realized, particularly in Belgium, Germany, Italy, and France. In their pristine form, however, the realization of neorationalist ideas was limited because, according to Lucan, "their increasingly dogmatic attitude of anti-industrial and pro-crafts resistance and their desire to remain separate from professional activity meant that they found themselves more and more isolated" (Lucan 1989, 126). Consequently, very few developments remained entirely loyal to the spirit of neorationalism, the closest perhaps being the reconstruction of Alma-Gare at Roubaix in France (1977–82) by Michel Benoit and Thierry Verbiest and the plan for Bologna in Italy (see Cervellati et al.) in the 1970s.[16] Other projects developed aspects of its tenets, most notably the architectural competitions for the reconstruction of Berlin (1978–)[17] and for the building of nine new cities in France (Ellin 1986, 1994).

NEOCLASSICISM

Other archetypes used to reconcile city design with architectural design refer to the forms of antiquity and of the Renaissance. These have been variously identified as neoclassicism, classical revivalism, academicism, romantic classicism, and neosocial-realist megaclassicism (Frampton 1985, 310). The revival of such classical languages has been attributed to a desire to return to a public order but "without a shared metaphysics or a belief in a single cosmic symbolism" (Jencks 1980, 5). Especially prevalent in Italy and Spain,[18] this mannerist style refers to the classical notion of imitation being the highest aesthetic ideal. Like neorationalism, neoclassicism focuses on physical form and its associated meanings, assuming timeless design features which can be discovered through the study of precedents and typologies (Attoe and Logan).[19] But whereas neorationalism produces collage, neoclassicism produces hierarchy and axial ordering. And while neorationalism applies incremental action, neoclassicism applies extensive restructuring (Jencks 1980, 5).

The urbanistic neoclassicists hark back to the spatial concatenation (*enchaînement*) of the Baroque city of the sixteenth and seventeenth centuries. French architect Joseph Belmont explains:

> After the sixteenth century, architects conceived of a building or a city in terms of strongly related elements which constituted a single "composition." This sequence led, little by little, to a dominant element which was the "head" of the composition: this was the dome of a church, the central hall of a palace, the belfry of a city hall. It was always limited by very well-marked "boundaries". walls around a city, angle piers at the ends of buildings. This hierarchy and this delimitation of space expressed a very faithful image of the hierarchy and the constraints of societies in that epoch. The baroque sequencing was directly inspired by natural sequencing: the parts of a building or a city were assembled like the branches of a tree or like the limbs of the human body. . . . Spatial concatenation always favored decoration and ornament: columns, cornices, the framing of bay windows, and sculpted motifs that were not just fantasies. These decors contributed to the unity of a building or city. Ornament served as the tool of spatial concatenation. Such preoccupations led the baroque architects to value symbol over necessity, the useless over the useful, monumental architecture over domestic architecture, in a word, to think symbol rather than function (Belmont 1987, 29–30).

Challenged initially by the revolutionary architects, and then by the modern movements of the early twentieth century,[20] baroque urbanism was not resuscitated until the rise of neoclassicism in the 1970s. Neoclassicists expressed contempt for the fundamental principle of autonomy and rediscovered baroque spatial concatenation with its principles of composition governed by rules of hierarchy and delimitation. Belmont describes this attitude, saying, "No more isolated buildings in green parks, but buildings carefully inserted in an urban fabric. No more windows dispersed over facades, but openings linked by ornament. No more functional preoccupations, but a constant concern with symbol. No more domestic architecture, but a monumental creation" (Belmont 1987, 65).

Many neoclassicists came to monumental design via the megastructures of the 1960s and 1970s. Ricardo Bofill is one example. Taking off from Adolph Loos's entry for the Chicago Tribune building (1922), shaped like a Doric column, Bofill has created whole building groups of columns and entablatures on an inflated scale from prefabricated reinforced concrete construction (Barnett 1986). Bofill's motto is that each piece of "construction is a monument, each plaza a theater, each building a temple" (cited by Fernandez-Galiano, 60). According to Bofill's *Taller de Arquitectura*, "The only way to create new cities is to create monumentalities in which the subconscious dreams of man are interpreted" (in Le Dantec, 56). This attitude draws from an architectural palette expressive of a strict social hierarchy, usually a monarchy, and when applied to public housing (as most of it has been), it enacts a reversal that might be understood as tongue-in-cheek, a travesty, or a political intent to empower the inhabitants. But since it is the architect who is responsible for the reversing—not the inhabitants—it is the architect who symbolically comes to occupy the apex of the hierarchy or who is the interpreter of people's subconscious dreams.

The neoclassicist Manuel Iñiguez asserts that "the city, ancient or modern, has some characteristics that define it forever: the street, the square, the public buildings, the residences, have established between them, through a slow and uninterrupted process, laws of composition. . . . If such compositional laws are forgotten, as in recent years, the City, deprived of measurement and proportion, corrupts the architectural components within it, creating a monstrous medley which can never be called a true City" (Iñiguez, 89). Neoclassicism is an "architecture that is based on the critical knowledge of its own history" and that "has its origins

La Belvedère, Cergy-Pontoise, France; Ricardo Bofill and Taller de Arquitecture, architects, 1986–87

Le Viaduc sur Lac, St Quentin-en-Yvelines, France; Ricardo Bofill and the Taller de Arquitec-tura, architects, 1982

in the rational imitation of itself" (Iñiguez, 89). It "should be understood as Quatremère de Quincy describes it in his book, *De l'Imitation*, as a rational construction of one image, which searches for resemblance in a previously known and analyzed object" (Iñiguez, 89). Classicism seeks to recover natural and essential patterns. To convey the sense of permanence associated with the classical city, Iñiguez cites the poet C. P. Cavafis, who wrote: "You will never find new lands, you will wander on the same streets and in the same quarters, you will become old; and between the same streets you will grow grey. You will always arrive at this City. For another land you don't wait, there is not a ship, there is not a land" (cited by Iñiguez, 88). With A. Ustarroz, Iñiguez redeveloped the village of Château Pichon-Longueville near Bordeaux along with its château and winery to create "a new place where old fragments and new architecture look as if they had been together from the beginning" (Iñiguez, 90).

At the same time as historicist urbanistic trends of neorationalism and neoclassicism gained credence, a more broad-based conservation movement throughout Europe focused on existing urban fabrics, particularly the prewar ones.[21]

OPEN ARCHITECTURE

A different breed of architect and planner reacted to the alienation produced by modernist solutions by opposing the rigidity of both the architectural mode of production and its product. This response sought to include the prospective users in the design process or to provide them with structures that could be easily transformed according to their own needs and tastes. It resulted in a cohousing movement (Marcus, McCamant and Durrett), experiments with movable partitions, and various forms of community design. The most well-known participatory work is that of the Belgian architect Lucien Kroll, who collaborated with inhabitants on the design of the medical faculty at Woluwé-Saint Lambert in Brussels (1969), the revitalization of a housing project in Alençon, France (1963–69), townhouses at the Vignes Blanches in France (1976), and houses at Emèrainville, France (1979).[22]

A variation on this theme was that of providing "open" or "half-determined" structures, which the user finishes. While sharing the goal of encouraging inhabitant intervention, this strategy sought to provide "supports" upon which users could build rather than to work directly with them. The attempt to provide "open architecture" paralleled calls for an "open society"[23] in the wake of the Second World War. While the "open aesthetic" plied by members of Team X in the 1950s sought to allow for indefinite growth and change, it also sought a clean break from the past. The Dutch architect Herman Hertzberger, a student of Aldo van Eyck, aspired to "polyvalent space," saying in 1963 that we should have prototypes which allow for individual interpretations of collective patterns (Frampton, 1985). He realized this intent in his Centraal Beheer insurance office building, 1974, which he left deliberately unfinished to encourage appropriation by its users. Another notable contributor to this kind of design is Nikolaas Habraken (and his Foundation for Architectural Research—SAR—in Eindhoven, Holland), whose Supports system offers personalized mass-produced housing (Habrakan).

THE FRENCH VERSION

Centrally situated within this western European urban design ferment, French architects and urbanists synthesized various influences and added their own special imprint. Beginning in the early 1970s, the questioning of modernist architectural ideals led to borrowings from neorationalism, neoclassicism, and the various open architectures, as well as from the British townscape movement and the American work of Christopher Alexander and Robert Venturi (see chapter 3). Knitting all of these strands together with their own concerns for preserving preindustrial urban fabrics (see below) and retaining the merits of modernity, French architects and planners grew intent upon creating an urban architecture (*architecture urbaine*) in the 1970s. Along with their American and other European counterparts, they shifted their attention away from megastructures and toward (re)discovering the actual scale and typology of the old city. Architects and planners began looking back to the pre-industrial rural villages and urban courtyard housing which modernists had abandoned for slab buildings and towers. The attitude of architects toward housing shifted from the collective monumental housing of the modernist city to individual houses within a "traditional" urban fabric. As Bernard Huet explained, "when everything becomes a monument, there is a crisis of monumentality and a loss of meaning" (Huet 1986, 12).[24]

Under the banner of *"Le groupe 7,"* a group of architects and architectural historians which formed in 1973 made references in their work to the French interwar garden cities, the Viennese Hofe, and the city block (or *ilôt*). This group included Christian de Portzamparc, Jean-Paul Dollé, Jean-Pierre Buffi, Antoine Grumbach, Roland Castro, Guy Naizot, and Gilles Olive (Le Dantec, 48–51). Other important contributors to this brand of urban design thinking and practice included Bernard Huet, Philippe Panerai, Jean Castex, and François Laisney.

The prominent place of the typo-morphology school in France was signaled by the appointment of Huet as editor-in-chief of *Architecture d'Aujourd'hui* (AA) in 1974. In this role, Huet helped to direct the course of architectural debates in France.[25] A series of important theoretical and historical studies were being undertaken in the mid-1970s that examined urban morphologies and architectural typologies. Probably the most influential was *Formes urbaines: De l'ilôt à la barre* (1977) by Jean Castex, Jean-Charles Dépaule, and Philippe Panerai,[26] which attempted to explain the slow decline of the city block (*ilôt*) by describing five of its seven incarnations: Haussmann's Paris, English garden cities, the expansion of Amsterdam under Berlage, Ernst May's Siedlungen in Frankfurt, and Le Corbusier's *Ville Radieuse*. According to David Mangin, this book played an important role in the diffusion of these ideas but was largely misunderstood. "The real subject of the book, still timely," says Mangin, "is in fact that of the relationship of buildings to the ground, to the public space and the private yards" (Mangin 1985) and not the creation of city blocks themselves devoid of context.

Other works of the "typo-morpho" genre included *Eléments d'analyse urbaine* (1980) by the same authors;[27] *Lecture d'une ville: Versailles* (1977, revised 1980) by Katherine Burlen, Jean Castex, Patrick Céleste, Catherine Furet, and P. Panerai; *Morphologie urbaine et typologie architecturale* (1977) by Ahmet Gulgonen and François Laisney; and *Le Creusot* (1981) by Christian Devillers and Bernard Huet with a preface by Louis Bergeron. Much of the work produced around this time bore the imprint of Michel Foucault's influence. Bruno Fortier's *La Politique de l'espace parisien à la fin de l'ancien régime*, for example, examined the way in which late-eighteenth-century public-health and penal disciplinarian initiatives led to "functional" planning. Le Dantec described this "renewal of criticism," claiming that "without the resurgence of an intellectual movement around architecture in France, the catastrophe of the 'thirty black years' [1945–75] would have been irreversible" (Le Dantec, 58).

This new ideal was evident in a series of government-sponsored architectural competitions that marked a turning point in French urbanism. The competition for the La Roquette neighborhood (1973–4) located in the 11th *arrondissement* of Paris elicited a number of projects from young architects[28] that diverged radically from the prevailing dogma. These projects suggested that "rediscovering the urban . . . can result not from the simple addition—or superimposition—of private spaces but, on the contrary, from the definition of public space [to produce architecture] which would no longer be an isolated object lording over a residual space, but part of an ensemble forming an 'urban room'" (Le Dantec, 62). Although the jury did not select any of these and opted for a more standard approach, Le Dantec contends that "on the ideological front, this competition was nonetheless a great victory" (Le Dantec, 62). For the first time, he explains, a great weekly (*Le Nouvel Observateur*) sided with this "new wave" and published a photograph of the model by Roland Castro. Having resonated with a large sector of the French public, this new wave proceeded to win competitions, obtain commissions, and change the ideological course of French urbanism.

The second important architectural competition was the seventh Program for New Architecture (*Programme d'Architecture Nouvelle*, or PAN) in 1974. Coinciding with the fiscal crisis and a decrease in construction, this competition encouraged "the creation of a new architecture and a new environment through the improvement and modification of new construction or of existing buildings" (Guiheux). The guidelines explained that the housing unit should be considered in relation to the site and should give back to inhabitants their "right to the city" (after Lefebvre). Christian de Portzamparc entered the project he had previously proposed for the La Roquette competition and won. After having designed only a water tower at Marne-la-Vallée, he was selected in 1976 to design the low-income housing project Les Hautes-Formes in the 13th *arrondissement* of Paris. Le Dantec remarked "Oh, that seventh session of the PAN! That already legendary seventh session of the PAN! . . . Not only did those young architects not propose models, '*céllules*,' or combining constructive systems, they also spoke words which were almost forgotten: . . . city, history, urbanity" (Le Dantec, 64–65).

Subsequent competitions explicitly prescribed urban form *a priori*, with the goal of regenerating traditional urban qualities. The French government held the first townhouse competition in 1974 for Les

Côteaux du Val Maubuée (in the new city of Marne-la-Vallée), award-
ing first place to AREA (*Atelier de Recherche et Études d'Aménagement*,
including Alain Sarfati, Stanislas Fiszer, and the late Bernard Hamburger), who proposed a picturesque solution; it awarded second place
to Paul Chemetov, Yves Lion, and Fernando Montès, who proposed a
more rigorous rational design. In 1976, a much larger townhouse competition was launched for Jouy-le-Moutier (in the new city of Cergy-
Pontoise) for which the government selected nineteen architectural
firms, all but one (Vasconi–Pancréac'h) proposing picturesque designs
(Ellin 1994).[29] Then, a traditional city-building (apartment building)
competition was held in 1978 for the neighboring municipality of
Cergy-St Christophe (Ellin 1986). A more restrained, and realizable,
version of reconstructing the European city in France was that of generating an "urbanism of houses," a strategy which has been extensively
investigated and realized by the firm AREA.[30]

This tendency was also apparent in private sector building, the most
well-known example being the resort of Port Grimaud, which François
Spoerry designed and developed near Saint Tropez in 1973 to resemble
a fisherman's village. Since then, Spoerry has gone on to produce mixed-
use neotraditional developments in Switzerland, Mexico, and the United
States (see chapter 3), as well as in France. An advertisement for Spoerry's Port Cergy, begun in 1990 and located just 20 miles outside Paris,
explains that it displays the charm and traditional character of the local
villages of the area (Port Cergy, 1988).

Another example of private sector neotraditional urbanism in
France is the "Provincial Urbanism" of developer Jacques Riboud, as
realized in 1966 at La Verrière-Maurepas within the new city of Saint
Quentin-en-Yvelines in the western suburbs of Paris (Riboud 1968,
1981). Riboud described his goal for this neighborhood, which he named
La Nouvelle Amsterdam (New Amsterdam), as that of rediscovering "in a
new city, created all at once, the traces, the arrangements of streets and
plazas, the types of housing (and especially individual houses with yards),
the perspectives, the source of architectural composition which made our
cities so pleasing, particularly our provincial cities before being submerged, first by the growth of suburban tract developments, then by the
brutal push of the '*grands ensembles*' with their density and severe geometry" (Riboud 1968). Provincial Urbanism achieves this, he explained, by
resurrecting "squares decorated with statues, . . . curving streets, little

alleyways that lead in unexpected ways to a boulevard and then to a vast open landscaped space offering wide perspectives. Boredom, that frightening enemy of new cities, finds its antidote in the alternation of narrow streets and open ones, in an original detail on a facade which doesn't necessarily conform to the reigning canons of taste, but which brings variety and breaks with monotony; that is also the objective of the streets open to cars without the fashionable concern for separating expressways from pedestrian paths. Along the sidewalks: stores, cafes, places to play *'boules,'* houses with little yards in which children can play under the eyes of their mothers while they take care of other things" (1968). The features which distinguish this neighborhood from typical suburban development include well defined and varied public spaces; connected houses (townhouses) with a small front lawn and larger backyards; a "picturesque" style of architecture with varied façades, and the spectrum of colors found in the old villages of the area.[31]

While new construction in France emulated traditional urban fabrics, a great deal of official and grassroots efforts were directed toward conserving existing buildings and streetscapes. Objections to the destruction of French central cities during the 1950s (in the name of redevelopment) incited legislation for the preservation of historic districts (*secteurs sauvegardés*) in 1962. This law— the *Loi Malraux* (because it was sponsored by then Minister of Culture André Malraux)—declared the twelve central *arrondissements* historic landmark districts, assuring their preservation and in some districts, such as the Marais, their rehabilitation (Evenson, 315). With the economic recession of 1973–75, this law also helped to justify cutting back on new construction. In addition, the creation of the *Agence Nationale pour l'Amélioration de l'Habitat* (ANAH) in 1970 encouraged the rehabilitation of old housing, and the *Nora Report* (1972) encouraged the rehabilitation of old buildings for public housing. All of these conspired to produce what came to be known as a movement for the *conservation du patrimoine*, a movement supported by the French Ministry of Culture and its socialist minister Jack Lang, who undertook this cause in the name of populism and environmentalism.

As was occurring elsewhere and had previously occurred in French history, however, such efforts also worked to displace the poor and to gentrify Paris. Beginning during the redevelopment of Paris under the direction of Baron Haussmann from 1853 to 1870, the poor were displaced from central Paris in order to house middle- and upper-middle-income

residents, with another wave of gentrification—or *embourgeoisement*—
occurring after the Second World War with the building of vast amounts
of public housing in the suburbs, and then another during the 1970s. The
population of central Paris decreased significantly while the population
of the near and far suburbs grew rapidly. It was primarily the Parisian
petit monde (shopkeepers, artisans, workers) who left Paris, while the percentage of yuppies (or *jeunes cadres dynamiques*) grew. This changing
social complexion occasioned the conversion of erstwhile low-income
housing units (including the *chambres de bonnes* or maids' rooms) into
upper-income housing or offices and the construction of new housing,
especially from 1950 to 1975 when 340,000 new units were added, comprising one-quarter of the entire housing stock in 1986 (Garcías and
Meade). Corresponding to this shift in the social composition of Paris,
the city grew more politically conservative. The *Loi Malraux* served to
justify as well as sustain this gentrification of Paris.

Zoning changes also assisted in the gentrification of Paris. Beginning with the reign of Louis XIV, building regulations required that the
alignment of the street be respected, along with the continuity of eaves-
lines, the solid-to-void ratio, and the depth of courtyards. These regulations ceased being strictly enforced around 1900. New zoning regulations
established in 1967 eliminated height restrictions and building-line regulations, admitting the construction of the Montparnasse Tower and the
new Central Business District (*le front de Seine*) in the 15th *arrondissement*. The uproar provoked by these skyscrapers incited a stricter zoning code in 1974 which attempted to resurrect or preserve traditional
blocks with certain alignments and volumes, but which has been criticized for producing "mere pastiche or facadism of a painfully cardboard
character" (Garcías and Meade).

When the wholesale food market, the *Marché des Halles*, moved out
of central Paris to the suburbs of Rungis and La Villette in 1969, the
pavilions which had housed the market, designed by Victor Baltard (during Haussmann's redevelopment of Paris), were used for cultural and
social activities and then demolished in 1971, despite impassioned
protests to save them. In 1974, with the Pompidou Center under construction nearby, the new president Giscard d'Estaing commissioned
Ricardo Bofill to design a project for this site. Finding Bofill's project
too "baroque," the president invited two more architectural teams to
submit proposals and mounted a public exhibition of these works in

April 1975 at the Hôtel de Ville. A combined project was assembled and construction started, but when Jacques Chirac became the first mayor of Paris in 1977, he assumed responsibility for this site and halted construction. In 1979 he presented the plan which was to be built (elaborated by the APUR, *Atelier Parisien d'Urbanisme*) featuring an underground shopping Forum and massive subway station designed by Georges Pancréac'h and Claude Vasconi.

The French Union of Architects (*Syndicat de l'Architecture*) opposed this decision and held a counter-competition in which over 600 architectural teams participated. In January 1980 an international jury convened—including Philip Johnson, Diana Agrest, Henri Lefcbvre, Bruno Zevi, and Jean Nouvel—and selected the project of Steven Peterson, a New York architect who "used a collagist figure-ground technique derived from the morphology of the site and surrounding fabrics to arrive at a tight, picturesque combination of medieval and classical forms" (Lesnikowski 1990, 40). Mayor Chirac, however, refused to acknowledge this counter-competition and proceeded with the Pancréac'h–Vasconi project, which was later complemented by additional projects by Paul Chemetov and others (Evenson; Lesnikowski 1990; Lucan 1989).

Frustrated with the state of architectural production and largely inspired by northern European initiatives, a number of French architects and planners undertook experiments in community participation (for example, P. Lefevre and Biriotti[32]) as well as in cohousing (Bonnin). Other French architects shared the goal of encouraging inhabitant intervention, but instead of working along with the inhabitants, sought to produce an unfinished architecture or "open work" (*l'œuvre ouverte*), so that its users could personalize it. The firm AREA has developed this idea most fully, especially Philippe Boudon, Alain Sarfati, and Bernard Hamburger, who acknowledge being influenced by the writings of Robert Venturi, Umberto Eco, Jacques Derrida, and Gilles Deleuze.[33] Sarfati has described the open work as a composition made from accumulation, juxtaposition, and the superimposing of actions, intentions, events, and chance (Sarfati). It takes advantage of serial (or "open") industrialization by using mass-produced building components. In an effort to achieve the open work, Sarfati seeks to include references that are recognized by a wide public—such as porches, ironwork, and other decorative features—and to incorporate a variety of materials, textures, and colors. Hamburger has asserted, we must abandon "the illusion that beauty . . . is the

La Verrière-Maurepas, St Quentin-en-Yvelines, France; developed by Jacques Riboud

Neighborhood designed by architects in collaboration with residents; Cergy-Pontoise, France; organized by architect Pierre Lefevre, 1976

reflection of a universal and transcendent order" (cited by Lucan 1989, 147) and substitute for it another aesthetic project, that of diversity.

Inspired by the work of Kevin Lynch (1960) and Kroll, the architect Jean-Paul Girardot designed a new townhouse development called *Sous les Jouannes* in the new city of Cergy-Pontoise. Referring to the Parisian villa, about which Girardot wrote in 1978, he sought to provide a setting in which both community and privacy as well as diversity and unity (both aesthetic and social) would be achieved (Girardot 1986).[34] To do so, he designed a strictly ordered public space of green arcades and pink columns and balustrades and divided the rest of the parcel into strips of 1.2 meters, or four feet (of which residents could purchase any number), allowing inhabitants to build any kind of

LE LOGIS SOCIAL DU VAL D'OISE
SOCIÉTÉ ANONYME D'HABITATIONS A LOYER MODÉRÉ

HLM
Octobre 1984.

2, RUE DES CORDELIERS, 95300 PONTOISE   ☎ 038 14-42

A tous nos locataires..

CONSTRUIRE ENSEMBLE A VAURÉAL

Notre société lance un nouveau programme de maisons de ville à Vauréal (ville nouvelle de Cergy Pontoise).

Ce projet original est destiné à ceux d'entre vous qui aimeraient participer à la conception de leurs logements, au choix de leur voisinage, et à la définition des espaces collectifs.

Nous vous proposons 2 formules :
— 20 logements en location
— 10 logements en accession à la propriété.

Pour mener à bien ce projet, les intéressés sont invités à se réunir avec des architectes une fois par semaine jusqu'au dépôt du permis de construire en février 1985.

L'emménagement est prévu courant été 1986.

Des séances d'information à votre intention sont prévues, suivant le calendrier.

Jeudi 4 octobre à 21 h.	— Maison de Quartier des Hauts de Marcouville à Pontoise Tél. : 030.04.36.
Mardi 9 octobre à 21 h.	— Maison de Quartier des Louvrais à Pontoise Tél. : 031.12.43.
	— L.C.R. des Bourseaux à Jouy-le-Moutier Tél. : 443.14.39.
Mardi 16 octobre à 21 h.	— L.C.R. des Larris à Cergy Sud Tél. : 032.42.35.
	— Maison de Quartier des Hauts de Marcouville à Pontoise Tél. : 030.04.36.
Mardi 23 octobre à 21 h.	— Maison de Quartier de Cergy Saint-Christophe Tél : 038.74.22.
	— Maison de Quartier des Louvrais Tél. : 031.12.43.
Mardi 30 octobre à 21 h.	— Maison de Quartier des Louvrais à Pontoise Tél. : 031.12.43.

Si vous ne pouvez pas participer à l'une de ces séances d'information renvoyez-nous le coupon ci-dessous ou remettez-le à votre gardien.

Je suis intéressé par le projet "Construire ensemble à Vauréal".

Nom : _____   3.18 _____

Adresse : _____

Téléphone : _____

Announcement for a neighborhood to be built in collaboration with residents, in the new town of Vauréal, France. Organized by architects Pierre Lefevre and Roger Biriotti

townhouse they chose. As Girardot explains, this project sought to reduce the gap "between the reality and the plan, between the buried desire and the constructed reality, between the culture of the demanders/inhabitants [*demandants*] and the cultivation of the commanders/designers [*comandants*]" (Girardot 1981). The carefully designed public space was to act as a support for personal creative expression and for the formation of a community spirit (ibid.). It was to comprise an "urban writing" with repeated elements which would endow the neighborhood with a certain character. Explaining this principle, Girardot said that "it is a little bit like advertising";[35] in other words, repeatedly seeing something makes a subliminal impression.

But the Lynch-inspired project of Girardot was never completed. Although the elaborate public space was built, as well as a model of the potential neighborhood for prospective buyers, no one purchased the lots. While all of the adjacent neighborhoods of the new city were built and populated, Girardot's project became an instant ruin amidst an overgrown field. A decade after the competition, the Public Development Corporation of the new city sold this land to a public housing developer whose standard townhouse development subverts Girardot's vision by turning its back on the public space rather than facing it. For Girardot, the product is a palimpsest of a suburban nightmare superimposed upon an urban dream.

Most people who moved into neighboring areas and had seen the model before purchasing their own homes said they preferred to buy a house that was already built rather than design one with an architect. Those who saw the model found it "very pretty" and even "extraordinary," but said they would not consider purchasing a lot there, afraid that no one else would and that theirs would eventually have to be torn down so that the whole parcel could be replaced with something else. Those who never discovered the purpose of these columns and arcades generally regarded them as "scary" or "bizarre." Lucien Kroll, who has a project adjacent to Giradort's, remarked, "The idea is not a bad one, though it is entirely literary and does not rest upon any reality. . . . But I do not think it is ugly" (Kroll 1986b).

In 1981 newly-elected President Mitterand initiated the Grands Projets (see Fachard, Chaslin, Kramer), sometimes referred to as "Mitterand's Monuments." These large and prestigious commissions changed the focus of architectural debate because they hark back to a traditional sense of monumentalism without being contextual or socially responsive (Lucan). These projects include the Great Arch of La Défense designed by Johann Otto von Spreckelsen; the Grand Louvre project by I.M. Pei; the Musée d'Orsay conversion by Pierre Colboc, Renaud Bardon and Jean-Paul Philippon, with interior design by Gae Aulenti; the Arab World Institute designed by Jean Nouvel; the Ministry of Finance designed by Paul Chemetov and Borja Huidobro; the Bastille Opera designed by Carlos Ott; and the Park of La Villette by Bernard Tschumi. The Park contains the Grande Halle conversion by Philippe Robert and Bernard Reichen, the Center of Science and

The public space of Les Figures, 1985; Jouy-le-Moutier, France; designed by Jean-Paul Girardot

The public space of Les Figures, overgrown, 1987; Jouy-le-Moutier, France; designed by Jean-Paul Girardot

New Opera at the Bastille, Paris; designed by Carlos Ott, 1983-1989

Institut du Monde Arabe, Paris; designed by Jean Nouvel, Pierre Soria, and Gilbert Lezenes, 1981–1987

Parc de la Villette, Cité des Sciences et Industries; designed by Adrian Fainsilber

Industry designed by Adrian Fainsilber, the Zenith concert hall designed by Philippe Chaix and Jean-Paul Morel, and the Music Center by Christian de Portzamparc.

ARCHITECTURAL EXHIBITIONS

The western European recasting of architectural and urban design theory during the 1960s and 1970s was expressed in a series of architectural exhibitions in the early 1980s. The Venice Biennale in July 1980 inaugurated the first international architectural exhibition along the theme "The Presence of the Past: The End of Prohibition." Under the direction of Paolo Portoghesi, this exhibition featured twenty-two, three-story townhouse façades aligned along a mock street called the Strada Novissima, inspired by an amusement park in Berlin. Held at the Corderia of the Arsenal, some of the participating architects were Hans Hollein, Oswald Mathias, Bofill, J. P. Kleihues, Venturi, Scott Brown & Rauch, Skidmore Owings & Merrill, Michael Graves, Stanley Tigerman, L. Krier, Allan Greenberg, Jean-Pierre Buffi, Antoine Grumbach, and TAU (Huet's firm).

Portoghesi described the intent of the exhibition, saying "we hope to take hold of a phenomenon which has its symptoms in the fifties, in the courageous turn of direction in the research of the masters of modern architecture, but has carried on, with a slow and arduous rhythm, transformed only in the past few years into a radical and definitive effort" (Portoghesi 1983, 14). He continued, "the past whose presence we claim is not a golden age to be recuperated. . . . The past with its 'presence,' that can today contribute to making us children of our time . . . is the whole system of architecture with its finite but inexhaustible sum of experiences connected or connectable by a society which has refused a monocentric culture, a main tradition with no competition" (Portoghesi 1983, 26). This exhibition, Portoghesi said, offers "a gallery of architectural self-portraits made for play, for rediscovering the very serious game of architecture, a game on which even the quality of our life depends somewhat" (Portoghesi 1983, 29). Aldo Rossi created his most well-known work for this exhibition, the Teatro del Mundo, a brightly-colored wooden structure set upon a barge in the Venice canals (Trachtenberg and Hyman, 577–78).

With the exception of Krier's façade, the Strada Novissima was built from temporary materials and realized by the Organization for the Administration of Cinema in the laboratories of Cinecitta. Portoghesi was correct in predicting that this "happily scandalous result . . . promises to stir up discussions and arguments, and to involve visitors not in a useless and anachronistic agreement, but in a critical adhesion, in a reawakening of a conscious question of the imaginary as an antidote to urban sterility" (Portoghesi 1983, 29; originally in catalogue 1980). Indeed, Kenneth Frampton condemned the exhibition as an "uncritical absorption of American Populism into the European mainstream" (Frampton 1985, 293) and he declined an invitation to participate. Frampton also withdrew his essay from the catalogue, saying "I see this Biennale as a pluralist-cum-postmodernist manifestation; I am not at all sure that I subscribe to this position, and I think I will have to keep my distance from it. . . . The critical position it adopts is so extremely opposed to all that could be summed up under the category Postmodernist, that I realized it would be absurd for me to advance the essay in this context" (cited by Portoghesi 1983, 17). Nonetheless, Frampton underlined the exhibition's significance when he affirmed that it "announced in various ways the emergence of Post-Modernism at a global level" (Frampton 1985, 305). It also ushered in a more critical approach to urban design.

The Paris Biennale sponsored its first architectural exhibition in the same year, this one with the theme "In Search of Urbanity: Urbanity is Knowing How to Build the City and Live in the City" (*À la recherche de l'urbanité: L'Urbanité, c'est le savoir faire la ville et le savoir-vivre en ville*). The catalogue for this exhibition explained that the search for urbanity is a reaction to the International Style. It defined urbanity as that aspect of a place which illustrates its identity, memory, conflicts, and changes while expressing and nurturing its inhabitants' lifestyles and aspirations. Urbanity, it pointed out, also bespeaks a harmonious form of urban intervention, tending "to put people in relation to the city through culture and a *'genius loci.'* Both people and the city can be endowed with urbanity" (Nouvel 1980a, 7). Emphasizing that the "project of urbanity" has to do with people as much as the built environment, Jean Nouvel, who organized this exhibition, wrote that it "is a political matter in the initial [Aristotelian] sense of the term" (Nouvel 1980a, 20).

The French Festival of Autumn took place in 1981, entitled *"Architectures en France: Modernité Post-Modernité,"* the first exhibition to be held in the newly-opened French Institute of Architecture. It was also the first architectural exhibition in France to attract an audience outside the design field. It reviewed the previous ten years of French architecture and virulently condemned the *grands ensembles.* At the same time, the Venice Biennale exhibit of 1980 opened in Paris at the Salpétrière as "The Presence of History" (*La présence de l'histoire*), not of the past, as in Venice. The French architects Alain Sarfati, Bernard Paurd, and Fernando Montès added their own contributions to the Strada Novissima and Christian de Portzamparc created an entranceway to the exhibit. The exhibition traveled to San Francisco in 1982 with the title "The Presence of the Past," and was pronounced a superficial postmodern "stageset" by Paul Goldberger (Goldberger 1983).

In Fall 1982, the *École Nationale Supérieure des Beaux-Arts* in Paris held an exhibition called "Modernity, An Unfinished Project" (*Modernité, un projet inachévé*), which had been the title of an address and article by Jürgen Habermas in reaction to the Venice Biennale of 1980 (see chapter 6). The architect Paul Chemetov organized this exhibition, largely in response to the one in Venice. He remarked, "Shouldn't we just call post modernism by its real name: neoconservatism?" (cited by Lucan 1989, 176). This exhibition gathered examples of contemporary architecture that referred back to the modernism of the European avant-gardes in the 1920s and 1930s. Its catalogue featured a contribution from Habermas entitled "The Other Tradition" (Habermas 1982).

While "Modernity, An Unfinished Project" was still mounted, the 1982 Paris Biennale opened with a less partisan theme, *Modernity or the Spirit of the Times* (*La Modernité ou l'esprit du temps*), presenting the work of about thirty "young" architects including Robert Venturi, Lucien Kroll, and Cedric Price. The selection jury included François Barre, Olivier Boissière, Patrice Goulet, Pierre Granveaud, Damien Hambye, and Luciana Miotto, who chose works that defended modernism but were detached from doctrine and dogmatism, as well as the search for universal models. Jean Nouvel, who was one of the principal organizers, described this attitude, "To be modern is to do/make; in order to have a chance, should the occasion arise, to make History" (Nouvel 1982, 20). As demonstrated by such expressions of political and aesthetic convictions, the European debate between the ancients and the moderns has continued to rage and to drive urban design theory and practice.

NOTES

1. The typological approach, Delevoy said, "involves simultaneously a problem of reading and writing, likely to lead to a production 'based on the recognition of cultural models'" (Huet, cited by Delevoy, 21). "Archetypologies" are "the types which signpost our journey backward" (Delevoy, 21). "Would this then be the future backwards? [allusion to Bellamy's socialist vision for the year 2000 described in *Looking Backwards* written in 1888]. We must hope so. . . . If only to drive back the specter of apocalypse. And to curb the ecological disequilibrium. And the progressive ideal? A myth. Which needs to be emptied of the enormous load of nonsense it conveys. . . . For it is based on a notion . . . of development . . . in the strict sense as growth phenomenon and not as method of social change" (Delevoy, 20).

2. For more on structuralism and deconstructionism, see chapter 8.

3. A similar argument was advanced by the American anthropologist Alexander Lesser in the 1930s. Lesser accused functionalism in the social sciences of denying the complexity of culture and of failing to explain "survivals," or the persistence of a certain aspect of culture even after its "function" has disappeared, been altered or forgotten. And since the 1960s, symbolic and structural anthropologists have, like Rossi, been asserting the relative autonomy of culture. (For more parallels between urban design and social theory, see chapter 8.)

4. The city, said Rossi, is the "human creation par excellence" and should be seen as a "totality," as a "repository of history" (Rossi 1966). After Savinio (the author of *Clio* and brother of Giorgio de Chirico), Rossi maintained, "Our memory is our culture."

5. According to Diane Ghirardo, this exhibition ignored the social, political, and professional contexts of architecture (Ghirardo 1992, 444).

6. Although Portoghesi is referring to formal archetypes, these are not unrelated to psychological archetypes. He writes that in the ancient world, architecture [*arkhē*] meant "art, or the craft of transforming the earth in function of man's needs" (Portoghesi 1983, 59). He says, "In Greek mythology the Muses were born from Mnemosyne, to mean that there is no art except that originating from memory, and in some way a repetition" (Portoghesi 1983, 37). Portoghesi contends, "The result of the discovery of the sudden impoverishment produced in architecture by the adoption of technologies and morphologies separated from places and traditions has been the reemergence of architectonic archetypes as precious instruments of communication. . . . The Postmodern in architecture can therefore be read overall as a reemergence of archetypes, or as a reintegration of architectonic conventions, and thus as a premise to the creation of an architecture of communication, an architecture of the image for a civilization of the image" (Portoghesi 1983, 11).

7. Portoghesi asserts, "In a future prospect—divested of the great totalizing illusions but not of the tension toward justice—architecture will be able again to assume its ancient role as mediator between man and nature, as guardian of the conventions and experiences characterizing the places of the world in their infinite diversity . . ." (Portoghesi 1983, 48). He contends, "In a certain sense, these are the years of 'refound time,' to use a Proustian image" (Portoghesi 1983, 20).

8. This third typology, Vidler claimed, "is evidently born of a desire to stress the continuity of form and history against the fragmentation produced by the elemental,

institutional, and mechanistic typologies of the recent past. The city is considered as a whole, its past and present revealed in its physical structure" (Vidler 1978, 31). This typology is an "ontology of the city" (Vidler 1978, 29), with "no clear set of rules for the transformations and their objects, nor any polemically defined set of historical precedents" (Vidler 1978, 32).

9. Vidler continued, "In this sense, it is an entirely modern movement, and one that places its faith in the essentially public nature of all architecture, as against the increasingly private and narcissistic visions of the last decade. In this it is distinguished from those latter-day romanticisms that have also pretended to the throne of postmodernism—'townscape,' 'strip-city,' and 'collage-city'(that in reality proposed no more than the endless reduplication of the flowers of bourgeois high culture under the guise of the painterly or the populist" (Vidler 1978, 32).

10. Krier and Culot said, "We must begin by rediscovering the forgotten language about the city which achieved formal perfection in the eighteenth century" (cited by Lucan 1978b).

11. Krier and Culot do not denigrate Le Corbusier, but seek to further develop certain aspects of his thought. Krier, for instance, has incorporated elements of modernism into his projects, such as a portico in the style of Le Corbusier (Barnett).

12. Rob Krier, eight years older than Leon (and a graduate of the Technical University in Vienna, 1975), tends to be more utopian and traditional than his brother. He designed the Ritterstrausse (1977–80) or the "white house" in Berlin, which bears similarities to the Karl Marx Hof in Vienna by Karl Ehn. It was intended to be low-income housing but is not. For more on Rob Krier, see R. Krier (1979, 1984) and Berke (1982).

13. Schoonbrodt was also the founder of *Inter-Environnement Bruxelles*.

14. One of these letters was from Gérard Bauer and Jean-Michel Roux, architects of the French firm AREA (Dethier).

15. Charles Moore won this competition.

16. With regards to architecture specifically, the Tendanza has realized very little in Italy. Most Tendanza realizations are by the Ticino School, so-called because it is based in Ticino (or Tesscin) in Switzerland, its most prominent member being Mario Botta (see Frampton 1980, 322–24).

17 Initiated in 1978, this International Architecture Exhibition in Berlin (Internationale Bauaustellung or IBA) was initially scheduled for a 1987 completion. For more on IBA, see Miller (1993), Wise (1994), Lampugnani (1991, 113–14), Rossi, Kleihues, and Grassi (1991), and Ghirardo (1996, 107-36).

18. There has also been an Anglo-American neoclassical strand as revealed in the writings and designs of the Prince of Wales, Quinlan Terry, and Charles Jencks.

19. Often, the neorationalist and neoclassicist trends are lumped together, as in Jencks's larger category of Post-Modern Classicism.

20 Spatial concatenation was challenged by the rationalist philosophers and the utopian and revolutionary architects of the late-seventeenth-and eighteenth centuries. These philosophers, especially Descartes and Kant, and architects, especially Ledoux, Boullée, Lequeu, and Durand (the revolutionary architects), substituted autonomy for sequencing. Rejecting the hierarchy implied in Baroque design, they

created buildings that were linked to nothing else. They proposed forms which were round (Ledoux's ideal city at Salines-des-Chaux in Arc-et-Senas), spherical (Boullée's project for Newton's cenotaph), and square, as well as cities of individual houses with no links between them or to their sites. They also rejected ornament and symbol in an effort to rediscover basic principles and function. But the ideas of these revolutionary architects were not widely adopted because the French Revolution of 1789 incited a conservatism in architecture and urban design which referred back to the Baroque. This wave of Baroque-influenced urban design lasted until around 1900 when the eighteenth-century style of rationalist thought began to flourish in the modern movement (see Kaufmann).

21. See Appleyard (1979) and Hewison (1987).

22. For a discussion of the Vignes Blanches, see Ellin (1994). For more on the work of Kroll, see Hunziker, Schuman (1987), and Dutton and Grant (1991, 42–43).

23. On the relationship between "open architecture" and Karl Popper's *The Open Society and its Enemies* (1945), see Jencks (1973, 332–34, 345–46).

24. Huet asserted: "Deprived of the aid of typology, isolated from all context, liberated from constraints imposed by convention and by urban regulations, architecture as a work of art can not depend on the usual means of postmodern art (commentary, transgression, and exception) except in referring to its own history, and in situating itself within the accelerated movement of fashion and the cycle of stylistic nostalgias. . . . Architects are reduced to relying upon their own subjectivity and the monuments which they draft can only exalt autobiographical values, which are at times interesting for art historians and specialized journals but not necessarily of interest to the majority of inhabitants of a city" (Huet 1986, 12).

25. Huet's first issue (no. 173) focused on housing. In his second issue (no. 174), Huet explained that he wished to remain faithful to the ideas of AA's founder André Bloc without adopting his ideas about modern architecture to the letter.

26. This was a revised version of a study originally commissioned by the *Comité de la recherche et de développement en architecture* (CORDA) in 1975, entitled *De l'îlot à la barre: Contribution à la définition de l'architecture urbaine.*

27   This was also a revision of a study originally done for the CORDA, entitled *Principes d'analyse urbaine* (1975b).

28. Among the architects who entered this competition were Roland Castro, Christian Devilliers, Edith Girard, Yves Lion, and Christian de Portzamparc.

29. Other townhouse experiments in France included the one at Lille-Roubaix-Tourcoing (1979–80), which sought to apply the traditional typology of the northern region of France and to respect the existing urban fabric (directed by J.-P. Guislain, see Melonio), and a low-income townhouse development designed by Jean Fatosme at Paron near Sens in the Yonne on the Route de Nemours (Fatosme).

30. This firm has put these ideas into practice and has written about them in *Un Urbanisme pour les maisons* (1979) by Bauer, Roux, and Renaud; *Banlieues de charme* by Bauer, Baudez, and Roux (1980); and in the collection *Paysage pavillonaire* (IFA, 1982).

31   Riboud contended, "It is not necessary to hide the fact that this kind of urbanism . . . differs profoundly from the conceptions which have governed urban creation over the last twenty years and [that this type of urbanism] has—inevitably—been subject

to criticism and opposition from certain professionals who see it as a 'return to the past'" (Riboud 1968, 35). Riboud responds to such criticism by saying that one should not "in the passion of being modern—refuse a means of expression for the simple reason that it has been used before" (Riboud 1968, 36). He also asserted that "far from being a return to the past, this conception of urbanism obeys recent notions and translates the concern for making certain choices ... on the basis of psychology, biology, and an understanding of the people who will use these spaces rather than on the basis of arbitrary aesthetic principles. ... It is now recognized that ... places should offer their inhabitants not only pleasure but also a 'factor of security.' This demands an architecture which evolves slowly and prudently; it rules out facades of a severe uniformity; it rules out bold experiments with uncertain results" (ibid.). Riboud claims that this kind of architecture is "recommended by psychologists who see in it a means for protecting the new inhabitant against reactions, often painful ones, to uprootedness [*déracinement*], in a city where all is new, and who see in it a means of accepting new cities more easily" (ibid.).

32. On the work of Lefevre and Biriotti, see Ellin (1994).

33. Other architects who have explored this potential include Stanislas Fiszer, Gilles Bouchez, Dominique Montassut, and Bernard Trilles.

34. Interview with the author, February 5, 1986, Paris.

35. Ibid.

3

URBAN DESIGN THEORY:
THE ANGLO-AMERICAN AXIS

SINCE GLOBALIZATION is an integral feature of postmodern urbanism, precise sources and flows of influence remain largely elusive. Suffice it to say that postmodern urbanism has not evolved within national vacuums, but is a product of substantial cross-fertilization across the Atlantic in both directions and increasingly across the Pacific as well through journals, books, travel, and extended visits. So much so that tracing origins and influences tends to become an exercise in futility. Indeed, some of these efforts trace its origins to Europe, others to America,[1] while others still regard these as independent and simultaneous developments which are either complementary[2] or at odds.[3] The division presented here, then, between the European continent and the Anglo-American world is mainly an heuristic one, intended only to suggest an impressionistic geography of ideas and practices regarding urban design. With this disclaimer, I proceed to describe the predominant theories guiding urban design from the 1960s to the 1980s, this time emanating primarily from Great Britain and North America: the townscape movement; advocacy planning, community participation, environmentalism, and feminism; regionalism and vernacular design; Venturi and contextualism; historical eclecticism; historic preservation and gentrification; critical regionalism; master-planned and gated communities; neotraditional urbanism; and edge cities.

THE TOWNSCAPE MOVEMENT

Led by the *Architectural Review* in the 1950s, the townscape movement reacted to the modernist tendency to regard the city "as a kind of sculpture garden" (A. Jacobs and Appleyard 1987, 114).[4] An editorial by J. M. Richards appearing in 1953 criticized the British new towns for their lack of urbanity, and Ian Nairn's "Outrage" in 1955 stated that "if what is called development is allowed to multiply at the present rate, then by the end of the century Great Britain will consist of isolated oases of preserved monuments in a desert of wire, concrete roads, cosy plots and bungalows" (cited by Hall 1988, 222). Art editor for the *Architectural Review* Gordon Cullen developed the idea of townscape in 1949 to describe the "art of relationship" among all elements of the landscape. He emphasized that our experience of a place is a result of "serial vision" or of the unfolding sequences of street scenes (Relph 1987, 238) and he offered a compendium of optimal qualities for a townscape including the architectural, the painterly, the poetic, and the practical (Cullen).[5]

In reaction to modernism's "architectural objects," the townscape movement emphasized the relationship between buildings and all that surrounds them, and encouraged designers to enclose buildings around public space rather than sit buildings in the center of it. This concern with the urban experience found inspiration in the past: in the eighteenth-century picturesque, the love of disorder, the cultivation of the individual, distaste for the rational, passion for variety, pleasure in idiosyncracy, and suspicion of the generalized (Rowe and Koetter, 34); in the romanticism of nineteenth-century French utopian socialism, and perhaps the anarchism of Kropotkin (Dyckman); in the nineteenth- and early-twentieth-century contributions of the Arts and Crafts movement, Andrew Jackson Downing, Frederick Law Olmsted, Camillo Sitte, and Raymond Unwin; and in "the wave of European postwar expressionism, existentialism, and bohemianism" (Dyckman).

This holistic view of the city was simultaneously being embraced on the other side of the Atlantic, particularly by Paul Goodman,[6] Kevin Lynch, and Jane Jacobs, although not necessarily described in terms of townscape.[7] An important impetus to the American concern was the confusion and fear generated by modern architecture and modern society and a desire to assuage these through humanizing the city. A widely touted means for doing so became that of making the city legible, in order to "read" the landscape. The text thus became a metaphor for the city. Through interviews and questionnaires, Kevin Lynch (1960) found that people come to understand places through five major features of the physical landscape: paths (to direct movement), edges (boundaries to limit one's "world"), districts (zones for each activity), nodes (points of intense activity), and landmarks (points of reference). In *The View from the Road* (1964), Donald Appleyard and J. R. Myer explored the new urban experience of highway driving and its implications for urban design.

The desire to make the city legible and alleviate urban fear led to an emphasis on resurrecting the social and symbolic function of the street and other public spaces. In contrast to the prevalent postwar planning practices, for instance, Jane Jacobs's widely-read critique of the postwar American city asserted, "It is futile to try to evade the issue of unsafe city streets by attempting to make some other features of a locality, say interior courtyards, or sheltered play spaces, safe instead" (Jacobs 1961, 35).[8] Instead, she maintained:

> A city street equipped to handle strangers, and to make a safety asset, in itself, out of the presence of strangers, as the streets of successful city neighborhoods always do, must have three main qualities: First, there must be a clear demarcation between what is public space and what is private space. Public and private spaces cannot ooze into each other as they do typically in suburban settings or in projects. Second, there must be eyes on the street, eyes belonging to those we might call the natural proprietors of the street. The buildings on a street equipped to handle strangers and to insure the safety of both residents and strangers, must be oriented to the street. They cannot turn their backs or blank sides on it and leave it blind. And third, the sidewalk must have users on it fairly continuously, both to add to the number of effective eyes on the street and to induce the people in buildings along the street to watch the sidewalks in sufficient numbers. (ibid., 35)

Serge Chermayeff and Christopher Alexander similarly bemoaned the decline of meaningful public space, foreshadowing the contexualist's trend: "Extinct are the intimate, the special, the strange experiences of the great cities of the past where once the solitary, the adventurer, or the poet in camouflage could mingle at will with the crowd and find pleasure by very reason of his anonymity" (Chermayeff and Alexander, 73).

Foreshadowing the contextualist trend, they intoned, "The time may soon come when planners, designers, developers, and others will recognize and act on the simple notion that the spaces between buildings are as important to the life of urban man as the buildings themselves" (66). This concern with the declining quality and quantity of public space paralleled a concern with the decline of the public realm among historians, philosophers, and social scientists such as Lewis Mumford (1961), Jurgen Habermas (1962),[9] and Richard Sennett (1973).

During the latter part of the 1960s, this discussion was largely overshadowed by American involvement in the Vietnam War and the Civil Rights Movement (Walzer, 470) as well as a pre-energy crisis infatuation with the technological utopias of Buckminister Fuller (1970), Yona Friedman (1968, 1975), the Japanese Metabolists, and Archigram.[10] But the products of urban renewal, the energy crisis, and the shattered idealism of the 1960s incited both reactive planning and anti-planning sentiments. Examining the tower and slab housing projects built during the previous decade, the planner Oscar Newman argued for the need to produce a "defensible space environment" (O. Newman 1972, 22) by heightening security measures, including building walls and fences as well as installing surveillance cameras, keep-out signs, and security patrols. Among those espousing anti-planning sentiments figured Richard Sennett (1970) who accused planning of stifling creativity and diversity and called for the abolition of zoning controls and professional bureaucracies. Robert Goodman (1971), meanwhile, accused planners of being "soft cops," proposing instead "guerilla architecture." And Douglas Lee (1973), in an influential article, predicted the demise of large scale comprehensive planning.

In a more proactive vein, the 1970s also saw a renewed interest in reconstituting the public realm, along with a return to valuing the contributions of Sitte, Unwin, and Olmsted.[11] Lynch emphasized the perceptual coherence of landscapes and their "sensuous forms" (Lynch 1971) and called for the creation of "place character," that which lends a sense of identity, security, pleasure, and understanding to a landscape (Lynch 1976). Charles Moore similarly called upon designers to take responsibility for more than an individual building: "If architects are to continue to do useful work on this planet, then surely their proper concern must be the creation of place—the ordered imposition of man's self on specific locations across the face of the earth. To make a place is to make a domain that helps people know where they are and by extension who they are" (cited by Hines).[12] In *Body, Memory and Architecture* (1977), Moore and Kent Bloomer called for humanizing design by making it both "haptic"—or highly sensory—and "syncretic"—combining historical references and other decorative features in a way which is meaningful to a general public (Russell, 32).[13]

Christopher Alexander and his co-authors adopted Sitte's and Lynch's methodologies in an effort to create a sense of historical identity in new settings. Asking how this "timeless way of building" can be expressed in new design (Alexander 1977, 8, 159), they developed 253 related "patterns" constituting a "pattern language," which seeks to discover preferred design solutions. Christian Norberg-Schulz addressed this concept in terms of "recovery of place" or respecting the *genius loci*. We should not copy the old, he said, but determine the identity of a place and interpret it in new ways (Norberg-Schulz 1979, 182). "Only then we may talk about a living tradition which makes change meaningful by relating it to a set of locally founded parametres" (ibid.). In contrast to the functionalist land-use diagrams, this humanistic approach to design is usually illustrated with street-level diagrams that include people, and annotations explaining how something is to look or function or what vernacular or historical element is being recalled.

The townscape movement and its North American counterpart have left deep imprints upon urban design theory and practice. In central cities, this approach contributed to supplanting smaller interventions for the large-scale planning undertaken after the Second World War, and by 1976, planners inspired by Jane Jacobs were described in the *New York Times* as "mainstream" (June 13, 1976, cited by Harvey 1989, 40). This attitude towards planning contributed to the implementation of new zoning ordinances (for example, in New York, San Francisco, and Pittsburgh) to encourage street walls, clearly defined plazas, and other aspects of urban design which had been legislated away in the 1960s to accommodate towers-in-the-park (Barnett). Outside of central cities, there was a return to the garden suburb of the 1920s (see Stern and Massengale 1981). The concern with the way in which people experience space also led to more programmatic attempts to design in collaboration with people.

ADVOCACY PLANNING, COMMUNITY PARTICIPATION, ENVIRONMENTALISM, AND FEMINISM

The massive application of new transportation, information, and building technologies after the Second World War led many architects and planners to question the elitist assumptions of their professions and to re-envision their clients and their tasks. Among planners, the 1965 American Institute of Planners (AIP) conference led to a revision of its statement of purpose in 1967, to enlarge the purview of planners beyond physical planning and include social, economic, and environmental issues as well.[14] In 1968, Robert Weaver called for "a new kind of urban generalist," a "new kind of modern Renaissance Man," leading to the development of interdisciplinary planning degree programs at the university level (M. Scott, 616). Also in 1967, the American Institute of Architects (AIA) established Regional/Urban Design Assistance Teams (or R/UDATs), interdisciplinary volunteer teams which would be invited to communities to study particular problems and propose solutions through working with local students, business and town leaders, and other town members (Russell, 102).[15]

On both sides of the Atlantic, a number of other challenges toward the authoritarian planning by-numbers in use since the 1940s appeared in the late 1960s and 1970s, such as social planning, community-based planning, participatory architecture, process architecture,[16] advocacy planning, self-building, and sweat-equity, efforts recalling some earlier initiatives of Patrick Geddes (1910s) and Frank Lloyd Wright (1930s). This brand of populism sought to enlist people in the design of their own environments, regarding style as elitist. Lynch's *The Image of the City* (1960) provided inspiration for much of this work since his method of interviewing suggested that designers discover people's images of the city in an effort to reinforce his five elements. Applying Lynch's method in the Venezuelan new town of Ciudad Guayana, Donald Appleyard revealed the wide gap between the planners' and inhabitants' views of the city (Appleyard 1969). Drawing from the work of Ivan Illich, John Turner (1970) explained that he sought to provide housing which was "convivial" in contrast to the "manipulative" intent undergirding modernist urbanism. Other theoretical contributions to this undertaking were offered by Alexander (1964, 1966, 1977), Davidoff (1965), Gans (1968), Mazziotti (1971), Kaplan (1973), Hartman (1978), Peattie (1978), Hague (1982), and Hester (1985).

Realizations of this theory include John Turner and William Mangin's work on squatter settlements (1963, 1972); Christopher Alexander's Mexicali projects and his plan for the University of Oregon (Alexander, 1977, 1985); the developer Michael Corbett's Village Homes in Davis, California in 1972 (Corbett); Moore and Turnbull's Kresge College at the University of California, Santa Cruz, in 1974; Moore, Grover, and Harper's use of television programs called "Designathons" to elicit popular opinion about how to develop 4-1/2 miles of riverfront in Dayton, Ohio, in 1976; David Lewis's multiple-use buildings for Pontiac, Michigan, and Pittsburgh, Pennsylvania; Ralph Erskine's Byker Wall in Newcastle-upon-Tyne in the 1970s; David Slovic's Student Union at Temple University in the 1980s; and Randy Hester's plan for the island of Manteo, North Carolina.

These challenges to authoritarian planning have met with varying fates and have themselves been challenged by the profession, local communities, and architects charged with carrying them out. Nonetheless, they have left indelible imprints on architectural theory and practice as well as on the landscape. One of these is the movement for cohousing, which began in northern Europe in the early 1970s before migrating to the United States. Usually consisting of 15 to 35 single-family houses surrounding one common house that has shared facilities, cohousing developments are typically designed in participation with their inhabitants.[17]

At the same time that architects and planners were reaching out to their constituencies, "post-occupancy" studies were being conducted (e.g. Gans 1967; Cooper 1975; Boudon 1969; Keller 1986) to find out what people think about the places in which they live and thereby inform future designs. Meanwhile, urban sociologists began accusing urban designers who neglected to consider the ways in which people perceive place, of "environmental determinism." Countering the growing presupposition that technology is rendering traditional notions of community and neighborhood obsolete, urban social theory was asserting the continued relevance of these, albeit overlain with the new kinds of communities and settlement patterns which were evolving in response to new communication technologies. This sentiment was apparent in Herbert Gans's study of an "urban village" in Boston (1962) and in the controversy sparked by Harvey Cox's *The Secular City* (1965) described in *The Secular City Debate* (Callahan 1966).

Also at this time, psychologists began directing their gaze to the environment. The new subfield of environmental psychology defined the concept of place identity as "a substructure of self-identity that defines an individual's personal identity in relation to the physical world through memories, ideas, feelings, attitudes, values, preferences, meanings, and conceptions about behavior relevant to the physical settings in his or her daily life" (Proshansky).[18] Based on psychological findings, the architectural historian Christian Norberg-Schulz (1964) asserted that form is perceived in ways which are culturally-derived and thus relative, and, as a corollary, that architecture is never value-free.

The late 1960s saw a renewed interest in "ecological planning" (for example, McHarg in 1969, and Bookchin in 1974),[19] a sentiment largely influenced by Rachel Carson's *Silent Spring* (1962) and expressed in E. F. Schumacher's *Small is Beautiful* (1973), which proposed a return to self-sufficient small-scale communities. Manifest primarily in a grass-roots movement promoting communal and rural living, this interest initially registered only marginally in urban design, as in the example of Arcosanti begun in 1970 by the architect Paolo Soleri, with the assistance of many student "workshoppers" outside of Phoenix, Arizona. At Arcosanti, Soleri sought to realize his concept of Arcology, a synthesis of architecture and ecology which he began developing when studying with Frank Lloyd Wright at Taliesen West. Constructed largely below ground and from local materials, this solar-powered mini-city was to combine housing, work, and leisure activities, making the car unnecessary (Russell, 97).[20]

By the 1980s, however, these concerns had become more broad-based, evolving into "environmentalism" or planning for "sustainability" (Partridge 1985, Van der Ryn and Calthorpe 1986, Bartone 1991, and Orr 1992). The description of a 1994 ACSA/AIA teachers' seminar articulated this concern as follows: "Architecture, once just a matter of style, is now a matter of survival. After eleven thousand years of building to protect ourselves from the environment, we are discovering that our designs are diminishing our health and well being, as well as the carrying capacity of the planet Earth. Many believe a major ethical and cultural shift is required, and that the beauty and power of nature may unlock the key to our future" (ACSA News 1994).[21]

A final related impact on urban design during this period was the feminist contribution, which began to appear in the 1960s alongside revisionary interpretations of American urbanism and urbanization that sought to correct the egregious omission of women from most accounts of American urban history and sociology.[22] As feminist scholars emphasized the importance of redressing this balance by incorporating women's history into American history, they also challenged certain assumptions of mainstream American history, especially the separations of male/female, workplace/home, public sphere/private sphere, and city/suburb, which led to an emphasis on the male/workplace/public sphere/city. This emphasis obfuscated the very powerful interrelationship between these and the female, the home, the private sphere, and the suburb. As a corrective, feminists reminded us that the "personal is political" and called for a more comprehensive and accurate interpretation of American history and society by reincorporating her-story into his-tory. This sensitivity toward the neglect of women extended to other silenced groups such as the poor, non-WASP ethnic groups, the physically-disabled, the elderly, children, gays and lesbians, and inhabitants of less developed countries, comprising the majority of the world's population. And finally, this sensitivity extended to the environment in which we live, a concern sometimes referred to as "eco-feminism" (see chapter 6).

Feminist revisions of urbanization and urbanism seek the source and trajectory of women's historical role in society. From Freidrich Engels (1840s) to the contemporary work of people such as Kenneth Galbraith (1973), many have attributed the subjugation of women to industrialization. When the home and workplace were one, they say, men and women participated equally in both. But industrialization altered this arrangement, shifting women's work from the communal workspaces of the village to the private spaces of the individual home, nuclearizing the family, and making the workplace (the public sphere) the domain of men. With this shift, the communications networks and political skills of women declined. In addition, industrial capitalism's need to generate larger markets for its greater production led to the creation of needs for home products and appliances which made housekeeping an obsessive, expensive, and extremely time-consuming occupation. Although women entered the labor force in large numbers during wartime, the shift of industrial activity from national defense to domestic appliances and house-building (after World Wars I and II) renewed the need to enlarge or create new markets such that vast advertising campaigns were launched to get women out of the workforce and back into the home. As

Dolores Hayden has pointed out, capitalism and sexism fused in campaigns for homeownership and mass consumption.

Suburbanization and the political economy which sustained it contributed to trapping women into the roles of caretaker (of home and children) and consumer (of mass-produced items).[23] But the suburban ideal proved far from ideal, despite its persistent popularity among suburban dwellers as well as those yet to attain it. It was not ideal because: (1) the isolation from neighbors, services, and places of employment rendered it difficult to satisfactorily combine housework, childcare, paid work, and a social life; and (2) this difficulty contributed to separating the public from the private sphere and men from women, with negative repercussions for equal political and economic participation as well as for domestic harmony. As Hayden contended, such single-family houses in suburban areas "constrain women physically, socially, and economically" and "acute frustration occurs when women defy these constraints to spend all or part of the work day in the paid labor force" (Hayden 1980b). She added that millions of angry and upset women were treated with tranquilizers. One drug company advertised, "You can't change her environment but you can change her mood" (ibid.).

In search of better alternatives, Hayden searched the historical record for instances where men and women shared housework, childcare, and paid work (Hayden 1976; 1980a).[24] She then applied elements of these to propose a solution for contemporary America with the understanding that most people do not want to live in communal settings or have state bureaucracies run their lives (Hayden 1980b; 1984). Hayden recommended designing so that cooking, cleaning, laundry, childcare, and transportation might be undertaken collectively. She proposed the formation of small participatory organizations called HOMES (Homemakers' Organization for a More Egalitarian Society), which would involve men and women equally in the unpaid as well as the paid labor force and where unpaid labor would be minimized as well as other forms of energy consumption that are wasteful. Hayden's HOMES would also eliminate residential segregation by class, race, and age and following from this, expand the possibilities for recreational and social activities. They would do this by incorporating private housing and private gardens for each household as well as collective spaces and activities such as day-care, a laundromat, a kitchen (for children at day-care, the elderly, and others not wishing to cook), a food cooperative, a garage with vans providing cab service and meals on wheels, a garden, and an office with helpers (for children and the elderly). In addition to new construction satisfying these requirements, Hayden suggested retro-fitting existing suburban blocks by converting single-family units into multiple-family housing; pooling interior land to create parks at the center of the block, and adding pedestrian paths and sidewalks to link all units with this park; fencing front and side lawns to create private outdoor spaces; and converting a select number of private porches, garages, tool sheds, and family rooms into community facilities.[25]

Feminist urban design theory also challenged assumptions inherent in the language we use, pointing out that many common terms are sexist. The term "bedroom suburb," for instance, is sexist because the home is only a bedroom for adults working full-time away from their residence. It is not just a bedroom for children, for adults who do not work outside the home (mainly women), or for the elderly. And the home is also a place of work (not only sleep), even if it is unpaid work, which remains an essential though often overlooked piece of the economic puzzle. The only people for whom suburbs are exclusively places to sleep are those who work full-time elsewhere, the majority of whom are adult men. Use of the term "bedroom suburb," then, grants greater legitimacy and value to the primarily adult male perspective than to the experiences of others.

Feminist urban design theory also questioned the use of the term "family" and why so many have asserted, and continue to assert, that the family and marriage are universal institutions,[26] an assertion which implicitly discriminates against those who do not fit the prescribed molds. To correct this, feminist urban design theory borrowed the distinction between household and family from anthropology (for example, Rapp, Collier, Rosaldo, Yanagisako), the household being a residential unit of production, reproduction, and consumption and the family being a subjectively defined group of people, and emphasized the need to acknowledge the wide range of these, which diverge from the prototypical household comprising a male wage earner, a female housewife, and children. By 1975, 39 percent of U.S. households had two workers; 13 percent were comprised of one parent (usually a woman) and children; 70 percent of all working women were working because of financial need (Hayden 1980b), and over 50 percent of all children between the ages of one and 17 years had mothers in the paid labor force. Today, less than 7 percent of all households constitute the prototype. Nonetheless, the design of the American single-family dwelling persists as the basic building block of most homebuilders and as the "dream" to which most people aspire. Any real innovations, such as the nineteenth-century apartment house with its communal kitchen, laundry, and day-care facility, have tended to be victims of critical attacks based on fear of "feminine rebelliousness, communistic sentiments, or warped children" (Wright 1981, 151).[27]

Despite this resilience to change, some new models have been infiltrating the housing market over the last two decades to serve the needs of constituencies who are currently more numerous, more articulate, and politically stronger than they have been in the past: the poor, single heads of households, the elderly, and singles—all groups of which women constitute the majority (Wekerle). And feminist thought has contributed to rethinking "the foundations of the [planning] discipline, its epistemology, and its various methodologies" (Sandercock and Forsyth, 55) in light of "both the need for and the resistance to a gender-conscious approach to the teaching of planning" (ibid.), and to the writing of planning history.[28]

These wide-ranging efforts—from advocacy planning to citizen participation, post-occupancy studies, environmental psychology, environmentalism, and feminist urban design theory—posed a challenge to the twin assumptions of architecture and planning regarding rationalism and environmental determinism. They revealed a reflexive turn within the professions, a self-critique, acknowledging that architects and planners are interested actors (and are not above politics), that there is no single overarching public interest (but diverse and contested interests which do not all have equal voice), and that urban design should not focus solely on issues of aesthetics and land use but should be defined more broadly. The role for urban designers, according to this self-critique, should be less authoritarian (more humble) and more overtly political, with the goal of empowering people to improve their communities and their environment. Rather than simply designing and realizing plans, these architects and planners would also engage in a critical examination of the status quo and in becoming advocates for unrepresented interests (Peattie 1978; Burchell and Hughes 1978, xxix). This kind of activity was to serve as a springboard for transforming society on a larger scale.

A simultaneous transformation was occurring among the public at large, which was increasingly demanding a voice, as was apparent in grassroots activities that shared many of the same dissatisfactions and radical goals of the design professions, such as the homesteading and squatters' movements. Closer to the mainstream, the number of citizen groups increased exponentially. In Davis, California, one of these groups succeeded in winning a majority in the 1972 city council election and substituted an environmentally-sensitive majority for rampant development in the face of rapid growth (Russell, 111). The American public generally was becoming increasingly opposed to developers' projects, as vividly illustrated by the success of citizen groups in Manhattan, over the last decade and a half, in derailing a number of large-scale projects including Westway,[29] additions to the Whitney and Guggenheim museums, and the demolition of Lever House.

Today, then, at least some degree of designing with the community is commonplace.[30] Efforts to design in harmony with nature have also become part of the standard design rhetoric and legislation has been adopted to assist these efforts, such as cluster-zoning ordinances to protect undeveloped areas.[31] But both community participation and designing for sustainability can be abused, particularly when invoked for the principle purposes of preserving one's own neighborhood, business, and property values.

While still seeking to provide people with urban design they like and to design in harmony with the site, other attempts dispensed with user input entirely and looked to local vernaculars or mass culture. For these designers, style remained within the domain of design professionals (Tzonis and Lefaivre 1984, 182). I turn to these now, looking first at regionalism and vernacular design and then at the influence of Robert Venturi and the contextualists.

REGIONALISM AND VERNACULAR DESIGN

Attempts to design in harmony with a site's surroundings have been present throughout human history. In the early part of the twentieth century, the British planner Patrick Geddes was a strong advocate of preserving architectural and cultural traditions and was opposed to the imposition of Western planning practices onto non-Western societies (Goodfriend).[32] Influenced by Geddes, Lewis Mumford wrote two books (1924, 1926) in which he offered "a vision to live by again" (Mumford; cited by Thomas,

226) by proposing a usable past via "regional reconstruction." Located in the past, Mumford explained that regionalism represents an escape from the feeling that "we live in a spiritual chaos" (ibid.) since the "last dying of the medieval ember" (Mumford; cited by Thomas, 227).[33]

But the adamant anti-regionalism of most modern urbanism largely foiled these attempts until the ill effects, especially the perceived rootlessness, of post-World War II urban design incited a re-emergence of efforts to preserve or create a sense of place during the 1960s. One means for doing so became that of designing in regional styles, or in the "vernacular."[34] Moshe Safdie, for instance, exclaimed that "the people who built their villages, the man who designed his own house and built it himself, worked in a simple situation. Today we have great factories and industries and organizations producing the environment. What is lacking today is a vernacular, our own vernacular. We need to create one which is an expression of our life and technologies" (Safdie 1970).

Bernard Rudofsky's book and exhibition at the Museum of Modern Art (MoMA) in 1964 entitled *Architecture without Architects* greatly stimulated this interest in vernacular architecture. Rudofsky introduced this, until then, rarely-discussed topic saying that the exhibition "attempts to break down our narrow concepts of the art of building by introducing the unfamiliar world of non-pedigreed architecture. It is so little known that we don't have a name for it. For want of a generic label, we shall call it vernacular, anonymous, spontaneous, indigenous, rural, as the case may be" (Rudofsky 1964, 1).[35] In an ironic twist, however, now it was architects who would lead a movement to "design in the vernacular" by gathering inspiration from non-architect-designed landscapes. There could not have been a clearer rebuke of the preceding generation of urban design.

Vernacular design has two main referents: (1) the past (historicism), and (2) the locale or site (regionalism). While the European neorationalists generally refer to the first referent, American contextualists (see below) usually refer to the second. One architectural critic described the division, saying that in England and France, "vernacular architecture is synonymous with preindustrial rural architecture" while "in America it has come to mean ordinary buildings and landscapes of all kinds from all historical periods" (Carter, 202).[36]

An important figure in urban design theory who does not fall neatly into a category or school of thought is John Brinkerhof Jackson (1970, 1977, 1980). Founder and editor of the journal *Landscape* (1951–68) and popular teacher at the University of California at Berkeley and other schools, Jackson examined the reciprocal relationship between people and the built environment, taking a humanistic approach toward evaluating landscapes. Jackson's iconoclastic contributions, which were influenced by the tradition of French geography (especially that of Vidal de la Blache), have nurtured an appreciation among architects and planners for the common landscapes of vernacular and commercial buildings.

The most recent spate of discussion along these lines has been described as the "new regionalism."[37] The impact of this kind of thinking on urban design in the West has been far-reaching, present in virtually all strands of Western urbanism since the 1960s. A number of efforts to design in the vernacular have also been undertaken in the non-Western world, the most well-known of these (among Western audiences) being Hassan Fathy's undertaking in New Gourna, Egypt (Fathy).

VENTURI AND CONTEXTUALISM

Freud said that he was not a Freudian and [Venturi and I] say that we are not postmodernists (Denise Scott Brown 1991).

We are modernists, not postmodernists. No one is a postmodernist. Maybe postmodernism is dead (Denise Scott Brown 1990a).

The postmodern period belongs to [Venturi] even if most post-modern architecture does not (Paul Goldberger 1991).

Recipient of the 1991 Pritzker Prize, Robert Venturi is widely regarded as the "father" of postmodern architecture and urban design in both the United States and Western Europe, despite claims to the contrary by his partner, Denise Scott Brown, and himself. Venturi made his initial mark in 1966 with the "gentle manifesto" *Complexity and Contradiction in Architecture*, in which he proclaimed: "I am for messy vitality over obvious unity. . . . I like elements that are hybrid rather than 'pure,' compromising rather than 'clean,' distorted rather than 'straightforward,' ambiguous rather than 'articulated,' perverse as well as impersonal . . . conventional rather than 'designed,' accommodating rather than excluding, redundant rather than simple, vestigial as well as innovating, inconsistent and equivocal rather than direct and clear. . . . I include the non-sequitor and proclaim the duality. . . . Blatant simplification means bland architecture"(Venturi 1966, 22).

In response to Mies van der Rohe's "Less is more" doctrine, Venturi replied, "Less is a bore." Whereas modernism maintained an either/or attitude with the ultimate goal of purity, unity, and order, Venturi proposed a more inclusivist "both/and" attitude with the goal of a "complex and illusive order of the difficult whole" (Venturi 1966, 22). Venturi aimed for "unity rather than simplification" (Venturi 1966, 80), aspiring to "simultaneously recognize contradictory levels" (Venturi 1966, 103). He thus privileged complex programs over simple ones, and multifunctional buildings and materials over the specialization of materials, structures, programs, and space. Whereas modernist orthodoxy emphasized continuity and sought to create flowing space in which the outside flows from the inside, an architecture of complexity and contradiction would incorporate enclosed spaces with exteriors that might contrast with the interiors to produce "decorated sheds" or "ducks." While modernist orthodoxy disregarded the street, Venturi's architecture would accommodate it. While modernist architecture led to finished free-standing objects, the architecture Venturi proposed would be unresolved so that it might evolve. The designer, Venturi suggested, should assume a modest role, unlike the heroic modern architect with utopian visions.

In contrast to modern orthodoxy, which condoned only engineering and industrial references, Venturi sought to communicate to a larger public by drawing from conventional symbolism, conventions, clichés, advertising, and cinema, as well as from industrial design. In *Learning from Las Vegas*, Venturi, Scott Brown, and Steven Izenour (1972) maintained that it was time to build for people—rather than some undefined ideal Man—and to stop pursuing abstract doctrinaire ideals. They suggested that architects gain inspiration from popular and vernacular landscapes, such as those of commercial strips and suburbs, because those are what people seem to like.

Venturi described his attitude toward history by saying, "As an architect, I try to be guided not by habit but by a conscious sense of the past" (Venturi 1966, Preface). He explained that he understood tradition as did T. S. Eliot, who said, "if the only form of tradition, of handing down, consisted in following the ways of the immediate generation before us in a blind or timid adherence to its successes, 'tradition' should be positively discouraged. . . . Tradition is a matter of much wider significance. It cannot be inherited and if you want it you must obtain it by great labor. It involves, in the first place, the historical sense, which we may call nearly indispensable to anyone who would continue to be a poet beyond his twenty-fifth year; and the historical sense involves perception, not only of the pastness of the past, but of its presence. . . ." (Eliot c. 1920; cited by Venturi 1966, 13).

Other contributions to this discussion were made by Charles Jencks and George Baird (1969), Christian Norberg-Schulz (1969), Charles Jencks and Nathan Silver (1972),[38] Alexander Tzonis (1972), and Vincent Scully (1974). Urging designers to be sensitive to the context in which they are working, this body of work constituted an architectural counterpart to social and advocacy planners. But this reaction to modernism tended to concern itself more with individual buildings than with urbanism. Mary McLeod (1986) has called attention to the fact that Venturi makes only two references to urban design in *Complexity and Contradiction*, one regarding Times Square billboards and the other regarding Main Street. She notes that in *Learning from Las Vegas*, he and his co-writers reject the notion of the traditional city entirely, adopting Pop Art as a model.

In the United States, an important forum for debate during this period was the Institute for Architecture and Urban Studies (IAUS) in New York City, co-founded by Peter Eisenman, Kenneth Frampton, and Mario Gandelsonas in 1972 and later joined by others, including Anthony Vidler in 1977. Initially an offshoot of MoMA's design department, the IAUS quickly became an entity unto itself whose mission continually evolved. The guiding purpose of the IAUS was to stimulate debate around architecture and it was largely ecumenical, including architects and historians of all stripes on its Board of Directors.[39] Its journal *Oppositions*, anti high modernism and architectural discourse, had a more strictly modernist/rationalist tendency (Pecora; Ockman 1988).[40] The IAUS provided the main conduit through which the ideas of the European neorationalists came to North America, by translating their works into English as well as by hosting them for extended visits. Two significant research projects undertaken at the IAUS which bore imprints of neorationalist thought and addressed urban scale included an inquiry into streets[41] and a study of low-rise high-density housing, which produced a prototype built in the Bronx.[42] The IAUS disbanded and *Oppositions* folded in 1984.

Typological theory was also disseminated in the United States through *Perspecta* (the journal of the Yale Department of Architecture) and through visiting professorships offered by Yale University and Princeton University. In the United Kingdom, typological theory was disseminated mainly through *Architectural Design* after it softened its critical stance in 1977 and became a glossy journal emphasizing graphic layout (Goode, 4).

Although they described themselves as the New York Neorationalist School, the work of Peter Eisenman, Michael Graves, Charles Gwathmey, John Hejduk, and Richard Meier—also referred to as the "Five" or the "Whites"—differed from the European neorationalists in that they disregarded the urban scale. Instead, they shared "a determination to reject the social concerns of the 1960s in favor of an inquiry into pure esthetics" (Goldberger 1993), just as the French structuralists were seeking to discover a fundamental order of language (as well as behavior and thought). In opposition to the Whites, another group of architects that included Venturi, Stern, and Moore "claimed that their work expressed the reality of shades of gray, not the false perfection of pure white" (Goldberger 1993).[43] But, as Goldberger contends, the "Whites and Grays alike, had more in common than they had dividing them: at the end of the day they were all profoundly elitist, concerned mainly with the esthetics of the single-family house, and determined to make architecture in a fairly traditional way. They shared an indifference to megastructures, computer design and other examples of super technology. What separated them was style more than substance" (ibid.).[44]

European neorationalism has had less impact on practice in the United States than in Europe, a fact which Frampton attributes to its "lack of relevance to the American city, which has nowhere the same typological and morphological complexity as its traditional European counterpart" (Frampton 1985, 299). Another factor has to do with the market-driven development in the United States, which lacks the necessary public support required for large-scale urban design innovation. These ideas have nonetheless been adapted to the American context, but largely stripped of their political and social intentions as, for example, in neotraditional developments (see below).

Colin Rowe became the prime mover in contextualist thought in the United States after his arrival at Cornell University in 1962 from Great

Britain. In *Collage City* (1978), Rowe criticized the utopian component of modernism which had impelled many to propose eradicating older cities, and he urged architects not to ignore the importance of the street, the axis, and the role of building mass as a definer of urban space. Rowe emphasized that city design is more like collage than like drawing and he encouraged designers to use all elements at hand including the existing urban fabric. He applied the collage metaphor to suggest that the diverse elements of the city should be woven into a cohesive whole—a "collage city"—containing polar opposites: utopia and anti-utopia, past and future. In the line of European "open architecture," he described it as an "open city [which] discloses no intimation of urgent belief in the value of any all-validating principle" (Rowe and Koetter, 132).

Reflecting on the impetus for modern architecture and its reconceiving of traditional urban space, Rowe asked "Why was it that after 1945, the street [as a social nexus] suddenly disappeared?" (Rowe 1989, 12). Noting that "the attack on the street predates the dissemination of the automobile," Rowe attributed the disappearance of the street to "the object fixation which was endemic in modern architecture" (ibid.). His contextualist approach corrects this by treating streets and squares as room-like spaces and by celebrating the outdoor public nature of these spaces at a pedestrian (not automotive) scale, paying homage to the consumer and the *flâneur* engaged in "an unprogrammed enjoyment of the city," rather than ideal forms seen from a car (Holston, 316). In an effort to revive interest in the relationship between built space and open space, Rowe applied the figure-ground map as a didactic tool, referring to Giambattista Nolli's 1748 map of Rome as a prototype. This map depicts open space as positive (in white) and building mass as negative (in black). A figure-ground reversal reverses these colors. This tool was intended to teach architects not to consider buildings merely in isolation or as objects, but also as backgrounds. It was also a way of urging architects to abandon megalomaniac visions of planning huge areas, and to concentrate on smaller areas, to link buildings with their contexts, and to forgo personal displays in favor of public commitment.

Stuart Cohen, a student of Rowe, was the first to actually use the term contextualism, in a Master's thesis written under the direction of Rowe and then in an article published in *Oppositions* (1974). To Rowe's virtually exclusive aesthetic and physical considerations, Cohen added a cultural dimension and proposed contextual solutions as "working strategies for architects who must . . . cope with a significantly re-evaluated position in our society," a "new and vulnerable role" (Cohen 1974, 22). In contrast to Rowe, Cohen's strategies "stress the relativity of value judgment rather than its suspension" (ibid.).

Tom Schumacher, another student of Rowe, explained that contextualists do not see architecture "as possessing a life of its own, irrespective of use, culture and economic conditions" (Schumacher 1971, 81), but as a mimetic art with the goal of communicating. To assure the fulfillment of this goal, he said, "an 'overplus' of communication is a necessary constituent of both buildings and cities" (ibid.). According to Schumacher, then, contextualists agree with Venturi that buildings should be "both/and": "Both responsive and assertive, both figure and ground, both introverted and extroverted, and both idealized and deformed" (Schumacher 1971, 86).

Contextualism thus evolved to encompass the wider contexts of history and culture, recognizing built form's symbolic as well as functional aspects. While emphasizing the vitality of traditions, the contextualists did not wish to merely emulate the past, but to incorporate new elements. They understood history, as well as urban design, as compromises between utopian aspirations and actual constraints and their idea of the "vest pocket utopia" consisted in striving for the ideal, even if ideal forms only exist on paper and in fragments of built form. These fragments, they maintained, could be "collaged," or adjusted into a context, and divergence from the ideal can ultimately enrich the work. From the anthropologist Claude Lévi-Strauss, urban design contextualists adopted the notion of the "*bricoleur*," someone who is adept at performing a wide range of tasks with whatever is at hand (McLeod 1984). And from the historian Isaiah Berlin, they adopted the contrast between "hedgehogs," artists with a single vision, and "foxes," artists with many visions, and they claimed the latter designation for themselves in contrast to modern architects and planners whom they regarded as hedgehogs (ibid.).

In sum, contextualism reacted to the singularity of the modern movement's "architectural object," the belief that buildings should be "pure" centerpieces that are created by one architect and stand alone, that do not have preferential façades, and that do not refer to their context. Analogous shifts of emphasis were simultaneously occurring in the social sciences and humanities, particularly with the rise of symbolic anthropology in reaction to functionalism, which had undertaken scientific studies of social and human needs (for example, Malinowski's functionalism, Radcliffe-Brown's structural-functionalism, Maslow's hierarchy of needs), and with the renewed popularity of the French *Annaliste* school of history and the general re-emergence of social and cultural history.

HISTORICAL ECLECTICISM

I am not at all sure that this is what Jane Jacobs had in mind when she launched her criticism of modernist urban planning (Harvey 1989, 82).

Whereas modern urbanism emulated the machine to accommodate an industrial society, postmodern urbanism seeks inspiration from pre-industrial townscapes to accommodate a post-industrial society. The meager American pre-industrial urban fabric may help to explain the relatively unfettered historicism of American urban designers in contrast to their European counterparts, whose borrowings from the past tend to be more academic. In architecture, the American attitude was perhaps best articulated by Robert Stern, who exclaimed: "Mies said less is more, Venturi said less is a bore, and I'm adding to that: More is more! . . . Nothing succeeds in America like excess" (Stern in Williams 1985, 13). Jencks celebrated this free borrowing from other times and places, saying that "it seems to be desirable that architects learn to use this inevitable heterogeneity of languages. Besides, it is quite enjoyable. Why, if one can afford to live in different ages and cultures, restrict oneself to the present, the local? Eclecticism is the natural evolution of a culture with choice" (Jencks 1977, 127).

Subsequent to organizing the "modern architecture" exhibition at MoMA in 1932 [45] and to designing the modernist icon, the Seagram Building, with Mies van der Rohe in 1956, Philip Johnson announced in 1975, "Modern architecture is a flop" (cited by Blake 1977, 10). Johnson described his personal evolution when he said, "I am a historian first and an architect only by accident and it seems to me that there are no forms to cling to, but there is history" (cited by Hines). He began expressing this in his work first through a stripped classicism and then through a more explicit quoting of historical references, as in his AT&T headquarters in New York City (designed with John Burgee 1981).

In similar fashion, Charles Moore's "architecture with a memory" (Bloomer and Moore 1977) applied historical allusions as well as color and wit, all of which modern architecture had banned. This historical eclecticism of American urban designers revealed a renewed concern with aesthetics—with art for art's sake—reminiscent of the City Beautiful Movement at the turn of the century. As Thomas Hines asserted, Daniel Burnham's "aesthetic commitment to historical forms would be resuscitated only in the 1960s and 1970s by the postmodern school of radical eclecticism." In the assessment Paul Goldberger, *New York Times* architecture critic, "If there is anything that has marked the buildings of the 1980s, it is a sense of romanticism toward the past; all the post-modern architects, those who choose to imitate the past literally and those who only allude casually to it, share a sense of fondness, and sometimes even awe, about what has come before" (Goldberger 1988a).

HISTORIC PRESERVATION AND GENTRIFICATION

The infatuation with the past among architects was paralleled among the general public, resulting in an efflorescence of historic preservation movements that extended around the globe. These movements to preserve the existing urban fabric began appearing in the 1960s in reaction to the enormous obliteration of urban fabrics in the United States (in the name of urban renewal) and to the rebuilding of war torn Europe, both adhering to modernist precepts. In the United States, popular opposition to the demolition of New York City's Pennsylvania Station in 1963 contributed to spearhead the establishment of a municipal Landmarks Commission in 1965 and the passage of the nationwide 1966 Historic Preservation Act. Prior to this Act, which called for the protection of districts "having special meaning for the community," either historic or architectural (Relph 1987, 221), only twenty cities had such districts, but by 1975 over 200 had enacted them (ibid.). In New York City, Herbert Muschamp contended, the popularity of historic preservation since 1974 has meant that architectural history "has taken the place of architecture" (Muschamp 1993b). In Great Britain, the Civic Amenities Act was passed in 1967, requiring local authorities to designate districts which should not be destroyed, but should be adapted to new uses (Relph 1987, 221), an activity non-euphemistically referred to as the "heritage industry." In order to professionalize and further legitimize these undertakings, a number of colleges and universities have established academic degree programs in Historic Preservation.

An example of the preservationist attitude is found in a study entitled *The Breath of History* by Paul Henry Gleye.[46] With the eye of a preservationist of the old—not a designer of the new, Gleye undertook a Lynchian analysis to discover which elements of a townscape "enhance the sense of historical identity in a place" (Gleye, 12) so that preservationists could produce this sense of historical identity, and along with it a sense of security and meaning. Focusing on the German town of Munster, which was almost entirely destroyed during World War II and subsequently rebuilt, Gleye identifies seven elements of responsible preservation: (1) reconstruction of major monuments; (2) repetition of traditional architectural motifs; (3) reaffirmation of the center and periphery; (4) incorporation of historical clues; (5) retention of perceived city scale; (6) adoption of historical design ordinance (a design guide); and (7) retention of traditional land uses in the town center (Gleye, 375–45). Although new, Gleye finds that these elements create "a sort of urban palimpsest" (Gleye, 12) by recalling previous urban forms and thus lend a sense of historical identity and security.

The feeling of a loss of center ("decentered-ness") accelerated after World War II, both sustained by and contributing to massive suburbanization. While some found what they were looking for in the new suburbs,[47] others found suburbia to be "disturbia" (R. Gordon et al.) or "subtopia" (Nairn 1955; cited by, P. Hall, 223).[48] And for many of the baby boomers born to these postwar suburbanites, the old city began to hold an appeal once again, a sentiment expressed in the works of Jacobs (1961) and Gans (1962), which waxed nostalgic for prewar urban fabrics and their neighborhoods. After the suburban boom, then, there was a move back to the central city in the 1970s and 1980s, a demographic shift that, although statistically small, was highly visible and effective in changing the appearance and the image of central cities. This grassroots movement was incited in part by the stall in building and the concern for conserving fuel which attended the 1972 fiscal crisis as well as by a general dissatisfaction with what the urban design professions were offering. Resulting in the upgrading of urban fabrics, this movement coincided with the rise of the historic preservation movements and was facilitated by landmark districting. Even real estate agencies capitalized on the widespread infatuation with the past, taking on names such as Old House, Restoration, Renaissance, and Revival (Kasinitz, 175).[49]

Though ostensibly "preserving" the past, the undertakings of preservationists and gentrifiers alike may be more accurately described as rewriting or inventing the past since buildings and districts are "renovated," "restored," or "rehabilitated" to correspond to ideal visions of the past and to satisfy contemporary needs and tastes by incorporating new technologies, floor plans, and more. To give just one among a multitude of examples (for more on this, see chapters 4 and 5), the "restoration" of the Old Town in Quebec City resulted in an assemblage of buildings which had never existed at the same time before (Relph 1987, 223).

Gentrification usually results in the displacement of people and businesses because it increases land values and rents even when occurring in already abandoned sections of town, due to the "domino" or "spillover" effect. In some instances, this has occasioned the rise of counter gentrification movements organized by people living and working in the area, who ironically make similar pleas for preservation. If the community is predominantly identified with a particular ethnic group, this group may make ethnic claims to the area because these are "recognized as potentially legitimate" (Kasinitz, 178) in the context of contemporary urban politics. Another twist which gentrification can incur is the return to the central city neighborhood of people who have only recently sought greener suburban pastures, now that these neighborhoods are being renovated and re-valorized, as has been occurring in the predominantly Italian-American neighborhood of Carroll Gardens in Brooklyn (Ellin 1995b).

One kind of gentrification is the re-use of abandoned warehouse buildings for housing, or loft living. Loft living is one attempt to achieve urbanity, historicism, and a combination of home and workplace. This breed of historic preservation or rehabilitation involves a re-valorization of the industrial past. Sharon Zukin has pointed out that increased automation and the decline of manual labor inspired an "artistic appreciation of older mechanical devices" (Zukin 1982, 74) as artists played with constructing their own machines using obsolete industrial parts. To display this work, MoMA hosted the Bauhaus-inspired "Machine Art" exhibit in 1934, just two years after the "Modern Architecture" exhibit. Although architects such as Frank Lloyd Wright, Walter Gropius, and Le Corbusier were greatly inspired by industrial design, they adapted it for residential buildings by prettifying it (for their primarily female consumers) and adapting its scale appropriately. It was not until the 1970s that a less disguised industrial design began to appear in non-industrial markets, suggesting a changed aesthetic that reflected a quest for beauty without artifice and for authenticity and efficiency. The search for a more human habitat, Zukin deftly observed, turned to factories (Zukin 1982, 68). Ever solicitous to consumer desires, some developers began offering new construction with features of lofts, and merchandising it as "new lofts" (for example, in New York City and Paris), for some, the best of both worlds.

As the housing stock was being gentrified, so was the retail sector, either in a piecemeal fashion or through larger-scale interventions. Most influential in the historic "re-use" of central city retail districts has been James Rouse. The developer of the 1960s new town of Columbia, Maryland, first oversaw the conversion of Boston's Faneuil Hall Market Place (originally built in 1742) and its adjacent Quincy Market (built in 1823) into a new kind of urban shopping mall combining shops, restaurants, small cart-boutiques, and street performers. Rouse thus created the new typology of the "festival marketplace," which in the words of the architect for several of these, Benjamin Thompson, were to be "settings for festive human interaction, made of food and clothes as well as buildings" (cited by Russell, 115). Various interpretations of the same formula followed in the conversion of a former chocolate factory into Ghirardelli Square (1964) in San Francisco by landscape architect Lawrence Halprin and the architectural firm of Wurster Bernardi and Emmons (Ghirardo 1996, 172), and the building (from scratch) of Harborplace in Baltimore and South Street Seaport in New York City. These so-called "urban revitalizations" entailed a "creative partnership" between the public and private sectors and succeeded in replacing declining manufacturing industries with a new economic base and generating a renewed sense of pride in downtowns. But in gentrifying central city districts, it also accentuated the polarization between rich and poor.

In the meantime, planners of a certain "anarchist" persuasion were recommending the implementation of Enterprise Zones (EZs), in which free enterprise would have free reign (see P. Hall). Various governments have embraced this opportunity to invest in older central cities, but the intended benefactors of EZs (central city residents, the poor, the unemployed) have been, for the most part, pushed aside by these initiatives, which usually benefit the already middle- to upper-income businesses that take advantage of EZ subsidies. And the scope of these plans remains largely restricted to formal attributes, as social ambitions (such as achieving social diversity) and land-use recommendations (for mixed use, for park space, for cultural centers) are consistently turned aside in favor of solutions which bring higher returns on investors' dollars.

Transformations in interior design during the 1970s, though not strictly constitutive of urban design, parallel it and deserve mention here. The modernist opening up of interior space, made possible by steel frames eliminating the need for structural walls, reflected a desire to be released from traditional social constraints and from barriers between social classes, ethnic groups, the generations, and genders. It corresponded to the mass ownership of cars in the United States along with massive road building and, as Vincent Scully (1988) suggests, reflected the American love of movement. Subsequent to World War II, it corresponded to a period of affluence that allowed more people than ever before to own their homes and to enjoy larger living spaces. These conditions encouraged the pursuit of opened, undefined, flowing interior space in the modern house by architects and non-architects alike.

More recently, however, a number of factors have contributed to a return of separate rooms with specific purposes, paralleling the urbanistic trend to create enclosed "room-like" public spaces. The fashion cycle and the perennial search for the new, offer one explanation for this shift, but there are more substantial reasons as well. With the 1972 fiscal crisis, new construction grew smaller and the desire for privacy called for the partitioning of spaces. At the same time, the postwar babyboomers reached childbearing age, producing another babyboom that contributed further to cramping living spaces and to the need for privacy. On a more abstract level, the coincident loss of faith in progress and lack of an organizing myth (see chapter 4) led to a re-valorization of more traditional living spaces. So whereas the opening up of spaces reflected a desire to break with the past, the partitioning of spaces perhaps reflects a desire to re-kindle the past. If the opening up of spaces engendered a sense of emptiness, void and meaningless, their partitioning would perhaps bring meaning back. And if the flowing space was to suggest and facilitate the elimination of social differences, perhaps the enclosed space is to vindicate and reassert these distinctions during a time of pervasive insecurity: a place for everything and everything in its place (see chapters 4 and 5). Nonetheless, the trend has not been toward recreating pre-modern spaces, but toward a compromise between these and the modernist open plan.[50]

CRITICAL REGIONALISM

Annoyed by the glibness with which history and the vernacular were being invoked, some began calling for a more reflexive or critical approach in the early 1980s, particularly with regard to regionalism.[51] Although "associated with [local] movements of reform and liberation," wrote Alexander Tzonis and Liane Lefaivre in 1981, regionalism had also become "a powerful tool of repression and chauvinism" (cited by Frampton 1983a). To avert this, they called for a more "critical regionalism." Kenneth Frampton elaborated upon this notion and further diffused it, saying that the idiosyncratic and symbolic elements of traditional cultures should be assimilated with the rational and normative aspects of universal culture to generate "regionally based world culture[s]" (Frampton 1985, 327) in order to avoid the "unreasonable reason" (Frampton 1985, 9) which accompanies the modern project if left unchecked. Acknowledging that there really is no such thing as an authentic local or national culture due to centuries of culture contact and interfertilization (Frampton 1985, 313), Frampton advocated that these be "self-consciously cultivated" by valorizing local materials, crafts, topographies, climate, and especially light. While avoiding the naive utopianism of modernism, he said that these efforts should also avoid the overly sentimental qualities of more recent design.

Critical regionalism, Frampton maintained, should "'deconstruct' the overall spectrum of world culture which it inevitably inherits" (Frampton 1983a, 21), specifically the *fin-de-siècle* eclecticism which "appropriated alien, exotic forms in order to revitalize the expressivity of an enervated society" (ibid.). This deconstruction might entail the production of a more sensual architecture which addresses more than just sight so as "to balance the priority accorded to the image and to counter the Western tendency to interpret the environment in exclusively perspectival terms" (ibid.). And since the central principle of critical regionalism is "a commitment to place rather than space" (Frampton 1983b, 150), a "general model to be employed in all future development is the enclave—that is to say, the bounded fragment against which the ceaseless inundation of a place-less, alienating consumerism will find itself momentarily checked" (ibid.).

Frampton explained that *critical regionalism* "is not intended to denote the vernacular, as this was once spontaneously produced by the combined interaction of climate, culture, myth and craft, but rather to identify those recent regional 'schools' whose aim has been to represent and serve, in a critical sense, the limited constituencies in which they are grounded" (Frampton 1983b, 148). Critical regionalism, Frampton asserted, "favors the small rather than the big plan" (Frampton 1985, 327) and virtually all of the examples he offers are of individual buildings rather than larger-scale interventions. Pointing out that these instances "flourish sporadically within the cultural fissures that articulate in unexpected ways the continents of Europe and America," Frampton described these borderline manifestations (after Abraham Moles) as the "interstices of freedom" (ibid.).[52] Three of the borderline manifestations which Frampton cites as examples of critical regionalism are the Catalonian nationalist revival of the early 1950s represented by the early projects of Oriol Bohìgas and Ricardo Bofill, the contributions of the Japanese New Wave especially Tadao Ando, and the work of Mario Botta.

MASTER-PLANNED COMMUNITIES, GATED COMMUNITIES, AND DEFENSIVE URBANISM

Since transformations in the already existing urban fabric are not sufficient for growing populations, new areas must also be developed. Large-scale plans for new "communities" since the 1970s[53] have been incorporating features of the townscape movement, regionalism, contextualism, neorationalism, neoclassicism, historical eclecticism, and the historic preservation movement in a variety of ways. Those discussed here include master-planned communities, gated communities, the New Urbanism, and Pedestrian Pockets.

Although virtually ignored by specialized design journals, master-planned communities (MPCs), also referred to as Planned-Unit Developments (PUDs), currently house 10 percent of the American population[54] and increasing numbers abroad. Ranging from one to 53,000 acres, MPCs diverge from the typical post-World War II suburban tract development by virtue of their building and design guidelines, shared amenities, and a zoning plan which includes outdoor public spaces, sometimes in exchange for moderate-density housing in one part of the development (Langdon, 50). Following nonetheless the earlier suburban pattern of curvilinear streets, cul-de-sacs, and collector roads, each pod of the MPC usually contains households on the same rung of the socio-economic ladder and MPCs as a whole are homes to the middle class and up, virtually devoid of rental or low-income housing. Some MPCs cater to the second-home market and offer a resort environment, often specializing in activities like horseback riding or golf, as in the "equestrian community" of the Palm Beach Polo and Country Club or in the "golf communities" of the Polo Club Boca Raton and Boca Pointe. The emphasis on creating a sense of "community" is usually important to the developers and designers of MPCs. As the planner of Sterling Forest, New York, explained, "The idea is to have a community that's really a community, that has a sense of place" (cited by Peterson).[55] But in order to create this sense of community, MPCs turn their backs on adjacent areas and are usually surrounded by greenbelts as well as walls.[56]

New developments large and small, as well as individual homeowners, have been installing security systems and gates. These gates, come in all sizes and shapes from the relatively unobtrusive and unguarded gates, to those operated by security codes or remotes, to highly-patrolled and ornate gates which sweep back from the street, are extensively landscaped, and in the exclusive MPCs are often accompanied by a cable television channel received by inhabitants which reports on security issues in the development around the clock. A recent survey revealed that almost one of every three new housing developments built in Orange County, the Palm Springs area, and the San Fernando Valley (all in California) are gated (Feldman). In many MPCs, such as Green Valley south of Las Vegas, walls surround neighborhoods as well as individual houses, a requirement clearly defined in the CC&Rs (Covenants, Conditions, and Restrictions) embedded in the deeds (Guterson). In a telling sign of the times, a gated townhouse development called Celebration at Rainbow Hill was built in Staten Island, New York, upon a site which had previously served as a prisoner-of-war camp during the Second World War (Oser, 1990). In search of security, the high-rise condominium development of Desert Island, outside of Palm Desert, California, features a 25-acre moat surrounding the community rather than a gate (Flusty). In addition to security systems, gates, and moats, homeowners and community builders have been planting "security oriented gardens," which are intended to avert thieves by obscuring the house and by clumping thorny plants beneath windows and along property lines (Flusty). Inside houses, the number of "safe rooms" is growing, armored rooms to retreat to in case of unwanted intrusions, usually concealed in the house plan and accessed by secret doors (Brown 1997).

Aerial view of Regency, the master-planned community designed by the SWA Group, Omaha, Nebraska

In existing cities, the pursuit of safety has led to the formation of neighborhood associations, that take action ranging from volunteer neighborhood watches to the hiring of private security companies.[57] In many cases, residents resort to "Cpted" (pronounced SEP-ted), which stands for Crime Prevention Through Environmental Design.[58] Usually, this translates into street closures or the gating of neighborhoods. The townhouse and apartment-tower complex (4,213 units) of Park Labrea in Los Angeles, for instance, built from 1941 to 1948, added gates in 1990.[59] The planner Oscar Newman (whose book *Defensible Space* appeared in 1972, see above) was recently asked to assist in designing gates for Five Oaks, Dayton, Ohio (Owens; Pietila), a neighborhood of 5,000 residents who live in homes built during the first half of the twentieth century. And he has received a grant from the United States Justice Department to improve security in fifty neighborhoods around the

Entry gate, Polo Club, Boca Raton, Florida

country (Owens). This movement to privatize city streets by gating off neighborhoods has incited controversy, particularly in Los Angeles[60] where, following the largest civil uprising in modern American history in 1992, hundreds of neighborhoods applied to the City Council for permission to install gates or construct street closures (McMillan 1992; 1993).[61] Another measure which has been taken to curb crime in the central city is the installation of seven-foot turnstiles in seventeen high-rise public housing towers in downtown Baltimore after previous efforts using door alarms, time-lapse cameras, and security guards proved ineffective (Simmons).

And such measures are not restricted to residential areas. Retail districts have been using gates, private security guards, and video cameras to spruce up security. The four shopping centers developed by Alexander Haagen in the 1980s in South-Central Los Angeles, for instance, were retrofitted with 7-foot-high wrought-iron fences around their peripheries and patrolled by a private security force (Mitchell). When built anew, shopping malls are usually designed in a panopticon fashion around a police substation, which in addition to becoming the hub of the mall, often becomes the "hub for community policing and neighborhood watch operations" (Flusty). The theme park can be seen as a mere variation on the shopping mall since it is a clearly-bounded and highly-controlled place for spending leisure time, not to mention money. In downtown Los Angeles, the development agency responsible for the design of Grand Hope Park has sought to avoid security problems by not providing restrooms (regarded as magnets for transients) and by

Gates added in 1990 to Park Labrea, Los Angeles. Originally designed by Leonard Schultze & Son and E. T. Heitschmidt for Metropolitan Life Housing Development, 1941–1948

asking the park architect Lawrence Halprin to design an eight-foot-high fence, the gates of which would be closed after dark, paralleling a trend around the country toward privatizing park space (L. Gordon).

This obsession with security has also incited architects to design "defensive architecture." [62] One example of this is a new kind of apartment complex which is reminiscent of the older typology of courtyard housing because arranged around common spaces. These fortress-like complexes diverge from the traditional form, however, in their retreat from the surrounding urban fabric. Accessed by patrolled gates, they turn their backs to the community around them, focusing inward upon the common spaces, which may include amenities such as swimming pools and community centers with gymnasiums. Like the MPCs, of which they are the urban or apartment analogue, these complexes feature architectural components that allude to the past or to the local vernacular, and that seek to offer inhabitants a sense that their own dwelling is somehow unique from the others and that the development as a whole is legible through, in part, providing focal points (often described as "landmarks") such as landscaped fountains, gazebos, or clock towers. [63] Individual house design has also taken on defensive components, either by appearing inconspicuous in order to hide the residents' wealth or by projecting a "don't mess with me" attitude. For the Dixon House in Venice

Hopper House, Venice, California; Brian Murphy, architect

(California), architect Brian Murphy retained the exterior shell of an existing dilapidated house and spraypainted the address number across the facade. And for Dennis Hopper's house in Venice, Murphy set a bunker-like structure with a windowless corrugated metal facade behind a white picket fence mimicking those in the neighborhood. Mike Davis considers these part of "an entire species of Los Angeles 'stealth houses'" (1990, 238).

An office/retail manifestation of defensive architecture has been the atrium building, the prototype being the Citicorp Tower in New York City designed by Hugh Stubbins. Capitalizing on the success of Rouse's festival marketplaces and on new "incentive" zoning laws that have allowed greater height in exchange for public amenities such as plazas, gardens, or renovated subway stations, the Citicorp Tower incorporates arcades of indoor shops referred to as "The Market," and a skylit stage offering free performances, into a huge office tower (Russell, 114). In central cities which have lost much of their population to the suburbs, the design of office and retail buildings may satisfy zoning regulations that require "public amenities" while at the same time remaining largely inaccessible to the public owing to siting, lack of parking, illegible entryways, or explicit signage. As Steven Flusty maintains, the security provisions of these buildings "are directed at maintaining the preferred 'user mix' by preventing non-professionals and the obviously less affluent from becoming so prevalent on site as to intimidate tenant office workers and executives" (Flusty).

The epitome of the fortress impulse is found in the work of architect/developer John Portman, which combines housing, retail, and offices in central city megastructures.[64] The first of these was the Peachtree Center (1976) located in downtown Atlanta where Portman is based. Turning its back on the surrounding city, this complex includes a multistory atrium, retail, offices, restaurants, bars, clubs, a hotel, and a conference center (Russell, 99). Portman was awarded an AIA medal for innovations in hotel design in 1978 (ibid.) and has reproduced this formula in a number of cities from San Francisco, Los Angeles,[65] and Detroit, to Shanghai.

NEOTRADITIONAL URBANISM OR THE NEW URBANISM

"[The] vast and seemingly inexorable process of suburbanization must be challenged, even though it seems so inevitable, so inexhaustible and so hopelessly far gone—a little like nuclear power once appeared and nuclear arsenals still seem (Kelbaugh, viii).

Dissatisfied with the conventional post- World War II suburban tract development as well as the master-planned and gated communities which succeeded them, others have proposed a neotraditional urbanism more recently dubbed the New Urbanism (see Katz)—which draws inspiration from townscapes of the past in an effort to engage their surroundings rather than retreat from them. In order to achieve this, neotraditional urbanism seeks to provide quality public spaces that are semi-enclosed, legible, and connect places that people use, in contrast to the amorphous, illegible, isolated, and largely unused public spaces of the MPC. Rather than increase the fortress mentality and fear, it is hoped that these measures will alleviate the sources of insecurity themselves.

The central motivation behind these efforts is to avoid the excessive separation of functions of modern urbanism along with the social and environmental harm that accompanies it. Though inspired by pre-industrial environments, these urban designs also seek to acknowledge current needs and tastes—including the preference for the individual house—and to take full advantage of new technologies for achieving these ends. This strategy for designing new communities might be regarded as an outgrowth of the historic-preservation movement or as an historic "invention" movement. As the senior vice president of the Regional Plan Association Robert D. Yaro commented, "The preservation movement of seeking out historic villages and towns has been so successful that they're too expensive for most people. [The building of new communities] is an opportunity for the market to produce new developments that have the same character and appeal of traditional villages and towns" (cited by Peterson). The two most well-known American variations on this theme are the Traditional Neighborhood Development or District (TND) and the Pedestrian Pocket (PP).

The TND is a new development, inspired by the local prewar urban fabric, which was developed by the husband-wife architectural firm of Andres Duany and Elizabeth Plater-Zyberk (DPZ).[66] In contrast to the conventional suburban tract development and the MPC, the TND is designed with people in mind rather than cars through the elaboration of design guidelines (or urban codes). In the place of "pods" of housing "clusters," office "parks," and shopping "centers" assembled along "collector roads," the TND is based on grids of straight streets and boulevards (instead of highways) which are lined by buildings in order to generate clear and enclosed public spaces. Buildings are grouped by scale and architectural expression but house a variety of functions, social classes, and age groups. These towns have a finite size and should be easily traversed on foot.

The first and most well known TND is Seaside, an eighty-acre community along the coast of the Florida panhandle, initiated in 1981 by the renegade developer Robert S. Davis. Duany and Plater-Zyberk developed the building code and town plan; a wide array of architects designed the houses and public buildings; and Léon Krier served as a consultant. The code aspired to harmonious diversity by including guidelines for proportions, dimensions, and materials and by designating features that are required, such as deep front porches, tall narrow windows, straight narrow streets which frame a view or have visual terminations such as a gazebo or community pool and bathhouse, on-street parking, separate garages situated toward the back of lots, galvanized steel roofs, screen porches that cover a certain percentage of the façade, picket fences, underground utility cables, and colors which fall within a specified range of pastels. The code encouraged other features such as "outbuildings"—small cottages located beside or behind the houses that could be used for older children, elderly family members, or as a rental

Rector Park in Battery Park City, New York City. Landscape design by Innocents and Webel with Vollmer Associates

unit—and it prohibited aluminum siding, sliding glass doors, bay windows, and design fakery such as inoperable shutters.

Not content with merely altering the shape of communities, Duany and Plater-Zyberk have also been concerned with influencing town politics. In order to encourage popular decision-making, they have been working with an attorney to develop town charters that would take the place of homeowners associations, which tend to discourage public participation because of their excessive legal-ese. Duany describes this as "the last brick in the arch" (cited by Langdon, 50) and Krier describes its importance saying, "The small-town philosophy of the TND is not just an architectural paradigm, but a social synthesis which, if applied nationally, will allow a much larger range of people and talents to become active citizens, in the full meaning of the phrase" (Krier, 1991, 119).[67]

Since Seaside, Duany and Plater-Zyberk have received commissions for over forty town designs, including Kentlands in Maryland, Blount Springs in Alabama, Charleston Place and Avalon Park in Florida, and Mashpee Commons on Cape Cod. They have also been among the designers for two very large projects, Playa Vista in Los Angeles (900 acres)[68] and Daniel Island in Charleston, South Carolina (4,500 acres).[69] And their work has been variously adapted by a number of developers and designers such as the developer Pioneer and the SWA Group, whose Green Meadows West in Johnston, Iowa was designed along neotraditional lines (in 1988) in contrast to its earlier development Green Meadows, begun in 1978, despite the financial success of the latter (Kagi).

The Pedestrian Pocket, as promulgated primarily by architect Peter Calthorpe (1989; 1993), seeks to incorporate elements from the European school of typology, critical regionalism, advocacy planning, and energy-conscious design in an effort to develop "new, compelling typologies for our suburbs—ones that take the low-density, homogenous net that has been thrown over the outskirts of our cities and gather it into finite knots—bounded, contained, lively, and pedestrian communities" (Kelbaugh, viii). Criticizing "the sanitized anti-urban world of [post-World War II America as] a place of diminished experience and diminished insight for its inhabitants" (Solomon, 29), this "suburban project" (Kelbaugh, vii) entails the retro-fitting of existing suburbs along with some new growth to produce concentrated pockets that are situated around public transportation hubs, ideally light railroad stations.[70] Adjacent to the stations are mixed-use areas of medium-high density, including affordable housing and offices.

A prototype PP "houses approximately 5,000 people with jobs for 3,000 on no more than 100 acres" (Calthorpe, 1989, 4) and it contains "housing, offices, retail, daycare, recreation and parks" (Calthorpe, 1989, 11) within a quarter-mile walking radius of a transit system. The housing is low-rise high-density (mainly townhouses, duplexes, and small apartment buildings) and many of the jobs are located in computerized "back offices" and in regional shopping malls. Well-placed pedestrian paths allow for comfortable and safe access to many destinations as well as a means for integrating groups separated by age, ethnicity, or class (Calthorpe 1989, 13, 15). Each PP is restricted in size (both physical and demographic). In sum, the PP is a recipe for urban growth and development which seeks to preserve open space, energy, and resources while reducing commuting time and traffic and widening the available range of working and living choices.[71]

In contrast to the TND, then, the PP has a more regional scope, is mass-transit-oriented (and sometimes referred to as a Transit-Oriented Development or TOD), and includes suburban infill as well as new building. Also in contrast to the TND, the PP does not have architectural guidelines, in an effort to achieve aesthetic diversity and to keep housing costs as low as possible. Rather, the guidelines for the PP focus only on public space, and Calthorpe would eventually like to see the public sector take over the implementation of both these guidelines and the mass-transit system, leaving development to the private sector (Calthorpe 1989, 12). Precursors to Calthorpe's Pedestrian Pocket idea include Ebenezer Howard's Garden City plan (1898), which was rail-oriented, self-contained, and expanded only through the founding of new garden cities, as well as Arturo Soria y Mata's Linear City idea (1882).

Battery Park City from the water

In 1989, Calthorpe was selected to design Laguna West, located twelve miles south of Sacramento. His design includes 66 acres of lakes, 35 acres of parks, and thousands of shade trees as well as 3,300 housing units and a town square surrounded by a town hall, community center, shops, offices, and apartments (Del sohn, 21).[72] Calthorpe has also drawn up a plan for Placer Villages, a new town for a population of 80,000 comprised of 10 villages situated along a proposed extension to Sacramento's rail system (Bressi, 102).[73]

A contemporaneous urban version of these design principles was

Winter Garden in Battery Park City;
Cesar Pelli, architect

taking place for the new city of Battery Park located on the southwestern tip of Manhattan. Situated on a 92-acre landfill, created in part (25 acres) from digging the foundations for the World Trade Center, the master plan for Battery Park City was elaborated in 1979 by Alexander Cooper and Stanford Eckstut. It organized the site as an extension of Lower Manhattan by extending the existing streets to the Hudson River and by establishing design guidelines intended to generate traditional spaces, a human scale, and aesthetic diversity. In particular, the guidelines recommended that prime locations be reserved for public spaces, which are meticulously landscaped with a variety of trees and shrubs, cobblestone paving, black iron railing, Central Park street lamps, 1939 World's Fair benches, and public art. The guidelines indicate that buildings should shape these public spaces rather than vice versa by creating streetwalls. In addition, the building façades should emulate prewar buildings by incorporating stone bases topped by masonry walls, prominent cornice lines, and varied rooflines (Ellin 1995a).[74]

A number of other projects have been initiated for redeveloping "under-utilized" urban sites—often abandoned industrial areas—with an emphasis on contextualism, historicism, and public space. Also along the Hudson are the French architect/developer François Spoerry's Port Liberté and plans for the Spanish architect Ricardo Bofill's Port Imperial. One advertisement for Port Liberté, which is located on the shoreline of New Jersey facing the Statue of Liberty, asserts that its "winding canals and arching bridges, and its panoply of boats give this new waterfront community in New York Harbor the atmosphere of your favorite Continental port or Riviera resort" (Port Liberté Partners).[75] Bofill was commissioned by the American billionaire Arthur Imperatore to design a city in the "Greco-Roman tradition" (Kleinfield) on 400 acres of Hudson waterfront facing midtown Manhattan. Another waterfront development, PortAmerica, located along the Potomac River on a 223-acre site adjacent to the Capital Beltway, was designed by Philip Johnson and John Burgee along neoclassical lines.[76]

Establishing separate firms in 1986, Cooper (Alexander Cooper + Partners) and Eckstut (Ehrenkrantz Group & Eskstut) have been involved in redeveloping a number of industrial sites along neotraditional lines both in the New York metropolitan area and elsewhere.[77] Other firms undertaking such projects include The Gruzen Partnership and Beyer Blinder Belle (Langdon, 56). Not incidentally, most of this industrial re-use is taking place in the eastern US where more industrial wasteland exists and where land is at a premium.

Other instances of neotraditional urbanism in urban settings seek to create or reconstitute an urban center. One such example is the recent major addition to the 1960s new town of Reston, Virginia, which starkly contrasts with its earlier curvilinear street plans in an effort to "embody the cosmopolitan character and charm of Washington's Georgetown and Boston's Newbury Street" (Rensbarger). In already existing towns and centers, a number of initiatives are seeking to reorganize the urban fabric to this end. The most recent efforts to redevelop downtown Los Angeles, for instance, are reacting to the earlier Bunker Hill development —which was conceived in the modernist spirit—by applying many neotraditional principles.[78]

Both DPZ and Calthorpe have spread their words with a missionary zeal, actively attending conferences and participating in the lecture circuit where they speak to packed houses, such as the "Rethinking the Suburbs" conference held in Baltimore and Duany's talk at the Million Dollar Theatre of Los Angeles. Both regard the revision of zoning ordinances of prime importance and they both participated in the elaboration of "The Ahwahnee Principles," neotraditional planning guidelines which are being promoted by the Local Government Commission of California. The first Congress for the New Urbanism was held in Alexandria, Virginia, in October 1993.

Calthorpe was successful in having his transit-oriented development ordinance for San Diego adopted. In California, these ideas have become so popular that "the general perception among developers seems to be that no large project stands a chance of being approved if it does not contain the grid street patterns and pedestrian orientation" (Fulton, 1993). Both the historic preservation movement and neotraditional urbanism have contributed to the adoption of contextual zoning ordinances in cities and towns throughout the US "to encourage uniform street walls and dignified, orderly public places" (Langdon, 56). Synthesizing neotraditional and environmental concerns, the planner Ronald Lee Fleming, who is president of the Townscape Institute in Cambridge, Massachusetts, called for urban policy which encourages urban designers to "retrofit suburbia into energy-saving, mixed-use villages, increase housing in the inner city, and build transit infrastructure that reinforces population concentration and saves what is left of the countryside" (Fleming). The New Urbanism has been incorporating a concern for ecological design in many recent projects, perhaps the most ambitious to date being Civano, outside of Tucson, Arizona (see Katz).

Neotraditional urbanism was concurrently emerging in Great Britain. Under the leadership of Melville Dunbar, Essex new town was designed in the early 1970s in reaction to what had been built in England after the war, which was widely criticized for its monotonous uniformity and its lack of local character. The city adopted a design guide to encourage a more imaginative approach to urban development

(County Council of Essex 1973). Essex new town was planned for a 450-hectare site—purchased by the county in 1973—adjacent to the town of Basildon (80 hectares and 1,000 housing units), located 60 kilometers east of London. The site for Essex new town was an area of small week-end houses built around the turn of the century that had been requisitioned during the war for food production and then abandoned. The master plan called for 5,500 housing units (10 per hectare) and a population of 17,000. The 450 hectares were divided as follows: housing, 200; commercial and industrial, 20; parks, playgrounds and ball fields, 160; and streets and public indoor spaces, 70. The county sold parcels of land of 4,000–40,000 square meters to developers, who agreed to follow the design guidelines. Housing was to be comprised primarily of town-houses and a few small apartment buildings. Ten percent of the housing stock would be for rent and the rest for sale. Commercial and industrial land was leased from the county on 100-year leases or more. Artisanal villages would combine housing, studios, and stores. The commercial area would be inspired by older cities, especially medieval ones. The factories would resemble eighteenth-century warehouses and houses.

The Essex plan and its realization were highly regarded and emulated.[79] The most extensive urban version of neotraditional urbanism in Great Britain is the redevelopment of Canary Wharf, Docklands, in London (1981–),[80] for which the firm of Skidmore Owings & Merrill designed the master plan.

The vogue for neotraditional architecture and urbanism has been aided and abetted by Prince Charles whose opinions have garnered attention and incited controversy. He has said: "I always feel that people get on best if they can live in an area that is like a village community within a city . . . . If you have things on too vast a scale, you lose the human dimension. The trouble is, of course, who designs these things, who makes the decisions and who the planners are" (His Royal Highness). The Prince of Wales believes "architecture should respect the landscape, that a building's size should reflect its public importance, that buildings, 'must relate to human proportion,' that buildings should be in harmony with surrounding structures and that buildings should create a sense of privacy and safety" (Trucco). He also thinks that "buildings should be made from local materials, that new architecture should respect the landscape, that decoration on buildings helps 'to enrich our spirits,' that art should accompany new structures, that signs and lights should be part of the architecture and that buildings should encourage a sense of community" (Trucco).

Prince Charles admires Seaside and has embarked upon his own mission to build four "traditional Dorset towns or villages" (each one consisting of 500–800 households on no more than 100 acres) in the area around Dorchester which is part of the Duchy of Cornwall, comprising the Prince's estate of Poundbury and Middle Farm. He commissioned Léon Krier in 1988 to advise him on this undertaking and Andres Duany to provide the building code (Krier 1989). This code is inspired by the eighteenth-century English village "with housing of all income levels close to shops and public squares, a direct relationship between the heights of buildings and their public significance, and rules governing such things as materials, signs and the proximity of buildings to the curb" (Steiner). The *Sunday Telegraph* criticized the Prince's efforts to return to a world "where squires and gentlefolk live happily alongside the artisan class" (cited by Steiner) and in the Prince's own words, he was subjected to "a torrent of criticism and abuse that was beyond all belief" (cited by Hoge). The recession delayed construction of these towns, but the first 142 houses (55 of which are scattered subsidized units) of Poundbury were built between 1995–98. Now built and inhabited, many of the skeptics are becoming converts as, "the town has recently begun to gain favor with the writers, designers, architects, planners and backpacking day-trippers who swarm all over the project in growing numbers" (Hoge). The influence of these planning ideas may grow if Prince Charles's recommendations to the European Community for urban reform are adopted.

To publicize his ideas, Prince Charles wrote a book entitled *A Vision of Britain: A Personal View of Architecture* (1989), which had a companion exhibition at the Victoria and Albert Museum, and he wrote and narrated a 90-minute television program in which he offered guidelines for good architectural design. The president of the RIBA, Maxwell Hutchinson, wrote a rebuttal to the Prince's book entitled *The Prince of Wales: Right or Wrong? An Architect Replies* (1989), in which he referred to the Prince's principles as "The Ten Commandments." This book has, in turn, inspired a few others, including an issue of *Architectural Design Profile* entitled "Prince Charles and the Architectural Debate" (1989). In October 1992, the Prince of Wales Institute of Architecture began offering its first course to 30 students. Located in two classical stucco buildings designed by John Nash on the edge of Regent's Park, this school is intended, according to Prince Charles, to reintroduce students to "the delicate thread of wisdom that connects us with the works of our

Stonybrook, New York, developers built a new "old town"

forebears" (ACSA News 1992). The director Brian Hanson said that the Institute would emphasize the "timeless approaches to design, planning and building" (ACSA News 1992), and Christopher Alexander has served on the faculty.

In addition to new towns and extensive redevelopment of existing cities, the impact of neotraditional urbanism is also apparent in smaller snippets of cities, suburbs, and small towns in both North America and Western Europe. It is sometimes interpreted in a merely cosmetic or rhetorical fashion, as in the regional façades applied by national chains and franchises, the adding of a few historical allusions to an otherwise standard shopping mall, or in calling a shopping mall a "Town Center."[81] The so-called "corporate campus" or "office park" designed by Kevin Roche [Dinkeloe & Associates] for General Foods headquarters (when it moved to Rye, New York 1977–82) included "office neighborhoods" and a "Main Street" in an effort to recover some aspects of the pre-industrial workplace. And instead of the tightly controlled office environments of high modernism—where windows could not be opened, blinds adjusted, or personal items brought to the workplace—the workspaces encourage personalization. Roche's design for the Bouyges headquarters in the French new city of St Quentin-en-Yvelines referred to the nearby *château* of Versailles. An advertisement for an exclusive community of 38 homes (with prices starting at $1,000,000) designed by Robert Stern describes

Two Rodeo Drive, designed by Kaplan McLaughlin Diaz Architects/Planners, Beverly Hills, California

these homes as "country French chateaux" and asserts that "Milwin Farm exemplifies that which you seek in quality and tradition. A setting that rivals the Normandy coast of France . . . Milwin Farm is properly located just minutes from the Atlantic in West Allenhurst, New Jersey."

Other examples go beyond cosmetics and rhetoric to more substantially emulate building forms of the past. In Manhattan and in Baltimore, for instance, townhouses and apartment buildings are being contextually designed to fit in with the adjacent older structures.[82] In New Jersey, the firm Beyer Blinder Belle designed 130 townhouses and 56 apartments called Montclair Mews, which Blinder described as "reminiscent of an old New England village square [while carrying] the feel and sophistication of New York City's Grammercy Park" (Garbarine, 1986). In the New Jersey planned community of Hidden Lake in the

Janss Court building, designed by Johannes Van Tilburg & Partners and developed by Janss Corporation, Santa Monica, California

Middlesex Township, a shopping and office mall called Towne Center seeks to replicate a village square with its clock tower and traditional design. An advertisement for Murray Hill Square in New Jersey reads: "Each distinctive home is a one-of-a-kind reproduction of Colonial and Victorian landmarks . . . set in a fairy-tale-like, turn-of-the-century village, complete with brick-lined courtyards, formal boxwood gardens, gaslights, and village squares." On the western end of Cape Cod in the town of Mashpee, a London-based developer built Stratford Pond, a "68-acre English theme community that includes cobblestoned streets, ornamental post boxes imported from Britain and a village green" (Hummel). A Connecticut developer built a neotraditional townhouse development in Krasnagorsk, a suburb of Moscow, intended for foreign companies in Moscow. And Two Rodeo Drive (or Via Rodeo), built adjacent to Rodeo Drive in Los Angeles, collages a variety of European building typologies reproduced at 9/10 their original scale along a pedestrian cobble-stoned street.

Other efforts go even further by seeking to include the functions of traditional urbanism through the combination of shops, offices, and housing in a single building or on a larger scale. The architect Roger Ferris has designed 90 Main Street in Westport, Connecticut, with retail on the ground level and housing above, and has overseen the conversion of the Gilbert and Bennett mill in Georgetown, Connecticut, into a community with 400 homes, offices, and shops, and the creation of a town center for Somers, New York. The architect Maria V. Popova-Kerbel has designed 15 units in five Carpenter Gothic townhouses called Partridge Hill which combine business spaces on the ground floor with the owners' living quarters on the upper one and one-half floors, also located in Westport (Charles). For Fairfax City, Virginia, another working/living environment was proposed which its architect described as "an almost historic 18th-century village with indigenous materials—brick, slate, oak shingles—each building different from the other" (Charles).[83] In the Voorhees Township of New Jersey, a mixed-use project called Main Street also allows people to live above or near their workplace (Garbarine 1988). And the Janss Court building on the Third Street Promenade of Santa Monica, California, combines cinemas (basement), two restaurants (ground level), offices (floors 2, 3, and 4), and housing (floors 5 and 6). These efforts look to earlier successful models like the Country Club Plaza in Kansas City developed by Jesse Clyde Nichols in 1923, which successfully accommodates the pedestrian and the car, without displacing either.

EDGE CITIES

Development trends in the United States since the early 1980s have favored urbanization on the outskirts of cities to form what have come to be know as "outer cities," "urban villages" (Leinberger and Lockwood), or most popularly, "edge cities" (Garreau). Rivaling traditional downtowns or central cities, these edge cities usually include business centers, with high-rise buildings often housing high-tech activities, an enclosed shopping mall surrounded by parking lots, and perhaps some designated outdoor public space. They are accessed by high-speed thoroughfares from low-density residential areas. As these suburban "cities" have been taking on certain urban attributes, central cities have been acquiring certain suburban attributes such as fast-food restaurants, suburban-style shopping malls and cinemas, and new middle-class residential districts (Leinberger and Lockwood).

Though closer to modern urbanism than to the contextualism of postmodern urbanism in their function, there is a concerted effort to render these developments more user-friendly than their modern predecessors. This is done through attention to providing quality public spaces; through the architecture itself, which applies more color, ornament, narrative (themes), and wit; and through using names which recall traditional cities, such as town center, business center, Main Street, downtown, plaza, agora, town hall, marketplace, food court, and so forth.

The edge city of Las Colinas, located five minutes from the Dallas/ Fort Worth Airport, offers a prime example. Begun in 1974, this vision of rancher/businessman Ben Carpenter[84] became a reality and, by 1989, had become home to over 900 companies including GTE, Xerox, and the international headquarters of Exxon. The resident population at this time was approximately 25,000, most of which was living within PUDs, which are gated and additionally protected by surveillance cameras and other security devices. The centerpiece of Las Colinas is the Canal Walk and Williams Square, a pedestrian walkway lined by a townscape which makes references to Texas's past, and an overscaled square plaza framed by office towers recalling the great civic plazas of Europe. This nostalgia for both the Texan and European pasts is evident in a Las Colinas real-estate brochure that reads: "Where Las Colinas grows today, once grew the maize and squash of the Tejas Indians. Over the hills and prairies came buffalo herds, Spanish adventurers, wagon trains, cattle drives to Kansas, ranchers, farmers and the mustang descendants of Spanish horses gone wild. The preservation of the heritage of Texas is an integral part of the commitment which Las Colinas makes to the future" (cited by Dillon, 8). Begun during the real-estate recession, when little was being built and the new town idea was regarded as no longer viable, Las Colinas became a model for edge cities elsewhere in the United States[85] as well as abroad, particularly outside of Tokyo (Dillon).

Attitudes toward this trend vary. Some regard it as simply a physical expression of the service and information economy, just as the traditional city was an expression of the era of manufacturing. According to this view, the last real surge of growth was a century ago with the manufacturing city and now there is another surge with the service economy, but this time the beneficiary is the outer city, turning the traditional metropolis inside out. In *Edge City*, Joel Garreau describes this urbanization as a utopian quest to bring home, work, and play together. Others regret this kind of urbanization, pointing out that these job-generating places are located in affluent areas and that most of the workers live in central cities or poorer suburbs, thus accentuating the gap between rich and poor. As Oliver Byrum contends, "the same process that creates 'edges' is also dividing us by race, income, and culture and

Food court, Owings Mills Mall, Rouse Company, 1985; edge city of Owings Mills, MD

may pose a threat to our future well-being that far outweighs the wonder of these places" (1992, 396). Some argue that these edge cities will
never achieve "true urbanity,"[86] while others disagree, pointing to the
appearance of libraries, theaters, schools, hospitals, and other public
amenities and cultural facilities in these areas.[87] But whether pro- or
anti-edge city, the edge is where much building is taking place and thus
deserves the attention of urban designers.

POSTMODERN ARCHITECTURE VIS-À-VIS URBAN DESIGN

Most of the trends adumbrated in this chapter and the previous one
have been developed by architects rather than planners.[88] This is
because architects have largely been the ones to generate visions for
change, while planners have tended more toward offering piecemeal
band-aid solutions after the fact. This tendency of architects to constitute the vanguard and planners the rearguard may be attributed to tem-
perament, training, and the conditions of their respective professional
practices. The relatively recent designation of "urban designer" usually
denotes an architect who is designing a fragment of a city (with or

without the buildings) or someone with a degree in "Urban Design," a prerequisite for which is usually a degree in architecture.[89] In this capacity, architects have been reappropriating the role of town planner which had been theirs in the days of the master builder prior to the emergence of the planning profession. This reappropriation has been made possible, and in part necessary, by the fact that planners have largely been relegated to the allocation of "resources according to projections of future need" (Barnett 1982, 237). The elaboration of postmodern urban design theory, then, has gone hand in hand with the elaboration of postmodern architecture theory. Although emphasizing building on a large-scale in this book, then, I cannot ignore concurrent theory regarding individual buildings. The nature of postmodern architecture being thoroughly discussed elsewhere,[90] I simply review here some of the more synthetic treatments of this discussion which directly pertain to urban design and are not already addressed above.

Although the term *postmodern* was first applied to architecture by Joseph Hudnut in the title of a 1945 article, it was Charles Jencks who began popularizing it in 1975.[91] Jencks defines *postmodernism* in architecture as "double coding: the combination of modern techniques with something else (usually traditional building) in order for architecture to communicate with the public and a concerned minority, usually of other architects" (Jencks 1978, 14; 1980, 14). Architecture, Jencks says, should contain two codes, "a popular traditional one which like spoken language is slow-changing, full of clichés and rooted in family life," and one which is rooted in a "fast-changing society, with its new functional tasks, new materials, new technologies and ideologies" and rapidly-changing fashions (Jencks 1977; cited by Harvey, 83). These dual meanings—or multivalency—led Jencks to suggest that this architecture "speaks on at least two levels at once" (Jencks 1981, 6). He describes it as exhibiting "a marked duality" and requiring a "plural definition." "Key definers are a pluralism both philosophical and stylistic, and a dialectical or critical relation to a pre-existing ideology" (Jencks 1978, 23). In addition to multivalence and pluralism, other characteristics Jencks ascribes to postmodern architecture are dissonant beauty, anthropomorphism, and a return to the absent center (Jencks 1977). It should, he maintains, be involved in "the imaginative transformation of a shared symbolic system" (Jencks 1978, 43). Jencks's prototype of double coding is James Stirling & Michael Wilford's addition to the Staatsgalerie in Stuttgart

(1977–84), in which classical forms are ironically applied to produce a building which is both functional and meaningful to its wide variety of users (Jencks 1978, 18–19).

Jencks attributes the advent of postmodern architecture to new technologies such as computer modeling, automated production, and market research and prediction, which have allowed for the mass production of "almost personalized products" along with a less dense and centralized built environment (Jencks 1977, 5). He also attributes it to the failure of modern architecture to communicate with its users (Jencks 1977) and to make effective links with the city and with history (Jencks 1978, 14). Jencks traces the beginnings of postmodernism in art and architecture to the 1950s and 1960s when it reacted to modernism (Jencks 1987 and 1988). The early 1970s, he says, witnessed the second stage of architectural postmodernism, which featured pluralism and eclecticism. Then, the third phase—or classical phase—of postmodernism, according to Jencks, began in the late 1970s and included Metaphysical Classicism, Narrative Classicism, Allegorical Classicism, Realist Classicism, and the Classical Sensibility. Acknowledging a debt to both modernism and classicism, this stage featured "a return to the past, a harkening back to tradition but to a tradition with a difference, one that has an awareness of the intervention of our modern world" (Jencks 1988).[92]

Jencks maintains that the modern secular world is nostalgic for a center and that this breed of architecture seeks "to recover the center for our de-centered world" through deliberate symbolism (Kimball, p. 28). Postmodern Classicism is distinct from Renaissance Classicism, according to Jencks, because new technologies allow for more precisely emulating past forms, as seen, for instance, in the building of the Getty Museum in Malibu to emulate a Pompeian villa (see Appendix B). These copies can be even more precise than the original, leading Jencks to propose the additional category of Superrealist Classicism. But since such precision is too easy, boring, expensive, or conformist, Jencks says that most Postmodern Classicists "have an antipathy to explicit revivalism, and a tendency to make their recollections veiled if not altogether invisible" (Jencks 1980, 14).

Writing in 1977, Robert Stern described three "principles" or "attitudes" of postmodern architecture: (1) Contextualism, which recognizes the individual building as a fragment of a larger whole and the inevitable "growth" of buildings over time; (2) Allusionism, which draws from history, culture, engineering, and behavioral science in order to render architecture more familiar, accessible, and meaningful to its users; and (3) Ornamentalism of vertical planes (walls) (Stern 1977, 127–35). An editorial in the *Harvard Architectural Review* explained that postmodern architecture seeks out the "messiness and imperfectability of the present rather than the clarity and order of an ideal world" (1980, 6) and that it spurns a strict set of tenets, accommodating instead many different—and often contradictory—ideas. Accordingly, it stated, postmodern architecture does not single out heroes or leaders, and contemporary architectural theory is primarily concerned with communication, rejecting a narrow "universalistic" language generated from within the profession and seeking instead to develop a rich and flexible language by referring to extant symbolic systems.

Philip Johnson expressed this new sensibility at the American Institute of Architects (AIA) meeting in May 1978 saying: "We are at a watershed, at the end of modernism as we have known it. We have new attitudes today, a new pluralism, a new belief in many streams flowing at once. There are no certitudes today. And we have a new willingness to use history, to use symbols—we don't want everything to look like a glass box anymore" (cited by Goldberger 1983, 10). In *The History of Postmodern Architecture*, Heinrich Klotz explained:

> The final goal is to liberate architecture from the muteness of "pure forms" and from the clamour of ostentatious constructions in order that a building might again become an occasion for a creative effort, attuned not only to facts and utilisation programmes but also to poetic ideas and to the handling of subject matter on an epic scale. Then the results will no longer be repositories of function and miracles of construction, but renderings of symbolic contents and pictorial themes—aesthetic fictions which do not remain abstract "pure forms" but which emerge into view as concrete objectivisations to be multisensorially apperceived. (Klotz 1988, 239)

The emblem of the modern movement was the "pure" architectural object, the centerpiece created solely by one architect in inspired isolation. Postmodern architecture rejected this, seeking instead to reinstate attention to the cultural, historical, geographic, and symbolic contexts. An onslaught on the sterility of the International style was launched along with an effort to promote a healthy regional individualism. As

Wojciech Lesnikowski contended, "The machine and technology ceased to be appropriate motives for architecture, and architects turned their attention to humanism conceived in part as the rediscovery of history . . . , or to the discovery of the modern vernacular, or finally to individual whims or caprices" (Lesnikowski 1982, 294). Unlike modern architecture, which is "simultaneously pure materiality, and pure sign, [and] does not refer to anything outside itself" (Harvey 1989, 70), postmodern architecture has been described as multivalent, or containing many meanings. It also draws from a variety of styles, celebrating difference and pluralism. It features ornamentation, often suggestive of the human body. And it reflects a desire for communal space along with an admission that there is nothing quite adequate to fill it.

These changes within architectural theory, along with the concurrent evolution described above, recast urban design theory from the 1960s to the 1980s. Articulated in terms of reactions to modern urbanism, the components of postmodern urbanism may be summarized as follows:

1 In reaction to modernism's clean break with the past and regarding of the future as a model →Historicism; historical quotation; an architecture of memory and monuments; the search for urbanity (in its pre-industrial incarnation).

2 In reaction to decontextualism, internationalism, models, neutrality, razing and flattening of sites, the International Style →Contextualism; importance of site/place; regionalism; vernacular design; pluralism; a search for "character," urban identity, unique features, visual references, creation of landmarks, genius loci, and urban legibility; populism.

3 In reaction to totalizing rationality, functionalism, Taylorism, the machine metaphor (mode of production as model for the city and for architectural practice), "Less is more," "Form follows function," technological "honesty," separation of functions (the city divided into its constituent parts) →Use of symbolism (with that being its only function), ornament, superfluous elements, wit, whimsy; the metaphors of collage, bricolage, assemblage, text, or simply older cities (Vidler's "third typology"); emphasis on human scale (the human figure re-enters the design); "More is more"; "Form follows fiasco"; no zoning or "mixed-use" zoning.

4 In reaction to the political agenda of the Modern Movement, the utopian belief that a new architecture will engender a new and more egalitarian society along with the desire to bring this about (assuming environmental determin-

ism), the belief in salvation through design, the belief in a perfectible world, the search for truth and purity, faith in linear progress, faith in science and reason, faith in technocratic solutions, a certainty and hubris among architects and planners ⇒Apoliticism, humility, a lack of faith and a search for something to believe in; anti-utopianism; belief perhaps in "vest pocket utopias" or "hetero-topias."

a. From anti-capitalism, egalitarianism, a reliance on State authority and large-scale interventions, democratic socialisms ⇒To anti-autocratic; anti-authoritarian; small-scale plans, or, if the intervention is large, collage-like using a number of architects and a design guide; participation of users or at least an effort to accommodate people rather than change them; a favoring of political decentralization and non-interference from the central State authority, liberal political economy, neoconservatisms.

b. From art as a tool for achieving political ends and the planner/architect as artist foremost ⇒To art as a commodity and therefore not as pedagogic, but catering to consumer tastes; the planner/architect as dutiful provider, public servant, or alternatively, panderer-to-the-rich.

c. From new building types for a new egalitarian society ⇒To a return to traditional building types.

d. From shock techniques (defamiliarization, strange-making) as a means to achieve these political ends ⇒To familiarity, use of "familiar" elements to make people feel immediately at home; legibility.

This distillation of urban design theory is not intended to imply that the reactions to modern urbanism have been monolithic. In fact, the diversity of postmodern architecture and urbanism of this period has led observers to describe it as "schizophrenic" (Jencks 1977), "a hybrid style" (Jencks 1977), "an odd pastiche" (Huxtable, 1981a, 75), and the "Frankenstein effect" (ibid.). For its proponents, however, the many and varied concerns of contemporary architectural and urban design theory are unified by a single thread, "a coherence . . . based on the heterogeneous substance and nature of modern society" (Stern 1981, 87). The art critic Martin Filler perceives this integrity, saying: "The fact that there are many different approaches . . . is not a sign of disarray, but rather an indication of a healthy and promising diversity" (Filler, 102). August Hecksher describes this coherence saying that it "maintains, but only just maintains, a control over the clashing elements which compose it. Chaos is very near; its nearness, but its avoidance, give . . . force" (cited by Venturi 1966, 104). Similarly, Jencks maintains that the built form inspired by this theory should suggest a climax but never reach it (Jencks, 1981). This synthesis which is never final—the dialectic—is often regarded as the objective of art.[93]

Rather than insist on permanent solutions, then, this theory aspires instead to achieve a dynamic unity, acknowledging the need for flexibility in architecture and urbanism, which entails an on-going self-critique, making evolution obligatory and revolution unlikely. In an effort to achieve dynamic unity, architects and planners have been experimenting with color, applied ornament, monuments, historical references, historic preservation, restoration, rehabilitation, adaptive re-use, participatory design, and the application of ideas from the social and behavioral sciences and the humanities. Rather than provide pat answers, postmodern urbanism seeks to raise questions and provoke or simply to accommodate post-industrial society rather than shape it. The chapters which follow situate these reactions to modern urbanism since the 1960s within their wider historical, social, and political contexts.

NOTES

1. As Andreas Huyssen sees it, postmodernism (generally) began in the United States in the 1960s and was exported to Europe in the 1970s. He maintains that it "could not have been invented in Europe at the time" because it "would not have made any sense there" (Huyssen, 190). Huyssen says that in France, "Where they talk about the postmodern at all, as in the cases of Lyotard and Kristeva, the question seems to have been prompted by American friends, and the discussion almost immediately and invariably turns back to problems of the modernist aesthetic" (Huyssen, 214), usually revolving around the issues of "*le texte moderne*" and "*la modernité*" (ibid.). Indeed, Lyotard attributes his use of the term postmodernism to American scholars (Lyotard 1985, xxiii). According to French architectural historians Jacques Lucan and Jean-Louis Cohen, the concern with "urban architecture" and other strands of postmodern urbaism in France were inspired by Americans, particularly Kevin Lynch, Christopher Alexander, and Robert Venturi, whose mid-1960s works were translated into French in the early 1970s (Lucan 1989; Cohen 1984, 92). Marc Emery asks "Who would have thought that an architect from Philadelphia would have had so much influence on the Parisian landscape in the end of the twentieth century? Of course, Robert Venturi never constructed anything in the capital but his formal influence predominates there ever since that curious cultural revolution set off by that little book *Complexity and Contradiction*" (Emery 1986).

2. For Alan Plattus, "architectural postmodernism [is] a phenomenon whose roots . . . are deep in Italian and American soil, and fertilized by a sprinkling of French theory" (Plattus, 69).

3. In Lesnikowski's view, "French and American post-modernism had little in common beyond similar historical sources. American post-modernism was associated with eclectic mannerism, superficial historical collages, a search for pluralistic fragmentation and contradiction, and straight historical imitation. In France, contrarily, this movement was based more upon French historical tendencies, that is, a return to grand classical principles of integrated planning, stylistic monumentality, and traditional architectural language. The French expression of this movement, which descended from the Beaux Arts legacy, produced results far different from American efforts. One could say that, in comparison to American tendencies, French post-modernism involved a modernist take on historical language" (Lesnikowski 1990, 40).

4. Jacobs and Appleyard contend that with more and more modernist cityscapes, "Many began to look through picturesque lenses back to the old preindustrial cities" (Jacobs and Appleyard, 114). Steven Daniels describes the picturesque as "a critical sensibility that actively engages political and social issues, indeed articulates them comprehensively in landscape terms" (cited by A. Kahn, 48).

5. Other contributors to this discussion included Kenneth Browne and Thomas Sharp.

6. Writing in 1962, John Dyckman asserted that "The most sophisticated critic and ideological leader of the new romantics of the city . . . is Paul Goodman." About Goodman's *Communitas* (1947), Dyckman writes: "While its emphasis on the integration of work and leisure and its search for meaning in these activities seems to build on the earlier craft romanticism of 19th-century French utopian socialism, or on Kropotkin, it is actually part of the post World War I reaction against the

destructive use of modern industrialism—a view that has accumulated momentum after World War II and atomic warfare." Goodman's work, Dyckman says, "is the only integrated statement of the romantically reconstituted city . . . , a kind of amalgam of Freud, the Bauhaus, and the Berlin theatre. . . . The ideal world of Paul Goodman shares with the expressionists of post World War II Germany a humanistic neoromanticism. Mindful of the dangers of sexual repression identified by Freud, it is tolerant towards dirt and disorder, clash of color and smells, and 'organicity.' It is neofunctionalist in its architecture and physical order, and is at its most romantic in attitudes towards work, leisure, and the environment: it is existentialist in its demands upon immediate experience."

7. These American contributions barely mentioned the concurrent European ones, and vice versa.

8. This articulation of Jacobs's ideas was directed specifically against the ideas and practices of the Regional Planning Association of America, which Jacobs characterized (or caricatured) as: "The street is bad as an environment for humans; houses should be turned away from it and faced inward, toward sheltered greens. Frequent streets are wasteful, of advantage only to real estate speculators who measure value by the front foot. The basic unit of city design is not the street, but the block and more particularly the super-block" (J. Jacobs 1961, 20).

9 Habermas's discussion about "the structural transformation of the public sphere" appeared in 1962 in German, but not until 1978 in French and 1989 in English.

10. The English group Archigram was most well known for its attention-grabbing city designs, particularly the walking Plug-In City, which first appeared in 1963 at a London exhibition (see Jencks 1973, 280–92).

11. The resurrection of Sitte owes greatly to the work of George Collins and Christiane Crasemann Collins, particularly their reissuing of Sitte's work in English along with a biographical survey (Collins and Collins 1986). The revived interest in Olmsted was evident at the celebration of his 150th birthday in 1972, for which ten thousand admirers gathered in Central Park. It was also apparent in the "New Olmsted Movement" christened by Grady Clay at the fourth convocation of the National Association for Olmsted Parks in 1984 (D. White).

12. Moore exclaimed: "The psychic spaces and the shape of buildings should assist the human memory in restructuring connections through time and space . . . so that those of us who lead lives complicatedly divorced from a single place in which we can find roots, can have . . . through the channels of our memories, through the agency of building, something like these roots restored" (cited by Lash 1990a, 65).

13. Moore and Bloomer sought to achieve this in their design of the Wonder Wall at the 1984 New Orleans Expo.

14. This was codified by eliminating the last phrase of their original 1938 statement, which had described the planner's activity as "the planning of the unified development of urban communities and their environs and of states, regions, and the nation, as expressed through determination of the comprehensive arrangement of land uses and land occupancy and the regulation thereof" (in M. Scott, 616). The 1967 revision eliminated the phrase referring to land uses.

15. Over the following twenty years, more than eighty teams elaborated these reports

(usually 60–100 pages) and presented them to the communities (Russell, 102).

16. Charles Moore and William Turnbull described their tactic for designing Kresge College (part of the University of California at Santa Cruz) in 1974 as "Process Architecture" since they worked closely with both college officials and students to discover their needs and tastes (Russell, 104).

17. In the United States, three of these have been completed and over eighty are in progress (E. Smith). For more on cohousing, see McCamant and Durrett (1988) and Marcus (1989).

18. Harold Proshansky, a prime mover in environmental psychology research, explained that it grew out of a realization "that it is not only the physical properties of the setting that determine why and how space is used" (Proshansky, 1990). He maintained that "because any physical setting is also clearly a social one, other people and their attitudes about the physical world, as well as the social meaning associated with particular places, influence an individual's place identity" (ibid.).

19. Garrett Eckbo was already expressing such sensibilities in his *Landscape for Living* (1949) and subsequent works, all focusing on development in California. But while contributing to spearhead an environmentalist movement in the Bay Area, his admonitions had little lasting impact on the Los Angeles region (see M. Davis 1994) or elsewhere.

20. The concern with protecting the environment was also registered in public policy such as the National Environmental Policy Act (1969, United States), which required Environmental Impact Assessments/Statements prior to building. This Act stipulated that all agencies of the federal government must "utilize a systematic, interdisciplinary approach which will insure the integrated use of the natural and social sciences and the environmental design arts in planning and decision making which may have an impact on man's environment" (cited by Barnett 1982, 15). Many states (such as Florida and California) have adopted their own environmental impact regulations. It may be argued, however, that these measures have done more to bureaucratize and politicize building than to protect the environment.

21. Held in June 1994 at the Cranbrook Academy of Art, this seminar grew in part out of priorities established at the Environmental Protection Agency (EPA). As the annoucement for the seminar read, "The United States Environmental Protection Agency has recently provided funding to reevaluate program content in architectural education in response to the demands of sustainable design principles, changes in social and cultural patterns, the state of the economy, available technologies and the need to restore architects to leadership positions in the world community . . . ." (ACSA News 1994).

22. This omission can be attributed to three factors: (1) Most research is based on observation and men have been more visible—spending more time in public spaces—than women, who have spent more time in the home. (2) Most secondary resource materials document this more visible and more public gender. (3) Most researchers had been male themselves, thus either incognizant of women's roles and influences on society or unable to gain access to women's realms (Lofland).

23. As Hayden pointed out, the Hoover Commission on Home Ownership and Home Building established the detached single-family home as a national goal in 1931, but

it wasn't until after the Second World War that this goal was achieved, with over half of the US population residing in suburban areas. This postwar suburban boom, she contended, reinforced the role of woman-in-the-home as the suburbs provided settings for the sexual division of labor, with men engaged in paid work away from the residential community and women engaged in unpaid labor in the home. At the same time, neighborhood-based services to the home were gradually being eliminated (such as the delivery of milk, other staples, and diapers), making housework and childcare more arduous and time-consuming. The increased isolation of families in individual houses allowed the impact of mass media to grow, while isolation rendered these suburbanites more reliant upon the mass media for news and information and more suggestible to advertising claims. In order to consume more, greater numbers of women began joining the paid labor force. As Hayden maintained, "Just as the mass of white male workers had achieved the 'dream houses' in suburbia where fantasies of patriarchal authority and consumption could be acted out, their spouses entered the world of paid employment" (Hayden 1980b).

24. In *Seven American Utopias: The Architecture of Communitarian Socialism* (1976), Hayden examined instances of communal living from 1790 to 1975, including the communes of the 1960s and 1970s. In *The Grand "Domestic" Revolution: Feminism, Socialism, and the American Home, 1870–1930* (1980a), Hayden focused on the late nineteenth- and early twentieth-century communities where childcare and housework were regarded as community activities. She found that by the late 1920s, very few of these experiments were still thriving, and attributed this to their failures to (1) recognize the problem of exploiting other women workers when providing services for those who could afford them; and (2) consider men as responsible parents and co-workers in the home.

25. For such a proposal to be realized on a larger scale, Hayden explained, all programs and laws which reinforce the unpaid role of the female homemaker—either explicitly or implicitly—must be eliminated. Ideally, Hayden maintained, people of all socio-economic groups could benefit from this solution. If instituted on a wide basis, it could also be a tool for reducing poverty by inciting a more efficient use of government subsidies, which almost always assume that people should live in households comprised of a male worker married to an unpaid homemaker with approximately two children, living in a self-sufficient apartment or house. For instance, public housing programs, Aid for Families with Dependent Children (AFDC), food stamps, and campaigns to support "family values" all attempt to support this image of the "family."

26. One explanation is sought in the Victorian insistence upon clearly distinguishing people from animals by engaging in "civilized" as opposed to "barbarian" behavior, including a monogamous and sedentary life within a nuclear family (especially after Darwin's work on evolution appeared in the 1850s and 1860s, in which he suggested that the human species is descended from animals). Another explanation for why so many fail to question the institutions of family and marriage and assume they are "natural" and universal features of the human species holds that such a belief is socially necessary in capitalist societies because it provides a "shock absorber" for the inherent inequalities of capitalism. By institutionalizing the split between the

home and the workplace, the nuclear family provides a stable non-rebellious work-force, both paid and unpaid. And the individual house provides an ideal stage set upon which a capitalist society can perform, so to speak, by housing the nuclear fam-ily, by having a front lawn for display and a back lawn for family leisure and togeth-erness, and by separating the nuclear family from places of (paid) work and from the larger public realm.

27. At least since the Progressive Reform Movement of the turn of the century, a "family crisis" has been said to exist, along with a consequent call for a "return to family life." Even though the term "family" means different things to different people, there is a tendency not to question it, for to do so would pose a challenge to some basic and sacred assumptions about social organization, social status, and social morality. The romanticization of the family, marriage, and the individual house serves to buttress the status quo and to mediate or obscure the contradictions inherent in capitalism.

28. Other contributions to feminist urban design theory include Saegart; Ardener (ed.); *Heresies*, no. 11 (1981); Franck and Ahrentzen (eds); Roberts; Spain; *Design Book Review*, v. 25 (1992); Colomina (ed.); Seager; Weisman, and Wekerle, Peterson, Morley.

29. On the discrediting of Westway, see Wiseman (1986).

30. As E. Smith has said, "It has now become commonplace for public and private inter-ests to seek community involvement and support from the outset of a project, in part because of the numerous instances where community groups have succeeded in derailing or causing major changes to projects after the fact. By the same token, architects and urban planners have, of necessity, become increasingly cognizant of and responsive to such articulated needs and desires in their vision of the shaping of the public realm. Indeed, the interaction between the design professional and the untrained, yet committed, layperson is a crucial component of the successful out-come of today's work in urban planning and design" (E. Smith, 15).

31. This has occurred, for instance, in the cities of Glen Cove on Long Island (New York) and Kent in the Berkshires (Connecticut).

32. Geddes developed these ideas while working in India from 1914 to 1924.

33. Frampton (1985, 319–20) offers a brief history of the architectural component to this spate of regionalism.

34. A vernacular is simply the language or style of a particular place or culture, for instance, the modernist vernacular. If intended to denote a familiar rather than for-mal kind of building, a more appropriate term might be "colloquial" architecture.

35. The success of this book prompted a sequel, *The Prodigious Builders* (Rudofsky 1977).

36. This sometimes subtle distinction is perhaps reflected in the translation of Marcel Proust's "*A la recherche du temps perdu*" to *In Remembrance of Things Past*. From searching for lost time in French, it becomes remembering things past in English.

37. See Hough (1991); Spirn (1984); and Riley (1992).

38. In this book, *Adhocism*, the authors advocated re-use of the industrial landscape. Lefaivre describes it as "a contextualist manifesto in a less polished vein than *Learn-ing from Las Vegas*" (Lefaivre 17).

39. Among those serving on the board of the IAUS were Vincent Scully, Robert Stern, Philip Johnson, Richard Meier, Charles Gwathmey, and Harvey Cobb.

40. *Oppositions* was edited by Diana Agrest and Joan Ockman, who were joined by Vidler

in 1977. The IAUS also sponsored other publications including *Skyline*, as well as a year of study for undergraduates in schools without architecture programs, a continuing education program, and large symposia and public fora.

41. This project was funded by the US Department of Housing and Development and published in a condensed form in *On Streets* (S. Anderson 1991; Vidler 1991).

42. Designed by Kenneth Frampton et al., this was the subject of an exhibition entitled "Another Chance for Housing."

43. See Rowe (1972); Frampton (1972); and Eisenman and Stern (1974).

44. This may be attributed to the fact that most architectural commissions in the United States during the 1950s and 1960s were for isolated buildings on the outskirts of cities. But even though architects began obtaining more urban commissions by the late 1970s, the emphasis on individual buildings, façades, and signage largely remained.

45. Organized by Johnson and Henry Russell Hitchcock, this exhibition, which introduced the "International Style," was officially titled "Modern Architecture—An International Exhibition" (G. Wright 1994).

46. Gleye went on to become a historic preservationist for the State of Nevada.

47. See, for example, Bennett Berger (1960), and Herbert Gans (1962).

48. In 1957, the editors of the *Architectural Review* launched "Counter-Attack, A Campaign against Subtopia" (Hall 1988, 223). These pejorative labels represent the attitudes of intellectuals and artists regarding the suburbs, not those of suburbanites themselves.

49 These agencies were located in the gentrifying neighborhood of Boerum Hill in Brooklyn, NYC (Kasinitz, 175).

50. This discussion of interior design draws in part from Goldberger (1990c).

51. The Team X critique might be regarded as a precursor to this one, with its emphasis on place and a subtle regionalism rather than abstract space and with its attention to high-density low-rise building (see Appendix A).

52. The existence of these critical regionalisms, Frampton maintained, suggests that "the model of the hegemonic center surrounded by dependent satellites is an inadequate and demagogic description of our cultural potential" (Frampton 1983b, 150).

53. These new communities followed upon the heels of various waves of efforts to design "new towns," from the late nineteenth- and early twentieth-century company towns, to the towns designed by the Regional Planning Association of America, to the 1960s new towns such as Columbia (Maryland), Reston (Virginia), and Miami Lakes (Florida). Widely regarded as the most successful of these, Columbia (which was developed by the Rouse Company) is comprised of "villages" each of which contains 3–5 neighborhoods, which together house a population necessary to support an elementary school. Near each school is a community pool, a community center, and a convenience store which all inhabitants can walk or cycle to without crossing any major streets. The village offers a supermarket, bank, and other businesses. The scale of these new towns, however, has proven unwieldy and usually unprofitable for developers, particularly since the 1972 fiscal crisis. The MPCs and neotraditional urbanism that succeeded these new towns retain some elements while rejecting others.

54. According to *Builder* magazine, about 100,000 PUDs were built in the United States

between the late 1960s and the late 1980s (Langdon, 50). Moudon reports that there were 605 MPCs in the United States by 1989, covering a total of 2,193,936 acres (Moudon, 9).

55. Sterling Forest is an MPC that is being developed by the corporation of that name near Suffern, New York, on 17,000 acres for a population of 35,000. The planner quoted here is Thomas Cooke.

56. For the new town of Shorehaven in the Bronx, the Leibman Melting Partnership sought to reinforce a sense of community in part through providing "a central entry point with a gatehouse and a surrounding fence" (Oser 1988a).

57. See Clare Collins (1994).

58. See *Crime Prevention Through Environmental Design*, by Timothy Crow (1991), as well as related books published by Butterworth-Heinemann, "a leading publisher of security books" (e.g. Underwood 1984; Poyner 1983).

59. While successful in averting through traffic, residents of Park Labrea complain that the gates have not succeeded in averting crime.

60. The elaboration of a defensive urbanism has been particularly marked in Los Angeles, a theme developed by Steven Flusty in *Building Paranoia* (1994). Flusty identifies five "paranoid typologies" of defensive urbanism in Los Angeles: the "blockhome," which is a defensive house (of both rich and poor), the "luxury laager," which is a gated community; the pocket ghetto, which is a low-income residential area patrolled by police and the inhabitants themselves and outfitted with street barricades; "strongpoints of sale," which are highly-controlled commercial areas; and "world citadels," which are high-rise office buildings.

61. On the defensive character of Los Angeles, see Mike Davis (1990), chapter 4, "Fortress L.A."

62. See Ellin (1997) and Corwin (1992).

63. Two examples of these apartment complexes are Studio Colony (in Studio City, Los Angeles), designed by the Berkus Group Architects, for the Forest City Dillow & Bluffside Development Company; and Bridgeport (in Miami), designed by Rafael Portuondo, Rolando Llanes, and Lariano Forero, for the developer Interdevco (Langdon, 59). Langdon considers the quality of the public spaces of the former as far less successful than the public spaces of the latter (ibid.).

64. In contrast to the earlier megastructures of the 1960s and 1970s, which were modular and extensible, taking modernist tenets to an extreme, Portman's version has a definitively postmodern look—tall glass buildings with glass elevators surrounding atriums replete with landscaped fountains and shops—as well as function, intended more for the tourist and shopper than for the inhabitant. Nonetheless, both kinds of megastructures have few street entrances and are not hospitable to the pedestrian. The effect, says Relph, is that "the street is rendered lifeless and pedestrians avoid it if at all possible" (Relph 1987, 243).

65. On Portman's Bonaventure Hotel in Los Angeles, see Jameson's widely-translated piece (1984b).

66. Duany and Plater-Zyberk worked for Arquitectonica before starting their own firm.

67. Krier continues: "Only when this possibility is secured will the dreadful welfare bureaucracy wither away; only then can states and governments take up their

original constitutional aim as guardian and patron of the *res publica* of the civic realm and its welfare" (Krier 1991, 119).

68. DPZ designed the master plan for Playa Vista along with local architectural firms Moule & Polyzoides and Moore Ruble Yudell, as well as Ricardo Legorreta of Mexico and landscape architects Hannah/Olin of Philadelphia. Initiated in 1989, the plan for Playa Vista is both contextual and environmentally-sensitive (Fulton 1993).

69. For more on the work of Plater-Zyberk and Duany, see Duany and Plater-Zyberk (1992), Langdon (1988), Audirac and Shermyen (1994), Krieger (1991), Lennertz (1991), Mohney (1991), Krier (1991), and Katz (1994). See also the newsletter, *New Urban News*.

70. Since the initial capital investment for light rail can not always be met, Calthorpe offers an incremental plan: "The Pedestrian Pocket is located on a dedicated right-of-way which evolves with the development. Rather than bearing the large cost of a complete rail system as an initial expense, this right-of-way facilitates mass transit by providing exclusively for car pools, van pools, bikes, and buses. As the cluster matures, transit investments are made for light rail in the developed right-of-way. But the growth of this land-use pattern is not dependent on this investment; the system is designed to support many modes of traffic and to phase light rail into place when the population is great enough to support it" (Calthorpe 1989, 12).

71. Calthorpe explains that Pedestrian Pockets "are meant to weave back together the currently isolated parts of our suburban environment; to put the elderly and kids without cars within reach of old downtowns as well as new shopping malls, parks and other Pockets; to allow workers access to existing and new job opportunities throughout a transit region, not just within a single town. Pedestrian Pockets are intended to balance growth in a developed region, enhancing and extending the diversity, complexity and history of the area" (Calthorpe 1989, 5). As in the modern suburb, Calthorpe says, inhabitants of Pedestrian Pockets would come to see themselves as "citizens of the larger region rather than as participants in the fiction of an isolated town or city" (ibid.).

72. See Calthorpe, Isley, and Kelbaugh (1989) for a more detailed description of this project.

73. In addition to his suburban interventions, Calthorpe was given an opportunity to transpose his ideas onto an urban setting for the 12-acre residential component of a mixed-use development in downtown Brooklyn (Oser 1986).

74. Battery Park City was developed by the Battery Park City Authority (BPCA), a public benefit corporation created by the New York State Legislature in 1968. Its development is the result of a public—private partnership wherein the BPCA initially used state bonds to finance the landfill, parks, and infrastructure, and then selected private developers for the commercial and residential areas, applying the profits to providing public amenities as well as to the construction and rehabilitation of low- and moderate-income housing elsewhere in New York City. Bounded by Pier A, Battery Park, West Street, Chambers Street, and the Hudson River, the site plan allocates 30 percent of the land for open space, including a grand esplanade along the river, 19 percent for streets and avenues, 42 percent for housing, and 9 percent for commerce and offices. The BPCA named Olympia & York as the sole developer of the commercial

area—the World Financial Center—which is adjacent to New York City's Financial District and connected to it by two pedestrian bridges. Designed by Cesar Pelli Associates, this Center includes four office towers rising 33 to 51 stories, two 9-story octagonal buildings, commercial and retail space, an enclosed glass Winter Garden, an outdoor plaza (designed with landscape architect M. Paul Friedberg & Partners) and a marina accommodating 26 ocean-going yachts. Architects of the housing include Charles Moore; Davis, Brody & Associates; Conklin Rossant; Mitchell/Giurgola; The Gruzen Partnership; Bond Ryder James; Ulrich Franzen/The Vilkas Group; James Stewart Polshek & Partners; Ehrenkrantz, Eckstut & Whitelaw; Costas Kondylis; and Gruzen Samton Steinglass. The new Stuyvesant High School, designed by Alexander Cooper & Partners, is located on the northernmost parcel of Battery Park City. The eight-acre waterfront park adjacent to the high school was designed by Carr Lynch Associates and Oehme, van Sweden & Associates in the tradition of Frederick Law Olmsted's Riverside Park. The three-acre park at the southern tip of Battery Park City was designed by Alexander Cooper, Nicholas Quennell, and the artist Jennifer Bartlett as a microcosm of one thousand years in garden design. Other artists whose work adorns Battery Park City include Siah Armajani, Scott Burton, Mary Miss, R. M. Fischer, and Richard Artschwager. Targetting a residential population of 25,000 and a working population of 35,000, the new city had attained a residential population of 5,000 and working population of 20,000 by 1989.

75. The Spoerry Group served as developer for this project and initially commissioned the Ehrenkrentz Group as architects. It was designed on over 100 acres to include housing, marina slips, office and commercial space, and a hotel, all on a man-made estuarial-canal system.

76. PortAmerica was designed to include a 22-story World Trade Center (scaled down from its initial 52 stories) and other office buildings, a marina, a hotel, a 12-foot-wide pedestrian promenade, waterfront pavilions containing retail and recreational space, and 1,200 townhouses and condominiums around a series of small parks meant to recall the crescents of Georgian England (Daniel).

77. Eckstut has been involved in two waterfront projects in New Jersey: the redesign of Newport, a 300-acre complex in Jersey City rising above and alongside the Holland Tunnel, and the redevelopment of the decaying piers in Hoboken for the Port Authority of New York and New Jersey. He has also been involved in the plan for redeveloping the 19-acre site for Baltimore's Inner Harbor East (Gunts, 1988a, 1988b), a waterfront project in Long Beach, California, and the development of a housing complex in Arverne on the waterfront in Queens, New York—this last is being designed by Ehrenkrantz, Eckstut & Whitelaw along with the Leibman Melting Partnership (Goldberger 1989c; Oser 1988b) .

78. This "Downtown Strategic Plan" has been elaborated by a team of design firms led by Moule & Polyzoides and including Duany and Plater-Zyberk. Elizabeth Smith explains that the goal of this team "has been to augment the evolving pedestrian and transit orientation of downtown, thus allowing for greater connection among its often distinctly physically and socially separated districts, and to propose several 'catalytic projects' as infill for sites in particular need of regeneration" (E. Smith, 12). See also Betsky (1993) and M. Davis (1991).

79. Translated into French in the architectural journal *Créé* (1981), the Essex plan influenced a number of French urban design projects.
80. See Zwingle (1991), Jencks (1991, 44, 47), and Ghirardo (1996, 176–94).
81. Despite this effort by developers to generate an urban ambiance, shoppers are rarely convinced and usually refer to it as "the mall."
82. In Manhattan, the builder Sheldon Solow hired the firm Attia & Perkins to design eleven 5-story townhouses on East 67th Street. In Baltimore, the 196-unit apartment building Waterloo Place, located across from the Peabody Institute, was designed to resemble the twelve townhouses that had been standing on this site but were demolished in 1970 to make way for a proposed redevelopment project that was never built.
83. The architect is David Cohey of the Robert Berkus Group.
84. In 1989, when much of Las Colinas was threatened with foreclosure, the Teachers Insurance and Annuity Association of New York and JMB Realty of Chicago bought out Carpenter (Dillon, 11).
85. For example, John Portman's suburban development subsidiary, Portman-Barry Investments Inc., is building Northpark Town Center, an edge city 20 miles north of Atlanta, on 100 acres (Finotti).
86. Such as Byrum (1992) and Sharpe and Wallock (1992).
87. Such as Garreau (1991).
88. Although some of these architects are also planners, particularly in Europe.
89. For definitions of urban design, see chapter 7.
90. See, for instance, Jencks, Klotz, Portoghesi, Crook, and C. R. Smith.
91. The etymology of the term postmodern is fully addressed elsewhere. See Jencks (1984, 8; 1986, 3–15); Connor (1989, 6, 65); Best and Kellner (1991, 5–20); and Rosenau (1992, 8, 16–18).
92. Jencks discerns six major traditions of postmodern architecture: historicisms, straight revivalism, neovernacular, ad hoc urbanism (e.g. Krier's breaking up of buildings into smaller discrete parts), metaphor metaphysical, and post-modern space (1978, 26). This study focuses on the first four and includes planning trends that fall outside of Jencks's purview. Other trends not included here are neofunctionalism, neomodernism, late modernism, and the Science Fiction-inspired movement (term of Rowe and Koetter, 28) which includes the space-age imagery of Buckminister Fuller's geodesic domes as well as the high-tech imagery of architects such as Norman Foster.
93. The composer Leonard Bernstein, for instance, has said that: "A work of art does not answer questions; it provokes them, and its essential meaning is in the tension between their contradictory answers."

4

THE POSTMODERN REFLEX

THE INFATUATION WITH THE PAST and with mass imagery in urban design might be understood as part of a larger search for meaning and security in a world that appears increasingly meaningless and scary. An obsession with the past is interpreted, on the psychological level, as a desire to return to the womb, to the mother, to nature, to archetypes, to some paradise or state of bliss which has been lost.[1] In its collective manifestation, the nostalgic impulse might be understood as a response to rapid change. The interest in primitivism and exoticism which accompanied the French Revolution and the rise of a bourgeoisie,[2] for instance, has been interpreted as an effort to consume the past in order to compensate for the sense of estrangement in an increasingly mechanized and segmented world.[3]

   With the transition to a post-industrial society, the sense of insecurity seems to have grown along with the intensity of the nostalgic impulse.[4] And the late-twentieth-century version brings an infatuation with mass imagery to join that with the past. This more recent wave of confusion and fear may be attributed to the acceleration of change and of globalization, along with a concomitant challenge to the dominance of the modern world view, a decline of the public realm, widespread access to information technologies, and the consequent obscuring of power. In this chapter, I describe the postmodern reflex generally before addressing its specific implications for urban design in chapter 5.

THE CHALLENGE TO MODERNITY AND
THE GROWTH IN PRIVATISM

During the Enlightenment, a "project of modernity" (coined by Habermas) emerged and grew dominant in the Western world. This project sought to discover that which is universal and eternal through the scientific method and human creativity, in order to dominate natural forces and thereby liberate people from the irrational and arbitrary ways of religion, superstition, and our own human nature (Harvey 1989, 12–13). The goal of the modern project was to break from the past in pursuit of freedom and progress and it inspired both the American (1776) and French (1789) Revolutions. But the use of power and technologies for destructive purposes (of both people and nature) to which the modern project ultimately led challenged its continued legitimacy.[5] (Simultaneous with the challenge to the modern project was a crisis in the architectural and planning professions, see chapter 7, as well as the academic disciplines, see chapter 8.)

Also contributing to challenging the modern project and to the reigning sense of insecurity have been the increased access to new technologies of transportation and communication and the related decline of the public realm.[6] As new technologies have facilitated the rapid movement of people and information, they have also profoundly transformed the perception of space and time, lifestyles (urbanism and suburbanism), and our sense of community and self. Having begun in the eighteenth century with the rise of a bourgeoisie (Habermas 1989a; Sennett 1974), the decline of the public realm was accelerated by the emergence of a mass society during the early part of the twentieth century. Each aided and abetted the other: the decline of the public realm allowed the market to grow in influence while the incursion of the market into our personal lives in turn contributed to eclipse the public realm.[7]

As knowledge, information, and entertainment derived increasingly from mass-mediated sources rather than from personal experience, the decline of the public realm and rise of a mass society reconfigured our sense of reality.[8] In architect-writer Martin Pawley's analysis, the intolerable primary reality of nineteenth-century industrial urbanism led to the creation of a "secondary reality" through marketing and advertising[9] to find "new meanings in the anonymity of city life" (Pawley 1973, 156, 14). This secondary reality was aided by the concurrent development of the communications and entertainment media and suburbanization

(Pawley 1973, 157). Entailing "a kind of willful self-deception about the nature of events" (Pawley 1973, 13), Pawley maintained, this superficial level of life relies upon the media and operates by the "visual deception" of these media, which are "changing the very basis of truth via the process of perception itself" (Pawley 1973, 14).

Widespread access to television accelerated these perceptual changes. As Pawley contended, television "absorbs the deceptions and evasions of the real world, mixes them with its own inherent deceptions, and thereby creates a new reality of its own" (Pawley 1973, 160). The secondary reality made possible by television provides "the synthetic social glue of consumer society" (ibid.) such that the "crisis of television begins when you stop watching it" (Pawley 1973, 60). Diffused to homes around the world, television has contributed enormously to the globalization of ideas, creating a "community of consumption" of television. Marshall McLuhan (1967) foresaw that the widespread use of electronic media was creating a global village and diminishing diversity while engendering a "retribalization," a distrust of distant authority, and a desire for "in-depth" participation, along with regionalist, separatist, fundamentalist, and reactionary sentiments.

While homogenizing the world, then, the media have also reinforced differences because they are assimilated (received or "read") differently, because they take the place of communal activities, and because of the need they instill for distinction and for the preservation of one's own identity in the face of globalization. In this context, the popularity of tradition and history, along with the search for "roots," can all be seen as efforts to distinguish or define oneself in an ever-cozier global village. Invoking Gertrude Stein's comment about Oakland, California, Todd Gitlin interprets the infatuation with the past as a desire to resist the leveling impact of globalization: "Postmodernists ransack history for shards because there is no 'here' here" (Gitlin 1989, 352). The anthropologist Kathleen Stewart further elaborates upon this point saying, "threatened with a deadening pluralism that makes us all just an 'other' among others (Ricoeur 1965), in which difference erases into an utter indifference (Foster 1983), and where the self is a pastiche of styles glued to a surface, nostalgia becomes the very lighthouse waving us back to shore—the one point on the landscape that gives hope of direction" (Stewart, 229).

The proliferation of television viewing (more than seven hours a day for the "average" American) has also had an impact on attention spans and aesthetic preferences. As Harvey notes, it is not surprising that "there has emerged an attachment to surfaces rather than roots, to collage rather than in-depth work, to super-imposed quoted images rather than worked surfaces, to a collapsed sense of time and space rather than solidly achieved cultural artifact" (Harvey 1989, 61). Because of its deceptions and its influence, Pawley claims that television is "the principal assassin of public life and community politics" (Pawley 1973, 160) because it makes ostensibility "the hallmark of contemporary social praxis" (Pawley 1973, 55).[10] The content of television programming also makes us fearful: news reports, police dramas, thrillers, and other programs with frightening content. In actuality, television—and particularly CNN—has altered the very nature of politics and has been instrumental in instigating a number of mass movements including those that occurred in Tiananmen Square, Beijing (1989), and in Los Angeles (1992).

In the Western world, we might even interpret the postwar quest for a "full" life as a characteristic of the first generation raised with television in the home. Exposing us to many new worlds and aspirations, television programming and advertising also made these appear attainable and encouraged the search for fulfillment by filling one's life with as much as possible, in terms of both experience and consumer goods. This quest was pursued to its extreme by the so-called counter-culture through experimentation with mind-altering substances, religions, travel, and alternative households. And it set the stage for the pluralism, complexity, eclecticism, and inclusivity of postmodernism in its various manifestations.

The enormous role which the media have come to play in political imaging is one example of the tremendous influence it can exert.[11] Former US president Ronald Reagan embodied the postmodern sensibility in that his popular support derived largely from his "television friendly" image as well as the collective memory of him as a star of the silver screen. This movie persona tends to be not just larger, but more real than life in the postmodern age. His popular support also derived from his nostalgia for the good ol' days and his staunch support of the family and traditional values. The editor of *Harper's Magazine*, Lewis Lapham, commented, "President Reagan proved the post-modernist thesis of the presidency as 'the living movie.' For eight years he read scripts, smiled or frowned on cue, [and] rummaged through American history as if it were a theatrical trunk from which he could borrow an attitude, a hat, or a quotation out of context" (Lapham).

The obsession with surfaces has also been evident in other realms. In the fine arts, the missionary and therapeutic intentions of the avant-garde were largely supplanted by an accommodation of the status quo through simply following fashion (Kuspit). In literature, Charles Newman contends that the "sense of diminishing control, loss of individual autonomy and generalized helplessness has never been so instantaneously recognizable . . . the flattest possible characters in the flattest possible landscapes rendered in the flattest possible diction" (cited by Harvey 1989, 58). In photography, Harvey finds the "interest of Cindy Sherman's photographs (or any postmodern novel for that matter) [in their] focus on masks without commenting directly on social meanings other than on the activity of masking itself" (Harvey 1989, 101). These postmodern cultural expressions suggest that Louis Wirth's 1938 prognosis of life in modern society as one in which people are particularly adept at wearing an array of social masks, but lack an enduring personal identity underneath, has grown ever more apt. The difference now, perhaps, is the heightened self-consciousness regarding these masks.

While private transit (the automobile) accelerated privatization during the first half of the twentieth century, widespread access to communication technologies—particularly the television, VCR, and personal computer—cast a new dimension on it. When the screen became more interactive, perceptions of time and space were altered yet again and furthered privatization. With the emergence of a mass society, style (the signifier) was separated from substance (the signified, the referent) (Benjamin). But, as Jean Baudrillard suggests, the post-60s information society led to the disappearance of certain referents entirely such that style (or simulacra) became everything (Baudrillard 1975).[12] Baudrillard applies the term simulacra to describe "the generation by models of a real without origin or reality, a hyper-real. The territory no longer precedes the map, nor survives it. Henceforth, it is the map that precedes the territory—PROCESSION OF SIMULACRA—it is the map that engenders the territory" (Baudrillard 1983a, 2).[13] Simulation, as distinct from resemblance, has no original or referent, for the model replaces the real "as exemplified in such phenomena as the ideal home in women's or lifestyle magazines, ideal sex as portrayed in sex manuals or relationship books, ideal fashion as exemplified in ads or fashion shows" (Best and Kellner, 119). With hyperreality, the simulations come to constitute reality, leading to what Baudrillard has called "the death of the subject." When something is produced artificially, such as a simulated environment (Disneyland being the prototype), it does not come to be regarded as "unreal, or surreal, but realer-than-real, a real retouched and refurbished" (ibid.).

What this means for Baudrillard is that perception and pleasure are altered such that the body, the landscape, time, and public space all disappear as scenes. He calls this loss of private space the "extroversion of interiority" because there is no more distinction between *self* and *other*. These become blurred because the society of consumption is also a society of spectacle. Since these distinctions are blurred, all becomes transparent, visible, and "obscene" because our intimate lives become feeding grounds for the media, which vomits the public domain into the private one. Obscenity does away with the mirror and with representation; it does away with secrets. There is no more drama of alienation, only an "ecstasy of communication" (Baudrillard 1983a).[14]

This disappearance of the referent—or the real[15]—contributed to a desire to return to a past or recover an original while simultaneously rendering this return more difficult if not impossible, yet easier than ever to simulate. Historicism has long been a means of legitimization and/or inspiration in the face of insecurity and fear. As Marx exclaimed in 1852, it is precisely when people "seem engaged . . . in creating something entirely new [that] they anxiously conjure up the spirits of the past to their services and borrow from them names, battle cries, and costumes in order to present the new scene of world history in this time-honored disguise and this borrowed language" (Marx 1959, 320; also 1987, 15).[16] Emerging states, for instance, have often invoked a certain past in an effort to convey an image of a unified nation and thereby legitimize their authority. Established states as well as other hegemonies also invoke the past as a means of preserving their status, especially during times of rapid change which may incite a nostalgia for the past while challenging the continued legitimacy of the power structure. As Hewison maintains, "The nostalgic impulse is an important agency in adjustment to crisis; it is a social emollient and reinforces national identity when confidence is weakened or threatened" (Hewison 1987; cited by Harvey 1989, 85—86).[17] In turn, resistance to hegemonic impositions quite often takes the form of tribal, ethnic, religious, or regional movements, which similarly tend to invoke certain pasts to justify their claims.

Invoking tradition,[18] then, is a means for securing social and group identity. In *Fiddler on the Roof*, the popular musical written by Joseph Stein and produced in 1971, the lead character Tevya laments, "Without tradition, our lives would be as shaky as a fiddler on a roof." Although usually articulated as the preservation or resurrection of a tradition, what usually transpires is the "invention" of tradition, according to historian Eric Hobsbawm. Changing the context or a break in continuity, says Hobsbawm, "movements for the defense or revival of traditions . . . can never develop or even preserve a living past . . . , but must become 'invented traditions' " (Hobsbawm, 7–8).[19] In addition, the vested interests of those invoking the tradition influences its invented incarnation. As John Berger observes, "The past is never there waiting to be discovered, to be recognized for exactly what it is" because "a privileged minority is striving to invent a history which can retrospectively justify the role of the ruling classes" (J. Berger, 11) in the face of a perceived threat to their rule.[20] The political subtexts of invented traditions are latent if not manifest, even though evoking the past can serve to disguise any political intent.

According to Harvey, "The ideological labor of inventing tradition became of great significance in the late nineteenth century precisely because this was an era when transformations in spatial and temporal practices implied a loss of identity with place and repeated radical breaks with any sense of historical continuity" (Harvey 1989, 272). The invention of tradition at this time was epitomized by the rise of a museum culture, international expositions, and the emergence of a historic-preservation movement.[21] The rapid change of the more recent past has generated a new wave of inventing tradition, but this time it may be a simulacrum for which there is no original, thus contributing to disguise what is actually occurring.

THE POSTMODERN TEMPER

The celebration of dissonance rather than consensus and the ready accusation of politically incorrect behavior (because it maligns a certain group or assumes authority) have rendered ethics as well as visionary thinking problematic, thus discouraging political engagement. This reticence with regard to envisioning a desirable future[22] and trying to make it real during the post-1968 period, combined with the altered perception of time ushered in by new technologies, marks what Habermas has described as an "exhaustion of utopian energies" (Habermas 1986).[23] In its extreme, this retreat from political engagement can turn into an over-riding sense of disillusionment, cynicism, and despair.

This loss of faith in working collectively toward a better world has occasioned a turning inward,[24] a privatism, a retreat facilitated by the television, walkman, VCR, and personal computer.[25] In response to the encroachment of the marketplace into our private domain (spawning a society of consumption), the collective idealistic vision of the modernist project has been replaced by a more personal search featuring an increased defense of the self, a romantic "quest for personality," a cult of the family, and a search for origins and roots, epitomized by the transnational wave of family research sparked in part by the television mini-series "Roots."[26] Christine Boyer (1994) describes the "inversion of values" which has occurred, valuing the private sphere over the public one. At the same time, there was a shift to the political right and a fascination with personal power.[27] Rather than address the sources of insecurity, the more common reflex has been avoidance and self-protection.[28]

As the proponents of neotraditional urbanism Andres Duany and Elizabeth Plater-Zyberk have observed, American suburbanites "are happy with the private realm they have won for themselves, but desperately anxious about the public realm around them. Because of the radical malfunctioning of the growth mechanism, the late-20th-century suburbanite's chief ideology is not conservatism or liberalism but NIMBYism: Not In My Back Yard" (Duany and Plater-Zyberk). In a book entitled *Private Pleasure, Public Plight,* David Popenoe reports that the advanced industrial nations (USA, Sweden, and England are his examples) feature a progressive decrease of public life along with a magnification of private life to a degree that is historically unprecedented and socially harmful. Although new technologies and the decline of the public realm may perhaps generate new kinds of community—communities of consumption and of specific interests, not communities based on propinquity or the common good—they have chipped away at the traditional sources of collective identity and security.

Pawley has described this condition:

> In a sense choices made by the peoples of the West—for the private car and against public transport, for suburban life and against urban or rural community, for owner occupation and against tenancy, for the nuclear and against the extended family, for television and against the cinema and the theatre, for social

mobility and against class solidarity, for private affluence and against community life, for machine politicians and against charismatic leaders, for orgasm and
against conception, for eroticism and against reproduction, for pollution and
against regulation—all these are choices in favor of privacy, in favor of individual freedom, in favor of anonymity, but against the very idea of community.
The triumph of consumer society is a triumph of all private goals over all public goals. The citizens of consumer societies are apolitical in so far as they are
independent, political only when their lines of supply are threatened. . . . Western society is on the brink of collapse—not into crime, violence, madness or
redeeming revolution, as many would believe—but into withdrawal. Withdrawal from the whole system of values and obligations that has historically
been the basis of public, community and family life. Western societies are col-
lapsing not from an assault on their most cherished values, but from a voluntary, almost enthusiastic abandonment of them by people who are learning to
live private lives of an unprecedented completeness with the aid of the momentum of a technology which is evolving more and more into a pattern of socially
atomizing appliances" (Pawley 1973, 60–61, 12).[29]

Most citizens, he maintains, prefer fantasy over community (Pawley
1973, 49).

The turn to "traditional" values and social institutions incited by
privatism has been appropriated and assisted by the advertising industry, which has dubbed it "neotraditionalism." A full-page advertisement
placed in the *New York Times* for the magazine *Good Housekeeping*, for
instance, explained that neotraditionalism is "now being recognized as
the most powerful social movement since the sixties" (*Good Housekeeping* 1989). The New Traditionalist, this ad implies, is a housewife and
mother, perhaps with a career, who believes in "timeless quality" and
"commitment" and who is "simple, honest, real, unpretentious and genuine" (ibid.). Another of these advertisements explains that the New
Traditionalist "started a revolution—with some not-so revolutionary
ideals. She was searching for something to believe in—and look what she
found. Her husband, her children, her home, herself. She's the contemporary woman who has made a new commitment to the traditional values that some people thought were 'old-fashioned.' She wasn't following
a trend. She made her own choices. But when she looked over the fence
she found that she wasn't alone" (*Good Housekeeping* 1988a).

The New Traditionalist: She started a revolution—with some not-so revolutionary ideals; New York Times Magazine, *October 9, 1988*

In other realms, the desire for familiarity, for recalling one's own childhood or even someone else's, and the exhaustion of creative energies are evident in the popularity of such programs as "Nick at Nite" on the cable station Nickelodeon, which rebroadcasts for the 20- and 30-something crowds; in feature film versions of popular childhood programs; in movie remakes and sequels; new renditions of popular songs; advertising that attempts to make products seem old or established; "classic rock" stations; the popularity of "lounge" music and old nightclubs; retro-clothing and furniture; the comeback of the diner; and more. These allusions can reassure continuity, or can be homage or parody, as in high camp.

Enhanced access to material goods through increasingly sophisticated means of production and distribution (particularly with home
shopping via catalogue, television, and personal computer) has put a premium on having something before everyone else has it. Being able to
purchase an item that is fashionable no longer carries the cachet that
having already had it before it was fashionable does. So if you must buy
it, it is better to buy something which could be mistaken for something
that has weathered time, that could perhaps be an heirloom. This has
inspired producers of goods to "wear them out" in a mass-produced way
through, for instance, multiple washing of clothes or special finishes on
furniture or frames. And advertisers tout the "worn in" quality of their
goods. Nostalgic for the time before "television culture, agribusiness and
mass consumption invaded the countryside and virtually destroyed its
regional identification and material culture," according to Boyer, people
re-valorize "habitats, decor, eating habits, craftsmanship" (Boyer 1990,
87). They display a penchant for "manipulating already known and
familiar patterns, hence our urban vocabulary is filled with reiterations,
rehabilitations, recyclings, and revitalizations all based on the regeneration of already known symbolic codes" (ibid.).

The nostalgic impulse has been evident in music as jazz began a
hard-bop revival and rock and folk referred back to their earlier incarnations. And perhaps most significantly, there has been a major comeback of that quintessentially American musical genre, country music.
As this rural nation became a suburban one, country music also subur-
banized, so to speak. Subsequent to the de-twanging of country music
in the 1970s, which record producers called "countrypolitan," there was
an effort to "sound old-fashioned" in the 1980s, which producers
described as "neotraditionalism" (Pareles 1991) like the larger social
trend in which it is inscribed. Played with guitars and fiddles, this neotraditionalist country music recalls a time "when life was simple and
roles and choices were clear" (ibid.), for people who yearn for such a
time. As distinct from traditional country lyrics, however, which con-
soled the listener in hard times, it looks "to the past through rose-
colored binoculars" (ibid.), using it as "just one more comfy stage set"
(ibid.). In fact, two of these neotraditionalist songs are entitled "Home":
one by Alan Jackson and one by Joe Diffie (Pareles 1991).

This nostalgia for a simpler and saner past was poignantly expressed
by a San Diego record producer in search of a new place for his family to

live. In a letter to the editor printed in about half a dozen newspapers, he described it as a place "with stately old homes and buildings; it should have a tree-lined main street of shops and businesses that the locals still support; there should be a park for summer concerts where senior citizens can gather on the benches to pass the time and the local gossip; four seasons (without too much of any one); and, hopefully, all this will be within an hour or two of big-city transportation and entertainment" (Gorman). The San Diego man wrote: "We want to live somewhere where people care about their community, about their families, about each other and about their country. Somewhere where there's space for kids to run, to play, to grow. Somewhere where people greet one another on the street. Somewhere where we can get to know the local policemen, the grocer, the postman, the minister, the doctor, the vet and the mayor" (ibid.). His search for the "old American Dream" (ibid.) elicited over one hundred responses from around the country, by people recommending their town or by people who wished to be informed of his findings.

With the challenge to the modern project, the shift from believing in rational solutions, to believing only in a self-imposed order, if any at all, finds parallels in science fiction. While visionary literature of a century ago generally posited an improved planet Earth (usually through new technologies), more recent visionary and science fiction/cyberpunk literature posits some kind of escape from our own present and future through time machines, space machines, and computer technologies (particularly through virtual reality), or through the emergence of new communities of computer users in cyberspace.

This escape or turning inward, however, only contributes to the very problems from which people are escaping. This is because the retreat from the public sphere leaves a void into which the marketplace or an authoritarian regime (with essentialist claims) can easily step. The decline in ideals and the desire to work towards them creates a *horror vacui*, leaving us increasingly vulnerable to fashion and fascisms. Foucault has described this condition as the "death of man."[30]

In the United States, according to sociologist C. Wright Mills, this transition began in the 1920s as the country shifted from being a "properly developing nation" (in which decisions about standards of living are made according to debated choices among cultivated styles of life, and industrial production is an instrument for increasing the choices among such styles of life) to an "overdeveloped nation" (where the standard of living is more important than the style of living). In an overdeveloped society, Mills maintains, democracy cannot flourish because "history-making decisions and lack of decisions are virtually monopolized by elites who have access to the material and cultural means by which history is now powerfully being made" (Mills 1963a, 242). With regards to authoritarian regimes, Harvey discerns parallels between the recent rejection of universalizing machine rationality and the "aestheticization of politics" which occurs in reaction to the universalizing impulses of the 1930s, of which Nazism was one variant (Harvey 1989, 35). The more recent version, Harvey suggests, could bring more of the same.[31]

With regards to the marketplace, Theodor Adorno foresaw that in an overdeveloped society, the commodity becomes its own ideology. In the words of Fredric Jameson, "the practices of consumption and consumerism . . . themselves are . . . enough to reproduce and legitimate the system, no matter what 'ideology' you happen to be committed to. In that case, not abstract ideas, beliefs, ideologies, or philosophical systems, but rather the immanent practices of daily life now occupy the functional position of 'ideology' in its other larger systemic sense" (Jameson 1985, 77). Not only has this process continued, it has expanded in scope thanks to the intensification of global flows (of capital, labor, products, media, ideas, and people) and the related emergence of flexible capital in the 1970s (see Chapter 7, note 18).With regards to expressive forms of culture, Douglas Crimp maintains that "whatever role capital played in the art of modernism, the current phenomenon is new precisely because of its scope. Corporations have become the major patrons of art in every respect" (Crimp, 85; cited by Harvey 1989, 62). The postmodern sensibility might be understood as an adaptation to the flexible accumulation of corporate capitalism since the 1970s, along with a desire for "symbolic capital," Pierre Bourdieu's term to describe the taste and distinction ascribed to owners of status-conferring possessions (Bourdieu). Keeping pace with rapid changes in the fashion cycle requires one to relinquish much of oneself, including a coherent sense of identity and tradition.[32]

Globalization and the emergence of a mass culture have contributed to supplanting traditional identity markers (such as class, ethnicity, and community) with market-related ones (Angus and Jhally). They deprive us of endowed identities (individual and group) and give us the duty—or opportunity depending on one's perspective—of selecting an identity for ourselves. This active identity-formation leads us to regard our identities and those of others as fluid, as capable of changing at any moment, inciting Baudrillard to proclaim the "death of the self." The aspired-to modern coherent sense of self has thus been supplanted by a more chameleon-like (or fragmented) sense of personal identity, a sentiment reflected in revisionary "postmodern psychology."[33] The insecurity ensuing from this lack of an anchor or "center" renders ideals and working towards them virtually impossible[34] and it encourages, like postmodern forms of cultural expression, the facile borrowing and collaging of facets from the past and mass imagery to compose a self.

At the same time, the contemporary challenge to Enlightenment ideals and the corresponding privatism may also devolve into fetishism, or disguising what is really happening.[35] Postmodern culture tends to mask disturbing or disruptive facts of life through irony, humor, and shallow optimistic sound-bytes, as epitomized by Bobby McFerrin's popular tune which hypnotically repeats "Don't worry; be happy," a message rapidly appropriated by the T-shirt industry and emblazoned upon people's chests. Social theorist Stjepan Mestrovic developed this theme, saying "postmodern audiences are exposed routinely to apocalyptic themes that are camouflaged in 'fun' images, so that they are not permitted to feel indignation, outrage, real concern, nor even a desire to act. The threat of the apocalypse is converted into entertainment" (Mestrovic, 3). He concludes, "The postmodernist mixing and borrowing of diverse themes from scattered contexts ensures that no one can ever distinguish fully the sinister from the benign themes. In responding to the popular media, we laugh at the same time that we are filled with horror. Much the same difficulty exists in everyday relationships among persons" (Mestrovic, 4).

Although the prevalent postmodern habit of borrowing from the past or from mass imagery bespeaks dissatisfaction with the present, this is suppressed, repressed, denied, or superimposed through consumption, particularly of entertainment. Indeed, the discussion surrounding postmodernism has itself been regarded as a means of deflecting pressing political and social concerns given its preoccupation with the signifier rather than the signified, with the medium rather than the message, with fiction rather than function, and with aesthetics rather than ethics (Harvey 1989, 102).[36] Edward Said has observed that this progressive withdrawal from asking questions and assuming responsibility in a world in which knowledge is increasingly specialized and fragmented disallows any radical or effective engagement with general issues (in Connor, 13).

In postmodern forms of cultural expression, the decline of ideals has been manifest as a lack of standards by which to judge something and a consequent reluctance to take a stand. As a result, postmodern forms of cultural expression tend to spurn originality and to be derivative. They tend to seek affirmation by borrowing and recombining already sanctioned things rather than creating anew. With the shift to a postmodern sensibility, Crimp explains, "The fiction of the creating subject gives way to frank confiscation, quotation, excerption, accumulation and repetition of already existing images" (Crimp 1987, 44–45; cited by Harvey 1989, 54–55). For Crimp, the postmodern artist has dispensed with the modernist "aura" (in Walter Benjamin's sense) of artist-as-producer and simply reproduces. Whereas pre-modern and modern works aspired to unity, Gitlin maintains that postmodern works have abandoned the search for unity. "Instead of a single center, there is pastiche, cultural recombination. . . . Modernism tore up unity and postmodernism has been enjoying the shreds" (Gitlin 1989, 350–51). Whereas modernism was "a series of declarations of faith," he says, postmodernism "is an art of erosion" (Gitlin 1989, 360).[37]

Although "making something appear as though it were something else" might seem to be in the tradition of modernism's "strange-making" or "defamiliarization," the pervasive culling from and collaging the past and mass culture ultimately achieves the opposite effect, numbing its audience rather than shocking it into awareness. Rather than defamiliarize, contemporary forms of cultural expression may dull the senses: when all is strange, nothing is. And when nothing can provoke or shock, we become blasé and complacent, rather than perceptive, creative, and capable of constructive criticism. In this sense, the postmodern pretense of speaking to everyone may end up speaking to no one at all.[38]

The reduction of time and experience by new technologies to a series of presents renders immediacy, superficiality, images, appearance, and spectacles all-important. In Harvey's words, "The immediacy of events, the sensationalism of the spectacle (political, scientific, military, as well as those of entertainment), become the stuff of which consciousness is forged" (Harvey 1989, 54). Boyer has observed that speed "has erased the fragmentation and hierarchies of space and time, homogenized everything to the absolute present. To roll on, to travel, erases our memory, for the world becomes an excess of things, places, and characters once transversed they can be forgotten" (Boyer 1988, 102). With such rapid change and simulacra, the present fuses with the past and the future. Our time conception is altered and there is a sense of pervasive ephemerality and transitoriness. Nothing seems permanent, exacerbating the longing for stability and permanence. The result, according to Gitlin, is that "Space is not real, only time" (Gitlin 1988, 35). The extensive use of brand names and designer names, including those of architects, as well as familiar names for new housing developments, shopping districts, and streets might be seen as an effort to resurrect "real" spaces. While blurring the distinction between past, present, and future, the apparent lack of permanence also renders other distinctions dubious, such as those between fact and fiction and between scientific evidence and fantasy.

One manifestation of the pluralistic postmodern temper is the tendency to discern sub-species of postmodernists, though usually still in the modernist dualistic–antagonistic mode. David Griffin, for instance, describes "constructive or revisionary" and "deconstructive and eliminative" postmodernists (1988, x–xi), while Gitlin (1989) distinguishes between "hot" and "cool" postmodernists; Andreas Huyssen (1986) between "affirmative" and "alternative" postmodernists; and Pauline Marie Rosenau (1992) between the "affirmatives" and the "skeptics" (see chapter 6). The current pervasive sense of fragmentation has led many to characterize postmodern artifacts and/or society as schizoid (for example, Jameson, Eagleton, Hassan). Gilles Deleuze and Felix Guattari, for instance, conclude that "our society produces schizos the same way it produces Prell shampoo or Ford cars, the only difference being that the schizos are not saleable" (in *Anti-Oedipus* 1983, 245; cited by Harvey 1989, 53). In architectural design specifically, Charles Jencks distinguishes many breeds of postmodernists and he contends that the schizophrenia of architecture today exists because schizophrenia exists in society generally (1977).

THE IRONIC RESPONSE

A prevalent means of responding to the lack of consensus and image-orgy characteristic of the postmodern condition is that of irony. The ironic response is a defense mechanism against a world in which ultra-relativity reigns, in which there are no truths or answers. This response acknowledges that one's words, thoughts, or actions are just a selection from many that are neither better nor worse. It also acknowledges that these are borrowed (for example, from the past or from mass imagery). This response is manifest through quoting (literally or figuratively), tone of voice, tongue-in-cheek, the wink of an eye. It reflects an attempt to acknowledge that it has been done before but that it retains (at least some) meaning nonetheless and to acknowledge the fragmentation of contemporary life yet craft a wholeness for oneself (at least for the moment). For people involved in creative work, this attitude allows having it both ways: free self-expression and satisfying market demand, being both traditional and modern, local and global, and so forth, an attitude epitomized by Jencks's "double coding" (defined, chapter 3, 108–09).[39]

In culture at large, Gitlin contends, "Self-regarding irony and blankness are a way of staving off anxieties, rages, terrors and hungers that have been kicked up but cannot find resolution" (Gitlin 1988, 36). He describes the postmodern attitude: It "neither embraces nor criticizes, but beholds the world blankly, with a knowingness that dissolves feeling and commitment into irony. It pulls the rug out from under itself, displaying an acute self-consciousness about the work's constructed nature. It takes pleasure in the play of surfaces and derides the search for depth as mere nostalgia for an unmoved mover" (Gitlin 1988, 35). Gitlin maintains that one way to make sense of the postmodern play with surfaces is to see it as a means of evading the "large cultural terrors that broke into common consciousness in the 1960s" (Gitlin 1989, 353). For Gitlin, "Postmodernism is above all post-1960s; its keynote is helplessness. It is post-Vietnam, post New Left, post-hippie, post-Watergate. History was ruptured, passions have been expended, belief has become difficult; heroes have died and been replaced by celebrities. The 1960s exploded our belief in progress, which underlay the classical faith in linear order and moral clarity. Old verities crumbled, but new ones have not settled in" (Gitlin 1988, 36).

The ironic response involves a simultaneous attachment to and detachment from the world of experience and occurs, because, "In the postmodern world, belief is both impossible and unavoidable" (M. Taylor 1989, 21).[40] This sentiment, however, is not unique to the postmodern world. Leo Tolstoy in his 1882 *Confessions* wrote, "The only thing that we can know is that we know nothing and that is the highest flight of human wisdom" (Tolstoy). One half century later, poet Wallace Stevens similarly maintained, "The final belief is to believe in a fiction, which you know to be a fiction, there being nothing else. The exquisite truth is to know that it is a fiction and that you believe in it willingly" (1957; cited by M. Taylor 1989, 21). And more recently, a retired tailor and Holocaust survivor living in Venice, California, in the 1970s expressed this sensibility: "The wise man searches, but not to find. He searches because even though there is nothing to find, it is necessary to search" (as told to anthropologist Barbara Myerhoff 1979, 74). This valorization of process over end is also apparent in the transfiction of literary theory, for example novelist John Barth's "The key to the treasure is the treasure itself" (Barth 1986; see chapter 8 on transfiction).

Paul Fussell pointed out that irony became standard in English writing after World War I as a means of navigating around the unspeakable (Gitlin 1988, 36). Along similar lines, Gitlin has observed, "The blank, *I've-seen-it-all* post-modernist tone . . . is self-imposed cultural anesthesia, a refusal to feel (except for punkish rage, in which only one thing can be felt: loathing). The fear is that what's underneath hurts too much; better repress it. . . . To grow up post-1960s is an experience of aftermath, privatization, weightlessness; everything has apparently been done. Therefore culture is a process of recycling; everything is juxtaposable to everything else because nothing matters. This generation is disabused of authority, except, perhaps, the authority of money; theirs is the bumper sticker, THE ONE WITH THE MOST TOYS WINS. . . . The culture they favor is a passive adaptation to feeling historically stranded— after the 1960s but before what? Perhaps the Bomb, the void hanging over the horizon, threatening to pulverize everything of value. So be cool. In this light, post-modernism is anticipatory shell shock" (ibid.)

This declaration recalls Baudrillard's claim that the postmodern is "characteristic of a universe where there are no more definitions possible . . . . It has all been done. The extreme limit of these possibilities has been reached. It has destroyed itself. It has deconstructed its entire universe. So all that are left are pieces. All that remains to be done is to play with the pieces. Playing with the pieces—that is postmodern" (Baudrillard cited by Best and Kellner, 128). For Harvey, what "appears to be the most startling fact" about the postmodern condition is "its total acceptance of the ephemerality, fragmentation, discontinuity, and the chaotic" (Harvey 1989, 44). Postmodernism, he claims, does not try to transcend, counteract, or even define the "eternal and immutable" elements that might lie within it. Instead, it "swims, even wallows, in the fragmentary and the chaotic currents of change as if that is all there is"

The academic left in 1968 and in 1990

(ibid.). Consequently, its efforts to legitimize itself by reference to the past typically hark back to thought which emphasizes the deep chaos of modern life, such as that of Nietzsche (Harvey 1989).

The sense of cultural leveling due to globalization, according to Gitlin, has generated postmodern forms of cultural expression in which "Everything takes place in the present, 'here,' that is, nowhere in particular. Not only has the master voice dissolved, but also any sense of loss is rendered deadpan. . . . The work labors under no illusions: we are all deliberately playing, pretending here. . . . There is a premium on copies; everything has been done. Shock, now routine, is greeted with the glazed stare of the total ironist. . . . Where there was a passion, or ambivalence, there is now a collapse of feeling, a blandness" (Gitlin 1989, 350). Postmodernism, Gitlin contends, differs from modernism in "its blasé tone, its sense of exhaustion, its self-conscious bemusement with surfaces" (Gitlin 1988, 35). Unlike modernism, it "self-consciously splices genres, attitudes, styles. It relishes the blurring or juxtaposition of forms (fiction/non-fiction), stances (straight/ironic), moods (violent/comic), cultural levels (high/low). It disdains originality and fancies copies, repetition, the recombination of hand-me-down scraps" (ibid.).

Among intellectuals, the contemporary emphasis on the cultural construction of everything as opposed to the universal truisms of modernism also contributes to making the ironic response obligatory. With meaning regarded as a product of arbitrary choice, Charlene Spretnak points out, "one can merely strike self-conscious postures as if one's responses had meaning. Anything more would reveal a dated naiveté. 'Enormously suggestive,' rather than 'accurate' or 'truthful,' is the highest accolade for an analysis or conclusion" (Spretnak, 15). In academia, the challenge to modernity has been manifest in an abandonment of activist pro-revolutionary, Marxist-inspired politics (Bernstein 1990), the turn to reflexivity, and a heated debate about the proper role of the Western "canon." Steven Watts describes this as the outcome of an exhaustion of 1960s political radicalism among academics, saying, "Facing an apathetic or hostile public, radicals have turned steadily inward both in their politics and their scholarship" (Watts, 631). Their self-exile to academia in the face of a growing conservatism in society generally, he maintains, produced "a sophisticated political disengagement" (ibid.) featuring an outpouring of scholarship on the theme of poststructuralism. Poststructuralism, according to Watts, "has gathered and sheltered a great many radical survivors by playing a powerful mediating role . . . between radical desires for a public role and simultaneous fears of political impotence [and between] the Leftist academic's felt necessity of posing a radical critique of the dominant culture, on the one hand, and the evident fact of the Leftist academic's embourgeoisment, on the other" (ibid., 163).

THE NEW SENSIBILITY

Emerging from a worldview that believed in truths and answers and that sought consensus, extreme relativity and the celebration of differences can be unsettling. Consequently, the very pluralism, anti-authoritarianism, and multi-centrality of the postmodern moment have also contributed to exacerbating the prevalent sense of insecurity.[41] Other contributors to this heightened state of insecurity include the concurrent decline in idealism and visionary thinking, retreat from political engagement, turning inward (privatism), obscuring of power, greater vulnerability to fashion (the market) and to fascisms (authoritarian regimes), fluidity of identities, and the increased sense of fragmentation. In cultural forms of expression, these are manifest as a lack of standards by which to judge something and a consequent reluctance to take a stand or to be original. This in turn incites a decline in creativity with the result that art loses much of its potential for provocation and inspiration, contributing instead to the overriding complacency and cynicism. Despite the touted democratizing potential of pluralism and "*décloisonnement*," then, their coinciding with (economic) liberalization, the rise of a new right, and the general de-politicization (or co-option) of expressive forms of culture suggests that there may be more than meets the eye.

While the postmodern reflex might be regarded as an effort to find meaning and to be contextual, it usually entails discovering meanings and inventing contexts in order to cope with the peculiar fear of the postmodern condition. The fear we sense today is no longer a fear of the "dangerous classes" or vice versa since social class is no longer clearly identifiable by one's relation to the mode of production. In contrast to the fear accompanying the industrial revolution, fear accompanying the post-industrial (or, more accurately, hyper-industrial) revolution is more elusive and the means for dealing with it appear further out of reach. Fear has come home (as manifest in privatization), but home has disappeared in both its figurative sense (the longing for a paradise lost) and its literal sense (with the increased frequency of relocating as well as of actual homelessness). New technologies have simultaneously generated nostalgia for the past and facilitated the repackaging of past images for present consumption, while rendering any true return impossible.

Georg Simmel suggests in his seminal essay about the impact of urbanization on people (1902) that overstimulation leads to a blasé attitude and political disengagement.[42] As urbanization has proceeded apace, so has our blasé attitude. Artist Barbara Kruger describes the current scene as a vacuous state of being: "To put it bluntly, no one's home. We are literally absent from our own present. We are elsewhere, not in the real but in the represented. Our bodies, the flesh and blood of it all, have given way to representations: figures that cavort on TV, movie and computer screens. Propped up and ultra-relaxed, we teeter on the cusp of narcolepsy and believe everything and nothing" (Kruger).

The positive side of the postmodern sensibility is that the challenge to the modern worldview signals more humility and less dogmatism among experts. It also signals more humanitarianism and pragmatism, more willingness to work in teams, and more faith in instincts than in science. There is a shift from envisioning society as homogeneous (as exemplified by CIAM 8) to seeing it as diverse, and from aspiring toward a universal language to affirming multiple languages (multivocality) as well as multiple meanings (multivalency). This translates into a shift from regarding others (non-experts) as in need of guidance to valuing all perspectives and engaging in dialogue or "multilogue," i.e. seeking to communicate with others by making one's ideas and work accessible through empathy and deep listening.

"We are now in the process of wakening from the nightmare of modernity," according to Terry Eagleton, "with its manipulative reason and fetish of the totality, into the laid-back pluralism of the post-modern, that heterogeneous range of life-styles and language games" (Eagleton 1987; cited by Harvey 1989, 7–8).[43] Rather than reach the "end of philosophy," Stephen Toulmin argues that reawakened interests in history, rhetoric, narrative, the oral, contextuality, the particular, the local, and the timely (or applied knowledge) (Toulmin, 180, 186–7) indicate a move back "from a theory-centered conception, dominated by a concern for stability and rigor, to a renewed acceptance of practice, which requires us to adapt action to the special demands of particular occasions" (Toulmin, 192).[44]

Regarding the aesthetic realm specifically, Leslie Fiedler proclaimed and celebrated the death of the avant-garde and the modern novel, and the emergence of a less elitist art which was "closing the gap" between the artist and the public (in the 1960s; cited by Best and Kellner, 10). Jameson raises the "possibility that with postmodernism a whole new aesthetic is in the process of emerging" (Jameson 1985, 86),[45] whereby "an aesthetic of homogeneity is here displaced in the service of a new kind of perception for which tension, contradiction, the registering of the incompatible and the clashing, is in and of itself a strong mode of relating two incommensurable elements, poles, or realities" (ibid.). The critique of high modernism, Jameson points out:

> . . . coincides with its extinction, its passing into history, as well as with the emergence, in the third stage of "consumer capital," of some properly postmodernist practice of pastiche, of a new free play of styles and historicist allusions now willing to "learn from Las Vegas," a moment of surface rather than of depth, of the 'death' of the old individual subject or bourgeois ego, and of

the schizophrenic celebration of the commodity fetishism of the image, of a now "delirious New York" and a countercultural California, a moment in which the logic of media capitalism penetrates the logic of advanced cultural production itself and transforms the latter to the point where such distinctions as those between high and mass culture lose their significance (and where the older notions of a "critical" or "negative" value of advanced or modernist art may also no longer be appropriate or operative). (Jameson 1985, 75)[46]

Huyssen has interpreted the recuperation of history and the re-emergence of narrative in the 1970s not as "part of a leap back into a pre-modern, pre-avantgarde past, as some postmodernists seem to suggest," but "as attempts to shift into reverse in order to get out of a dead-end street where the vehicles of avantgardism and postmodernism have come to a standstill" (Huyssen, 174), recalling the French aphorism "*Il faut reculer pour mieux sauter*" (You have to step back in order to jump better). Huyssen describes this as part of "a slowly emerging cultural transformation in Western societies, a change in sensibility" (Huyssen, 181), which marks a departure from "the great divide" between high culture and mass/popular culture, a divide which implies exclusion and elitism (Huyssen, ix).[47] While acknowledging the validity of Adorno's claims regarding the negative aspects of the culture industry, Huyssen emphasizes the positive component to the various mergings of high and mass art and is sanguine about the possibilities of a counterhegemonic project, saying that:

Even under the conditions set by the capitalist culture industry and its distribution apparatus, art ultimately can open up emancipatory avenues if only because it is granted autonomy and practical uselessness. The thesis of the total subjugation of art to the market . . . underestimates possibilities for emancipation inherent in consumption; in general, consumption satisfies needs, and even though human needs can be distorted to an amazing degree, every need contains a smaller or larger kernel of authenticity. The question is how this kernel can be utilized and fulfilled. (Huyssen, 152)

Ultimately, the sanctioning of multiple worldviews may offer alternatives to the destructive and oppressive components of the modern worldview. The challenge to the modern project holds potential for ending the imperial and colonial sensibilities of the last two centuries, as well as more recent neoimperialisms and neocolonialisms (of consciousness).

NOTES

1. Jameson writes: "The appetite for images of the past, in the form of what might be called simulacra, the increasing production of such images of all kinds, in particular in that peculiar postmodern genre, the nostalgic film, with its glossy evocation of the past as sheer consumerable fashion and image—all this seems to me something of a return of the repressed, an unconscious sense of the loss of the past, which this appetite for images seeks desperately to overcome" (cited by Robertson, 54). See also Viorst, "The Ultimate Connection" (Viorst, 9–23).

2. With the emergence and consolidation of a bourgeoisie, history was reified, change came to be regarded as inevitable, and time became a commodity of which there was never enough (Moravia), inciting sayings such as "Time is money," "*Le temps qui passe,*" "*pas de temps de vivre,*" "*Métro, Bulot, Dodo.*" This led to a valorization of "leisure" time and an anticipation of a future moment when time would be less tyrannical (retirement), along with a fascination for the past. Alberto Moravia dates the rise of "terror" to this period. He writes: "With the Revolution of '89, the bourgeois world, a materialistic world firmly bound to duration, that is, to the passage of time, superseded the feudal world, a world completely alienated from and immovably situated outside of time. If nothing stands still, then everything—opinions, styles, information, fortunes, success, groups, society—falls victim to continuous change. Snobbery comes to stand as the fickle and arbitrary surrogate of good taste, which is based no longer on the canon of the beautiful but on that of fashion, of whatever is in vogue. . . . It is here, in the realm of historical change, that terror comes into play as an instrument of power" (Moravia, 37–38).

3. See Lowe (1982) and Sennett (1984).

4. Prior to the nineteenth century, "one tended to find a more directly existential type of nostalgia, arising more 'naturally' from estrangement or alienation" (Robertson, 55). By the late part of that century, this combined with a more willful, synthetic, and politically driven nostalgia (Robertson, 54) which became "incorporated—for the most part capitalistically—into consumerist, image-conveyed nostalgia" (Robertson, 55). This late-twentieth-century nostalgia both universalizes particulars and particularizes universals; it is "both collective on a global scale and directed at globality itself" (Robertson, 56).

5 In one of the earliest uses of the term "postmodern," C. Wright Mills described this development in 1959, saying that the postmodern age diverges from the modern one in that the two major orientations of the modern age—liberalism and socialism — both products of the Enlightenment—"have virtually collapsed as adequate explanations of the world and of ourselves" (C. W. Mills 1963a, 242). Based on the assumption that "freedom and reason will coincide, that more rationality will bring more freedom" (ibid., 244), Mills claimed that neither ideology remains appropriate for a time which questions whether rationality and scientism guarantee increased freedom and a better world for all. In Mills's analysis, the overdevelopment allowed by pursuit of the modern project ultimately challenges this project because it results in a situation of "rationality without reason" and of "human alienation" (ibid.), recalling the "dialectic of Enlightenment" (Adorno and Horkheimer).

6. According to Hannah Arendt (1958), the public realm satisfies three criteria: (1) By

outlasting mortal lives, it memorializes and thereby conveys a sense of history and society to individuals. (2) It is established collectively and is an arena for diverse groups of people to engage in dialogue, debate, and oppositional struggles. (3) It is accessible to and used by all. Sennett contends that "A *res publica* stands in general for those bonds of association and mutual commitment which exist between people who are not joined together by ties of family or intimate association; it is the bond of a crowd, of a 'people,' of a polity, rather than the bonds of family or friends" (Sennett 1974).

7. Sennett attributes the decline of the public realm to changes "that began with the fall of the *ancien régime* and the formation of a new capitalist, secular, urban culture" (Sennett 1974).

8. In order to create a market for mass-produced goods, marketers need to influence the way in which people perceive themselves. Through the metropolitan press and advertising, they work to supplant traditional social markers (involving ethnic, regional, and class allegiances) with market-related differences (Angus and Jhally, 4–6). This process accelerated after World War II and again since 1972. With social identity now deriving largely from what and how much one consumes (ibid.), the emergence of a mass society largely blurs the distinction between images and the real thing, altering our perception of "reality." Advertising's creation of needs merged culture and consumption into the "culture of consumption" so that the languages of culture and consumption resemble one another closely as "culture and economy have merged to form a single sphere" (Angus and Jhally, 5).

9. Pawley traces the origins of this secondary reality to "the absorption of surrealism and psychoanalysis [which like the French Symbolist poets of the late nineteenth century sought to convey impressions by suggestion rather than direct statement] by the commercial art of advertising and marketing" (Pawley 1973, 14).

10. Television, Pawley contends, "makes things normal" (Pawley 1973, 160). He writes, there "is enormous pressure on the wizards of media to develop techniques powerful enough to effect a permanent orbit [and] to evade the uncertainties of democracy by abandoning primary reality altogether" (Pawley 1973, 171). Although politics has always done this, he says, now the public prefers that the media do it "in a world whose real possibilities are running out fast" (Pawley 1973, 173).

11. See Best and Kellner, 120–21.

12. Assessing the impact of the widespread use of new communication technologies, Baudrillard (1975) draws from structural linguistics to suggest that the code (signifier, sign) no longer refers back to anything but its own logic, so that reality becomes a simulation. This perspective shifts the locus of contradiction, control, and oppression from production (the Marxian focus) to the code. Use-value and needs thus disappear as simulation takes the place of ideology. The scene (signified/referent) and the mirror (sign), says Baudrillard, have been replaced by a screen and a network—involving connections, contact, feedback, interface—such that we become control screens and simulation becomes the end, rather than the means to communicate (1983a).

13. Roland Barthes in *Essais Critiques* (1964), explains, "The aim of all structuralist activity, in the fields of both thought and poetry, is to reconstitute an object, and, by this process, to make known the rules of functioning, or 'functions,' of this object.

The structure is therefore effectively a simulacrum of the object which . . . brings out something that remained invisible, or, if you like, unintelligible in the natural object" (cited by Best and Kellner, 18).

14. See C. Wright Mills's similar analysis (1963b). With the introduction of electronic media which has no original and no copy (Angus, 100), our complaints about simulacra replacing authenticity may not be valid as they would have been in Walter Benjamin's time. As Angus explains, with electronic media "there is no 'alienation' from an original identity to which one can authentically 'return.' It is possible to interpret this development as a utopian surpassing of industrial specialization" (Angus, 101).

15. Harvey describes how the "real" is shaped by the mass media: "Through films, television, books, and the like, history and past experience are turned into a seemingly vast archive instantly retrievable and capable of being consumed over and over again at the push of a button. . . . Reality, it seems, is being shaped to mimic media images" (Harvey 1989, 61).

16. In "The 18th Brumaire of Louis Bonaparte" (1959, 318–49; original 1852), Marx explains that change elicits a longing for the past as well as a need for legitimation and meaning. He writes: "Men make their own history, but they do not make it just as they please; they do not make it under circumstances chosen by themselves, but under circumstances directly found, given and transmitted from the past. The tradition of all the dead generations weighs like a nightmare on the brain of the living. And just when they seem engaged in revolutionizing themselves and things, in creating something entirely new, precisely in such epochs of revolutionary crisis they anxiously conjure up the spirits of the past to their service and borrow from them names, battle slogans and costumes in order to present the new scene of world history in this time-honoured disguise and this borrowed language. . . . The awakening of the dead in those revolutions therefore served the purpose of glorifying the new struggles, not of parodying the old; of magnifying the given tasks in imagination, not of taking flight from their solution in reality; of finding once more the spirit of revolution, not of making its ghost walk again" (Marx 1959, 320).

17. Hewison describes the "preservation impulse" as "part of the impulse to preserve the self. Without knowing where we have been, it is difficult to know where we are going. The past is the foundation of individual and collective identity [and] objects from the past are the source of significance as cultural symbols. Continuity between past and present creates a sense of sequence out of aleatory chaos and, since change is inevitable, a stable system of ordered meaning enables us to cope with both innovation and decay" (Hewison 1987; cited by Harvey 1989, 85–86). Benedict Anderson also develops the theme of national identity drawing from the past in *Imagined Communities*.

18. The definition of tradition proffered by Max Radin in the *Encyclopedia of Social Sciences* (1934) suggests that it is not the product itself or the process of transmission per se but the belief in the value of something and the desire to continue it.

19. According to Hobsbawm, there are two major categories of invented traditions: "innovatory movements" and "new political regimes" (Hobsbawm, 10), or artistic and political movements. Although initiated by different groups and variously expressed, both categories invoke the past to promote and legitimize group cohesion, identity, and

power through selectively culling and reassembling imagery, symbolism, and language. These two categories merge when art and politics join forces, as is often the case in city building. Hitler, for instance, who was an architect manqué, had the Bauhaus mutilated and closed while aggressively promoting a neovernacular cottage style under the Reich (Speer; Krier and Larson).

20. Berger maintains: "History always constitutes the relation between a present and its past. Consequently fear of the present leads to mystification of the past. The past is not for living in; it is a well of conclusions from which we draw in order to act" (J. Berger, 11).

21. Harvey says: "Historical preservation and the museum culture experienced strong bursts of life from the late nineteenth century on, while the international expositions not only celebrated the world of international commodification but also exhibited the geography of the world as a series of artefacts for all to see. . . . This was also an age when the artefacts of the past or from afar began to trade as valued commodities. The emergence of an active antique and foreign craft market . . . are indicative of a trend that was consistent, also, with the revival of the craft tradition pushed by William Morris in Britain, by the craftwork movement of Vienna, and in the art nouveau style that swamped France in the early years of the century" (Harvey 1989, 272).

22. Bertrand de Jouvenal has called such visions "futuribles."

23. With a communications zeitgeist replacing the labor zeitgeist (which prevailed from the French Revolution to 1968), Habermas says, the specific utopian idea based on social labor is over. That idea arose out of a new perception of time such that hopes for paradise shifted to this world (Habermas 1986, 3).

24. Examining the psychological implications of the decline of the public realm, Sennett declares: "Western societies are moving from something like an other-directed condition to an inner-directed condition—except that in the midst of self-absorption no one can say what is inside. As a result, confusion has arisen between public and intimate life" (Sennett 1974). This self-absorption, he says, "obscures the continuing importance of class in advanced industrial society" (ibid.) and leads us "to undervalue the community relations of strangers, particularly those which occur in cities" (ibid.).

25. Architect and environmental psychologist Sharon Sutton writes, "Struggling with extreme differences in wealth and deprivation and with the conflicts of increasing ethnic diversity, Jane Jacob's 'eyes of the street' have withdrawn into the electronic privacy of VCRs and cable televisions" (Sutton, 293).

26. Harvey reminds us that the "preoccupation with identity, with personal and collective roots, has become far more pervasive since the early 1970s because of widespread insecurity in labor markets, in technological mixes, credit systems, and the like" (Harvey 1989, 87).

27. This thesis is treated in Kenneth Galbraith's *Power* and Sennett's *Authority*.

28. This tendency toward privatization has resulted in a situation which Galbraith refers to as "private affluence and public squalor."

29. Pawley exclaims, "Privatization has become the Final Solution to all our social 'diseases' and our profoundly ambiguous attitude to that solution is reflected in the evasive thinking that surrounds it" (Pawley 1973, 49). He says that "privatization means a media-fed life of autonomous-drive slavery wherein every wish is gratified and every fear calmed

by means of sublimation. . . . Not only do we wish to exterminate community but we wish to do it secretly" (ibid.).

30. Similarly, Boyer points out that if we renege on the modern project, "We are locked into a mode of unreflective thought, and we fall into nihilistic abandonment of our claims for freedom and moral autonomy" (Boyer 1990, 93) and for "overall equity and progressive concerns" (ibid.).

31. Regarding the renewed interest in geopolitics and in the aesthetics of space within their historical contexts, Harvey warns, "Geopolitical and aesthetic interventions always seem to imply nationalist, and hence unavoidably reactionary, politics" (Harvey 1989, 283). He asks: if "aesthetic production has now been so thoroughly commodified and thereby become really subsumed within a political economy of cultural production, how can we possibly stop that circle closing onto a produced, and hence all too easily manipulated, aestheticization of a globally mediatized politics" (Harvey 1989, 305)? With the advent of simulacra, allowing for the commodification of images themselves, Harvey suggests that it is more difficult than ever before.

32. Gitlin asserts, "High-consumption capitalism requires a ceaseless transformation in style, a connoisseurship of surface, an emphasis on packaging and reproducibility. . . . In order to adapt, consumers are pried away from traditions, their selves become 'decentered,' and a well-formed interior life becomes an obsolete encumbrance [as] 'life styles' become commodities to be marketed" (Gitlin 1988, 35). Extending Foucault's (1980) notion of industrialism as employment of disciplinary power to describe post-industrial society, Zygmunt Bauman (1983) says that consumerism is a poor means of social integration because consumer drives and conflicts are so makeshift. Bauman suggests that this might account for the present unease, a crisis in disciplinary power, much as the conflicts of the early industrial society were related to the crisis of sovereign power.

33. A certain strand of postmodern psychology revises modern psychology's goal of recovering a coherent self, aspiring instead to facilitate the cohabitation of our many selves.

34. With postmodernism, Jameson contends, "alienation of the subject is displaced by fragmentation of the subject" (Jameson 1984a, 63; cited by Harvey 1989, 54). Harvey explains that people are no longer alienated in the classical Marxist sense "because to be alienated presupposes a coherent rather than a fragmented sense of self from which to be alienated. It is only in terms of such a centered sense of personal identity that individuals can pursue projects over time, or think cogently about the production of a future significantly better than time present and time past" (Harvey 1989, 53–54).

35. Gitlin contends that the whole discussion about postmodernism is "a deflected and displaced discussion of the contours of political thought" (Gitlin 1989, 348). Harvey similarly describes the means by which postmodernism deflects attention from the underlying realities as a "politics of distraction" (Harvey 1989, 61). He maintains that Marx "would surely accuse those postmodernists who proclaim the 'impenetrability of the other' as their creed, of overt complicity with the fact of fetishism and of indifference towards underlying social meanings" (Harvey 1989, 101).

36. Harvey submits that "postmodernism, with its emphasis upon the ephemerality of *jouissance*, its insistence upon the impenetrability of the other, its concentration on the text rather than the work, its penchant for deconstruction bordering on nihilism, its preference for aesthetics over ethics, takes matters too far. It takes them beyond the point

where any coherent politics are left, while that wing of it that seeks a shameless accommodation with the market puts it firmly in the tracks of an entrepreneurial culture that is the hallmark of reactionary neoconservativism. . . . Postmodernism has us accepting the reifications and partitionings, actually celebrating the activity of masking and cover-up, all the fetishisms of locality, place, or social grouping, while denying that kind of meta-theory which can grasp the political-economic processes . . . that are becoming ever more universalizing in their depth, intensity, reach and power over daily life" (Harvey 1989, 116–17). Harvey maintains, "The rhetoric of postmodernism is dangerous for it avoids confronting the realities of political economy and the circumstances of global power" (Harvey 1989, 117).

37. Charting the differences between modernism and postmodernism, Ihab Hassan (1975; 1985) ascribes to modernism: purpose, design, hierarchy, mastery, finished work, distance, totalization, synthesis, depth, metaphysics, and transcendence. To postmodernism, he ascribes: play, chance, anarchy, silence, process, performance, happening, participation, antithesis, deconstruction, surface, against interpretation, irony, immanence.

38. The seeds of this have been situated in the rise of mass culture. After spending time in the United States, Theodor Adorno described (in 1963) the workings of what he called the "culture industry" as forcing "a reconciliation of high and low art, which have been separated for thousands of years, a reconciliation which damages both. High art is deprived of its seriousness because its effect is programmed; low art is put in chains and deprived of the unruly resistance inherent in it when social control was not yet total" (cited by Huyssen, 145). Andreas Huyssen maintains that an "inherent contradiction of the postmodernist avantgarde" is "the paradox of an art that simultaneously wants to be art and anti-art and of a criticism that pretends to be criticism and anti-criticism" (Huyssen, 169).

39. A more self-conscious version of irony is the parodic response (for example, Hutcheon, 70).

40. M. Taylor writes: "The negation and reappropriation of the past is, therefore, the assertion of the subject's own ironic self-consciousness" (Taylor 1989, 21). Anthony Vidler (1992) suggests that irony is a dominant mode of emancipation in the "posturban" city.

41. This is not to suggest that there was ever a true consensus, but simply that the modern worldview enjoyed a dominance which has been challenged.

42. In similar fashion, Orin Klapp (1991) suggests that symbolic or cultural inflation occurs when oversupply, enlargement, or expansion lead to diminishing the value of a symbol through, for instance, exaggeration (by individuals), crusading (by a group, i.e. propaganda campaigns), or oversupply by the market or otherwise, for example an oversupply of credentials, smiles, kisses, greeting cards, fashions, and information.

43. Steven Connor writes: "The postmodern condition . . . manifests itself in the multiplication of centers of power and activity and the dissolution of every kind of totalizing narrative which claims to govern the whole complex field of social activity and representation. The waning of the cultural authority of the West and its political and intellectual traditions, along with the opening up of the world political scene to cultural and ethnic differences, is another symptom of the modulation of hierarchy into heterarchy, or differences organized into a unified pattern of domination and subordination, as

opposed to differences existing alongside each other but without any principle of commonality or order" (Connor, 9).

44. The humanizing of modernity, says Toulmin, entails a shift away from the de-contextualizing project which began with the Cartesian rationality of the mid-seventeenth century—subordinating rhetoric to logic and geometry—and lasted until the 1950s. It entails a shift "from a focus on the problem of preserving stability and preventing instability, to a focus on creating institutions and procedures that are adaptive. . . . In an age of interdependence and historical change, mere stability and permanence are not enough. Like social and political institutions, formal techniques of thought too easily lapse into stereotyped and self-protective rigidity. *Like buildings on a human scale*, our intellectual and social procedures will do what we need in the years ahead, only if we take care to avoid irrelevant or excessive stability, and keep them operating in ways that are adaptable to unforeseen—or even unforeseeable—situations and functions" (Toulmin, 186, emphasis added). Rather than choose between sixteenth-century humanism and seventeenth-century exact science, then, Toulmin recommends retaining "the positive achievements of them both" (Toulmin, 180).

45 In contrast to the modernist "aesthetic of identity or of organic unification" (Jameson 1985, 86)

46. Along similar lines, Gitlin identifies an emergent sensibility which features "jubilant disrespect for the boundaries that are supposed to segregate culture castes, but [which] does not imply a leveling down, profaning the holy precincts of high culture" (Gitlin 1989, 359).

47. This divide, says Huyssen, grew especially pronounced during "the age of Stalin and Hitler when the threat of totalitarian control over all culture forged a variety of defensive strategies meant to protect high culture in general, not just modernism" (Huyssen, 197). For postmodern artistic or critical sensibilities, Huyssen maintains, the great divide "that was codified in the various classical accounts of modernism no longer seems relevant" (ibid.). Now, Huyssen observes that "in an important sector of our culture there is a noticeable shift in sensibility, practices, and discourse formations which distinguishes a postmodern set of assumptions, experiences, and propositions from that of a preceding period" (Huyssen, 181). Contemporary postmodernism, Huyssen says, "operates in a field of tension between tradition and innovation, conservation and renewal, mass culture and high art, in which the second terms are no longer automatically privileged over the first; a field of tension which can no longer be grasped in categories such as progress vs. reaction, left vs. right, present vs. past, modernism vs. realism, abstraction vs. representation, avantgarde vs. Kitsch" (Huyssen, 216–17). These dichotomies, which are central to the classical accounts of modernism, Huyssen says, have broken down. One outcome of this is that "artistic activities have become much more diffuse and harder to contain in safe categories or stable institutions such as the academy, the museum or even the established gallery network" (Huyssen, 218–19). Huyssen contends that "postmodernism at its deepest level represents not just another crisis within the perpetual cycle of boom and bust, exhaustion and renewal, which has characterized the trajectory of modernist culture" (Huyssen, 217). Rather, "it represents a new type of crisis of that modernist culture itself" (ibid.).

5

THEMES OF POSTMODERN URBANISM

THE REACTIONS TO MODERNIST ARCHITECTURE and planning discussed in chapters 2 and 3 can be mapped along two axes, one indicating the formal ambitions of urban designers and the other the ways in which they perceive their role. These axes meet at the point where urban designers aspire to realize their personal artistic and financial ambitions, with little or no theoretical justification entering the mix, and the axes diverge along the designers' respective theoretical paths. The formal ambition axis moves from producing good and beautiful built forms to drawing inspiration from mass culture, the social context, the site, and the past. The urban designer's role axis proceeds from the businessperson and artist to the facilitator, political activist, and social engineer. Although the reactions to modernist architecture and planning might be mapped along these axes, such an exercise would ultimately reveal little since theory is often a mask or justification for personal ambitions or vice versa.

Rather than chart the rhetoric of these various approaches, then, this chapter peers beyond it, by reviewing and assessing the major themes which fall along the axes of postmodern urbanism as inscribed within the larger postmodern reflex outlined in the preceding chapter. These overlapping themes include contextualism, historicism, the search for urbanity, regionalism, anti-universalism, pluralism, collage, self-referentiality, reflexivity, preoccupation with image/decor/scenography, super-

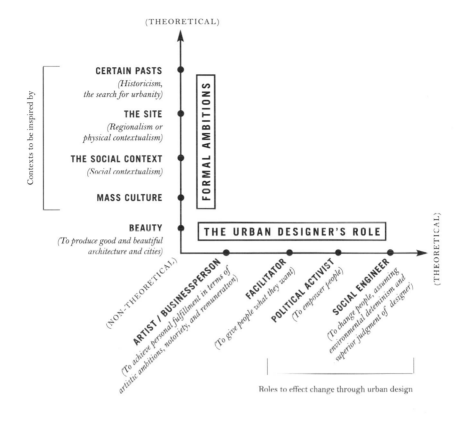

The axes of postmodern urbanism.

ficiality, depthlessness, ephemerality, fragmentation, populism, apoliticism, commercialism, loss of faith, and irony. The critique of postmodern urbanism advanced in this chapter is organized as follows: Form Follows Fiction; Form Follows Fear; Form Follows Finesse; Form Follows Finance; and The Result. The concluding section, On Balance, presents certain correctives of postmodern urbanism as well as promising initiatives that have emerged in the 1990s.

The challenge to the modern project and the decline of the public realm to which modern urbanism was accomplice called for new responses from urban designers. Whereas "modernism from the 1910s to the 1960s . . . responded to the challenge of establishing social order for a mass society; post-modernism since the 1960s . . . responded to the challenge of placelessness and a need for urban community" (Ley 1987, 40).

In contrast to modern urbanism's insistence upon structural honesty and functionality, postmodern urbanism sought to satisfy needs that were not merely functional and to convey meanings other than the building tectonics. In architectural theory, Ada Louise Huxtable observed, there was "a search for meaning and symbolism, a way to establish architecture's ties with human experience, a way to find and express a value system, a concern for architecture in the context of society" (Huxtable 1981a, 73–74).

As modernism's minimalist tendencies grew ever more stifling, urban designers embraced maximalism and inclusivity, as expressed in the maxims "Less is a bore" (Venturi 1966) and "More is more" (Stern in Williams 1985). The parallel shift occurring in literature is evocatively portrayed by the protagonist in John Barth's *Tidewater Tales* (1986), a writer whose increasingly minimalist style ultimately blocks his ability to write or dream until circumstances (including the birth of his first child) re-ignite his creative juices, this time in a maximalist form. Likewise in urban design theory, universalism and purism were gradually supplanted by pluralism and contextualism while the role of the urban designer shifted from that of inspired genius, artist, or social engineer to that of a more humble, and at times servile, facilitator.

FORM FOLLOWS FICTION

Whereas modernist architecture and urban planning derived inspiration from the machine to house an industrial society, many reactions to modernism since the 1960s have sought inspiration from pre-industrial townscapes for a post-industrial society. While certain outcomes of these efforts have been salutary (see "On Balance" below), the two-part denial inherent in them often render success elusive or merely partial. This denial entails a reluctance to acknowledge that post-industrial needs and tastes can differ vastly from pre-industrial ones, along with a related tendency to edit history, valorizing and idealizing selective pasts while denigrating and erasing others, particularly our most recent past, that of modernism.

In its determination to improve upon modernist urban design, postmodern urbanism often fails to acknowledge the irreversible changes wrought by the industrial revolution. In an early criticism of writers such as Jane Jacobs, John Dyckman (1962) contends that they "simply edit the factory out of the city and talk about neighborhoods in which the monster of industrialism never intrudes. . . . Dirt and disorder are powdered over, colors and smells are somehow blended as in the artist's palette or the master's cuisine, so that tolerance of their diversity is no affirmation of sensuousness, but is as respectable as a showing in an advanced gallery, or a good dinner in mid-town. Leisure is relaxed and reflective, because security underlies it, and work, with its meaning, is virtually out of sight. To build an urban aesthetic on this caricature of urban life is wholly without meaning for contemporary city planning."

A more recent proponent of historicism, Léon Krier, would also like to ignore industrialization, which he has described as a "total failure" (Krier 1984), as well as the institutionalized forms of education that evolved along with it, which he has referred to as "a tortuous necessity for all," the "decisive instrument" for social, cultural, and ideological control for social reproduction (Krier 1978a, 59). As a result, Manuel Castells maintains, although Krier's typology "has a nice appeal," it is "reductive and ultimately meaningless" (Castells 1983, 315). Thomas Dutton likewise observes "a wide gulf between Krier's urban perceptions and prescriptions" and contemporary realities (Dutton 1986, 22), rendering him guilty of misrepresenting the actual relationship between dominant and oppressed cultures, power and powerlessness, urban design and social change.[1] Ultimately, Dutton claims, the realization of Krier's proposals would only produce superficial change, "leaving the city to the reign of dominant institutions with business as usual" (Dutton 1986, 24).

The fact that new transportation and communications technologies have subverted the logic of the pre-modern city (with its high density and tight mix of building functions) has also been overlooked in the pursuit of urbanity, as has the impact they have had on reshaping the use and perception of public and private space.[2] The danger of this nostalgia is most blatantly manifest in the oversight of the car. As Richard Ingersoll contends, "Often, in the enthusiasm for a return to the city fabric, the city is treated as if postindustrial times were postautomobile times" (Ingersoll 1989c, 12). Interviewing Colin Rowe, Ingersoll asks, "Isn't the problem of the automobile, even if it was not the origin of the formal solutions of Modernism,[3] still central in a current urban scheme" (ibid.)? In a telling response, Rowe admits, "Here in Rome there are times, in fact every day, when I would prefer to get into an automobile and go shopping in a supermarket than go shopping around in these little stores. The ideal thing would be to have a good American suburb adjacent to a very concentrated Italian town, then you'd have the best of both worlds" (ibid.). Rowe's ideal of living and doing his errands in a well-appointed American suburb with an old European village nearby—for charm, character, and possibly status—is no doubt a widely-shared sentiment, albeit rarely admitted by those decrying the decline of the public realm and pursuing the "search for urbanity."[4]

Although pre-modern typologies and morphologies may appear quaint and may be fun to visit, they usually do not correspond to contemporary needs and tastes (see Ellin 1994). Ingersoll addresses this issue, saying: "While the objective of walkable streets and harmonious surroundings might appear to be universal, at the heart of this postmodern alternative lies a troubling paradox that is rarely taken into account and indeed calls into doubt the wisdom of what are essentially formal solutions: preindustrial forms and spaces are not necessarily suited to postindustrial ways of life" (Ingersoll 1989a, 21). Ingersoll asks, "If one proposes all kinds of nice public spaces, connected streets and figured piazzas, will there still be an audience in a highly technological society for their use" (ibid.)? The answer is often no, as attested to by many unused indoor and outdoor public spaces that have been carefully designed and inserted into existing urban fabrics or built in new towns and edge cities.[5]

The search for urbanity is misguided when it ignores the contemporary context, such as efforts to build "urban architecture" regardless of the site, suburban or urban.[6] Testament to the divergent reception of a similar building design in different locations: the poor reception (both critical and by inhabitants) of apartment buildings by Ricardo Bofill's Taller de Arquitectura in the French (exurban) new towns of Cergy-Pontoise, Marne-la-Vallée, and St Quentin-en-Yvelines, and the favorable reception of a similar building in the very urban Montparnasse (the 14th arrondissement of Paris), where it is coveted by Parisians and adulated by architectural critics. The French architect Roger Biriotti, for instance, said that he much prefers Bofill's work at Montparnasse than in the new cities, explaining that "it is a question of scale . . . it is better integrated in Paris where it is surrounded by buildings of the same measurements" (Biriotti 1986). American architecture critic Paul Goldberger also detected the "location-persuasion," excoriating Bofill's new town projects and praising his Parisian work (1985).

The search for urbanity is also misguided when it falls into the trap of environmental determinism, presuming that traditional urban forms will engender traditional urban lifestyles.[7] As James Holston has asserted, the problem with forays into contextualism "in today's city is paradoxically a question of context: they are out of context in their nostalgic references to (an imagined) social and economic order of the past" (Holston, 317).

Accordingly, the search for urbanity has been accused of placing a "brake on the imagination" (Lucan 1989, 145) because its fatuous adherence to the forms of the past discourage innovative solutions to the problems of a rapidly changing world. David Mangin maintains that while this new "false urbanity" may offer some advantages over modern urbanism, it is really about "managing mediocrity" (Mangin): since only good designers can create modern architecture, but all architects can work within the frame of urban architecture, which he regards as "an architecture of accompaniment" (ibid.).[8] Such management of mediocrity is apparent in the development of Battery Park City on Manhattan's southwestern tip (see chapter 4), which *New York Times* architecture critic Herbert Muschamp described as "a corrective to modern urbanism" (Muschamp 1994c), but a place where the design guidelines inspired by prewar New York constrained architects from exercising originality. The result, he concludes, is that "there isn't one building with something fresh or stimulating to say about urban life today" (ibid.). Another example of urban design that failed to elicit innovative approaches because of its nostalgia is the plan for revitalizing the waterfront of New York City. According to Muschamp, this plan failed to grasp its potential for environmentally-sensitive development and for blending nature with the city because it "was soaked in the thinking of an earlier day: the Industrial Age that treated nature mainly as raw material to be exploited for human use" (Muschamp 1993b).[9]

In part an outcome of exhausted creative energies, then, the infatuation with the past further hampers creative potential. Muschamp suggests that this mentality in the world of design generates "a climate of indifference to the imagination" because "it has apparently been decided in advance that every new building should look like the Art Deco apartment buildings of the 1930s. Bishop-crook lampposts should light every street. Every park should look like an Olmsted park" (Muschamp 1993b).

In addition to ignoring the vast impact of the industrial mode of production and the new technologies it has availed, postmodern urbanism also tends to edit the efforts by urban designers to accommodate these changes as manifest in modern urbanism. Rather than design in the context of modernist settings, postmodern urbanism turns its back on these. Indeed, if it were truly contextual, it would largely be accommodating modernist settings, since these constitute such a large percentage of the landscape the world around.[10]

Architects and urbanists such as Krier, Robert Stern, and Quinlan Terry, according to Doug Davis, "ignore the specific ideological or religious implications of the periods they quote [and] are in fact anti-historicist: they prefer history-as-arcadian-symbol, not history-as-reality" (D. Davis, 21). McLeod similarly criticizes the European typologists Aldo Rossi, Vittorio Gregotti, and Rob Krier for treating "architecture primarily as a static artifact, despite their purported interest in history and political transformation" (McLeod, 9). Although they call for contextualism, she says, their proposals are actually couched in a language of universality that views "type as a 'constant' in a context of changing productive relations" (ibid.). Indeed, their highly personal interpretations of type may reflect "a past that may not have existed" (Moneo; cited by Francescato, 8). The typologists claim that quoting familiar types is reassuring. Yet as Christine Boyer asserts, "This can be like walking on a thin tightrope, . . . for decorative pastiches do not necessarily arouse our collective memory" (Boyer 1983, 289). Not unlike the European typologists, Venturi is also guilty of being selectively contextual. As Lesnikowski maintains: "Venturi did not address the composition of the examples he described in their contextual (political, cultural, physical) totality but picked up fragmentary and secondary aspects to prove his points" (Lesnikowski, 1982). His interpretation of the great European mannerisms, says Lesnikowski, was personal, individualistic, detached, isolationist, and formalistic (ibid.).

Although certain designers seek a faithful return to the past, most of them justify their more stylized historicisms as intentionally ironic.[11] Like the more generalized ironic response (see chapter 4), its manifestation in urban design implies that it is aware of the fictions being applied but acknowledges their necessity. The strategy of "double coding" proffered by Jencks, for instance, suggests that we use past forms in an ironic way (Jencks 1978, 18). There is no alternative in our current mass media-inundated world.

Yet the denial of contemporary needs and tastes along with the tendency to reject the modern tradition rather than incorporate it have allowed for borrowings from the past which prove misguided and inappropriate. The particular references favored by urban designers are usually selected from their readings and travels on the basis of personal taste and are usually removed from their political and social contexts. Consequently, the meaning designers intend to bestow upon their architecture, so that it communicates, is usually lost.

The effort to re-center our de-centered world by creating centers offers one example. The Piazza d'Italia, designed by Perez and Associates and Charles Moore, was one effort to develop such a center, but it never became the vibrant public space that its designers had hoped it would be. Highlighting the deadliness (rather than vitality) of this plaza, Paul Walker Clarke points out that it has served as a stageset for two movies, both of which portrayed it as empty and with a corpse in the fountain. He contends, "The design never overcame the limits of its commission; the false notion that urbanity can be generated by the constitution of an 'urban center' " (Clarke 1988, 16).

The recent vogue for townscapes of the past is apparent in movements around the globe for historic preservation, adaptive use, rehabilitation, restoration, and renovation. But in most cases, these attempts to preserve built form are entirely revisionary, for instance, turning houses into museums and old factories into housing. This urban design trend is thus inscribed in the larger trend of "inventing traditions," described in chapter 4.[12]

In order to make something appear truly old or "authentic," it is often necessary to begin anew and to use materials and techniques which were not used for the original.[13] An architect who designed a seventeenth-century Tuscan villa on Long Island for one client remarked, "We thought of renovating the existing house, but it became clear that to make a house that would look old, we had to start anew" (*New York Times* August 30, 1990, C6). Given the emphasis upon image-making in urban design, developers not surprisingly have looked to the entertainment industries—the masters of "imagineering"— particularly for the design of hotels, theme parks, and restaurants. One entertainment executive explained that his company uses fiberglass rather than granite or stone to give the appearance of a rock because "you get a very artificial appearance with real rock" (cited by Huxtable 1992, 27).

The disingenuous nature of these efforts to look effortless (as though there had been no intervention by designers) and to make the new look old extends to interiors as well, as illustrated by the current predilection among city-dwellers for acquiring home furnishings which appear rural and old. To give new things the aged-look, a salesperson explained, their "paint finishes intentionally show signs of wear and aging" (cited by Slesin 1993). One shopowner explained this sensibility as a "nostalgia for the simple life" and another maintained, "I feel that esthetic is more important than authentic" (cited by Slesin 1993). This desire for an aged patina was also apparent in clothing fashion with the popularity of "vintage clothing" and worn-in blue jeans. California architect Brian Murphy poignantly commented, "Acid-washed jeans are a perfect metaphor for the perverse post-modern mentality. They take a perfectly good fabric and make it look old" (B. Murphy).[14]

The valorization of artifacts of the industrial era offers one significant example of the way in which the past is revised for current purposes. Since the 1970s, the factories, warehouses, machines, and products of our industrial past have been elevated to preservation status, and endowers of social status, as is apparent in museums devoted to displaying items from this period, loft-living, the rise of "industrial archaeology," and movements for preserving industrial landscapes. The "reason that people develop a sentimental—or a sensual—attachment to the industrial aesthetic," says Sharon Zukin, "is that it is not real. To be precise, it is no longer real" (Zukin 1988a, 73). Robert Harbison maintains that people "are choosing to return to a more manageable past. As each generation of machines becomes more complicated, we withdraw 'into dreams of obsolete machines and see ourselves among windmills, clipper ships, even trolley cars' " (cited by Zukin 1988a, 73). The smaller our machines become, the more the older larger ones evoke nostalgia and become part of a common folklore. We are also attracted by the durable quality of things such as reinforced steel shelving in contrast to the built-in obsolescence of so much that has replaced it.[15] While postmodern urbanism has largely overlooked changes set in motion by the factory system, it has at the same time ascribed new meanings to the industrial era by displacing historic artifacts from their original context.

Efforts at contextualism and preservation, then, are engaged in inventing a history that largely erases the chapter on the modern period, or re-valorizes it and idealizes selected earlier periods. Once the invention of tradition goes beyond a certain point, it produces "hyperreal" environments which, Umberto Eco explains, must be absolutely fake in order to be better than anything real (Eco 1986, 7, 8, 30). The pretense of historicism or preservation, referring to a certain original, is superseded by an attempt to produce an encompassing environment that transcends its source of inspiration. Much of our postmodern landscape has thus been described as "hyperreal," particularly master-planned communities, shopping malls, and theme parks or entertainment palaces.

The introduction of the magic marker in the 1960s, according to architect Daniel Solomon, contributed to the recasting of American urbanism by magically substituting MPCs for the gridiron town and, in so doing, transforming "the landscape of banality of the 1950s into a landscape of metaphor in the 1960s: Mariner's Cove, Tonga Gardens, Briar Heath, Broad Sunlit Uplands" (Solomon, 31). Solomon thus contends, "If history was the victim of the first generation of post-war development, reality was the victim of the second" (ibid.). New information technologies have also played an essential role in displacing reality, as they have influenced urban design, the design and building processes, spatial organization, and designers' aesthetic preferences.[16] Although some designers find CAD (Computer-Aided Design) and GIS (Geographic Information Systems) constraining and others find it liberating, there is no question that these technologies have contributed to an emphasis on appearance over substance and image over content.[17]

The enhanced power of the image introduced by these tools and by other technologies of communication has incited architects and planners to design, more than ever before, with an eye toward getting published; they pay keen attention to how a building appears in a two-dimensional frame. At the same time, architectural publications have altered their formats. Pointing out that the insides of buildings are no longer shown in architectural publications, only the exteriors, the French architectural historian Anatole Kopp sarcastically remarked: "Who cares how one is going to live inside? Is it not enough to have provided majestic Public Spaces, streets and squares? We will be able to take endless walks? We will go everywhere afoot. . . . How wonderful in the Paris or London climate!" (Kopp, 37). Magazines that focus on interiors, for their part, rarely include plans or even photographs of building exteriors, bespeaking the growing fragmentation of the design professions.

This "return of aesthetics" is distinct from its earlier incarnation, according to Boyer (1990), because it now features "a free play of all styles, with a general quoting, appropriating, recycling of images which

*Suburban tract house design in a "Victorian" barnyard style, 1990s;
Yellow Springs, Ohio*

easily slide over surface structures" (Boyer 1990, 100–101). Not necessarily referring to any original, what is often produced are simulacra. Such urban design, Boyer maintains, engenders a "blasé
attitude" (Boyer 1990, 97) for it implies that the city is "after all just
entertainment; we are only there to look and to buy. The city has
become a place of escape, a wonderland that evades reality, for there
is nothing more to think about in pure entertainment. There is no
outside world, no place from which we feel alienated, for this formalistic city is known and comfortable; it is above all a place to enjoy oneself. The pleasure is affirmative and far from oppositional and
negative" (Boyer 1990, 97–8). With consumption replacing production as the primary economic role of our central cities, Boyer explains,
they become places of "pure play" (1990, 97). Trevor Boddy describes
the product of postmodern urbanism as "the analogous city," largely
because its "urban prosthetics" (pedestrian bridges and tunnels)
which join towers, shopping centers, and festival marketplaces "provide a filtered version of the experience of cities, a simulation of
urbanity" (Boddy 1992, 124). By accelerating the stratification of race
and class, he says, they "degrade the very conditions they supposedly
remedy—the amenity, safety, and environmental conditions of the
public realm" (ibid.).

In theme parks, as well, Harvey observes, "it is now possible to experience the world's geography vicariously, as a simulacrum," in a way which conceals "almost perfectly any trace of origin, of the labor processes that produced them, or of the social relations implicated in their production" (Harvey 1989, 300). In a contemporary—and somehow unnerving—twist, these simulacra have become reality since many more people visit the simulacra of Africa and China presented in Disneyworld than actually visit these foreign lands and, for them, the simulacra are Africa and China more than the far-off places themselves.[18]

The emphasis on appearance has translated into the favoring of building façades that disguise the authentic materials, scale, history, and purpose. This is usually done in an effort to maintain or generate a sense of urbanity or tradition. Rather than reveal the true structure of a building, façades are often designed to make large buildings look like a number of smaller ones (sometimes explained as "building on a human scale"), to be decorative, or to make new construction look old. Thus, our cities today contain many examples of "prewar" facades, a term popularized by the real estate industry, usually referring to World War I and sometimes World War II. Prewar-styled townhouses, mansions, shops, and factories mask what are actually late twentieth-century luxury condominiums (for example, 79th Street near Park Avenue, Grammercy Place, and Soho lofts, all in New York City), hotels (Helmsley Palace Hotel above the Villard Houses in New York City), retail stores (Barney's in New York City), cultural institutions, sports arenas (Oriole Park at Camden Yard in Baltimore), and corporate office buildings (712 Fifth Avenue in New York City, and 2000 Pennsylvania Avenue in Washington DC). The new typology of "festival marketplaces" appearing in central cities since 1972 joins a variety of commercial uses in a rehabilitated prewar building or a new building designed in the spirit of the old.

Such design has been described disparagingly as "façadism" (Choay 1985, 269; Richards) or "façad-omy" (*New York Times* 1990, Editorial). A *New York Times* editorial asserted, "Modern America has turned facades inside out. . . . Small masks big. Old masks new. Elegant modesty disguises graceless pretension" (ibid.). Postmodern architectural theory and criticism have similarly been accused of "façadism" for their tendency to proffer analyses based solely on the formal aspects of buildings (Ley and Mills), and to obfuscate rather than clarify.[19]

This move toward playing with façades and appearances generally reacted to the over-serious corporate character of modern urban design, which ignored people's emotional needs and which led a number of urban designers to assert that form should follow fiction, rather than function.[20] Jacobs and Appleyard, for instance, complained that: "Architects and planners take cities and themselves too seriously; the result too often is deadliness and boredom, no imagination, no humor, alienating places. But people need an escape from the seriousness and meaning of the everyday. . . . One should not have to travel as far as the Himalayas or the South Sea Islands to stretch one's experience. Such challenges could be nearer home. There should be a place for community utopias; for historic, natural, and anthropological evocations of the modern city, for encounters with the truly exotic" (Jacobs and Appleyard, 116).

While invented tradition and hyperreal environments often offer an antidote to modernism's insularity, they can also devolve into bad taste, or kitsch, in their sentimental references to something else.[21] Most urban designers no longer seek to destroy the city, Patrice Noviant argues, but their objective is still not "the real city" (Noviant 1978, 4). Instead, he observes, it is what "one might call the kitsch-city, by which is understood the false city, more beautiful than real" (ibid.); "that which is aspired to is a certain comfortable level of false consciousness" (ibid.). According to Scott Lash, "Postmodern architecture exemplifies de-differentiation" (Lash 1990b, 36) in contrast to the modernist grounding in differentiation of signifiers from signified.[22] But, he maintains, the "signified or meaning that postmodern architecture signifiers latch onto is . . . substanceless and dissolves into a vacuum of kitsch" (ibid.).[23] With regard to postmodernism more generally, Mestrovic remarked that "postmodern themes of impulse, play, fun, and fantasy . . . are shallow, kitsch imitations of genuine compassion and emotionality expressed by the Romantics" (Mestrovic, 15).[24]

In addition, the dogged subjectivism of certain urban designers can distract them from the actual program in their "search for a fantasy world, the illusory 'high' that takes us beyond current realities into pure imagination" (Harvey 1989, 97). Harvey muses, "It is, perhaps, appropriate that the postmodernist developer building, as solid as the pink granite of Philip Johnson's AT&T building, should be debt-financed, built on the basis of fictitious capital, and architecturally conceived of, at least on the outside, more in the spirit of fiction than of function" (Harvey 1989, 292). Alluding to Marx's admonition that history repeats itself, "the first time as tragedy, the second as farce" (Marx 1987, 15), Boyer contends that "the current rescue of 'history' from the warehouse of society can be a farce" (Boyer 1983, 286–87). On the one hand, she maintains, "we often have historic preservation that looks like a near equivalent to stage designing or an emotional remembrance of a nostalgic past; and on the other hand postmodernism turns toward a past without any idea of how to use it" (Boyer 1983, 287).

FORM FOLLOWS FEAR

As the public realm has been growing increasingly impoverished, there has been a corresponding decline in meaningful public space and desire to control one's space, or to privatize[25] (see chapter 4). From a place that once combined production, consumption, and social interaction, public space has become compartmentalized. The social aspects of the street, for instance, have been suppressed over time in favor of movement (the road). And as public space has been transforming, so have private space and the relationship between them.

The privatization impulse is epitomized by the exponential growth in the West in the number of households living in individual houses, as well as in gated communities. As meaningful public space diminishes, private space—the home—has become increasingly important.[26] The French philosopher Jérome Bindé interprets the widespread desire to live in an individual house as "the postmodern moment where everyone is returned to himself. To his little games, to the scenery of his daily life, to his narcissistic anxiety of 'being liberated,'. . . . The individuals of societies in crisis, disoriented by the sudden devaluation of unanimous credos (capitalist 'abundance' or socialist 'emancipation') become thus refugees in a rediscovered opium, in this padlocked garden where one would like to forget the snubs/insults of real History" (Bindé).

The clear spatial and social distinction provided by the gated community (see chapter 3) replaces the former distinction of "vertical segregation" (which became blurred with the advent of the elevator, wherein all floors became equally desirable) and substitutes horizontal for vertical segregation. The number and size of these socially homogeneous ghettos has expanded along with America's road network. This marked social   segregation   allows   a   certain   ignorance,   and   therefore

CityWalk in Universal City, Los Angeles; designed by the Jerde Partnership

fears, regarding social differences, as well as the generation of myths, stereotypes, and stigmas associated with "the Other."[27]

The privatization impulse is also manifest in the appropriation of public spaces by private agencies, for example the inward-turning shopping mall which has abandoned the central city for the suburbs and which turns its back entirely on its surroundings with its fortress-like exterior surrounded by a moat-like parking lot; the indoor "atriums" of corporate office buildings; the proliferation of

CityWalk "code of conduct," Universal City, Los Angeles

theme parks in which "Main Street" and other recognizable features of the past are reproduced at a miniaturized 7/8's scale, scrubbed clean of their real contexts, and commercialized; and the expansion of franchises and chain stores which offer consumers familiarity wherever they may be.

Although the office and retail towers, shopping malls, theme parks, and central city mixed-use megastructures of postmodern urbanism provide new public spaces, entry and behavior are tightly restricted through sophisticated security systems, signage, and the design itself, leading Mike Davis to call them "pseudo-public spaces" (Davis 1990, 226). The compromised nature of these ostensibly public spaces is well illustrated by the sign posted at the entry to Universal Studio's new theme park, CityWalk—neither a city nor a place to which anyone can walk—which warns visitors against, among other things, obscene language or gestures, noisy or boisterous behavior, singing, playing of musical instruments, unnecessary staring, running, skating, rollerblading, bringing pets, "non-commercial expressive activity," distributing commercial advertising, "failing to be fully clothed," or "sitting on the ground more than 5 minutes." In all of these more recent forms of public space, participation is largely single-focused (in contrast to the more multifunctional traditional public spaces) and almost always consumer-oriented, limited to those with the ability to purchase.

Older public spaces have also been appropriated and controlled through increased gating; signage designating who should be using the space and when (for example, "We have the right to refuse service to anyone"); the expansion of curfews and police sweeps in transportation terminals and parks; the expansion of the public police force; the increased use of private police forces; and the pronounced anti-growth mentality. While certain parks, plazas, and commons remain places to escape from loci of production and consumption, their traditional social component is invariably circumscribed because the rising tide of fear has transformed them into controlled and guarded places, usually with curfews and/or gates and not accessible to all. These so-called public spaces, then, are places of exclusion as well as inclusion. The apotheosis of this escapist and exclusionary urbanism is found in the proliferation of "edge cities" during the 1980s (see chapter 3), an abnegation of the central city and the unique quality of life it promised.

Grassroots measures to secure property often make little pretense to create vibrant public spaces as demonstrated, for instance, by the sprinkler systems used by shopowners to keep the homeless from sleeping nearby (M. Davis 1990) and the Muzak used by 7-Eleven stores to keep teenagers from hanging out (Flusty). The rebuilding of shops after the 1992 Los Angeles uprising has taken defensive urbanism to its extreme. As Flusty recounts, "Wood frame structures, flammable and easily breached, have been replaced by single or double thick walls of concrete masonry. Parapets have been extended to deflect fire bombs thrown from street level. Display windows have been either omitted, or set into concrete bulwarks two to five feet above sidewalk level to prevent automobiles ramming through to the interior. Locking glazed entrys and steel lattice sliding burglar doors have been replaced with solid metal plate roll down gates, many pre-graffitied to discourage taggers" (Flusty).

The panopticon—and its successive refinements—offer a literal and figurative model for understanding this evolution. As Foucault posits, evolving technologies of power serve to maintain the status quo. From the seventeenth- and eighteenth-century political rationality of *raison d'état*, he maintains, "biopower" began to inform the disciplinary technologies employed by elites, and for the exercise of biopower, visibility was essential. Spectacles of terror and punishment as well as those of patronage and benevolence acted as a kind of "natural policing" (Corrigan and Sayer, 107). By the nineteenth century, this visibility was enhanced by the redevelopment of European cities with long, wide straight boulevards and strategically placed monuments and housing for the bourgeoisie. As disciplinary strategies have been progressively refined to the present, visibility of the ruled has continued to increase, but that of the rulers has decreased. This is because, as Foucault remarks, "power is tolerable only on condition that it mask a substantial part of itself. Its success is proportional to its ability to hide its own mechanisms" (Foucault 1980, 86). As the expression and exercise of power has become less and less visible over the last few centuries, its influence is more difficult to discern. And it is more difficult to resist. Whereas the plaza—or *place* (in French)—was the quintessential public space until the nineteenth century, today's place-lessness renders the exercise of power more elusive. It is everywhere and nowhere, assumed ubiquitous, or alternatively, assumed absent.

One example of disciplinary regional planning is offered by the splintering of the Parisian university in the wake of the student uprisings of May 1968. The university was not only factioned into many smaller ones, but these were located outside of the central city and designed to incorporate little or no public space for spontaneous or even planned student gatherings. Another example found in France was the building of five new cities in the outer suburbs of Paris to house the working class of the city (and thereby gentrify it) and to de-densify the inner suburbs (and thereby mollify their revolutionary tendencies). A parallel example, though this time undertaken by the private sector, was the exodus by many US corporate headquarters from central cities to more controlled and less costly suburban "office parks" or "corporate campuses" as well as the "edge cities" of which they form an integral part.

Disciplinary space is also encountered on the smaller scale in, for instance, atrium buildings, which could be regarded as evolved heirs to Bentham's panopticon, where the center is now occupied by a void rather than a supervisor. To take the example of New York University's Bobst Library, designed by Philip Johnson in 1972, the void serves to discourage unsanctioned behavior by library users, whether the stealing and abuse of books or physical assault. The historically disciplinary supervisor is rendered superfluous library users have become their own guardians. This protective strategy is less blatant than the earlier ones, as are its agents. Is it the architect, his client, or our fellow library users who are exercising the control?

The wielding of power today, then, is disguised and difficult to identify because it is not localized and often not personalized, because its agents are rarely self-aware, because it is internalized to a great extent, and because it therefore goes largely unnoticed. Jürgen Habermas has observed, "The distortions within such a regulated, analyzed, controlled, and watched-over life-world are certainly more subtle than the obvious forms of material exploitation and impoverishment; but [they] are no less destructive for all that" (Habermas 1986, 9). As the exercise of power grows more disguised and anonymous, agency becomes confused and people— unwittingly—become terrorists as well as terrorized. In the end, a growing perception of greater equality among people both nationwide and worldwide, plied largely by the various mass media, accompanies and legitimizes growing inequalities.

The contemporary built environment offers a dwindling supply of meaningful public space and that which exists is increasingly controlled by various forms of surveillance and increasingly invested with private meanings.[28] Activities that once occurred in the public realm have either been abandoned (for example, liberal discourse) or usurped by more private realms, as leisure, entertainment, gaining information, and consumption are increasingly satisfied at home with the television or computer. Or if one leaves home, these activities often take place in the strictly controlled uni-functional settings of the shopping mall, theme park, or variants thereof. Describing this condition, Jacobs and Appleyard noted that cities:

> have become privatized, partly because of the consumer society's emphasis on the individual and the private sector, . . . but escalated greatly by the spread of the automobile. Crime in the streets is both a cause and a consequence of this trend, which has resulted in a new form of city: one of closed, defended islands with blank and windowless facades surrounded by wastelands of parking lots and fast-moving traffic. As public transit systems have declined, the number of places in American cities where people of different social groups actually meet each other has dwindled. The public environment of many American cities has become an empty desert, leaving public life dependent for its survival solely on planned formal occasions, mostly in protected internal locations. . . . Fear has led social groups to flee from each other into homogeneous social enclaves. . . . It is an alien world for most people. It is little surprise that most withdraw from community involvement to enjoy their own private and limited worlds" (Jacobs and Appleyard, 114–15).[29]

Now more than a generation after the seminal works of Jane Jacobs (1961) and Chermayeff and Alexander (1963),[30] the rising tide of fear and privatization has continued to inspire efforts among urban design professionals to assuage feelings of fear through design.[31] Such efforts are found on the left in the name of egalitarianism and on the right as a means of social control. Pinpointing the decline of meaningful public space, and of the clear distinction between private and public space, as the source of much contemporary fear, many postmodern urban design strategies focus on reconstituting these. Usually, such strategies involve combining the familiarity and human scale of traditional spaces with the benefits of contemporary technologies (see chapters 2 and 3). The "illegible" quality of post-World War II urban development, and the fear this generated, also incited a concern for creating "legible" landscapes (see chapters 3 and 8).

A prevalent postmodern urban design strategy has been to enclose public space, as opposed to the modernist tendency to place buildings within public space.[32] Many urban designers have been attempting to recreate the physical and dimensional relationship between public and private space that existed in pre-industrial townscapes. These efforts focus on producing settings that appear to have evolved spontaneously over time, and that encourage inhabitants naturally to appropriate spaces.[33] Efforts to emulate pre-industrial colonial or medieval cities are apparent on a smaller scale in designs for shopping districts, theme parks, and other public or semi-public spaces.

A number of urban design initiatives have experimented with the design of public space. One of these is found in the town of Val d'Yerres (located 25 kilometers southeast of Paris), built in 1965 for a population of 30,000. In an effort to prevent social unrest, the public-private developer of this town decided to create a public space between a middle-income neighborhood of individual houses and a lower-income neighborhood of subsidized apartments. According to Manuel Castells, "Most residents reacted with hostility. . . . The home owners of Epinay-sous-Sénart petitioned to have their open space enclosed and separated, so that the children of the public housing units could not play with theirs. Immigrant families faced open racism, expressed through complaints against their smokey cooking and their noisy chatting. Youths were blamed for every possible mishap, and by 1972–73 many residents were asking for permits to own handguns as well as an increased police presence" (Castells 1983, 92). Various demonstrations took place from 1972 to 1974 and although the local police records did not indicate a significant increase in crime, a general feeling of insecurity prevailed.[34]

Historicism can be interpreted as an attempt to deny change rather than to adapt to it, because of the prevalence of fear and anxiety in postmodern society.[35] Supporting this contention, Huxtable interprets the re-creation of Main Streets in theme parks, saying: "'Main Street USA' is created even as main streets die across the country" (Huxtable 1992, 25). Historicism can also be interpreted as "an expression of nostalgia for an authoritarian past" (Tzonis and Lefaivre 1984, 185). In this vein, Doug Davis highlights the similarities between the contemporary appeal for classical architecture and the "cultural literacy" campaign (Allan Bloom, E. D. Hirsch et al.) as well as the spate of apocalyptic "neo-conservative crisis literature" (Daniel Bell, Christopher Lasch, Robert Bellah et al.). All of these bemoan the deterioration of "order" in post-industrial societies and usually invoke a return to some idealized past or to a certain morality or canon. This turn to the past, Davis suggests, is more about (re-)asserting dominance than a genuine reverence for the past. In urban design, historicism may be integrally related to the perceived loss of dominance within the architectural profession (see chap-

Main Street at Disneyland, Anaheim, California

ter 7). As Margaret Crawford suggests, the shift to classicist references (from populist and vernacular sources of imagery) could bespeak an effort by the architectural profession to acquire the trappings of prestige necessary to distance itself "from more pragmatically oriented professional groups" (Crawford, 41).

We must question the validity of referring back to an architecture which was built by and sustained a tyrannical elite, even when there is an attempt to subvert this order by, for instance, applying such references to the design of public housing. A propos, Kenneth Frampton questions the appropriateness of Ricardo Bofill's public housing complexes in France (see chapter 2), comprising "standard apartments which are willfully encased in ... false architraves and empty columns. Deprived of a terrace, since this does not accord with the assumed syntax, the upwardly mobile resident has to be satisfied with the operatic illusion of living in a palace" (Frampton 1985, 310–11). Léon Krier is not oblivious to the political and manipulative intentions lurking beneath architectural styles, contending, "Classical architecture has been the noblest instrument of politics and of civilizing propaganda for thousands of years and throughout all great cultures and continents" (1985; cited by D. Davis 1987, 17). While Krier regards this as one of its assets, others regard such urban design strategies as reactionary. Davis points out, "the assumption that the obsessively symmetrical classical language once taught to upper-class schoolboys in England (and in a handful of New England private schools) is 'universal' in its appeal to a multiracial world is xenophobic" (D. Davis, 19). Although appropriate for universities in late-nineteenth- and early-twentieth-century America, when Republican ideals were popular, Rosemarie Bletter suggests that neo-classicism's inflexibility renders it inappropriate for most other uses. Referring to its re-emergence in the United States in the early 1980s as the "Ronald Reagan Style," Bletter maintains that the pretense to monumentality usually ends up mocking whatever it is used for (Bletter). Another outcome of re-creating such landscapes today may be to buttress, or exacerbate, contemporary social inequalities.[36]

Although postmodern historical eclecticism, regionalism, and preservation are justified as expressions of pluralism or multicultural-ism, the modern version's imperialistic subtext is certainly latent as well, if not manifest. A number of recent efforts can be seen to resemble, for instance, the building of new cities in the French colonies from 1900 to the 1930s (Rabinow 1989; G. Wright 1990 and 1991; Eickelman, 72–73). The French technocrats responsible for the design of these new cities were trying to modernize without eradicating the local character of the colonies by applying strict building codes and design reviews. This strategy was intended to preserve the "native" society in such a way as to ensure French dominance over it and to offer the French a picturesque and exotic environment for their pleasure. It would also prevent or discourage the local society from evolving and, in the process, imply that its members were only of value in this museum-ified fashion. In actuality, the French intervention was destroying the local economies, increasing the gap between rich and poor, and alienating the indigenous populations from their cultural traditions. And by keeping the local culture un-modern, the French technocrats could ensure its dependence upon French services, markets, and technologies.[37]

In its postmodern manifestation, the effort to respect differences and to design with regards to regional contexts can additionally become a style, which defeats its very purpose of being anti-universalist and preserving "distinction." As Steven Connor asserts, "when hybridization itself becomes universal, regional specificity becomes simply a style which can be transmitted across the globe as rapidly as a photocopy of the latest glossy architectural manifesto. Paradoxically, the sign of the success of the anti-universalist language and style of architectural post-modernism is that one can find it everywhere, from London, to New York, to Tokyo and Delhi" (Connor, 80).[38] And needless to say, it fails to achieve its putative intent of celebrating pluralism.[39]

When that which is being "preserved" is nature, a Christian/Puritan morality can enter the picture, a morality which sees bodily pleasure and experience as amoral and which calls for the preservation of one's honor. This impulse bemoans the defiling of Mother Nature by the penetration of virgin countryside with man-made technologies, the worst case scenario being the skyscraper. The following reaction of Thomas Sharp in 1932 to the prospect of town expansion exemplifies this impulse: "The strong, masculine virility of the town; the softer beauty, the richness, the fruitfulness of that mother of men, the countryside, will be debased into one sterile, hermaphrodite beastliness" (cited by P. Hall 1988, 83). This may be understood as a reflex—not among those whose honor (whose countryside) is to be preserved—but among those (urbanites, colonials) who wish to deny others what they themselves already have and who wish to retain pockets of unspoiled nature or folklore for their own enjoyment and for maintaining their hegemonic position by preventing others from access to the same opportunities. Movements to "preserve" nature or wildlife may be thinly veiled attempts to preserve the intimacy of one's community as well as land values, such as anti-growth sentiments and NIMBY-ism.

The oft-applied phrases "adaptive re-use" and "the search for a usable past" (for example, in Stern 1986) are revealing. Indeed, postmodern urbanism often appears to "use" the past for present purposes, which have to do with imperialistic motives as well as with profit-making and the personal recognition of the designer or client. Holston has pointed out that the modernist aesthetic of "erasure and reinscription" (Holston, 5) is often criticized for masking realities and colluding with certain governments in their attempts "to rewrite national histories" (ibid.). In similar fashion, the architecture and planning of the last two decades may be criticized for denying contemporary realities and for rewriting history, excluding that which it wishes to be forgotten, or for being "Stalinian" (Noviant 1980, 13).[40] Like the eighteenth-century picturesque, to which it often refers, it can be accused of complacency, of regarding "landscape as something separate from and opposed to human society [and of deploying] its imagery to obscure social and economic issues" (S. Daniels; cited by A. Kahn, 48).[41]

Modern fear and the scientific climate in which it occurred led to efforts to cope with it through rational understanding and shaping the future. Prevalent responses to postmodern fear, amidst the reigning anti-technocratic climate, are nostalgia and attempts by designers to provide legible environments that are meaningful to their constituencies by referring to a certain context or to mass imagery. Are these efforts achieving their goals, particularly that of diminishing danger and providing a sense of security? Or does the concerted effort to plan for spontaneity, to invent traditions, to design in the vernacular, and to generate hyperreal environments subvert this intent? The answer is not clearcut.

Certainly gated communities, policing, and other surveillance systems, defensive architecture, and neotraditional urbanism contribute to giving people a greater sense of security.[42] But such settings no doubt also contribute to accentuating fear by increasing paranoia and distrust. In addition, the escapist nature of neotraditionalist urban design may emit signals that the present is too unsavory; let's pretend it's not here and go back to the good ol' days. Such reluctance to embrace the present and happily anticipate the future inevitably contributes to an atmosphere of foreboding which casts a pall upon the quality of life at all levels, from the most public to the most intimate (see Ellin 1997).

FORM FOLLOWS FINESSE

In search of meaning, one direction in which architecture and planning theory turned was toward the systematic study of signs, or semiology (for example, Eco, Broadbent et al., Choay, Gandelsonas), an outgrowth of structural linguistics. This turn injected a welcome dose of concern with the symbolic meanings of architecture and with context, content, and substance, rather than solely with style. But recourse to semiology and linguistics led to a theoretical impasse and was criticized for being misguided, pretentious at best and a distraction from more important issues at worst. Tom Wolfe, for instance, described "the current fashion of discussing architecture in the terminology of linguistics [as] solemn nonsense" (Wolfe 1980, 3), saying it "is mainly euphemism used to avoid such sensitive subjects as class, status, and the priestly ambition of the architect "when it isn't sheer brain fill" (ibid.) or an attempt to disguise the architect's real project of making architecture about architecture and of standing out in the crowd.[42] Though provocative, the inaccessibility of semiological and linguistic theory and the difficulties in applying it to urban design ultimately obfuscated issues more than it clarified them, and failed to produce a usable urban design theory.

Having grown disillusioned with the idealism of modernism and with the possibilities for semiology, there was a turning inward in the urban design professions, paralleling that in society at large. As Wojciech Lesnikowski contends, "Instead of speaking of any ideology or group approaches, architects started discussing their works in terms of their own attitudes and indulged in extreme individualism" (Lesnikowski 1982, 294).[43] The French architect Alain Guiheux observed, "from an architect supposedly giving to others [the modern architect], we have moved in a very short space of time to the 'artist' architect [the postmodern architect] who speaks of himself, of his own genius" (Guiheux, 21).[44] And Huxtable exclaimed: "The most fundamental change in architecture today is one of attitude. Scratch a postmodernist and you will find an apostle of architecture for art's sake, something that would have had any respectable and responsible architect drummed out of the profession not too long ago. . . . With the renunciation of traditional social responsibilities as beyond his capacities or control, the architect has finally been freed to pursue style exclusively and openly . . . without apology or disguise" (Huxtable 1981b, 104).[45] She bemoaned the current state of design as having "more pettiness and pedantry than passion in architecture today. . . . There are no heroes, and no architectural giants, because there are no causes" (ibid.).

Alexander Tzonis and Liane Lefaivre referred to this tendency as "narcissistic," suggesting "an act of regression due to acute frustration" (Tzonis and Lefaivre 1980a) with the prevalent urban design approaches of the 1960s. In reaction to the naive attitudes of scientism and populism, they contended, this narcissistic turn disregards or denies context entirely (ibid.) and features instead a preoccupation with the purely visual features of architecture (formalism), a fascination with the evocative power of drawings and models (graphism), a tendency to view design solely as an object of gratification (hedonism), the conviction that the architect is the supreme judge of the quality of the built environment (elitism), and the rejection of the functionalist aesthetic as well as the very idea of function itself (anti-functionalism) (ibid.). Venturi warned against such a tendency: "An architecture of complexity and contradiction . . . does not mean picturesqueness or subjective expressionism. A false complexity has recently countered the false simplicity of an earlier Modern architecture . . . it represents a new formalism as unconnected with experience as the former cult of simplicity" (1966, 18).[46] Once again, the emphasis was on surface rather than substance, or aesthetic rather than authentic, but this time it reflected a turning inward rather than an effort to be playful or protective. And like the tendencies to follow fiction or fear, this "false complexity" contributed to masking the shortcomings of postmodern urbanism as well as its social and political settings.[47]

Postmodern urbanism's resurrection of the street, avenue, boulevard, park, plaza, and square (taking the place of primary, secondary, and tertiary routes as well as the green or open spaces of modern urbanism) offers another example of insufficiently considering the context. These rhetorical changes do not always translate into formal ones and even when they do, they do not always translate into changes in function and perception. This is because the circumstances in which urban design is occurring have moved ahead, not backwards. These circumstances—including social relations of production (division of labor); techniques (for example, steel frame supports as opposed to load-bearing walls, even if made to look like load-bearing walls); materials (such as steel and reinforced concrete); and post-industrial lifestyles—usually foil any effort to hark back to pre-industrial towns, or effect only skin-deep changes. This has incited one critic to regard postmodern urban interventions as Villes Radicuses in medieval and baroque garb (Tempia 1977).

One outcome of the failure of postmodern urbanism to adequately consider the contemporary political economy was demonstrated in the building of False Creek (not a pseudonym!), a "self-conscious attempt to build a postmodern landscape" (Ley 1987, 46) in the 1970s within the city of Vancouver, Canada. For the building of this new community, David Ley maintains, "There was an unusually direct transfer of current social science and design theory to the built environment," (ibid.) including Herbert Gans's ideas about social diversity and urban villages, Jane Jacobs's four generators of diversity (J. Jacobs 1961), Christopher Alexander's pattern language and participatory design process (Alexander 1977), and Ian McHarg's view of ecological harmony in design (McHarg 1969). In an effort to humanize the city and to make it "livable," planners applied historical, vernacular, and regional allusions and devised a plan with an "orientation toward the picturesque" (Ley 1987, 46). It was a "conscious reaction against unimaginative urban design" and "nothing was left to chance; even street names would evoke continuity rather than transience" (Ley 1980, 254). At False Creek, there was to be a mixing of lifestyles and tenure types and the "income mix was to reflect the metropolitan area with approximately one-third low income, one-third middle income, and one-third high income" (ibid.).[48]

The problem with this "livable city strategy," however, was that it inflated housing demand while the policy of low-density housing and the resistance of private developers to invest in lower profit development limited housing supply (Ley 1980, 255). Consequently, land prices sky-rocketed, doubling from 1972 to 1974, and by 1978, 25 percent of the city's households were spending excessive amounts (over 30 percent of income) on housing. In sum, actions stemming from liberal ideology "disfavored a vulnerable income group and favored the more privileged" (Ley 1980, 256) and the "development boom followed by an economic downturn exposed this weakness with a vengeance" (Ley 1980, 258). Ley thus concludes, "A livable city ideology and an ideology of equity are only coincidental in special cases where economic strength is assured, public intervention is active, and private interests are con-strained" (Ley 1980, 257).

By the same token, efforts by architects and planners to involve their constituencies in the design process have suffered from an insufficient consideration of political and economic constraints as well as of the structural position of the architect or planner vis-à-vis the people. These efforts, which were particularly widespread during the 1960s and 1970s, included social planning, participatory design, community architecture, advocacy planning, and self-help (see chapters 2 and 3). Architects and planners discovered that if they chose to give clients what they wanted (regardless of whether or not they shared their tastes): (1) the task of understanding and satisfying the needs and desires of a diverse popula-tion proved daunting; (2) they were relinquishing their creative role along with its possibilities for enhancing the social and physical land-scapes; and (3) they became pawns in a larger political economy which they may not support.

Though intending to subvert the traditional mode of architectural production and thereby serve as a springboard for changing other aspects of society, these architects and planners discovered that the "acquisition of home, especially if one identifies with it, accelerates the privatization of self and intensifies conformist behavior and a passive attitude toward efforts that affect general social issues" (Tzonis and Lefaivre 1984, 184). Rather than politicize their participants, these projects tended to play "a socialization role in preparing the user for a consumer society" (ibid.). Crawford describes how the efforts of these radical architects and planners were misdirected, saying that they unwittingly "replaced modernism's welfare state with a marketplace, in which, unfortunately, their ideal client did not have the means to purchase architectural services" (Crawford, 39). Their critique of modernism, Crawford discerns, ended up "emphasizing the marketplace of taste" and allowing "the dominant economic tendencies to become the final arbiter" of what gets built (Crawford, 41). John Turner's work, for instance, has been accused of representing "nothing less than the now traditional attempts of capitalist interests to palliate the housing shortage in ways that do not interfere with the effective operation of these interests" (R. Burgess; cited by P. Hall, 255).[49] Even attempts to consider the local context of design intervention (social contextualism) without actual input from the local community has usually exceeded the grasp of urban designers.[50]

In the final analysis, such undertakings have proven relatively expensive to realize, largely unable to reach those intended (the poorest and least powerful), and although found mainly on the political left, guilty of colluding with uneven development and other injustices of the capitalist system rather than resisting or subverting these. Although leaving their imprints on theory and practice as well as on the landscape, these experiments have had little success owing to resistance from within the profession as well as from local communities. Both the modernist and postmodernist efforts at populism, then, ultimately ended up succumbing to market "forces" and pandering to the rich rather than serving the public good. Peter Eisenman expressed this view, remarking that participatory architecture "makes for an elitist fantasy masquerading as a populist game" (cited by Hines 1985).

Recoiling from these populist efforts, many architects and planners concluded that they were casting their net too wide and should return to focusing solely on buildings and physical planning. The attempt by professional architects and planners to become politically engaged and to treat urban problems holistically by drawing from the social sciences was thus in large part supplanted by a more insular and apolitical approach,[51] featuring an emphasis on aesthetics.

The postmodernist re-emphasis on aesthetics is often explained as a reaction to the modernist neglect of aesthetic issues for the sake of political ones (in its caricatured version). From a "social architecture" designed to resolve "collective problems" (Oscar Niemeyer 1955; cited by Holston, 38), postmodernism shifted to concerns that are less politically ambitious and more cosmetic and symbolic.[52] Indeed, the vociferous political agenda of the modern movement is often countered by extreme apoliticism among postmodern urbanists, with designers emphasizing the limits of changing society through architecture.[53] Whereas modern urbanism included a political stance critical of the unregulated capitalist economy, private property, and inegalitarian class relations, postmodern urbanism tends to regard these issues as outside the line of duty and sometimes even to champion them. Because of the decline of modernist ideals, those few designers who carry the modern torch and retain an emancipatory vision tend to be ridiculed, particularly in the United States. Proposals for buildings without ornament or for towers in a park rather than pre-industrial-looking townscapes are often condemned as fascistic. And in the few instances where an idealistic desire to make a better world persists, the ability to do so is diminished because of the fragmentation and thoroughly transnational nature of power.

FORM FOLLOWS FINANCE

The apoliticism of contemporary urban designers has impelled critics to accuse them of being anti-avantgardist (Harvey 1989, 76) or rearguardist.[54] Since urban design interventions invariably have an impact on people's lives, however, the work of urban designers is inevitably political whether or not they choose to be politically engaged. But the denial of urban design's political component[55] contributes to exacerbate existing inequalities, one of these being Euro-American hegemony.[56] Paul Walker Clarke, for instance, contends that postmodernism's claim "to embrace history, respect context, endorse 'popular' forms of culture, and elaborate vernacular typologies" raises certain questions: "Whose history? Whose notion of context? Whose vernacular? Whose 'popular culture'?" (Clarke 1988, 18). Left unaddressed, he asserts, history is objectified by an architectural or technocratic elite.[57]

Ultimately, the retreat from a political agenda into the invention of histories, the production of hyperreal environments, and subjectivism usually ends up accentuating the banes of capitalist urban development rather than checking its excesses. Not part of the solution, designers become part of the problem. Rather than bring historical forms and concepts to contextualize current issues, Mark Jarzombek observes, the contemporary brand of historicism favors "an uncritical alliance with mass culture that wants to neutralize history so that it doesn't threaten the day-to-day working of the world of marketing" (Jarzombek, 92).[58] Although the collage may in theory allow for a kind of popular participation by offering a double reading, it does so, as Harvey points out, "at the price of a certain incoherence or, more problematic, vulnerability to mass-market manipulation" (Harvey 1989, 51).

Rather than inform the present, then, the contemporary uses of contextualism in urban design often appear to mystify it. Likewise, the so-called search for urbanity may be regarded as a smokescreen for the growing gap between the rich and the poor. As the French architect Claude Parent writes: "The discussion about the city is a distraction, in the strong sense of the term . . . it is a manipulation of minds. We are camouflaging pauperization; it is extraordinary and insulting. It is propaganda in its pure state" (cited by Champenois 1986). This is also evident in the new typology of the festival marketplace, which Harvey has described as "an institutionalized commercialization of a more or less permanent spectacle" (Harvey 1989, 90) since its emphasis on architecture as theatre or spectacle is a deflection from dealing with other problems. This typology gives the public "bread and circuses" (Harvey 1989, 89–92) as did Roman leaders during the decline of their Empire in an effort to compete favorably against other cities and to distract the populace from their own corruption and other pressing issues. Finally, this is apparent in the gentrification and concurrent growth in homelessness since the 1970s as well as in the growth of "edge cities" during the 1980s, all symptoms and symbols of the growing gap between the rich and the poor.[59]

Instead of harnessing the potential of the first machine age, Martin Pawley contends (in reference to Banham), the second machine age (the contemporary period) has substituted a fascination with images for ideology and social concerns, as architects have succumbed to the evergrowing power of the mass media.[60] With the emergence of hyperrealities,

Jean Baudrillard claims, architecture became a monument to advertising rather than to public space (Pawley 1983).[61] Frampton notes that in *Learning from Las Vegas*, Venturi, Scott Brown, and Izenour "are brought to concede the superfluity of architectural design in a society that is exclusively motivated by ruthless economic drives; a society which has nothing of greater significance to represent than the giant neon-lit sky sign of the average strip" (Frampton 1985, 291). He contends that "the cult of 'the ugly and the ordinary' becomes indistinguishable from the environmental consequences of the market economy" (ibid.).[62]

This elevation of images over ideology has allowed an unprecedented complicity with the marketplace. Architecture, Barry Bergdoll remarks, "has become a booming subsidiary of the fashion market" (Bergdoll, 67). Frampton observes that "Today the division of labor and the imperatives of 'monopolized' economy are such as to reduce the practice of architecture to large-scale packaging. . . . At its most predetermined, Post-Modernism reduces architecture to a condition in which the 'package deal' arranged by the builder/developer determines the carcass and the essential substance of the work, while the architect is reduced to contributing a suitably seductive mask" (Frampton 1985, 307).[63]

The Walt Disney Company perhaps best epitomizes the commercialization of architecture in commissioning twenty well-known architects. According to Patricia Leigh Brown, Disney "cannily figured out that architecture itself was undergoing a vast change in the last decade, a change that could dovetail perfectly with Disney's corporate needs" (Brown, 24). One of the selected architects, Robert Stern, remarked that Michael Eisner (Disney chairman) "sensed architects were hot" (cited by Brown, 42). As architecture has become increasingly concerned with image and entertaining, so the general public has become more interested in architecture. Brown declared that "it is not only that Disney has come closer to the mainstream of architecture—it is also that the mainstream of architecture has become more like Disney. . . . It is in Disney that the worlds of architecture and entertainment, which have been moving closer to each other for years, have achieved their most powerful intersection yet—becoming so intimately intertwined that it is sometimes impossible to tell any longer which is which" (Brown, 24).

This subjugation of urban design to market forces was certainly present in modern urbanism and largely spelled the demise of its political agenda. But these forces have grown ever stronger since the 1970s with

the acceleration of change, featuring: the emergence of flexible accumulation (see Chapter 7, note 18); the rise of cities supported by global
economies, and "second tier" cities (with regional and national
economies (Boyer 1990, 40–41); the corporatization of the architectural
profession; heightened competition among firms; and the related concern among consumers to achieve "distinction" while simultaneously
investing money prudently in objects with resale potential, which look
"solid" or "traditional." These conditions have combined to render
norms and ideals virtually unthinkable,[64] ushering in apoliticism along
with a decline in creativity.

THE RESULT

A principal feature of postmodern urbanism is contextualism (historical,
physical, social, and mass cultural), in contrast to modern urbanism's
break from the past and the site. When contextualism is achieved in
urban design, it is usually appreciated (successful) unless somehow inappropriate or regarded by the users as a patronizing gesture. In most
cases, however, contextualism is not achieved, because of economic and
political constraints, the invention of histories, shortcomings of urban
designers (who may only be paying lip service to contextualism while
pursuing more personal goals), and other reasons. In short, these goals
usually prove elusive owing to urban designers's ironic failure to
acknowledge the larger contexts in which they build. When contextualism is not achieved, the urban design initiative is usually not appreciated
(unsuccessful), except in certain instances where people believe a place
is historically, physically, or socially contextual (even if it is not) or don't
care because the place succeeds for other reasons such as the standard of
living it offers, its prestige, and/or its location.

The contextual attempts to gain inspiration from the site, the social
context, and mass culture have more in common with attempts to gain
inspiration from the past than may initially appear to be the case. Indeed,
they converge where urban design draws from a fictionalized and media-
massaged past or vernacular.[65] Like the historicist tendency, these others
betray a sense of insecurity and/or confusion and suggest a desire for
self-affirmation, self-expression, self-discovery, and "rootedness." And
like historicism, these efforts also tend to be more rhetorical than real,
largely because their premises contain denials and because the formulation and implementation of these agendas by elites subvert their initial

claims. We might say that postmodern urban form follows fiction, finesse, fear, and finance as well as function. But then so did modern urban form.

Ultimately, despite its efforts to counter the negative aspects of modern urbanism, postmodern urbanism falls into many of the same traps. Despite its eagerness to counter the human insensitivity of modern urbanism, postmodern urbanism's preoccupation with surface treatments and irony makes it equally guilty of neglecting the human component. By denying transformations that have taken place, postmodern urbanism may even be accentuating the most criticized elements of modern urbanism such as the emphasis on formal considerations and elitism. Ingersoll has asserted: "To project a return to a 'traditional' city and with it a future of 'neovillagers' may be more of a fantasy than any science-fiction vision of a society dominated by robots. If the urban process is confined to aesthetic criteria alone, the social consequences, such as the elimination of emancipatory demands from the urban program, may be as unpleasant as those wrought by the functionalist fallacies of the postwar period. . . . It is as if *urbs*, the bound city form of the past, could be considered without *civitas*, the social agreement to share that lost urban promised land" (Ingersoll 1989b, 21).[66]

As Clarke has said, although its agenda suggests an antithesis, "postmodernism has a legacy from modernism it has yet to contradict" (Clarke 1988, 13). Although architects "may no longer be talking of the unadorned cube as the aesthetic model," he contends, their works are still divorced from the larger context, particularly social, in which they are situated (ibid.). Although this style may look different on the surface, it is just as fragmented as what it pretends to be criticizing, because flexible accumulation favors urban design interventions which distinguish themselves, thereby mitigating against contextualism.[67] The modernist refusal to acknowledge context, as epitomized in the reflecting glass wall (see Jameson 1989b; Holston; Harvey 1989, 88), might be interpreted as a refusal to acknowledge the emergent mass culture and culture of consumption.[68] But postmodern urbanism's continued denial of the conditions of a mass society, despite its efforts to acknowledge them through contextualism, merely exacerbates the problems of modern urbanism. This denial is epitomized by certain postmodernists' refusal to build any physical structure or place, only to design or theorize (see Chapters 2 and 3). Although justified as a form of resistance, this informed choice only perpetuates the conditions they oppose (Dutton 1986, 23).

ON BALANCE

While much ink has been spilled on pronouncing the banes of postmodern urbanism (along with postmodernism generally), there is also widespread sentiment that it offers a number of correctives to that which preceded it. Indeed, Relph has suggested that these reactions to modern urbanism have ushered in "a quiet revolution in how cities are made and maintained" with the result that "repressive architecture and planning by great corporate or government bureaucracies is being replaced by more sensitive and varied alternatives" (Relph 1987, 215; see Mangin and Muschamp above).

Although historicism can be "essentially elitist, esoteric, and distant" (Clarke and Dutton, 2) and can devolve into kitsch, it can also provide a sense of security and "rootedness" when judiciously applied, as in the reconstruction of European central cities (Gleye). The potentially creative component of borrowing from the past is suggested by folklorist Barbara Kirshenblatt-Gimblett, who maintains that "traditionalizing" or "restoring" (Kirshenblatt-Gimblett, 208) is a universal behavior which entails a process of giving form and meaning by referring to something old while creating "new contexts, audiences, and meanings for the forms" (Kirshenblatt-Gimblett, 211).[69]

Other contextualisms have also succeeded to some extent in achieving an urbanism that is meaningful to more people (i.e. a more pluralistic urbanism). Efforts to design in a physically contextual manner have, for the most part, been an antidote to the modernist emphasis on the architectural object and disregard for the site. Its close cousin, regionalism, has also proven to be a welcome departure from the high modernist contempt for existing styles even though, like historicism, it may appear as a caricatured, mass-produced travesty of the regional context, and/or a neocolonialist undertaking (by developers, technocrats, and urban designers) to prevent the "natives" from becoming more cosmopolitan (like the earlier French colonial urban design).

Residential design in postmodern urbanism offers certain advantages over that of modernism. The Athens Charter maintained that instead of connected low-rise housing lining the streets, housing should be provided in high-rise buildings located in the center of large lots away from streets and from each other in order to maximize open green space and natural light in the homes. Secondly, it maintained that these buildings should be raised onto *pilotis* to open up views from the ground and endow large buildings with a sense of lightness. Finally, it recommended that roofs be flat to offer additional living space. Urban design theory since the 1960s reverses each of these tenets, with towers and slabs (*tours* and *barres*) giving way to houses and apartment buildings and with superblocks supplanted by city blocks (*îlôts*). These changes have been applauded for providing a more human scale, offering more personalized and personalizable living spaces, and adding visual interest to the landscape.[70]

Concerted efforts to create high-quality public spaces have also produced some welcome results. In many instances, the "return to the street" from the shopping mall has been successful in bringing vitality back to street life. Increased attention to the provision of traditional public space—parks, plazas, and squares—as well as to landscaping has offered an antidote to the privatization and concreting of urban settings. Likewise, the effort to design "mixed-use" projects has provided an antidote to modernism's rigid and anti-urban separation of functions.

And while hyperreal environments may be criticized for being artificial, it can be argued that it is precisely that quality which people like about them. Accused of distracting people from the injustices and ugliness of their lives, of placating them, and of being places of "spectacle and surveillance" (as in Harvey's criticism of Baltimore's Inner Harbor, 1989), hyperreal environments might also be applauded for the diversion they offer, for simply providing places in which people can relax and have fun in the company of family and friends.[71] Other beneficial aspects of these environments are the vast multipliers they create in the local economy (Ley and Mills). And for urban designers, themed environments remain one of the few major opportunities to give full rein to their powers of creative expression.

The critique of postmodern urbanism as enhancing settings for consumption is a double-edged sword that really boils down to a critique of consumption. While critics of mass society highlight the extent to which the market dictates our sense of identity, forces us to consume, and exacerbates social inequalities, others point out the market's potential for empowerment since we can personalize or resist that which it offers us. There is no question that people worldwide prefer abundance over scarcity, full shelves over empty ones, and that they vindicate their "right" to select from a variety of options along with their "freedom" to shop. As Ley and Mills have pointed out, "Access to goods (as basic as bread) is as much a facet of democratization as free elections and guarantees for the rights of the marginalized. [The] hardback editions for the few become the paperback editions for the many" (Ley and Mills, 271). And as long as we are going to shop, why not do so in a pleasant environment?

While the preservation movement may be criticized for inventing histories (and therefore not really preserving anything) and for advancing the interests of certain elites, the valorization it bespeaks of the existing urban fabric (including industrial and commercial landscapes) represents a welcome corrective to modernism's obsession with forgetting the past and starting over on a clean slate. It also suggests a valorization of cultural traditions and of cultural differences that was largely absent from modern urbanism. Indeed, many developers would say we have gone overboard in this direction as local communities' attachment to existing forms and nostalgia for the past lead them to rally behind saving every fast-food restaurant in their neighborhood.

And while movements to "preserve" nature or wildlife may sometimes be thinly veiled attempts to preserve the intimacy of one's community as well as land values, no one would deny the importance of designing in harmony with nature. The growing sensitivity towards the environment represents a great advance in contemporary urban design theory, expressed in terms of "growth management" or "sustainable design." Such theory and practice focuses on design intervention that does not deplete any natural resources or impose hardship upon any people, and preferably enhances the environment and living conditions.[72]

Most of the more exemplary recent urban design initiatives are engaged in healing scars left by interventions of the modern era, when the building of railroads and highways was undertaken with little consideration for the surrounding communities and natural landscapes. Much of this work has to do with re-using abandoned transit corridors, designing new ones, and redesigning existing fabrics both urban and suburban, sometimes in collaboration with local communities. While sharing the emphasis on enhancing the public realm with the neotraditionalists, this tendency is not necessarily intent upon emulating past townscapes, but considers instead contemporary lifestyles and preferences and aspires to retain the valuable elements of modern urbanism and architecture.

And rather than direct its focus to the traditional center, this tendency is more often concerned with the edge between the city, suburb, and countryside; between neighborhoods; and between functional uses, as well as the more metaphorical edges between disciplines, professions, and local communities. In its more extreme versions, it even champions the elimination of the traditional center, which brings with it old social inequalities. Speaking generally (not about urban design specifically), Hal Foster describes this as a "postmodernism of resistance" or "reaction" entailing "a critique of origins, not a return to them" (Foster 1983, vii).

Rather than preserve, renovate, or create a center or a past, this urban design theory holds that we should focus attention on the edge/periphery/border with an eye towards the future. Acknowledging that most biological activity occurs in nature where different zones meet, for instance, Richard Sennett maintains that "urban design has similarly to focus on the edge as a scene of life" (Sennett 1994, 69). Sensitive to the fragmentation of the built environment as well as among the urban design professions and between these and their constituents, then, designers have been increasingly setting themselves the task of "mending seams."[73]

In Western Europe, ironically, the concerted search for urbanity and the creation of centrality has been largely played out on urban wings rather than on center stage, as suburbs increasingly become the site for urbanization, immigration, and government subsidy for building. Consequently, many architects and planners began adapting these ideas to the building of satellite cities, industrial re-use, and the reorganization of suburban sprawl, as exemplified by the French program *Banlieues '89*, launched in 1985. Carriers of the modern torch also turned their gaze to suburbs because, as François Barre[74] maintained, "Classic urbanity loses its logic there . . . , but modernity finds without a doubt a great many promising departures" (in Nouvel 1980a, 17). Barre asserted, "it is on the periphery that urban development is now taking place. The notion of center itself is dissolving. . . . If the suburbs interest people today, it is precisely because of the wild production there which does not refer to any model but instead to a sort of superposition or collage. . . . It is without doubt the most faithful representation of the present time. . . . The suburb offers an accumulation of modesty and a slightly wild abundance . . . ; this reality expresses itself more through music, film, and the city than any thing one could find in architecture" (Barre, 54-55). And the way one assesses the situation, he reminds us, depends on one's perspective, both geographical and ideological: "Things look different depending on whether you look at them from the periphery or the center" (Barre, 54).

Architects of all persuasions, then, grew interested in designing on the edges of cities, including Krier (Berlin project, see chapter 2), Rossi (1991, Berlin project), Rem Koolhaas (Euralille), and Steven Holl (1991, projects for American cities). The apotheosis of this attention to the edge and to integrating functionalist tenets with the traditional city is found in the restructuring of the Barcelona waterfront, as overseen by the architect Oriol Bohígas.[75] With this renewed focus on the periphery, Donald Olsen suggests, the central city "may revert to its pre-industrial role as a work of art, designed for ostentation rather than for use, a symbol of prestige, a center of specialized consumption, a place to indulge in luxurious vice, to spend money made elsewhere" (Olsen 1983, 266). Or, this interest in the periphery may be symptomatic of the growing irrelevance of distinctions between the city, the suburb, and the countryside and between urbanism and suburbanism as ways of life, as foreseen by Marx (1858), Arthur Schlesinger (1940), and Herbert Gans (1962) (see chapter 8).

The mending of seams has been central to a number of recent urban design initiatives in North America, as apparent, for instance, in the re-use of transit corridors. Landscape architect and urban designer Diana Balmori has proposed building a light rail system and greenway on the site of an abandoned canal and rail line connecting New Haven to the center of Connecticut and the Massachusetts border, to create a corridor that unites segregated communities and enhances pedestrian ways (E. Smith, 7). The Greenway Plan for Metropolitan Los Angeles similarly centers on revitalizing 400 miles of abandoned rail and infrastructure rights-of-way as well as river and flood control channels (E. Smith, 6).[76] And in Boston, where a tunnel is being substituted for the expressway which disrupted a formerly vibrant lower-middle-class neighborhood, Alex Krieger proposed restoring the urban fabric and interweaving it with open spaces in an effort to resonate with the past but also consider current and future uses (E. Smith, 7).[77]

The re-use of abandoned transit lines has been greatly assisted by the Rails-to-Trails Conservancy (RTC), a national nonprofit organization created in 1988 to assist local activists around the United States in converting abandoned railroad corridors into public "linear parks," also called rail-trails or rails-with-trails (Ryan and Winterich; Ryan). With a nationwide membership in 1994 of 60,000, RTC had conducted 13 assessment studies around the country and almost 1,000 miles of trails had been constructed, with others in progress. Studies of rail-trails in Baltimore, Seattle, and the East Bay of San Francisco reported that properties adjacent to the trails sold better than before the trails were built and that the trails also generate economic activity for the communities through which they pass (LAING).

The design of new transportation hubs and corridors is another instance of healing scars and mending seams. A number of proposals for subway and light rail stations for the Los Angeles metropolitan area, for example, aspire to retain that which the local community values while providing that which it desires. Johnson Fain and Pereira Associates devised a plan for a Chatsworth station which includes a replica of the historic Chatsworth Station, a child-care center, and other civic and commercial services, all linked to the natural landscape by pedestrian and bicycle paths (E. Smith, 6). For a more urban site, Koning Eisenberg Architects proposed a station in Hollywood which would retain the small scale of the residential blocks while providing market stalls clustered around the station along with a larger mercado, and necessary housing (including a single-room occupancy hotel) over shops at street level, all in an effort to enhance the neighborhood identity. California-based architects Marc Angélil and Sarah Graham sought to create a center for the town of Esslingen, Switzerland by clustering shops, offices, and housing around a railroad station, all heated and cooled by an extensive system of solar energy (E. Smith, 11). And in a plan for a highway corridor for the small town of Chanhassen in Minnesota, the architect William Morrish and landscape architect Catherine Brown aspired to retain the small-town character which its inhabitants valued, preserve the natural environment, and integrate the new road into the community rather than allow it to divide and conquer the community (Muschamp 1994a).[78]

A final emergent trend to note is the effort to go beyond shaping the physical environment, to also affect changes in public policy and in public opinion regarding the potential value of urban design. Along with DPZ and Calthorpe (see chapter 3), Morrish and Brown are also engaged in these efforts, as demonstrated by their 1987 master plan for the public art program in Phoenix, which "used art as a bridge between the public and those who make public policy" (Muschamp 1994a) and in two more recent efforts in Minneapolis, one to create jobs while also providing a series of small neighborhood parks at the Hennipin County Works, and the other to better integrate public housing with private-sector housing (ibid.).

A number of efforts to reclaim vacant lots for use by the surrounding neighborhoods also go beyond shaping the physical environment. The landscape architect Achva Benzinberg Stein, for instance, designed the Uhuru Garden in Watts, Los Angeles, to include gardens as well as facilities for instruction in gardening and for selling what is grown. Intended primarily for use by the local residents of a public housing project, students at the local public school, and members of a local drug rehabilitation center, this garden incorporates native California vegetation as well as indigenous irrigation techniques (E. Smith, 14). Other efforts to convert vacant lots into community gardens in South Central Los Angeles have been undertaken from the grassroots by the LA HOPE Horticulture Corps and the LA Regional Food Bank Garden.

In certain regards, then, we might consider contemporary urban design theory as the mature young adulthood emerging and benefiting from the mistakes of its rebellious modern adolescence.[79] To best seize this moment, however, the urban design professions must be vigilant, a subject addressed in the following chapters.

NOTES

1. Although "the characteristics of late-capitalism have significant spatial repercussions," Dutton says, "one searches in vain to see how Krier responds to them, except to reject them out of hand or pretend they need not be confronted" (Dutton 1986, 23).

2. Because of the changes effected by these technologies, Huertas questions the contemporary search for urbanity, saying, "The city is no longer contained by the rules of unity of place, unity of action, and unity of time of the Poetic Art. Human behavior is divided up in time and in space. There is the space of work, the residential space, the space of knowing, the space of culture, the space for leisure, the space for communications, etc. . . . The media have taken over from the city. The 'pastoral ideal' and the garden city are already dated concepts. Urban places have become magnetic bands [cassettes] that we can put in our walkmans" (Huertas).

3. According to Rowe, the origin was a fixation with objects.

4. In this vein, Deborah Berke points out (with reference to Rob Krier's work) that "the square is at present an anachronism, having succumbed to the popularity of the supermarket, the telephone, and the television" (Berke, 12).

5. Ingersoll thus admonishes: "The ascendance of Bel Geddes's gratifications of technocracy over Hegemann's [1922] virtuous defense of the urban spaces of the past should be a lesson to current champions of the past: the demand for automobiles and the dependence on technology for the reproduction of everyday life show no signs of subsiding. This is not a rejoinder to submit to consumer reality, but rather a suggestion that viable alternatives in urban design will only come from a confrontation with this reality, not an avoidance of it" (Ingersoll 1989b, 23).

6. The architect Joseph Belmont, who was the prime mover behind the building of the modernist new city of La Défense, outside Paris, maintains that even when "architects have recreated the urban fabric, they have not reinvented the city" (Belmont 1987, 71). "They have used existing forms without thinking about their reasons for existing. They have engaged in urban art (essentially visual) and not in urban development (essentially political)" (Belmont 1987, 72).

7. Mangin asks whether the attempt to produce "urban architecture" has lost sight of its initial objectives to produce an "urban tissue" and build for mass society without incurring the damages of the Modern movement (Mangin).

8. This plan, Muschamp said, "envisioned nature in 19th-century terms, as a scenic backdrop or as a wilderness to be segregated into parklike preserves" (Muschamp 1993b).

9. As James Holston maintains, "It is . . . not too great a generalization to say that the modernist vision of a new way of life has fundamentally altered the urban environment in which nearly half the world's people live" (Holston, 4–5). At a conference convened in Brussels to discuss the Movement for the Reconstruction of the European City, Jacques Lucan similarly criticized this denial of the modernist city (Lucan 1978, 49) which has left indelible marks on our minds and landscapes and cannot simply be ignored. Ingersoll contends that most architects would prefer to design for "lovely historic contexts" (Ingersoll 1989a, 3) instead of a site like Pruitt-Igoe. Should we, he asks, "continue to bomb the postwar contexts that are, like-it-or-not, the majority of our contexts"? (ibid.) Alain Colquhoun (1985) also develops this thesis.

10. According to Heinrich Klotz, the historicism of postmodern urbanism is neither a

reactionary response to modernism nor a nostalgic response to the loss of an idealized past, but an ironic response.

11. The motive behind such inventions of tradition is often the packaging of the past as a
commodity for present consumption aimed toward profit-making. In this instance,
historical tradition is at best "reorganized as a museum culture, not necessarily of
high modernist art, but of local history, of local production, of how things once upon
a time were made, sold, consumed, and integrated into a long-lost and often romanticized daily life (one from which all trace of oppressive social relations may be
expunged)" (Harvey 1989, 303). Harvey maintains, "tradition is not often preserved
by being commodified and marketed as such. The search for roots ends up at worst
being produced and marketed as an image, as a simulacrum or pastiche (imitation
communities constructed to evoke images of some folksy past, the fabric of traditional
working-class communities being taken over by an urban gentry)" (ibid.).

12. David Harvey contends that "With modern building materials it is possible to replicate ancient buildings with such exactitude that authenticity or origins can be put
into doubt" (Harvey 1989, 289).

13. Tom Wolfe thus situates postmodern architecture within the Modern Movement,
explaining that it serves the same purpose as Pop Art for modern painting. He says:
"Pop was not a rebellion. The Pop artists still religiously observed the central tenets
of Modernism concerning flatness, 'the integrity of the picture plan,' non-illusion-
ism. They were careful to do only pictures of other pictures—labels, comic strip pan-
els, flags, pages of numbers and letters—so that their fellow hierophants in the
Modern movement would realize that they were not actually returning to realism. . . .
Pop was a leg-pull, a mischievous but respectful wink at the orthodoxy of the day"
(Wolfe 1980, 3). In similar fashion, says Wolfe, "Post-Modernist architects use decoration . . . , camping it up and vamping it up" (ibid.).

14. The superseding of the industrial revolution by the information revolution was marked
by the 1968 exhibition "The Machine as Seen at the End of the Mechanical Age" at the
MoMA in New York City (Zukin 1988a, 74). The organizer Pontus Hulten asserted that
"the mechanical machine—which can most easily be defined as an imitation of our mus-
cles—is losing its dominating position among the tools of mankind; while electronic
and chemical devices—which imitate the processes of the brain and nervous system—
are becoming increasingly important" (cited by Zukin 1988a, 74–75). The artists exhibited here were suggesting that progress is inevitable and desirable in certain respects,
yet also entails a significant loss of the past and of meaning.

15. While these new technologies have recast the goals and tasks of urban designers,
they have also altered spatial perception, engendering what has been described as
"cyburbia" (Sorkin, Dewey).

16. Martin Pawley attributes the preoccupation with surfaces in urban design to "the
advent of domestic electronics and the massive spread of process control mechanisms"
(Pawley 1990, 3) which, he says, is what distinguishes the current "second machine
age" from Reyner Banham's "first machine age" (Banham 1960) of the early part of the
twentieth century. For Banham, the first machine age contained the potentially liberating promise of ending the control of machines by an elite. But according to Pawley,
"Banham stopped where the nightmares of technology began" (Pawley 1990, 3) and

the second machine age has been having socially atomizing effects.

17. Giandomenico Amendola exclaims, "Contemporary architectural theatrics turn shopping malls and suburban arcades into Victorian or bohemian environments. The transformation of a Holiday Inn into a noble English manor is a movie-set type of deception made possible by mass media culture. However, it deals not only with a neobaroque visual trick but also with a social trick" (Amendola, 254).

18. As Jarzombek asserts: "The art of building has degenerated into the art of collecting one-liners; criticism into a self-conscious display of 'learning'" (Jarzombek, 89).

19. In the catalogue accompanying the "Post-Modern Visions" exhibition, Heinrich Klotz (1985) asserts that the matter of postmodernism is "not just function but fiction" (cited by Harvey 1989, 97). Amendola also contends, "The shift is from function to fiction" (Amendola, 254). Deconstructivists have also rallied to the "form follows fiction" cry, but their fiction is a more self-referential one (see Chapter 8).

20. Kimball, for instance, criticizes the work of Charles Jencks (1985), saying that he has gone beyond camp—a conscious playing with sentimentalized products of bad taste—to kitsch.

21. Three ways in which it does this, according to Lash, are: "(1) an 'auratic' style is replaced by a populist and playful one, (2) the consistent working through of the possibilities of a building material, such as glass, or concrete, or a principle is abandoned in favor of pastiche, (3) it is once again historical" (Lash 1990b, 36).

22. Lash maintains that "The attempt of postmodern architecture to re-connect with historical meanings (or signifieds) has . . . wound up in the trivialization of the latter" (Lash 1990a, 72).

23. Mestrovic asks whether postmodernism has descended into "nihilism, kitsch, bad taste, and a delight in decadence?" (Mestrovic, 27). "In practice," he maintains, "it is very difficult to distinguish postmodern superficiality from genuine sentimentality" (Mestrovic, 155). He points out that "one person's kitsch can be another person's naive aura" (Mestrovic, 27, in reference to Walter Benjamin).

24. The French expression for this condition, *repli sur soi* (literally, folding in on oneself), is evocative.

25. For many members of postmodernist culture, Harvey says, "The home becomes a private museum to guard against the ravages of time-space compression" (Harvey 1989, 292).

26. As Jean-Paul Sartre provokes in *Huis Clos* (No Exit), *"L'enfer, c'est les autres"* (Hell, it is others). These myths emphasize, and often invent, that which distinguishes others from oneself.

27. Pawley maintains that the public realm has been taken over by "welfare bureaucracies" and "administrative terrorism" (Pawley 1973, 13), such that the arenas of public life are falling "prey to security restrictions which endanger their very practicality" (ibid.).

28. Manuel Castells describes this condition saying, "the new tendential urban meaning is the spatial and cultural separation of people from their product and from their history. It is the space of collective alienation and individual violence, transformed by undifferentiated feedbacks into a flow that never stops and never starts. Life is transformed into abstraction, cities into shadows" (Castells 1983, 314).

29. Chermayeff and Alexander recount the history of the impact of fear on urban design saying: "The earlier, coherently organized city was fortified against the invader and the

relative anarchy of the larger countryside; the individual buildings and houses were heavily armed against rebels, robbers, and the stranger. These precautions, which were clearly expressed in plan and structure, have slowly given way under the influence of economic improvement and social discipline, implemented by the organized enforcement of law. The great sheets of easily shattered glass, the picture window, the absence of walls and fences are all symbols of a short-lived confidence in the efficacy of things. . . . However *le cercle est bouclé*—civilization has come full circle. Now that law enforcers are largely engaged in wrestling with traffic problems, efficiency in protection appears to be diminishing, with the result that opportunities for invaders of the private realm are multiplying. And the robbers and strangers of the past have been joined by hoodlums and psychopaths, confidence men and salesmen, all seemingly respectable, turning up in standard clothes and standard cars" (Chermayeff and Alexander, 74). They acknowledge the role of electronic media in the changing nature of public and private space: "What was once a commonplace—the possibility of escape from the crowd for privacy and rest—has all but vanished. The crowds, once restricted to the streets and borders of the public domain, now follow unbidden into the solitary, private domain by means of electronic media intruding acoustically through the thin partition that fails to separate man from his noisy neighbor" (Chermayeff and Alexander, 73–74). Chermayeff and Alexander contend, "The very instruments that have given man increased dynamic power—total mobility and instantaneous communication—are destroying the equilibrium in the human habitat" (Chermayeff and Alexander, 79). Everywhere, they write, "wheels are turning at cross purposes to legs and other people's voices cut across our thoughts" (Chermayeff and Alexander, 73).

30. Architects, according to Sennett, "are among the few professionals who are forced to work with present-day ideas of public life, . . . and indeed are among the few professionals who of necessity express and make theses codes manifest to others" (Sennett 1974).

31. As Jacobs and Appleyard's 1987 urban design manifesto states: "Avoiding the temptation to ascribe all kinds of psychological values to defined spaces (such as intimacy, belonging, protection—values that are difficult to prove and that may differ for different people), it is enough to observe that spaces surrounded by buildings are more likely to bring people together and thereby promote public interaction. The space can be linear like streets or in the form of plazas of myriad shapes. Moreover, interest and interplay among uses is enhanced. To be sure, such arrangements direct people and limit their freedom—they cannot move in just any direction from any point—but presumably there are enough choices (even avenues of escape) left open, and the gain is in greater potential for sense stimulation, excitement, surprise, and focus" (Jacobs and Appleyard, 119).

32. Examples include the American Traditional Neighborhood Developments designed by Andres Duany and Elizabeth Plater-Zyberk; the Pedestrian Pockets of Peter Calthorpe, Doug Kelbaugh, and others; the British new towns commissioned by Prince Charles; and some French new cities (see chapters 2 and 3).

33. Castells concludes: "By bringing together profitable housing and public service, the [public-private developer] had broken the rules of segregation, while still trying to sell social status to the middle class. This was done in total disregard of the fact that distance is an essential component of symbolic distinction in a mass society where

cultural differences are less apparent between individuals. . . . By promising a good environment to the middle class, cheap rental housing to workers, and profitable investment to capital, the [developer] tried to demonstrate how urban contradictions could be superseded by urban design" (Castells 1983, 94). But these efforts were unsuccessful.

34. The philosopher Karsten Harries maintains that architecture is a defense against the tyranny or "terror" of time (in Harvey 1989, 206) since the creation of permanent and beautiful structures is a way of linking time and eternity. The aim of built form, he says, is "not to illuminate temporal reality so that [we] might feel more at home in it, but to be relieved of it: to abolish time within time, if only for a time" (ibid.).

35. E. M. Farelly maintained that "After the apparent failure of both heroic Modernism and '60s idealism, Western society of the '70s and '80s has been characterized increasingly by doubt, anxiety, and a general loss of nerve, which has allowed expedience and mendacity to replace any more altruistic social discipline: Post-Modern Classicism is the architecture of despair" (Farelly).

36. Concurrently the French provinces were seeking greater political autonomy from Paris and one expression of this was the application of regional design, especially to public buildings.

37. Boyer points out that "Mass production is serial so that it is not surprising to find the mass production of city spaces in late capitalism taking on a serial appearance, producing from already known patterns or molds of places almost identical ambience from city to city" (Boyer 1990, 96).

38. As Connor points out, once a heterotopia has been named, it becomes "controlled and predictively interpreted, given a center and illustrative function" (Connor, 9) and therefore closed off to "the very world of cultural difference and plurality which it allegedly brings to visibility" (Connor, 9–10).

39. Expressing this view, Relph exclaims: "it may be that post-modernism is little more than a disguise for ever more subtle and powerful types of rationalistic organization by corporations and governments alike. For all its pre-modern suggestions of quaintness, its apparently old materials and its revival of locality, the post-modern street is still usually a product of large-scale economics and intense design efforts. Its appearance is the consequence of arbitrary choice and fashion rather than tradition, and is rarely more than superficial. To that extent it is a lie, though it is a pretty lie" (Relph 1987, 259).

40. See Sidney Robinson.

41. And earlier efforts to invent traditions have been successful in giving people a sense of history, continuity, tradition, roots, and identity (Hobsbawm and Ranger).

42. Jacques Guillaume similarly maintains that the turn to enigmatic discussions about architecture merely served to assure the survival of architecture (as a profession) at a time when it was being threatened by the rapid postwar building (which made wide use of engineers) and by the modernist conflation of architecture with other arts and politics.

43. This was particularly acute in the US where politics and urbanism are conspicuously disassociated for the most part. David Bell reflected upon this situation in 1988 saying: "In this year of national elections, neither of the major political parties has given even lip-service to the nature and problems of our cities. It is curious that we have been so conditioned to accept that national government and those who run for national

political office should have so little to say about our cultural life and especially the life of our most profound cultural invention, our cities. . . . My speculations as to why these concerns are perpetually relegated to the rear of political attention are grounded in a sense that there is a tacit, widely-held belief that cultural concerns, such as the quality of our cities, are not really appropriate political concerns because these former, after all, have more to do with aesthetics, which is in our time considered by many to be an autonomous, beauty-is-in-the-eye-of-the-beholder domain. In other words it has, like much of everything else, been relativized and privatized" (David Bell, 2).

44. In assessing the results of the first European architectural competition (for young European architects) in 1989, for example, Guiheux finds that most competitors designed for "European nomads" like themselves (Guiheux, 21).

45. According to Huxtable, "Style, as it is being written about and embraced today, is no longer style as we have previously defined and understood it—as an attempt to give appropriate expression to a kind of life, or society, or collective need, or moment in cultural time" (Huxtable 1981b, 104). Instead, "Like so much else today, the emphasis is on self and the senses, with 'design' an increasingly hermetic and narcissistic process, serving as often to short circuit purpose and accessibility as to expand the horizons of constructive vision. Style is being dangerously confused with art" (ibid.). Today, Huxtable maintains, "There is no Zeitgeist demanding recognition and fealty, no unifying force or sentiment, no greater public good, no banner around which architects can rally. They can go in any direction and follow any muse. This is surely one of the most open, challenging, promising, and dangerous moments in the history of the building art" (ibid.).

46. Paul Goldberger described the 1980s historicist trend as ultimately glib and unsatisfying, saying: "Now, as the decade draws to a close, architecture that clings to the past as if it were a life raft seems increasingly unsatisfying. At its best, it is hopelessly sentimental. But in neither case can this kind of architecture project the sense of authenticity it needs to have credibility. We think so much in terms of image and marketing today that we instinctively feel this architecture has little power to convince us. It is simply too glib. The process of creating a building was much slower and more deliberate in the 1920s, so the final product seemed more substantial. Back then, architects could get away with designing a fake 16th-century Tudor mansion in a way that we cannot today" (Goldberger 1989c).

47. Goldberger contends, "now, in all fields of culture as well as architecture, the temper is romantic and conservative; form is what seems to matter most, not content, whereas a decade ago content seemed to be everything. It is a mood that is at best introspective and at worst self-indulgent" (Goldberger 1983, 15, orig. April 29, 1980).

48 There are nonetheless circumstances where low-rise, high-density building remains appropriate outside of urban fabrics. Clustered housing can be warranted on environmentally sensitive sites such as wetlands and wildlife conservancies. And, of course, it is also appropriate for any community where the people prefer it (particular age or ethnic groups). Wherever applied though, it is important that quiet and privacy are ensured through judicious design and that, optimally, the housing corresponds to its inhabitants' image of a home, whatever that may be.

49. See also Ellin 1994, chapter 5.

50. As Gwendolyn Wright points out, "Responding to local traditions entails serious appraisal of a complex culture, even for a small place—skills few designers have been taught" (G. Wright 1988, 10). Tempia similarly maintains that architects are not trained to design within a social context and suggests that this task requires the skills of a social researcher (1982, 28). With regards to Frampton's proposal for a critical regionalism which preserves local cultures while simultaneously benefiting from new technologies, Hal Foster maintains that this is difficult to realize "unless one lives in a relatively homogeneous society" (Foster 1990, 116) because of the expansion of the capitalist world system over the last thirty years.

51. Lefaivre attributes the decline of socially contextual urban design efforts (including Third World self-help projects, participatory design in Europe, and advocacy planning in the USA) to the "fiscal crisis" of the welfare state, the proliferation of terrorist activities, a waning spirit of populism, and the replacement of an industrial economy with a non-productivist post-industrial economy based largely on real-estate speculation which made the low-yield populist experiments unfeasible.

52. Frampton thus describes postmodern architecture saying "it tends to proclaim its legitimacy in exclusively formal—not to say superficial—terms, rather than in terms of constructional, organizational or socio-cultural considerations" (Frampton 1985, 305). He maintains that "the impulse is scenographic rather than tectonic, so that not only is there a total schism between the inner substance and the outer form, but the form itself either repudiates its constructional origin or dissipates its palpability. In postmodern architecture classical and vernacular 'quotations' tend to interpenetrate each other disconcertingly. Invariably rendered as unfocussed images, they easily disintegrate and mix with other more abstract, usually cubistic forms, for which the architect has no more respect than for his extremely arbitrary historical allusions" (Frampton 1985, 307). As sources for urban design, Clarke and Dutton maintain, the "concepts of history, context, public realm, and art . . . have become cleansed of their social, cultural, and political dimensions. Clasped within a parochial discourse, the profession has stripped these concepts of their potential to engage the political construction of society—a society disfigured by class, race, and gender discrimination and other forms of unequal power distribution" (Clarke and Dutton, 5).

53. Gosling and Maitland justify this re-emphasis: "To say that a city should be more concerned with the solution of grave economic issues and social injustices than with the niceties of urban design implies a narrow cosmetic view of the subject belied by experiences of communities in the Third World" (Gosling and Maitland). David Bell seeks to correct the opposite tendency to assume brute environmental determinism by reminding that "to suggest that some kind of connection [between the shape of cities and politics] does not obtain, precipitates the most self-absorbed notions of architectural autonomy" (David Bell, 2–3). Paolo Portoghesi argues for the postmodern tendency to de-emphasize the political impact of architecture: "Between architectural forms and political practice and theory, there can exist temporary reciprocal acts of instrumentality, convergences involving material interests, and elective affinities felt sincerely by someone or other in one of the two fields, but not much more. The rest consists of mystifications or news items having little meaning in the long run" (Portoghesi 1983, 37). Michel Foucault has pointed out the limits of social

reform through architecture, saying that architecture can only resolve social problems "when the liberating intentions of the architect coincide with the real practice
of people in the exercise of their freedom" (interviewed by Rabinow 1982b, 18).

54. Addressing architecture students at Columbia University in 1984, Percival Goodman (who graduated from the École National Supérieure des Beaux Arts in 1926
and co-authored *Communitas* in 1947) bemoaned this political apathy of contemporary urban designers, citing Henry Thoreau, who said: "What's the use of building
a house if you don't have a nice world to build it in?"

55. Robert Stern, for instance, opposes political interpretations of architecture, saying:
"Architecture is not a whipping boy for politics. It is not built nationalism, it is not
built sociology. I think most of today's critics make a tremendous mistake in seeing
architecture this way. They never look at buildings anymore" (Stern in Williams
1985, 11). But at the same time, Stern vindicates the profoundly political nature of
architecture, claiming: "The truism is that buildings are the single most permanent
artifact of man that directly affects each and every person every day of his or her
life. . . . Architecture, as an art, is raised to the level of cultural reflection when someone decides that he wants to build not just a box to accommodate a task but something that says something about himself, his corporation, his government or
whatever. If architecture(and not just a building)results, that is still one of the most
pervasive means of cultural expression. . . . Buildings are lives" (ibid.).

56. Portoghesi attributes criticism of the 1980 Biennale exhibit and of the postmodern trend
in general to four fears: the fear of heresy (toward the Modern movement), the fear of
hegemony (Euro-American), the fear of memory, and the fear of (political) regression
(Portoghesi 1983, 32). But what Portoghesi refers to as the "fear" of hegemony and
regression might also be regarded as "resistance" to hegemony and regression.

57. Clarke and Thomas Dutton point out that both academic and populist approaches
toward history fail to address questions such as: "What is history? How is it constructed and interpreted, and in whose interests do these constructions and interpretations serve? How are architects using history? By what criteria does an architect
select from history? . . . By what criteria does the architectural community—or anyone—make judgments about the appropriateness or inappropriateness of a particular
use of history? . . . Is not the teaching of skills in itself a teaching of history?" (Clarke
and Dutton). The failure to answer these questions, they say, results in "an historical
imperialism, a denial of people in their cultural and social relations and practices and
lived experiences. What is more, the objectification of history denies the political: the
social processes through which environments and artifices are brought into being
and the multiple meanings that are ascribed to them" (ibid.).

58. Jarzombek maintains that urban designers have variously regarded and "used" history over time, saying: "With the Renaissance, Historicists used historiographic
arguments to legitimize historical forms . . . ; Modernists used historiography to
kill historical forms . . . Post-Modern Historicists, however, use history to kill historiographic speculation, a much more dangerous proposition than either of the other
two both from a design point of view and politically" (Jarzombek, 94).

59. Philip Cooke describes the socio-economic landscape of postmodernism as "a new
stage of rentier-led overaccumulation based on third-world debt, military outlays and

capitalist flight to monetarist havens [featuring] a return to the social relations of the premodernist era as capital retrenches to its more dynamic redoubts in international finance, property, high technology and military production" (Cooke 1988, 490). Its manifestations in the built environment, he says, include "increasingly enclosed and isolated urban spatial structures, increasingly defensive architectural forms in the core of the urban environment, and through the juxtaposition of hyperspace and overconsumption with the unemployment, sub-employment and environmental decay of the superexploited poor, a new, degraded form of urbanity itself" (Cooke 1988, 491).

60. The "great weakness of theory and design in the Second Machine Age," says Pawley, is that "it has failed to produce any unifying theories at all" (Pawley 1990, 3) despite "the veritable explosion of writing about architecture that has taken place since the collapse of consensus support for Modernism some 15 years ago" (ibid.). This writing, Pawley suggests, "has not so much explained architecture as buried its driving force, the social purpose of building, a purpose that in the Modern era generated a model relationship between theory and practice" (ibid.). He continues: "The Second Machine Age is an age without ideology, and its books are not theoretical. As in the eighteenth century, at least until the French Revolution, they are more likely to be collections of images with a bland, soothing text laid like wall-to-wall Berber carpet between them. . . . This new way of looking at buildings without at the same time considering what they are for or how they are made has supplanted the analytical enlightenment of the Modern era" (Pawley 1990, 3–4). Pawley exclaims: "Architects too have learned to become visually instead of ideologically oriented, and the intellectual substance of their discourse has changed accordingly. Today they are not in the sociology business but in the imaging business, just as much as the magazine and book publishers, the TV producers, the art editors, photographers and writers of the media. All of them behave as though the old world of historical time has been telescoped by perfect color photography into a kind of illustrated catalogue of the built environment. . . . The architecture that results is exactly like one of the selective evocations of the past that appear in television commercials, with historical veracity achieved by a few bars of Dvorak and sepia-tone streetscape. On TV, as in architecture, this superficiality is enough" (Pawley 1990, 4).

61. Some postmodern urbanists who refer to the past and the site justify what they do by saying "that contemporary architecture based upon popular images and symbols [is] unavoidably consumerist and corrupt, and thus can only reflect accepted, commercially debased values as opposed to moving beyond them" (Clarke and Dutton, 2).

62. Lesnikowski is also critical of *Learning from Las Vegas*, saying: "it is disconcerting from the start to observe that in order to explore the principles of 'ordinary' architecture, Venturi [Scott Brown and Izenour] addresses the issue of 'extraordinary' circumstances, which Las Vegas . . . certainly is. Venturi's anti-heroic attitude ends up by promoting new elitism about Las Vegas's bad taste, which is indeed confusing. . . . His own sophistication denied him the capability of being an ordinary man and here his ideological fallacy lies" (Lesnikowski 1982, 299–300).

63. Frampton asserts: "If there is a general principle that can be said to characterize postmodern architecture, it is the conscious ruination of style and the cannibalization of architectural form" (Frampton 1985, 307).

64. As Clarke maintains, "Lost is the naiveté of universal norms and of ideal environments for living and working. There is little security in such when flexible accumulation makes long-range planning horizons unrealistic. Creative destruction no longer advances under the single umbrella of a grand, unified ideological system. Postmodernism is a cultural equivocation that allows for divergence and heterogeneity. The term conveys a direction from modernism, but signifies no destination" (Clarke 1988, 13).

65. Joseph Rykwert contends that history is back, but "It is a catalogue history, devoid of narration, in which the phenomenal past is digested to a set of timeless motifs on which the designer can call to deck out his project in a garb which will produce, so it is generally thought, the right kind of denotation response in the public. While market forces, the traffic engineer and the planning administrators operate as before, their sins are now covered by a skin of ornament borrowed from the history books" (Rykwert 1988, Preface).

66. Ingersoll's chilling question brings this home: "Is it only coincidence that the exploded housing blocks of Pruitt-Igoe, the icons that have come to symbolize the end of modernism, were blown up in 1972, the same year that the neutron bomb was unveiled as America's ultimate weapon?" (Ingersoll 1989a, 3).

67. Clarke elaborates: "Flexible accumulation has become the mobilization of image—the employment of spectacle within the urban arena. Disneyland becomes an urban strategy" (Clarke 1988, 14). Disneyland presents seductive images, he says, but these "seem alien and fragmented. While the style is new, the fragmentation is much like that of the previous architectural epoch. It occurs because symbolic capital must distinguish itself. It must define its edges to protect itself as both symbol and investment. As such it cannot be 'infill' within the urban continuum [cannot be contextual], it has to be a separate event" (ibid.).

68. The Athens Charter (1933) has been criticized for insufficiently acknowledging the cultural, historical, or topographical contexts of cities. Rather than design with regards to contemporary contingencies, this de-contextual approach posited "an imagined future . . . as the critical ground in terms of which to evaluate the present" (Holston, 9). As Holston maintains, this "teleological view of history dispenses with a consideration of intervening actors and intentions, of their diverse sources and conflicts. Rather, the only kind of agency modernism considers in the making of history is the intervention of the prince (state head) and the genius (architect-planner)" (ibid.). A fatal contradiction of the Modern movement, then, inhered in the putative desire to help usher in a more egalitarian society alongside a conviction that the architect/planner is infallible and must have unlimited power.

69. "The impossibility of perfect or complete replication," Kirshenblatt-Gimblett says, "offers opportunities for innovation, for reflection about the relationship between the proposed 'original' and the restoration, between the past and the present" (Kirshenblatt-Gimblett, 212).

70. These changes have been most apparent in the many new styles of public housing (for example, Moley; Querrien; Maitino and Sompairac; Barbe and Duclent), even though less public housing has been built during this period than the modern one. These changes have also been apparent in the effort to generate "traditional neighborhood developments" or an "urbanism of houses" (see chapters 2 and 3).

71. Ley and Mills highlight these practices, "which escape the imputed social control of spectacle" (Ley and Mills, 259). Even Harvey concedes that such environments might accomplish "the construction of some limited and limiting sense of identity in the midst of a collage of imploding spatialities" (Harvey 1989, 303–04).

72. An ACSA/AIA teachers' seminar on the theme of "Sustainability and Design" was held in May 1994.

73. This attention to the edge has nothing to do with the building of "edge cities" (see chapter 3), which instead of breaking down barriers, create new ones, and which are market-driven rather than the product of considered thought and action.

74. Barre was editor of *Architecture d'Aujourd'hui* before becoming Director of the Public Development Corporation of La Villette.

75. In addition to Bohígas, the other architects of the master plan for the Barcelona waterfront, called La Nova Icària, are Josep Martorell, David Mackay, and Albert Puigdomènech. See Lampugnani (1991, 114–17) and Bohígas (1991, 119–23). Michael Rotondi, Director of the Southern California Institute of Architecture, has described this interest in edges saying, "All the things talked about now . . . regardless of the title, are really about order and disorder, trying to understand the relationship of center to periphery. . . . It has to do with the redefinition of centers as a result of astronomical discoveries. . . ." (in G. White, 173). Anthony Vidler has described the "posturban sensibility" saying, "the margins have entirely invaded the center and disseminated its focus" (1992, 186).

76. This plan was developed by Johnson Fain and Pereira Associates.

77. The Boston Planning Department ultimately decided to dedicate 75 percent of this corridor as open space, rather than adhere to Krieger's proposal for more built space (E. Smith, 7).

78. Morrish directs the Design Center for American Urban Landscape in Minneapolis, Minnesota (founded in 1989), which emphasizes connections among people, built form, and nature, as well as among the design professions in the tradition of Frederick Law Olmsted. Other major influences on the Center's work include J. B. Jackson's emphasis on the integration of natural and human artifacts, Kevin Lynch's cognitive mapping, Ian McHarg's ecological planning, and earlier efforts at community participation (Muschamp 1994a).

79. Ada Louise Huxtable expresses this optimism, specifically with regards to architecture: "I have a feeling that when the scores are finally in and architects have stopped beating their father-figures and smashing icons, the art of architecture will have emerged into a new and very vital period," which she describes as "the natural if somewhat stormy evolution of modernism into something of much greater range and richness" (Huxtable 1981b, 104–05). Huxtable explains: "I see it as a much broadened phase of modernism— not as the undoing of modernism. I do not like the phrase post-modernism because it implies that something has been finished and replaced" (Huxtable 1981b, 104). In similar fashion, Lesnikowski interprets our misguided efforts as preparing the ground for more substantial and worthwhile change: "Undeniably the present developments in architectural thought—whether connected with promising consolidations of classicist attitudes or with the continuation of individualistic romantic postmodern attitudes, even if they are at the present shallow and naive—represent a necessary and unavoidable step in the direction of correcting modern architecture's mistakes, and this is why they are so encouraging and important" (Lesnikowski 1982, 318).

6

THE MODERN PROJECT:
CONTINUED OR ABANDONED?

THE MORASS OF POSTMODERN POLEMICS can be untangled to reveal two essential debates. The first asks where we are: Is postmodernism a continuation of the Enlightenment and Modern project of liberating humanity through science and rationality? Or is it a rebuke and rebellion against it? In other words, have we been witnessing a moment of hyper-rationality or indeed a shift toward romanticism? The second debate asks where we should we be: Should we be pursuing this modern project or should we reject it in favor of some better alternative? As the challenge to the legitimacy of the modern project has been mounting, intellectuals and artists have sought to theorize this moment, portray it, and sometimes prescribe directions for it. While they have the luxury of indulging in relatively insular debate/art, however, urban designers face very real dictates of financial, political, and pragmatic vagaries that truly test the validity of postmodern claims. After briefly reviewing the theoretical debates surrounding postmodernism, this chapter examines the implications of these for urban design theory and practice (description) and explores possible future directions (prescription).

SUPPORTERS AND DETRACTORS

Supporters of the modern project (described in chapter 4) believe that it continues to hold the greatest promise for human emancipation. The arguments that we should abandon the modern project hinge on the premise that the modernist pursuit of control over the forces of nature ultimately leads to and justifies the domination and destruction of the environment which sustains us and of the human species itself.[1] Max Horkheimer and Theodor Adorno described this in 1946 as the "dialectic of Enlightenment," whereby reason turns into its opposite as the rebellion against alienation and the pursuit of emancipation actually contribute to increasing domination and oppression. Modernist thinkers—from Stalin to Mao and Robert Moses—have reiterated that destruction is necessary for progress to occur. Their critics have questioned the relative value of the destruction compared with its merits.

Among the most outspoken recent critics of the modern project are Jean-François Lyotard, Jean Baudrillard, Michel Foucault, and Jacques Derrida, whose thinking has been loosely identified as *poststructuralism.*[2] Lyotard argues that, even if universal and eternal truths exist, we are not capable of accessing them. Likening language to a city which has grown incrementally (borrowing from Wittgenstein), he maintains that there is no single meta-narrative or meta-language, only codes depending on the context in which we find ourselves.[3] Along with Lyotard, Baudrillard claims that recent changes call for new theories of society which do not make universal claims or seek foundations of knowledge, which do not take representation to be a mirror of reality, and which do not seek causality or social coherence (a unified subject). Foucault similarly dismisses the existence of broad interpretive schemes, insisting instead upon the embeddedness of power relations in their particular discourses, histories, and sites. Discounting the viability of an overarching emancipating project, Foucault calls for localized resistances, specific to each site, which stem from open discourse and which might peacefully coexist to form a "heterotopia." Derrida argues that we must deconstruct the binary oppositions governing Western philosophy and culture that presuppose a hierarchy valuing reality over appearance, speech over writing, men over women, and reason over nature.

Other observers of post-industrial society largely accept the validity of the modern project, assess the extent to which it has been achieved, and continue to pursue its goals. Sometimes described as neoconservatives,[4] they see postmodernism as a positive evolution of modernism, maintaining that the conditions currently exist for eliminating poverty, ignorance, and wars among nation-states, and for bringing about worldwide unity and modernization (continuing the 1950s optimism regarding the use of technologies). For instance, in reaction to the repressive control and singularity of modernism, Daniel Bell finds that postmodernism unleashes repressed impulses and instincts, extending modern bohemianism to all society (Daniel Bell 1976).[5] Sometimes described as "neo-optimists," these social commentators tend to regard the rise of mass society as capable of ushering in a more democratic society, a post-scarcity or affluent society (for example, Daniel Bell, David Reisman, Philip Rieff, and Christopher Lasch). The new "communitarians," who, including Amitai Etzioni and Robert Bellah, define community as prior to individual rights and call for a return to traditional social institutions such as religion and the family (D. Bell 1992). Largely upholding the liberal Western tradition, this view criticizes deviations from or threats to this tradition.

Others still would like to see an "oppositional," "alternative," or "critical" postmodernism. This perspective acknowledges the deficiencies inherent in the modern project but maintains that we must continue to pursue it nonetheless, because if we do not, we renege on our possibilities for coherent action and improvement. The most notable proponent of this view is Jürgen Habermas. Habermas shares with his anti-modern project counterparts the belief that an excess of rational thought and behavior is detrimental. He bemoans the encroachment of instrumental rationalism into every realm and speaks of the necessity to preserve a world of values and meanings against the onslaught of the rational and bureaucratic world (Habermas 1970). In contrast to the anti-modernists, however, Habermas attributes the negative repercussions of Enlightenment thinking to improper application, rather than to flaws in the thinking itself, and he seeks a concept of rationality which allows room for critique, a certain sensitivity, and democratic practice.[6] He accuses the poststructuralists of not producing useful things (Jay, 28) and of being neoconservative by virtue of devaluing emancipatory modern theories and values (Habermas 1986).[7] In reaction to what he regards as their nihilistic and relativist stance, Habermas maintains that consensus and norms do arise in daily life and that this "communicative reason" should form the basis for action and change (Habermas 1987). To accomplish this, he proposes a brand of critical reason (as opposed to instrumental or positivistic reason), which seeks to nurture mutual understanding and agreement/consensus through free and equal access to rational discourse on all topics (Best and Kellner, 237–39).[8] Critical reason, Habermas contends, could re-unite the spheres of philosophy, morals, science, and aesthetics separated by modernism, and thereby finish an unfinished project. He does not really believe this can fully occur, however, without structural changes in the political economy.[9]

More proactive formulations of critical postmodernism include the ecological and feminist critiques (often fused as ecofeminism), also described as constructive or reconstructive postmodernisms in reaction to poststructuralism's deconstructionism. This critique, which I will refer to here simply as ecological postmodernism, holds that poststructuralism's assertion that there is nothing but cultural construction in human experience (as in Derrida's "There is nothing outside the text") denies anything outside human invention and thereby fulfills a desire for control (for example, over nature, over woman) (Spretnak).[10] The ecological critique faults poststructuralism for regarding any kind of communion and things that we share (like language, ritual, and customs) as "prison houses" or "repressive codes" from which we must release ourselves, pointing out that this attitude encourages an indifference and a cynicism towards others and the environment. The attitude of the poststructuralists, according to this critique, lazily assumes "that 'Mom' (Mother Nature) will always clean up any ecological mess we make and, besides, she would never really kill off her children no matter how badly we treat her" (Spretnak, 144). In contrast, ecological postmodernism encourages us to see the gestalt obscured by the modern project's attempt to scientifically control situations,[11] which ends up valorizing certain fragments while ignoring others such as nature or native peoples (Spretnak, 19).[12] In doing so, this perspective seeks to open a "passage beyond the failed assumptions of modernity . . . that preserves the positive advances of the liberal tradition and technological capabilities but is rooted in ecological sanity and meaningful human participation in the unfolding story of the Earth community and the universe" (Spretnak, 4).[13]

SIGNIFICANCE FOR URBAN DESIGN

When applied to urban design, the view that we should continue the modern project champions ever-greater mastery over the environment through the scientific method and creativity, with the goal of creating spaces which are rational, universally good, and conducive to emancipating discomfort and oppression. Aesthetically, this view tends to champion the functional design of buildings and cities valuing practicality and efficacy over emotional and symbolic attributes. The role of the urban designer is to make rational decisions, relying heavily on quantitative data, and to implement these with expedience.

The view that the modern project was misguided because its logical conclusion is the abuse of power is less optimistic about the potential for improving the built environment via an overarching theory and method. This view is skeptical about human mastery over nature, pointing especially to the environmental damage and human oppression incurred by efforts to date. Regarding utopia as a dystopia, this view settles instead for small-scale and grassroots interventions, the role of the urban designer being that of facilitator, privileging qualitative information over quantitative data. Proponents of abandoning the modern project tend to delight in ornament as well as color, whimsy, winding streets, and other features of the romantic aesthetic.

We know that there have always been voices in architecture and city planning that spoke out against the modern project. The number of these voices grew and their pitch intensified during the late-eighteenth-century romantic movement, which spoke of "radical subjectivism," "untrammeled individualism," and the "search for individual self-realization" (Harvey 1989, 19). With this shift to romanticism, the revolutionary architecture of Ledoux, Boullée, and others was rejected in favor of classical forms. The nineteenth century, particularly from the revolutions of 1848 to the 1890s, witnessed rapid urbanization and a return to favoring the modern project. Sometimes referred to as cultural modernism, this period was characterized by efforts "to represent the eternal and the immutable in the midst of . . . chaos" (Harvey 1989, 20) through methods such as shock tactics and montage or collage. The 1890s marked a shift to heroic modernism, which reached its apogee from 1910 to 1915, the period when urban planning became a profession and Frederick Winslow Taylor, Henry Ford, and Albert Kahn made their influential contributions to industrial production and consumption. Swept up in the euphoria of industrial progress, heroic modernism embraced and championed industrialization in contrast to cultural modernism's attempts to counter and criticize it. The Bauhaus, for instance, redefined "craft" as "the skill to mass-produce goods of an aesthetically pleasing nature with machine efficiency" (Harvey 1989, 24). Modernism, however, challenged the Enlightenment notion of a single unifying rationality, coinciding as it did with the dominance of industrial production and class struggles. It "took on multiple perspectivism and relativism as its epistemology for revealing what it still took to be the true nature of a unified, though complex, underlying reality" (Harvey 1989, 30).

Also during this period, the Athens Charter (written by Le Corbusier, based on the 1933 International Congress of Modern Architecture—CIAM) defined and codified modernist architecture and planning theory. The charter prescribed the separation and organization of functions (housing, work, recreation, circulation) through zoning regulations; regional planning; measurements based on the human scale; and professional standards of design carried out by experts with the assistance of modern technologies.[14] The eighth CIAM, held in London in 1945, took the Athens Charter to its logical extreme in declaring that industrialization had rendered social categories irrelevant. José Luis Sert organized the conference with the theme "The Heart of the City." Participants declared that the industrial mode of production had reduced everyone to *homo economicus*, yielding a monolithic mass society with widely shared aspirations and tastes. This conception of society at "degree zero" (Barthes) justified a functionalist approach which was to be pure, sterile, avant-garde, elitist, and esoteric.[15]

Louis Sullivan's dictum "form follows function," later adopted by Mies van der Rohe, succinctly expressed the ideology of functionalism in architecture and urban planning. Architects and planners who subscribed to this doctrine designed for an ideal Man rather than for real people, seeking to discover universal solutions. Architects aspired to create the architectural object, a building that stands alone without reference to its particular setting either physically or socially. Although this concept was not new,[16] the assertion that all building types should exist as isolated objects was new (T. Schumacher 1971, 81). Designers on the larger scale (urban planners) such as Ebenezer Howard, Patrick Geddes, Tony Garnier, and Le Corbusier proposed "ideal types" which could be applied anywhere, rather than specific plans appropriate for specific sites.[17]

Regarding the academic eclecticism of the Beaux-Arts as no longer evocative or symbolic of its time, modernism employed imagery related to machinery rather than to previous buildings, reflecting the faith in technology and the desire to create a technocratic utopia. Universalizing machine rationality provided a suitable organizing myth in the quest to contend with the disruptions and apparent disorder of industrialism. Anthony Vidler suggests that the machine/engine metaphor grew out of the need to confront mass production, especially the mass production of machines by machines. This new metaphor, he says, suggested that "buildings were to be no more and no less than machines themselves, serving and molding the needs of man according to economic criteria" (Vidler 1978, 30).[18]

With World War II and the growth of corporate capitalism in the 1950s, the international power system became relatively stable and so did the beliefs in linear progress, absolute truths, and rational planning. This condition ushered in universal or high modernism, in which the role of the market grew ever more influential.[19] With this period, cultural forms of expression, including urban design, were increasingly co-opted by the growing reach and power of the market. In the United States, this was epitomized by the Housing Acts of 1949 and 1954 and the Highway Act of 1954, which the real estate, building, and automotive industries had lobbied for, and which allowed for massive suburbanization along vehicular patterns. This appropriation of urban design by developers was also signaled by a symposium held at the MoMA in 1947, "What is Happening to Modern Architecture?," which derided recent regionalist design in the Bay Area and championed a return to essentialist modernism, Le Corbusier's Radiant City being the universal model (G. Wright 1994).

As a result, much of what was built after the war in both the US and Western Europe consisted of isolated towers as well as unending blocks of mass-produced single-family houses. Although modern urbanism may have been elegant and socially-responsible in the abstract, its realization "turned out to be repressive, ugly, sterile, antisocial, and generally disliked" (Relph 1987, 211) and by the late 1950s and early 1960s, criticism of modern urbanism began to mount. In its dogmatic insistence on purity, critics proclaimed, modernism bespoke its own death. Because of its inflexible tenets, it was neither conducive to evolving along with technology and cultural tastes nor could it reconcile biotechnical determinism with artistic intuition (McLeod 1983, 6–7).

In the late 1960s, the Six Day War (June 1967) in the Middle East and global economic restructuring set off fear of energy shortages, challenging the legitimacy of the modern project and urban designers' large-scale initiatives, a sentiment expressed by E. F. Schumacher in *Small is Beautiful* (1973).[20] Christopher Alexander's article "The City is Not a Tree" (1965) expressed the flaw in understanding the city in terms of mathematical models, and Lionel March's research demonstrated that the modernist preference for high-rise over low-rise housing was based on the mistaken assumption that it is space-saving (March 1967).

The challenge posed to rationality required reformulations of what urban design can and should be with regards to its formal components and the role of urban designers.[21] This contributed to the resurgence of anti-modernism, or to postmodernism, a reaction that featured a turn away from organic and mechanical models and a return to many aspects of traditional cities such as urbanity, mixed uses, and vernacular design. Urban designers took on a less authoritarian role and less ambitious attitude, often described as a humility, in part because the pressures of rapid development precluded the forethought required for rational thought.[22] The attempt to avoid a totalizing discourse in postmodern urbanism yielded concerted efforts to plan for a pluralistic society, to be populist, and to avoid colonialisms.[23]

But, as elaborated in chapter 5, these attempts to combat the negative aspects of modern urbanism have fallen into many of the same traps. This is because the critique of modern urbanism was large displaced and overly narrow, focusing on formal issues to the detriment of understanding the changing role of architects, planners, and the built environment in an evolving global political economy (a subject addressed in the following chapter). Although architecture and planning may appear to have come full circle as many recently built landscapes resemble pre-industrial ones, in actuality, these landscapes are now products of hyper-rational efforts.

Recent urban design inarguably advances the modern project because it refuses to relinquish the vast possibilities offered by new technologies and because it is embedded in larger market forces. Despite its prevalent romantic imagery, its mode of production, distribution, and consumption remain highly rational as do the lifestyles of the people who use it (with a few scattered exceptions). In architecture, an abandonment of the products and promises of the modern project would constitute an undeniable regression because its evolution has gone hand in hand with that of new technologies. And a challenge to the modern project on the part of planners would violate the very bases upon which planning rests since the profession emerged during the modern period and is predicated on modernist notions of rationality and progress. It is not surprising, then, that the architecture and planning professions have largely avoided reflecting too deeply upon the continued validity of the modern project.[24]

Pressed to ascertain whether this recent swing of the pendulum in urban design theory and practice has actually posed a challenge to the modern project or whether it has affirmed it, we must concede that as long as architects and planners seek technical and creative solutions to social problems in pursuit of progress, they continue to pursue the modern project. While contemporary urban design may break from the modern project formally and rhetorically, it actually continues it technologically, politically, and economically, perhaps with the exception of a growing sensitivity toward social diversity and toward the environment. Symbolically, contemporary urban design both continues and breaks from the modern project for it suggests to the general public a re-valorization of history, urbanity, the vernacular, and the community, while in fact only cosmetic changes are effected.[25] In sum, while contemporary urban design may constitute a symbolic break from modernism, in actuality, it continues the project, as is revealed by architects' and planners' goals, their means for implementing these goals, their products, and their means of assessing the relative success of these products.

Rather than avoid the drawbacks of modern urbanism, then, architecture and planning since the 1960s are guilty of much of the same, albeit unwittingly. This is largely because the political economy of advanced global capitalism and the continued prominence of positivistic thinking (despite challenges posed to it) impose constraints that limit its actual divergence. A reality which many architects and planners have preferred to ignore or minimize is that rather than following function, form has increasingly been following finance (see chapter 5). The prime mover, particularly in the more liberal economies, is less the architects and planners than the larger economic system in which they work and which functions according to the profit motive.[26] Like the initial claims of modern urban design to be populist,[27] those of postmodern urbanism have also been subverted, perhaps even more so. But designers are reluctant to acknowledge their ever-growing reliance upon the marketplace for it detracts from their potential for creative expression and for implementing change, not to mention their ability to preserve the legitimacy of their professions.

As a brief aside, even the deconstructivist trend falls subject to this critique, although pretending to break both from the Enlightenment project and from postmodernism by refusing to pave a path toward progress and by rejecting historical references except, perhaps, to industrial landscapes. In its reaction to postmodernism, deconstructivism mocks and steers away from pastiche historicism and "cutesy" picturesque architecture and urbanism which pretend to be something they are not. In this sense, it sees postmodernism as dishonest and calls for more honesty, like modernism. It is cynical in the extreme, however, for unlike both modernism and postmodernism, it does not really have a social agenda. It says the world is a mess, and that to design honestly, we should express that. And its coziness with elite benefactors permits a world that is heir to and progenitor of this project to appropriate it for its own agenda. Despite the media attention devoted to deconstructivism, its actual impact on the landscape, urban design professions, and evolving trends does not appear to be substantial or enduring. Rather, it seems more of a passing fancy of some designers dissatisfied with the bulk of what is being produced and seeking alternatives, commissions, and notoriety.

Postmodernism generally has thus been regarded by many not as post-paradigmatic, but as simply another swing of the pendulum. The rhetoric of modernity and postmodernity oppose one another, but since the underlying political economy has merely evolved rather than alter its course, many observers consider it more accurate to describe postmodernism as an evolution of modernism, rather than a rupture with it (for example, Zukin, Berman, Harvey). Gerald Graff, in an article entitled "The Myth of the Postmodernist Breakthrough" (1973), maintains, "postmodernism should be seen not as breaking with romantic and modernist assumptions but rather as a logical culmination of the premises of these earlier movements" (cited by Best and Kellner, 304).[28] Stjepan Mestrovic claims, "Despite its rebellious rhetoric, postmodernism, like modernity, takes a disparaging attitude towards the irrational aspects of life" (Mestrovic, 15) and, ultimately, extends modernity. Mestrovic finds that postmodernist writers rarely criticize bourgeois civilization as deeply as previous *fin-de-siècle* thinkers did (Mestrovic, 184), but have for the most part "continued the Enlightenment tradition by linking morality with the mind, not the heart" (Mestrovic, 108). He argues that "postmodern philosophy never truly rebels at the notion of rationality, never embraces compassion, and always maintains the commercialist, bourgeois status quo" (Mestrovic, x). Postmodernism, he concludes, is "one more bit of unnecessary jargon imposed upon humanity by intellectuals who suffer from excessive rationalism" (Mestrovic, 211).[29]

One way in which our intact bond to the modern tradition is revealed is in the resurgence of the Western idea modernity, or of history, such as national boundaries and imperialistic attitudes. Although it has been postulated that history has ended (Fukuyama 1989; 1992) and that we have transcended the dualisms characterizing modernity as well as its means of ascribing identities, the insecurity generated by the "time—space compression" (Harvey's term) of postmodernism incited a return to these (Robertson, 55). Consequently, we have been witnessing reassertions of national boundaries and imperialistic attitudes and behaviors, especially evident in the Gulf War. This perceived need to anchor ourselves in time and space (in the face of universalizing tendencies) is reminiscent of the "geopolitical" reflexes of the 1930s. Martin Heidegger, for instance, called for "rootedness in place and environmentally-bound traditions as the only secure foundation for political and social action in a manifestly troubled world" (Harvey 1989, 35).

With regard to expressive forms of culture, Huyssen asks, "whether this transformation has generated genuinely new aesthetic forms in the various arts or whether it mainly recycles techniques and strategies of modernism itself, reinscribing them into an altered cultural context" (Huyssen, 181). Maintaining that postmodernism "can now be described as a search for a viable modern tradition" outside of the canon of classical modernism, he exclaims that "the postmodernist search for cultural tradition and continuity, which underlies all the radical rhetoric of rupture, discontinuity, and epistemological breaks, has turned to that tradition which fundamentally and on principle despised and denied all traditions" (Huyssen, 169).

Contrary to stereotypical accounts, postmodern urbanism is not distinct from modern urbanism in its historicism but in its catholicism of historical references and its motivations for using the past.[30] While the modernists were partial to strict Classical architecture, postmodernists most commonly favor medievalism (Gothic and Romanesque), neoclassicism, and rationalism. Alan Plattus remarks:

> "Postmodernism has not only recapitulated many of the theoretical strategies of the 18th and 19th century, from typology to eclecticism to outright revivalism, it

has also had recourse to some of the same strategies invoked by modernism in its
quest for a stable source of order and authority that would transcend the vagaries
of style, taste, and the increasingly voracious art market. neotraditionalism and
neomodernism thus appear as more or less superficially different responses to the
same problem. More recent efforts to escape the crisis of authority by accepting—
and, in some cases, celebrating—its apparently radical consequences are heavily
indebted, both formally and intellectually, to the experiments and polemics of the
early 20th-century avant-gardes." (Plattus, 69)

In this vein, Jacques Lucan (1978) discerns instructive similarities
among Viollet-le-Duc, Le Corbusier, and the neorationalists of recent
years. In addition to all having strong roots in France, they share the belief
that architecture was suffering a crisis and invoked "reason" to remedy it,
considering themselves "rationalists." All three draw inspiration from a
past, albeit different pasts: Viollet-le-Duc from the Middle Ages, Le Corbusier from the Parthenons of ancient Greece, and the neorationalists
from eighteenth-century Europe. For all three, these pasts represent
moments of *"Harmonie"* in architectural form, production, and collective
reception that they wish to "re-conquer" [*reconquérir*]. These comparisons
highlight the continuities between modernism and postmodernism, with
the former seeking a return to an apocryphal "harmonious" past and the
latter carrying at least a part of the Enlightenment/modern torch.

As Frampton points out, early modernists such as Mies van der Rohe
and Kahn were not ignoring the past but reassembling "its precepts and
components in accordance with the technological capacity of the epoch"
and they "would have seen the advent of Post-Modernism as cultural
decadence" (Frampton 1985, 305) for its failure to acknowledge and
incorporate change. It was modernism's intent on accommodating the
changes wrought by industrialization which led to a neglect of the existing city and the human component that postmodernism has in turn been
seeking to correct. But postmodern urbanism's tendency to turn its back
on change casts it in a regressive rather than a progressive light.[31]

In the final analysis, the reactions to modernism since the 1960s
reveal themselves to be an evolution of modernist rationality, despite
their rhetoric which pretends to oppose it. Nonetheless, this continuity
is obscured, because contemporaries and historians of the modern
period tend to emphasize its universalizing tendencies while those of the
postmodern period highlight its concern with multivalence and

localisms. The largely monolithic and starkly opposing interpretations of these two periods might be interpreted as an effort by intellectuals and artists (including architects) to create a niche for themselves paralleling actual transformations in market capitalism, which targets the largest number of consumers, reduces complexity to slogans which will sell, and constantly revamps these slogans to retain a captive market interested and buying. With regards to urban design specifically, the widespread expressions of discontent in the late 1960s incited marketers, politicians, developers, builders, planners, and architects to propose something entirely new-and-improved, something which was in fact the opposite of what already existed. While the wrapper has vastly changed, however, the content remains largely the same.[32] And solutions to urban design dilemmas largely continue to elude.

Echoing Adorno and C.W. Mills (see chapter 4), Jameson interprets contemporary trends as simply the cultural logic of late capitalism and contends that both the rational and romantic tendencies derive from Enlightenment thought, in some ways paralleling Mills's socialist and liberal tendencies. Paraphrasing Tafuri, Jameson contends, "The Enlightenment attempt to think of urbanism in some new and more fully rational way generates two irreconcilable alternatives: one path is that of architecture as the 'instrument of social equilibrium' [social control, uniformity, equality]. . . . The other is that of a 'science of sensations,' a kind of 'excessive symbolism' which we may interpret as the conception of a libidinal resistance within the system, the breakthrough of desire into the grids of power and control" (Jameson 1985), which originated in Baudelaire.[33] Like Jameson, Harvey suggests that it is the coincidence of these apparently contradictory impulses that characterizes modernity and postmodernity (generally) and distinguishes them from pre-modernity (Harvey 1989, 240–41).

Stephen Toulmin describes the current temper as bearing a "strand of experience continuing ahead" and a "strand of doctrine closing back into an Omega" (Toulmin, 172). With the increasingly disguised profit-making and power-holding mechanisms of late-industrial capitalism, perhaps the two poles of rationalism and romanticism exist in greater extremes, so that we have an apparently paradoxical situation in which a pronounced anti-technocratic impulse (manifest as tribalism or geopoliticism) and a quest for intense passionate experience (physically, emotionally, and spiritually) exist side by side with an increasingly fragmented self-identity served up by increasing rationality (Lears's shift from a Protestant to a therapeutic world view). This quest favors unpredictability, spontaneity, complexity, and ineluctable experience that defies explanation. The concerted effort to know along with the pronounced skepticism of such authority has made irony (and sometimes despair) the tone of the day. Legitimacy crises abound and genres blur in an attempt to resolve them.

Very impressionistically speaking, if we examine the way in which order has been regarded in discourse over the years, we see not a linear progression toward decreasing tolerance for disorder and a greater desire for control, but something more like a pendular swing from such a desire for control over "disorder" to a value placed on tolerance for diversity, cultural pluralism, and relativism and then back to a need for some imposition of order. In the arts, in cultural theory, and in urban design we see a shift from a kind of formalism in the early part of the century to the more recent expressionistic multiplicity and amplitude, or in Robert Venturi's articulation, from either/or to both/and. Illustrating this changing temper, chaos theory was actually posited around the turn of the century but the intense desire for order, uniformity, and predictability led to a resistance to chaos theory, which did not become acceptable until the more recent shift to appreciating disorder and skepticism. From the perspective of control, however, the progression appears more linear: from less extrinsic control, to a form in which the mechanisms of control are apparent, to more illusive forms of control which are often mistaken for its absence.

The Marxian view sees the current situation as an extension of the past without prospect for improvement until there is a structural change in the political economy. This is why Manfredo Tafuri, who was instrumental in introducing radical alternatives in *Architecture and Utopia: Design and Capitalist Development* (original 1973, English 1976), is ultimately pessimistic with regard to the possibilities for effecting social changes through architecture. In his view, the hegemony of global capitalism will ultimately succeed in co-opting anything architects produce. Jameson similarly believes that architects can be political like anyone else, but that "their architecture today cannot be political" without "total revolutionary and systematic transformation" (Jameson 1985) of the political economy.

Postmodern urbanism tends not to challenge bourgeois society, but works within it, seeking inspiration from the history that the moderns rejected. That is why it is post- and not avant-. In this respect, perhaps it connotes a "selling out," an acknowledgment of defeat or of not even trying to finish an as yet "unfinished project." Yet current trends also demonstrate a greater concern with the meanings that environments have for their users and with quality of life rather than the more exclusive concern with functionality. In defense of postmodern urbanism, many of its products—such as pedestrian pockets, traditional neighborhood developments, courtyard housing and townhouse communities, the festival marketplace, the renovation of central city districts—are widely considered superior to products of modern urbanism, such as the tower-in-the-park, the suburban shopping mall, and the tract home. These new spaces offer possibilities for a lifestyle that was largely precluded from the urbanism of 1945–70, when the emphasis was on separating functions.[34] The fact that this lifestyle is not available to all is unfortunate and efforts on the part of designers to change this are admirable. But such change can not be accomplished through urban design alone.

PRESCRIPTIONS

The second debate as to whether or not urban designers should be pursuing the modern project is hotly contested. While abandoning emancipatory goals through design is not the answer, neither is strict adherence to the modern project, which has revealed itself as deeply flawed. The question thus becomes: How can we subscribe to an overarching interpretive framework if we oppose the centralized authority and scientific method implied by meta-narratives and rationality? Or, to contextualize this debate within the currents of historical change, it becomes a question of how best to combine local traditions with globalization. Paul Ricoeur articulated this dilemma as follows: "We have the feeling that this single world civilization at the same time exerts a sort of attrition or wearing away at the expense of the cultural resources which have made the great civilizations of the past. This threat is expressed, among other disturbing effects, by the spreading before our eyes of a mediocre civilization. . . . It seems as if mankind, by approaching *en masse* a basic consumer culture, were also stopped *en masse* at a subcultural level. . . . There is the paradox: How to become modern and to return to the sources; how to revive an old dormant civilization and take part in universal civilization" (1961; cited by Frampton 1983a, 16). Sometimes the goal of this search is described as "alternative modernities" (as in Gutiérrez 1994).

As elaborated above, wholesale abandonment of the ideals which stem from the Enlightenment[35] would present certain dangers, namely a subjectivism which loses sight of the larger good and which offsets a confusion as to goals, both of which confer greater power upon the marketplace and state and which usher in a decline in creativity and ideals, ultimately boding poorly for improving the world.[36] In urban design, as described in the preceding chapter, the contemporary challenge to modernist ideals has led to a turning inward, allowing the market ever greater sway, to the point where it largely determines what gets built. And the decline of the dominant world view of modernism with no consensus to replace it has generated a sense of insecurity, leading designers to generate environments which are photograph-able and increasingly hyperreal,[37] to justify their work with something else, and to seek power, prestige, and pecuniary rewards. These goals, in turn, mask the true sources of discontent with the contemporary landscape as well as among design professionals, thereby obscuring the path towards improvement.

For the planning profession in particular, the challenge to the legitimacy of scientism threatened its very *raison d'être*, which included the assumption that there exists a common good and that properly trained experts can access it (Appelbaum, 148). The reactions of planners to the challenge to the modern project, from which the planning profession emerged, varied. While some turned to the invisible hand of the free market, others pinned their hopes on new technologies, and still others allowed planning to serve the purposes of propaganda and repression (Friedmann, 311). A minority sought to identify the structural bases for unequal access to resources and uneven development and to propose structural transformations (for example, Harvey, Castells, Friedmann).

In society generally, the current sense of confusion has elicited a nostalgia for an idealized past and a desire to return to it, as well as an obsession with mass imagery. In academia, this reflex is manifest as a call to return to the canon of Western thought and a retreat from political engagement to focus more on issues of style. In urban design, it is manifest as historicism and allusions to mass culture. In all of these, the seen-it-all done-it-all sophistication combined with the choice to be disengaged has engendered a blasé attitude and a studied ironic response. In its extreme, this becomes a retreat from asking questions and from acting. Although sometimes touted as the only responsible course given the circumstances of the contemporary world, this tendency recalls the saying of the ancient Chinese philosopher Wang Yang-Ming, "To know and not to act, is ultimately not to know" (in Dutton 1986, 25).

At the other end of the spectrum, there are those who follow the modernist tradition by authoritatively positing new universals or paradigms or by seeking salvation in new technologies. Esa Saarinen, for instance, endorses "the shift from a logocentric and a cogito-centered culture of isolation to a world of cooperative and communicative action" primarily through exploiting media technologies and the possibilities created by them, a strategy he describes as "media philosophy"(Saarinen).[38] In urban design, this is manifest as a conviction that computer technologies, serial production, and other technologies hold the answers to our problems by combining the diversity and craftsmanship of pre-industrial production with the democratic possibilities of industrial production, without their respective disadvantages. But most are more circumspect about hedging their bets on new technologies, the classic science fiction theme of technologies coming to dominate their creators (expressing patricidal phobias) hovering ever nearer.

Another reflex has been the spiritual one. With the replacement of a communications zeitgeist for a labor zeitgeist (see chapter 4), Habermas has observed that utopian expectations seem to be taking on a religious guise once again. With the faltering of faith in the modern project, there has been a (re)turn to spirituality and mysticism throughout the Western world. In the tradition of earlier thinkers such as Kant and Nietzsche, a number of recent observers of the human condition have also called for a spiritual turn to mollify the harshness of the modern world, including Derrida, Lacan, Foucault, Kristeva, Barthes, Griffin, and Jencks.[39] To give one example, Spretnak suggests turning to wisdom traditions such as Buddhism, Native American spirituality, Goddess spirituality, and the Semitic traditions, which can "help us to nourish wonder and hence to appreciate difference, the unique subjectivity of every being and community, thereby subverting the flattening process of mass culture. Such awareness keeps hope alive. It protects consciousness from becoming so beaten down that it loses a grasp of what is worth fighting to defend" (Spretnak, 223). David Griffin describes this spiritual turn as a move from disenchantment to re-enchantment. Perhaps this return to a more mystical or religious utopian vision reflects a reconceptualization of space whereby symbolic space is privileged over physical space, which has been largely neutralized.

In an effort to recover the "civic society" we have lost, but without denying change that has occurred or reneging on the opportunities it offers, another impulse has been to identify or seek to create copasetic communities. Although this effort recalls the geopoliticisms of the modern period, this time, the "geo-" can be figurative. Proposals for doing so include Lyotard's "local determinisms," Fish's "interpretive communities," Foucault's "heterotopias," and the contextualist's "vest pocket utopias." While mindful of avoiding the dangerous consequences of the modern geopoliticisms, these posit spaces (literal or figurative) in which "otherness" can flourish. The novelist Italo Calvino expressed this reflex saying: "The inferno of the living is not something that will be; if there is one it is what is already here, the inferno where we live every day, that we form by being together. There are two ways to escape from suffering it. The first is easy for many: accept the inferno and become such a part of it that you can no longer see it. The second is risky and demands constant vigilance and apprehension: seek and learn to recognize who and what, in the midst of the inferno, are not inferno, then make them endure, give them space" (voiced through his character Marco Polo, Calvino, 165).

In urban design, this effort is apparent in Jencks's strategy of double coding (defined, chapter 3, 108–09). An effort to resist the universalizing tendency of modernism, yet offer nonetheless an explanation and model for the current scene, this strategy seeks to affirm and deny "the existing power structures at the same time, inscribing and challenging differing tastes and opposite forms of discourse" (Jencks 1992, 13). By simultaneously appealing to various audiences, double coded urban design is intended to preserve differences within "a new synthesis on a higher level" (Jencks 1992, 13–14). Although not necessarily intended to resolve the differences, Jencks maintains, this may occur (Jencks 1992).[40]

This tendency is also revealed by Frampton's effort to resist the negative aspects of globalization through "critical regionalism," a strategy which seeks to achieve "a manifest critique of universal civilization" by mediating "the impact of universal civilization with elements derived indirectly from the peculiarities of a particular place" (Frampton 1983a, 20) (see chapter 3). If urban design is to retain its critical capacity, Frampton asserts, it must assume "an *arrière-garde* position, that is to say, one which distances itself equally from the Enlightenment myth of progress and from a reactionary, unrealistic impulse to return to the architectonic forms of the preindustrial past. A critical *arrière-garde* has to remove itself from both the optimization of advanced technology and the ever-present tendency to regress into nostalgic historicism or the glibly decorative. It is my contention that only an *arrière-garde* has the capacity to cultivate a resistant, identity-giving culture while at the same time having discreet recourse to universal technique" (ibid.).

The ecological and the ecofemimist critiques seek to inject a sense of values which counter the traditional Eurocentric patriarchal values of rational objectivity, separateness, autonomy, and control with those of transactive subjectivity, togetherness, and the nurturance and protection of others as well as the environment. This attitude is seen, for instance, in Friedmann's departure from his initial understanding of planning as relying on scientific and technical knowledge to a radical approach relying on subjective knowledge (Friedmann, 413–15). It is also evident in the suggestions of many writers that local and global problems of urbanization and urbanism will only be resolved through a substitution of matrifocal for patrifocal values and assumptions or at least by redressing the balance. Seeking to avert the deleterious effects of economic restructuring, for instance, Logan and Swanstrom proposed replacing "the masculine metaphor of cutthroat competition for mobile capital" with "a more feminine image of nurturing the strength of the local context," "of economic development based on embeddedness" (Logan and Swanstrom, 21).

While contemporary urban design largely breaks from the modern project in theory, its implementation is nonetheless embedded in it. This disjunction between means and ends can be traced to an insufficient consideration of the context in which building occurs, and its unfortunate results include wasted resources and acute frustration among designers. A clearer understanding of the current scene could assist urban designers in aligning means to ends and in more fully realizing their ameliorative goals. To achieve this understanding, we must learn from our experience, past and present, by separating (or deconstructing) its various components, assessing them, and then reassembling them in a way which best applies the designer's creative capabilities to the problem at hand.

We must also rid ourselves of reductive political associations with either modern or postmodern urbanism, which inevitably bias debate. The conflation of modern urbanism with the modern project links the noble goals of "liberty, equality, and fraternity" with both undertakings and, by extension, imputes neoconservative values—or an "un-enlightened" condition—to postmodern architecture and urbanism. In Europe particularly, these associations have incited a reluctance to abandon modern architecture and urbanism[41] as readily as some of their North American counterparts.[42] This is why Habermas's critical address and article about the Venice Biennale (1981) made such a splash there.[43] It is also largely why the qualifier "postmodern" elicits snickers and pejorative connotations and why so many (particularly European) architects and planners plant themselves firmly in the modernist camp. And it explains a tendency among critics (both lay and professional) to simply describe urban design that they applaud, as modern, and that which they deplore, as postmodern.

In learning from modern urbanism, we must consider the wide variation among modernist townscapes in conception, realization, and inhabitation. And despite the shortcomings widely attributed to modernist townscapes, we must also remember that some are highly regarded by urban design professionals as well as laypersons. Indeed, sociological studies (for example, Castells 1983, 78–85) suggest that people who live in them report a sense of community and an attachment to their neighborhoods. At the same time, we should avoid overestimating the happiness people manage to summon in such settings. Indeed, coping—the ability to make the most of a situation and to ascribe meaning and value to the world in which we live—is a universal human attribute. In addition, over-zealous social scientists in search of knowledge about the Other have managed to discover a "sense of community" in virtually every group they study, an almost inevitable occupational hazard of their empathic and relativistic theory and method. Though there are undeniably grounds for averting the wrecker's ball from many of these settings, the oft-celebrated tenacity, resourcefulness, and sociability of the inhabitants should not be taken as proof that their built environment is optimal, cannot benefit from improvements, and should be emulated. Holston's close scrutiny of Brasilia, for example, leads him to conclude, "We have seen that modernist intentions end up dialectically reversed with enough regularity that we are justified in repudiating their utopian project and demanding an alternative" (Holston, 315).

But rather than reject modern urbanism outright, we should isolate flaws in the design logic, such as the decline of meaningful public space and the social and symbolic stigma associated with low-income housing for which modern urbanism was often applied. Likewise, we must isolate flaws in the design logic of postmodern urbanism from other expressed sources of dissatisfaction, such as the creation of places which are exclusionary and which heighten paranoia through omnipresent surveillance. Then we should adapt the good aspects of both modern and postmodern urbanism to contemporary design projects on a case-by-case basis, depending on the particular site, client, prospective users, and the program. And if we aspire to effect change beyond that which the program allows, such as altering zoning regulations, allocating more funds and better sites for public housing, or promoting social equality and harmony, we must avoid confusing ends with means and acknowledge that these goals, although they may be related to the project, are extrinsic to it and must be pursued independently.[44]

Although urban designers may bemoan the decline of modern ideals and of the public realm, it is folly to assume that certain forms will make these reappear. Moreover, it is inconsiderate to impose urban design that assumes a different way of life upon inhabitants unwilling to be guinea pigs (particularly for "affordable housing"). Like anyone else, architects and planners may engage in struggles for social change, but through political means, not urban design, unless they are experimenting on themselves. And until the social and political changes occur, they must settle upon an interim compromise in their professional practice. The only realistic exception to this would require a large piece of land, along with architects, developers, and investors who share a vision, and a sufficient number of inhabitants who are willing to take a risk and have the confidence that their property values will remain stable. But the belief that planners and architects might change society through changing built form is a conceit which, in most cases, only ends up frustrating users and designers alike.

To complete or to abandon the modern project? Architects and planners might best answer that query in a qualified manner. If they are to accomplish anything at all, they must retain a certain faith that improvement (or progress) is possible. In order to believe this, they must have some means of deciding what constitutes improvement. Sustained by an understanding of the potential applications of the modern project, they might avoid its negative uses—the domination and destruction of other people and the environment—without leaving the direction of change solely to market logic or the state. This is how we might define progressive urban design. Although contemporary urban designers rarely have the means to effect deep and lasting structural change, we nonetheless harbor the potential to make a limited and localized difference. And if we do not become part of the solution, we invariably become part of the problem.

NOTES

1. If the Enlightenment, or the modern project, is understood as "the domination of nature in order to produce a wealth of commodities which are intended to sustain a community of mutually recognizing free and equal subjects" (Angus, 96), then it can not be condoned, because people are a part of nature (Harvey 1989, 13).

2. Also contributing to poststructuralist thought were Roland Barthes, Julia Kristeva, and others. These predominantly French theorists continued the French counter-Enlightenment tradition rooted in the works of de Sade, Bataille, and Artaud among others (Best and Kellner, 22). Their critique also existed within the larger tradition described in chapter 1 (note 2). While furthering the structuralist focus on language as the key to meaning, poststructuralists asserted that signs are arbitrarily constructed instead of assuming a presumed unity between signifier and signified.

3. Lyotard defines the postmodern as "incredulity towards meta-narratives" (cited by Harvey 1989, 45).

4. For a history and inside perspective of the neoconservative movement, see Daniel Bell (1992, 83–86).

5. Bell sees current trends as the institutionalization of the creative impulses of modernism when high-brow authority over cultural taste gave way in the 1960s to pop art, pop culture, ephemeral fashion, and mass taste (Harvey 1989, 60).

6. Habermas's affinity for the modern project is perhaps revealed in his choice to live in a modernist house, which he had built in 1971, referring to the work of Adolph Loos (Stephens 30).

7. With regards to the "neoconservatives" proper, Mestrovic points out that Habermas "does not see that the West's neoconservative ideologies are an extension of the very project he proposes to complete" (Mestrovic, 203).

8. Habermas described this "thread" that runs through his work, saying: "I think that a certain form of unrestrained communication brings to the fore the deepest force of reason, which enables us to overcome egocentric or ethnocentric perspectives and reach an expanded . . . view" (cited by Stephens, 30).

9. Applying Marxian theory, which is itself an Enlightenment strategy, David Harvey largely shares this perspective. While appreciating the poststructuralist insistence upon acknowledging that all representations are historically and linguistically mediated, he finds it too relativistic and nihilistic, maintaining that the notion that coherent representation and action are repressive or illusionary precludes the prospect of global political engagement, leaving Dewey's pragmatism the only path of action (Harvey 1989, 52, 59).

10. This critique holds that the poststructuralist valorization of separateness, autonomy, and control values the individual who is nomadic, undomesticated, and unattached to a family, a community, or the Earth and casts all relationships in terms of a power struggle (Spretnak). Charlene Spretnak locates the origins of this attitude "in patriarchal culture's brutal and self-destructive divorce from the body—the Earthbody, the female body, the body of the mother" (Spretnak, 135). Perceiving an opposition between self and other, she says, the patriarchal attitude teaches us to "neutralize the other as being the same or complementary" (ibid.) and in doing so, it negates the female body (Spretnak, 122–24). The "aggressive surge of denial called

for by deconstructionism," Spretnak maintains, "leads to a flattened valuelessness in which nothing is left but the will to power" (Spretnak, 260). Deconstructive postmodernism, she maintains, is a philosophical justification for deeply engrained perceptions of profound separateness which yield "alienation, deep-seated rage, and reactive cravings for autonomy and control" (Spretnak, 260–61). Embracing this philosophical position, Spretnak says, is ultimately the most repressive act for it is a "cultural construction of the deepest loneliness" (Spretnak, 219).

11. Spretnak elaborates: "Just as modern scientists discounted and ignored perturbations observed outside of the accepted model, so modern economists ignored the effects of unqualified economic growth on the 'fragment' of the whole that is nature. Modern statesmanship proceeded by ignoring the sovereignty of native people, a 'fragment' that was clearly outside the accepted model, and modern rationalists denied any spiritual perceptions as anomalous quirks not to be mentioned. With the liberating sensibilities of ecological postmodernism, however, scientists engaged in chaos research now try to absorb into their conclusions everything they observe through their measurements; ecological economists consider the total costs of production, including the depletion of our primary 'capital,' the biosphere; advocates of a postmodern world order defend the precious diversity of cultures that comprise the planetary whole; and people no longer boxed in by the tight constraints of highly selective modern rationalism now allow themselves subtle perceptions of the grand unity, the ground of the sacred" (Spretnak, 19–20).

12. In similar fashion, the "alternative" postmodernism posited by Andreas Huyssen does not merely use history and tradition, but challenges the patriarchal presuppositions of Western civilization, which in turn calls for reconceiving notions about power relations among people, cultures, nations, and ultimately between people and nature. An alternative postmodernism, he explains, is one "in which resistance, critique, and negation of the status quo were redefined in non-modernist and non-avantgardist terms, terms which match the political developments in contemporary culture more effectively than the older theories of modernism" (Huyssen, 188). While acknowledging that the fascination with the past is shared by "the simple-minded rearguard assertion of traditional norms and values" (Huyssen, 172), he warns against confusing these diametrically opposed political intentions even though they exist side by side and often appear to support one another. Deriding poststructuralism as being just an extreme version of modernism (Huyssen, 209), he maintains that the critical potential for postmodernism lies "in its radical questioning of those presuppositions which linked modernism and the avantgarde to the mindset of modernization" (Huyssen, 183).

13. In an effort to synthesize postmodern views, Pauline Marie Rosenau (1992) discerns affirmative and skeptical tendencies. She describes the affirmative one (which roughly correlates with constructive postmodernism) by saying: "More indigenous to Anglo-North American culture than to the Continent, the generally optimistic affirmatives are oriented toward process. They are either open to positive political action (struggle and resistance) or content with the recognition of visionary, celebratory personal nondogmatic projects that range from New Age religion to New Wave life-styles and include a whole spectrum of post-modern social movements. Most affirmatives seek

a philosophical and ontological intellectual practice that is nondogmatic, tentative, and nonideological. These post-modernists do not, however, shy away from affirming an ethic, making normative choices, and striving to build issue-specific political coalitions" (Rosenau, 15–16). Their politics in the Third World "takes the form of populist, fundamentalist, nationalist" social movements which "call for returning to the primitive, sacred, and traditional society as well as rejecting First World ideologies, technologies and economics" (Rosenau, 24). "Although ambivalent about reason, few affirmatives are willing to abandon it altogether. They sometimes evaluate knowledge claims on the basis of normative preferences or community standards" (Rosenau, 23). This is one way in which they seek to be both intellectually consistent and relevant. The skeptics (which roughly correlate with the poststructuralists), by contrast, "are political agnostics, proposing that all political views are mere constructions and generally avoiding advocacy of any type. Some are pessimistic about the possibility of changing society. Hence they argue for nonparticipation as the most revolutionary position in the post-modern age. Others consider play and euphoria the best alternatives to traditional, modern political action. . . . In the extreme, some skeptics talk of terror, suicide, and violence as the only truly authentic political gestures that remain open" (Rosenau, 23–24). Daniel Bell encapsulates the current attitudes among Western society generally, saying that with the Enlightenment project now receded, people are "occupied by a cultural nihilism, a melioristic liberalism, and a conservative defense of traditional values" (1992, 107).

14. The ideas set forth in the Athens Charter were intended to resolve "the urban and social crises attributed to the unbridled domination of private interests in the public realm of the city, in the accumulation of wealth, and in the development of industry" (Holston). The Charter thus called for collective action and collective rights over private interests, including the power to engage in land reform (expropriations). It called for new typologies as well as new ways of living in these. By eliminating the street, this design ideology also eliminated "the type of urban crowd and public activity that streets support" (Holston, 52). In planning a city in a park, it proposed "a new focus on sports for the displaced public activity of streets" (ibid.). It reconceived the "relationship between residence, work, and commerce, and between market and marketplace" (ibid.) recommending, for instance, decreased dependence on family as an economic unit and increased reliance on the public sphere of collective services.

15. The appropriate role of the architect followed from these intentions. The modern era, says Alain Guiheux, saw "the emergence of an Architect with the desire to take in hand the salvation of humanity, a radically new role with the stated aim of transforming the conditions of life emanating from the apparently anarchic and cancerous development of towns from the industrial revolution. . . . Neither Vitruvius, Alberti, nor Perrault had envisaged for an instant that their science would extend beyond its limits" (Guiheux, 18.). For modern architects of the early twentieth century, however, "The project was total: art, politics, housing, the territorial and social aspects of life, everything in fact" (ibid.). For them, "the supposed model inhabitant was particularly basic: his needs were evidently primary. Above all he had no desires and certainly no fantasies. Transparent, he was also universal, whatever his culture, age, sex or profession. His size, his gestures in the kitchen were coded. Art was transformed

into an anthropometric laboratory" (ibid.). Le Corbusier described the new order of things as *l'esprit nouveau* and he maintained (until his political *prise de conscience*) that only the elite can comprehend this, for everyone else is immured in romanticism.

16. Alberti, Palladio, and others also designed architectural objects.

17. Modernism diverged from both the romantic and the classic traditions in its attitude toward public space: "The romantic and classic traditions may appear contrary, but they share one basic trait: the public space—either street, square, or plaza—is the dominant form. The buildings are subservient. Though less true of the romantic, both traditions use urban buildings as the 'walls' of great outdoor 'rooms,' with the facades ornamenting and unifying, and public art 'furnishing' these rooms. Garnier's plan expresses a totally new sense: the building becomes the object, not defining the public space, but situated in it. . . . The buildings become autonomous forms placed in a park-like setting" (Calthorpe 1986, 203–04). The proposals of both Le Corbusier and Frank Lloyd Wright were thus modern in their conception of form because they conceived of "the building as an autonomous object maintaining responsibility only to internal functions, rather than the old urban tradition in which the building defined the public space that it fronted" (Calthorpe 1986, 206).

18. Tracing the evolution of modernist thought, Vidler writes. "The natural analogy of the Enlightenment, originally brought forward to control the messy reality of the city, was now extended to refer to the control of entire nature. . . . A vision of Taylorized production, of a world ruled by the iron law of Ford supplanted the spuriously golden dream of neoclassicism" (Vidler 1978, 30). As Bernard Huet explains, the "functional" city was conceived as a "space of Euclidean abstraction regulated by quantity and industrial repetition, a space whose three fundamental characteristics are homogeneity, isotropy, and fragmentation, and which presents itself as the absolute antithesis of the space of the 'historic' city. The model of the 'functional' city is the most accomplished expression of a 'scientific' urbanism which progressively detached itself from the practices of urban art at the beginning of the twentieth century and whose exclusive object is the rational administration of housing the masses in industrial society" (Huet 1986, 12). The outcome, according to Vidler, was that "Architecture, in this final apotheosis of mechanical progress, was consumed by the very process it sought to control for its own ends. With it, the city, as artifact and polis disappeared as well" (Vidler 1978, 30).

19. Harvey describes the period of high modernism as "a corporate capitalist version of the Enlightenment project of development" (Harvey 1989, 35–36). Jameson contends, "The new utopianism of high modernism unwittingly and against the very spirit of its revolutionary and utopian affirmations prepared the terrain for the omnipotence of the fully 'rationalized' technocratic plan, for the universal planification of what was to become the total system of multinational capital" (paraphrasing Tafuri; Jameson 1985, 78). This period of modernism, he says, "ended up rationalizing the object world more extensively and ferociously than anything Ford or Taylor might have done on his own momentum" (Jameson 1985, 80).

20. These events provoked distrust in the "ideology of industrial building and technical improvement as a solution to the ills of the city" and "the conviction grew that economic growth was not the unmitigated social blessing it had been believed to be" (Rykwert, no page nos).

21. In his introductory statement to the catalogue, "Precursors of Postmodernism, Milan 1920s–30s," Emilio Ambasz describes this shift with regards to architecture specifically: "In their relentless pursuit of Utopian models, the architects of the Modern Movement engaged in a Long Journey they believed would lead, in the course of generations, to social justice and a humane world. The price paid for such a single— minded quest was the neglect of the Short Journey-the twenty-four hours of the day, the many daily routines and rituals of which Long Journeys are composed. In order to see the future clearly and run toward it lightly, these pursuers of Utopia unburdened themselves of architectural memories. Seeking to achieve purity as they approached their ever-receding goal, they also deprived themselves of the pleasures of ornament and texture. Hence, the Day, as the measurement of an individual's existential cycle, was sacrificed to The Generation as the earliest due date for social reckoning" (Ambasz). Ambasz remarks: "The tragic realization that for the sake of long term dreams, whole generations have rejected the heritage of their architectural forefathers has lately dawned on us—and with different degrees of response" (ibid.).

22. It was no longer "self-evident that rational, scientific knowledge of the social world is possible [and] that the presumed objectivity of the physical scientist provides an adequate model for the human sciences" (Appelbaum, 148).

23. I do not wish to imply in this discussion that the modern response was a consensually rational one. Because the modern condition is generally portrayed thus, however, discussions of counter trends have tended to classify them as "anti-modern" (for example, Lears). Analogously, more recent efforts at rationalizing are regarded as late modern or neomodern as distinguished from postmodern. Unlike the predominantly seamless descriptions of modernity which appeared earlier, however, the more recent chroniclers reveal a more postmodern temper which is less exclusive and prone to categorize and more tolerant of—even indulgent towards—chaos and contradiction, of diverse threads which don't necessarily weft and warp into a single cloth. Whereas the more typical modern accounts of modernity sought to somehow transmogrify perceived fragmentation into a unity, the more typical postmodern account of modernity and postmodernity appears to revel in and emphasize fragmentation.

24. James Mayo points out that few planning theorists have addressed the debates of postmodernism, citing Charles Hoch who explained that "the postmodern critique of the sort inspired by Foucault persuasively uncovers the productive quality of power relations at the very core of our moral practice but then seems to leave us no way to decide what political actions are better than others" (Mayo, 230).

25. Gwendolyn Wright develops this thesis from an opposite angle, arguing that some of the most interesting contemporary urban design proposals "are motivated by similar concerns and even expressed in comparable language" to those of the interwar period, particularly by American architects, many of whom "envisioned their buildings not as isolated objects, but as part of cohesive communities within existing cities and towns," "employed a vernacular diction that drew more from local history and ordinary speech than from abstract rhetoric," and "rejected the idea of universally beautiful forms or solutions" (G. Wright 1994, 27). These concerns were obscured, according to Wright's analysis, after World War II. Joan Ockman,

however, argues similarly for the post–World War II period (Ockman 1993).

26. Douglas Crimp maintains, "The present condition of architecture is one in which architects debate academic, abstract aesthetics while they are in fact in the thrall of the real-estate developers who are ruining our cities and turning working class people out of their homes" (cited by Harvey 1989, 114).

27. As Paul Goldberger explains, the 1932 Modern Architecture exhibition at the MoMA, which was largely responsible for bringing the modern movement to the United States, presented a set of rules for making modern architecture: "Nowhere but here did there seem to be such narrow dictates, nowhere but with the gurus of the International Style was there so much concern with pronouncing buildings acceptable or unacceptable. . . . The International Style was never really about much of anything except esthetics anyway, in the end. There was much talk about social responsibility, and about using new technology and modern materials, but these factors could never hold a candle to the question of how a building looked" (Goldberger 1983, 26, originally February 28, 1982). The co-optation of the modern movement by the marketplace (of finance and of style) occurred especially in the United States, a thesis popularized by Tom Wolfe in *From Bauhaus to Our House* (1982). Ultimately, then, the Modern Movement was co-opted by that which it was trying to subvert.

28. Describing the deconstructive or eliminative brand of postmodernism, Griffin maintains that it "could be called ultramodernism, in that its eliminations result from carrying modern premises to their logical conclusions" (Griffin 1989; cited by Jencks 1992, 33). Umberto Eco has similarly described postmodernism as resulting from a series of eliminations proposed by the avant-garde. Alex Callinicos (1990) also argues that most elements of postmodernism were anticipated by modernism.

29. Mestrovic asserts that although postmodernism appears "to be an extension and exacerbation of Gesellschaft values, other-directedness, anomie, and other elements of modernity [it is] not a genuine rebellion nor reaction against modernity" (Mestrovic, 29). Best and Kellner elaborate upon Mestrovic's thesis saying: "Perhaps postmodern theory was a fad and epiphenomenon of the 1980s, an expression of the failure of nerve and alienation of intellectuals in the face of the dashed utopian political hopes of the 1960s, their potential obsolescence in the new media and technological society, and their despair or cynical accommodation in the 1980s. The 1980s were an unparalleled era of corruption, cynicism, conservativism, superficiality, and societal regression and one could argue that postmodern theory expressed these trends, even when, upon occasion, maintaining a critical posture. From this vantage point, the postmodern frenzy was a mere ripple on the tides of history, a seduction for intellectuals which offered tempting new sources of cultural capital and which induced a desperate attempt for intellectuals to retain significance while becoming increasingly marginalized in the computer and techno-capitalist society" (Best and Kellner, 297).

30. See Appendix A for historicism in modernism. Indeed, all urban design is inspired by the past, for we always refer to what we already know. It may emulate the past or react to it and this reference may be explicit or implied, conscious or unconscious.

31. As Holston asserts, the utopias of postmodernism "are a regressive response to the progressive utopias of modernism" (Holston, 317).

32. Relph writes: "I begin to suspect that the only fundamental social advances [of urban

design] have been to do with sanitation. All the other changes—skyscrapers, renewal, suburban subdivisions, expressways, heritage districts—amount to little more than fantastic imagineering and spectacular window dressing" (Relph 1987, 265).

33. Jameson continues: "These two great utopian antitheses [the rational and the libidinal], Saint-Simon versus Fourier, if you like, or Lenin versus Marcuse, are for Tafuri the ideological double-bind of a thinking imprisoned in capitalist relations. . . . The first utopian alternative, that of rationalization, will little by little formulate its program in terms of overcoming the opposition between whole and part, between urban plan and individual architectural monument, between the molar and the molecular, between the 'urban organism as a whole' and the 'elementary cell' or building blocks of the individual building" (Jameson 1985, 78–80). This "supreme moment of Freud and Nietzsche, of Weber and Simmel, and of the birth of high modernism in all the arts ['the moment in which ideology is overtly transformed into utopia'] was in reality for Tafuri a purely destructive operation in which residual ideologies and archaic social forms were systematically dissolved" (Jameson 1985, 80). Regardless of their intentions, Jameson contends, the modernist impact "lay in the systematic destruction of the past. . . . Thus the emergence of secular conceptions of the city in the eighteenth century is first and foremost to be read as a way of clearing away the older culture" (Jameson 1985, 77). The second alternative, the libidinal strategy, "ends up training the consumer for life in the industrial city" (Jameson 1985, 81), substituting the consumption of an entire lifestyle for the opportunity to choose from an array of products. This strategy, Jameson contends along with Tafuri, "revitalizes itself in the postmodernist ideologies and aesthetics of the present period" (ibid.).

34. Lesnikowski maintains that contemporary trends "even if they are at the present shallow and naive—represent a necessary and unavoidable step in [correcting the mistakes of modernism] and this is why they are so encouraging and important" (Lesnikowski 1982, 318).

35. Enlightenment ideals held that "people could rationally control the future, that society was evolving progressively toward higher levels of civilization, that rational instrumental action always moves from a state of chaos toward that of control" (Boyer 1990, 99).

36. Best and Kellner, for instance, share the poststructuralist suspicion of foundationalist and universalist claims (because they serve particular groups), but assert that "the creation of a just society requires establishing certain universal rights like equality, rule by law, freedom, and democratic participation and those postmodern theories which scorn these notions ultimately help conservative powers who are all too willing to put aside democratic rights, freedoms, and values" (Best and Kellner, 243).

37. As Harvey maintains, "Refusing (and actively 'deconstructing') all authoritative or supposedly immutable standards of aesthetic judgement, postmodernism can judge the spectacle only in terms of how spectacular it is" (Harvey 1989, 56–57).

38. Against the insularity and ideological utopianism of academic intellectuals, Saarinen contends, "If there is any single source of energy to combat the global disasters facing us, it is that created by outrageous, anarchic, antihierarchical, unprejudiced, explosive interaction" (Saarinen, 70).

39. See Hebdige (1987, 67).

40. In a test of Jencks's hypothesis of double coding, Linda Groat and David Canter found that architects and non-architects do indeed have different sensibilities, but that very few buildings succeed in appealing to both of them (Groat and Canter).

41. To give just one example, Anatole Kopp maintains that the categorical rejection of all ideas and principles of modern architecture represents a desire for a straw man: "Whoever wishes to kill his dog says he has rabies" (*Qui veut tuer son chien dit qu'il a la rage*). Kopp mocks the recent desire to go back in time, saying that those pre-industrial times "were so good that one must go back to them as fast as possible. Let us forget, therefore, a century of research. . . . Let us go back to handicrafts, to mud blocks, to cut stone, to 'Democratic Vertical Windows'. Let us burn Giedion and Benevolo. Let hazard rule creativity . . . let us rehabilitate the *'Grand Ecole des Beaux-Arts'* murdered in 1968, . . . let us imitate, let us copy the ancients" (Kopp). In an attempt to learn from the past, Kopp identifies features we might retain from modern architecture, which for him was produced during the 1920s and 1930s only, such as the idea that there are models inherited from the past that are eternal; international cooperation and exchange; the attempt to respond to new ways of life and provide scientific and rational solutions to new problems through architecture; the judicious application of the industrial mode of production to architecture; and the joining of architecture and politics through the avant-garde. He also lists aspects of modernism that were not fruitful, mainly resulting from misguided efforts to apply quantitative and mechanical methods, such as the belief that good form automatically follows from function and the deliberate oversight of social function and of the interrelationship between different aspects of towns (due to functional zoning).

42. As Huyssen explains, in both France and West Germany, "the 1960s witnessed a return to modernism rather than a step beyond it" (Huyssen, 191). In contrast to their North American counterparts, he observes, European writers, artists, and intellectuals were "much more aware of the increasing co-option of all modernist and avant-garde art by the culture industry" (Huyssen, 165) in the 1960s.

43. Indeed, there sometimes appears to be a fear of abandoning modern architecture and urbanism because of its imputed political associations. While enumerating certain flaws of modern urbanism, for instance, Habermas (1989b, 8) calls nonetheless for its renewal, citing community architecture as a positive example of its expression for it applies the dialogical model he embraces. But community architecture is most definitively postmodern! While the philosophy espoused by Habermas suggests that he would favor aspects of both modern and postmodern urbanism and reject others, his politics obfuscates the issue (see Ley and Mills).

44. In pursuing such political ends, we might heed the recommendations of Best and Kellner, who contend that "in some situations it is best to engage in dissensus, to challenge hegemonic views, and to preserve differences, while in other contexts it is necessary to reach consensus to promote certain political or ethical goals" (Best and Kellner, 241). It is necessary, they say, to apply critical reason (which is critical of society) without applying instrumental or positivistic reason, which is part of a system of domination (Best and Kellner, 282, 238–39).

7

CRISIS IN THE ARCHITECTURAL PROFESSION

IT WAS IN THE LATE 1950S and early 1960s that we began to hear murmurings about a "crisis" in the architectural profession. In the United States, the crisis was triggered by a series of events: Urban Renewal projects, out-migration from cities to suburbs, protests by architecture students, the apocryphal granting of the National AIA Award to the Pruitt-Igoe housing project,[1] its subsequent dynamiting in 1972, and other instances. In Western Europe, the crisis was apparent in the massive amount of postwar rebuilding and new construction, the closing of the ENSBA (*École Nationale Supérieure des Beaux-Arts*) in 1968, and the controversy surrounding the razing and rebuilding of *Les Halles* in central Paris. Although the precise moment and source may be debated, the existence of a crisis in the architectural profession is not. This chapter examines the contours of this crisis and its relationship to the elaboration of postmodern urban design theory. Finally, it explores some opportunities this crisis may have availed for resolving professional problems while improving the quality of the built environment.

CONTOURS OF THE CRISIS

With the massive amount of building after World War II, it became increasingly apparent that something was dreadfully wrong. In peacetime, industries that had been mobilized for war shifted into highway building, community building, and the production of house appliances,

Impact of urban renewal on southeast Manhattan. East River, showing (clockwise)
Williamsburg Bridge, Manhattan Bridge, and Brooklyn Bridge

spurring a mass movement of the middle classes to the suburbs which
left central cities largely to the poor and left city coffers deprived of tax
dollars. In an effort to revitalize declining central cities, the federally
funded Urban Renewal program replaced many nineteenth-century
urban fabrics across the United States with tower-and-slab housing projects and large cultural and financial districts. Given the pace of construction during this period, both suburban and urban builders took
advantage of mass-production techniques, with housing construction
occurring almost in an assembly-line fashion. The pioneer in this regard
was homebuilder Abraham Levitt, whose firm could produce thirty
houses, from start to finish, in one day. A similar pattern was occurring
in Western Europe, except that most central cities remained intact (or

were rebuilt to resemble their prewar condition), tower-and-slab housing projects sprouted just outside the central cities, and suburban tract housing was built in the outlying suburbs. This postwar development in the United States and Western Europe has been widely accused of destroying much of our urban heritage; disrupting communities and displacing people from their homes and businesses; increasing social segregation on a regional scale; accentuating gender role distinctions and disfavoring that of the woman; diminishing the public realm; and of environmental insensitivity, aesthetic monotony, and downright ugliness.

Although these transformations in the physical and social landscapes may be accounted for in large part by demographic trends, economic policies, and the application of new technologies, architects and planners were not mere cogs in this machine of change. There is no question that the suburban and urban development of this period was informed, or at least justified, by architecture and planning theory elaborated over the prior fifty years, having to do with garden cities, greenbelts, neighborhood units, Broadacres City, towers-in-the-park, machines-for-living, and separation of functions. To be sure, the rapid rate of development and the various political and economic constraints that architects and planners had to contend with rendered it virtually impossible to realize their visions to the letter, particularly in the more liberal economies like that of the United States. We should not therefore surmise that the less than satisfactory building products of this period indicate theoretical flaws. But nor should we absolve architecture and planning theory of any guilt under the pretext that it was subverted by more pressing and powerful interests.

Whatever the precise culprit, whether design theory or the incompatibility of design with the political economy, dissatisfaction with the built environment abounded among urban design professionals[2] and the public at large. It was apparent in numerous publications[3] as well as in architectural and planning practices that began to challenge the authoritarian and rational models of modernism with experiments in participatory and advocacy architecture (see chapters 3 and 5).

It was also apparent in protests and manifestos of architecture students. In 1963, students at Yale University protested the new Art and Architecture Building, designed by Paul Rudolph in the Brutalist style, for imposing an undesirable "order" (Russell, 26). At Columbia University, students produced a manifesto in 1967: "We oppose stylistic and empty form-making. We oppose architecture that is whimsical, or for fun. We do not believe that the goal of architecture is to produce buildings as works of art" (cited by Goldberger 1983, 13). The following year, architecture students at the ENSBA in Paris declared: "We want to fight against the conditions of architectural production which submit it to the interests of public and private developers. . . . We want to fight against the particularly conservative content of the architecture curriculum which is particularly non-rational and non-scientific and in which personal impressions and habits continue to prevail over objective knowledge . . ." (*Comité de grève* 1968). Although the French statement was more politically couched than the American one, both protests were geared toward rendering pedagogy as well as the architectural product less authoritarian, more egalitarian, and more socially responsive and responsible. According to Kenneth Frampton, these protests reflected "the deeper and more significant dysfunctions of architectural practice and theory—the latter often serving to mystify the true network of power and exploitation permeating the entire society" (Frampton 1985, 279).

The most vivid symptom and symbol of transformations in architectural education resulting from this discontent was the dissolution of the 300-year-old ENSBA into eighteen geographically dispersed "pedagogical units" (nine in Paris and nine in the provinces), replacing the traditional patron system with new teaching practices. In the United States, where architectural education had already diverged from the Beaux-Arts model, reform was less drastic, consisting mainly of curricular modifications. In both the United States and France, these expressions of discontent coincided with an assault on traditional academic disciplinary boundaries (see Chapter 1), and architecture curricula grew more interdisciplinary by incorporating some of this emerging scholarship. While American students began to read works in urban sociology (such as Gans), urban anthropology (such as Rapoport), environmental studies (such as McHarg), and cultural geography (such as J. B. Jackson), French architecture students were reading the works of scholars such as Henri Lefebvre, Michel Foucault, Roland Barthes, Jacques Lacan, Pierre Bourdieu, and Jean Baudrillard. In both countries, however, many of the newly introduced courses were poorly enrolled or eventually regarded as unnecessary expenses and dropped.

Pervasive resistance to these reform efforts in both architectural training and practice ultimately purged this radical critique of its political and social components by the mid-1970s, turning it "into a relatively innocuous academic debate" (Pope, 83) about aesthetics and function. As a result, although the discussion about the built environment evolved at this time, transformations in architectural training and practice were not substantial, lending fuel to the crisis in the profession rather than extinguishing it. In order to understand why this critique was deflected, a brief history of the architectural profession is in order.

When architects dealt directly with patrons on a one-to-one basis, buildings designed by architects were clearly distinguishable from those that were not designed by architects. During the eighteenth and nineteenth centuries, however, architects gradually began reaching beyond the narrow confines of this elitist circle to the growing middle class in search of a larger market and greater creative freedom. In doing so, they adapted their wares to this new clientele and set out to demonstrate the superiority of their products and services over those offered by their competitors: engineers, professional builders, and self-builders. They also honed their craft by adopting new technologies until the machine and assembly line transformed it into a mass-produced commodity. Henry Ford had foreseen this potential after successfully applying mass-production techniques to car building and queried: "Why not apply assembly-line techniques to the antiquated building of houses?" (cited by Boorstin 1973). Abraham Levitt seized upon this prospect in 1946, initiating a trend that has spread around the world.

The extension of professional architectural design to include housing for all social classes, as well as the building types for an industrial/modern society (factories, warehouses, department stores, public schools, public libraries, museums, hospitals, and railroad stations) broadened the universe of architectural patrons. Just as mass production enabled more people to own automobiles, so the adoption of mass-production techniques by the architectural profession began reshaping ways of life, the landscape, and ways of thinking. But there was a paradox inherent in these "democratization" efforts through mass production. For the standardized products limited both the visual variety of the built environment and consumers' choices, a situation recalling Ford's well-known remark, "Everyone may have a car in the color of his choice, as long as that color is black." Since mass production relied upon mass distribution, consumers' needs and tastes became swayed by advertising campaigns, by available financial arrangements (such as installment plans, loans, and credit), as well as by the actual use of the item once acquired.

The implications of industrial production for the architectural profession were equally far-reaching. Just as Ford's assembly line had replaced the chariot-maker's craft with a greater number of more task-specific jobs within a socially stratified factory, so its adaptation to the construction industry—especially for housing—further threatened the architectural profession. As many new kinds of building-related jobs emerged on the scene, architects had to increasingly circumscribe their interventions and collaborate with other specialists on any given project. This transition was not unlike the deskilling of craftsmen for work in factories, particularly with regard to the loss of control over the product and the inhibition of innovation. While mass production of the built environment improved the overall standard of living, then, it also sacrificed choices for consumers and freedom of expression for architects.

In addition, this enlargement of the architect's task and market muddied the profession's waters as it marked the end of a clear distinction between what is architecture and what is not (but is simply building). If architects could now design virtually anything, then what did not belong within the category of architecture? And how would architects distinguish themselves from engineers and self-builders to justify their existence?

Architectural theory kept pace with these changes through the elaboration of various modern movements in the late nineteenth and early twentieth centuries which called for streamlining the design of buildings and cities (in part by applying mass-production techniques) to render them more functional and more accessible to all sectors of society.[4] But this body of theory failed to resolve the professional identity crisis. New-wave musician David Byrne (of Talking Heads) articulated the paradox inherent in modern architectural theory:

> If [modern architects] followed their own theories to the letter—form follows function, using mass-produced techniques to make cheap things with no frills—what you'd end up with is a metal building! . . . The reason no architect ever says that is because you don't need an architect to build metal buildings. You order them out of a catalogue. Just put down your color, the size you want, number of square feet, style, and what you need it for. It comes with a bunch of guys, they put it together in a couple of days, maybe a week, and there you go. You're all set for business. Just stick a sign out front (Byrne 1986).

French architect Guy Naizot voiced concern for the architect's role: "Currently, there is no longer any need for architects in order to build. So what does that mean for me? What am I going to do these days" (Naizot, 54)?

To avoid this kind of rationale and preserve their legitimacy, architects faced the task of convincing non-architects, other architects, and themselves that what they offered was unique and could not be provided by anyone else. One means of doing so was to cultivate a certain mystery about what architects do, in part by perpetuating their ambiguous artist–civil servant status and by generating a certain amount of controversy (and thus public interest) around architectural interventions. In addition to instigating turf skirmishes, then, the modernist recasting of the architectural profession also proved problematic because its lip service to raising the standard of living for all people contradicted its understanding of the architect as the ultimate arbiter of taste.

In an awkward attempt to reconcile these conflicting goals, the adoption of the industrial mode of architectural production and of the industrial aesthetic was accompanied by a desire to buck the fashion cycle and to design buildings that would not need alterations or replacement. This quest for universal solutions and the corresponding fascination with and emulation of the machine furnished a logical means and ideological justification for colonization abroad and proletarianization at home.[5] The insistence upon a universal aesthetic that would never become outdated probably also veiled the profession's denial that design was being increasingly usurped by advertising and other features of mass society. If so, professional architects ultimately defeated themselves because they not only countered market and consumer demand (for obsolescence and the consumption of new products) but also tested public esteem for architects, as modernist developments around the world grew infamous for their blatant disregard of local cultures and topographies.[6]

At mid-century, C. Wright Mills observed that the rise of mass society during the early twentieth century and the consequent subordination of art, science, and learning to capitalist institutions "explains the big split among designers and their frequent guilt; the enriched muddle of ideals they variously profess and the insecurity they often feel about the practice of their craft; their often great disgust and their crippling frustration" (C. W. Mills 1963b, 374). Serge Chermayeff and Christopher

Alexander also bemoaned the confusion plaguing the design professions (and architecture specifically): "The production processes in industrialized society have recently undergone profound changes. But architects and designers remain much the same; no body of specialists in our culture finds it so easy to seek refuge in generalities. None has found it easier to join the busy market-place activity while professing to speak from the forum" (Chermayeff and Alexander, 105).

In sum, the current crisis in the architectural profession can be traced to the threat posed by industrial production of the built environment. Modern architectural and planning theory, although elaborated in an attempt to adapt to the times, suffered from a confusion of terms which succeeded in preserving the architectural profession, but at the cost of exacerbating the crisis. By deifying the machine while trying to transcend the fashion cycle and by adopting a social and political agenda while insisting on the architect's role as an artist who acts independently, the modern movement succeeded only in offering a band-aid solution to the ills plaguing the architectural profession rather than a cure. The various expressions of discontent with architectural training, practice, and products registered during the 1960s attested to the persistence of the crisis.

MANIFESTATION OF THE CRISIS: THE GAP

Part cause and part result of the crisis in the architectural profession is a gap between architects and non-architects with regard to what constitutes a good and beautiful built environment. This is not to imply that the range of expression among architects is not wide. Nor is it to imply that non-architects do not share architects' tastes. Of course, some do.[7] Nonetheless, the gap between most architects and most non-architects is patent and widely apparent in architectural discourse. Huxtable, for example, praises certain contemporary architects for "moving architecture to a place where it has not been before" and achieving "a style beyond 'styles'" (1992, 29) while chastising "the public" for its "increasing unwillingness . . . to deal with anything but slickly merchandised substitutes that make instant contact" (1992, 29). She explains, "The chasm continues to widen between . . . a public expecting the effortless gratification of make-believe and a profession wrestling with the complexities of art and life" (Huxtable 1992, 29).[8]

This kind of commentary reinforces a distinction between buildings that qualify as "architecture" and those that do not. It also implies that the aesthetic judgment plied by experts in the field of architecture is more valid than that of people who do not benefit from such expertise. This narrow definition of architecture is, according to Hal Foster, "an extraordinary mystification" (Foster 1990, 112), which frequently relegates consideration of buildings outside of the design category to the "real-estate" and "business" sections of newspapers. "The powers that be," Foster writes, "could not devise a more perfect ideological mask than the one we produce and reproduce daily in the course of our own practices as architects, critics, and teachers—even (or especially) when we think we are at our most theoretically subversive" (ibid.). Although intended to affirm the continued viability of architectural contributions, this ideological mask actually restricts the percentage of buildings for which architects are commissioned.

But despite the dangers this gap poses to the architectural profession, there is a tendency among architects, critics, and teachers to celebrate and preserve it. Attesting to this is the feeling among so many architects that one of the highest compliments a user or critic can pay a work of architecture is incomprehension or even disdain, along with praise from the architectural cognoscenti. The following appraisal of Laurinda Spear and Bernardo Fort-Bresica's (the firm Arquitectonica) house for Spear's parents offers one example: "Located on Miami's sedate North Shore, the shocking pink house with its porthole opening onto a bright blue pool caused outrage in the neighborhood but was widely celebrated in the architectural press" (Nesbit). This sort of comment is widely regarded within the profession as akin to saying that a film was not a commercial success but won high critical acclaim and this is, no doubt, the model which the architectural compliment is emulating. In the case of architecture, however, it only reveals arrogance. For we are not forced to see a film and certainly not to live with one, as we can be condemned to live with a building.

While architecture bears similarities to cinema and other arts, it also diverges from them in that it bears certain responsibilities to its client and prospective users, among which figures that of serving a specified function. This essential difference allows other kinds of artists more license to shock, mock, criticize, cajole, and provoke their audience. Highlighting the distinction between architects and other kinds of artists is the convention of not quoting architects' works. We simply write Loos's Tzara House or Frank Lloyd Wright's Guggenheim Museum or Johnson and Burgee's AT&T Building. But we quote Charlie Chaplin's "Modern

Times," Mary Cassatt's "Mother and Child," and Robert Rauschenberg's "Odalisk." This convention not only expresses the fact that these artists name their works while architects usually do not (because the client does); it also suggests that these artists claim more ownership of their work (even if purchased by someone else) than architects. Public buildings become part of the common good and private ones become personalized and often vastly transformed. In addition, the name of a building can change as its owner or use changes, while the name of a film, painting, or sculpture generally remains that bestowed upon it by its creator. Also highlighting the difference between the role of architects and that of other artists is that the name of a building is usually more well known among the general public than the architect's name, whereas the name of a painting or sculpture is usually less well-known than its artist's name.

This desire to preserve the gap between what architects and non-architects consider good and beautiful despite the dangers it poses can be attributed to the profession's instinct for self-preservation through distinction. Like any profession, the architectural one cultivates its distinctiveness in order to preserve its legitimacy. For if everyone shared the skills and aesthetic notions of architects, there would be no need for them. But more so than in other professions perhaps, the gap between architects and their constituency becomes a source of frustration for both. Users of the built environment may find it impractical, unattractive, or even offensive while architects find it virtually impossible to design in a way that is at once socially responsible and responsive, as well as politically and economically feasible, technically sound, artistically rewarding, and respected by colleagues and professional critics. In short, the gap perpetuated by the architectural profession for its self-preservation is both debilitating for the architect, and the source of a good deal of inappropriate urban design. Edward T. Hall describes the angst resulting from this conundrum: "the talents of architects [separate] them from their clients and [cause] untold pain and agony" (E. T. Hall 1976, 174). (See also C. Wright Mills's comment above.)

Design schools have contributed to sustaining rather than bridging the gap since they have concentrated mainly on training students to insert themselves within the profession rather than to constructively reform it. As the *rite de passage* that transforms the mere user of the built environment into both user and designer, architectural training consists of adopting certain aesthetic tastes as well as certain assumptions regarding the role of the architect in society. As David Canter says, architectural training "is aimed at weaning [students] from their personal viewpoint and educating them in the more remote, abstract orientation of their profession" (Canter, 178). Ultimately, then, those who become architects tend to share the notions of their teachers to a large extent since those who beg to differ will probably not graduate, build, or influence future generations. In this way, the gap is self-sustaining and self-perpetuating.

What exactly are these tastes and assumptions taught in design schools? According to Chermayeff and Alexander (writing in 1963), these schools "try to perpetuate the traditional image of professional integrity and unique skill personified by the 'architect' guiding the 'cultured' and unique 'client' [and to] transform average students into universal men of the highest order—to graduate an annual horde of Leonardos. This makes pretentious pseudo artists out of fools and inhibits our best talents because they cannot be conveniently pigeonholed in a conventional manner" (Chermayeff and Alexander, 106). In a more recent study, Dana Cuff contends that design schools "highlight the importance of pure design by removing from its study key aspects of professional practice: the client or patron, the coordinated group process of design, and economic and power relations. . . . Architects are thus not trained to be alert to significant relations of authority, economics, power, group decision-making processes, management, and so on" (Cuff, 45). Describing his own conversion over the last three decades, the architect Dennis Alan Mann admits, "As a young graduate I felt that my responsibility, my quest, was to move out among the masses to educate their tastes. What I've come to realize is that I meant to impose my tastes on others" (Mann, 10). A generation hence, Cuff attests that with the Howard Roark myth "of the autonomous architect-hero in mind, I was caught off guard by my early ventures out of the university into the realm of actual architectural practice. What, I kept asking myself, is going on here" (Cuff, 1)?

Planted in design schools, the gap is nurtured by the peculiar reward system of professional practice. As Robert Gutman observes, despite the long tradition beginning with Pugin which "argues that the test of a building's aesthetic qualities is its effect on social relations, people and their satisfactions are not the primary concern of most architects. . . . The principal interest is architecture, and architecture, at least in its manifestation as an art, is believed by most advanced architects to exist in a realm by itself" (Gutman 1989, 106). Roger Montgomery similarly reports, "A page in the architectural press counts more than any other success symbol" (Montgomery, 31–32). Allen Jacobs and Donald Appleyard attribute the profession's shortcomings to conditions of architectural practice, saying: "Quick surveys are made, instant solutions devised, and the rest of the time is spent persuading the clients. Limits on time and budgets drive us on, but so do lack of understanding and the placeless culture. Moreover, we designers are often unconscious of our own roots, which influence our preferences in hidden ways" (Jacobs and Appleyard, 115).

Resistance to change is endemic to the architectural profession for a number of reasons. Beginning as the obedient and uncritical employees of princes, architects still require clients in order to work (Montgomery, 31–32). As Clarke points out, "The architect is, by convention, identified with the ruling powers of society, the only force capable of amassing and supplying capital, materials, land, and the authority to act; typically considered requisites for architecture" (Clarke 1988, 4). And since architecture is a means for these clients to distinguish themselves, they usually request the acknowledged distinguishing forms rather than experiment with new forms, rendering it difficult for architects to introduce innovation. The high cost of building also discourages risk-taking among clients as well as architects, particularly during times when architects have little work. Another reason for resistance to change is the desire among architects to fulfill expectations they had upon entering the field, which are often misinformed by romanticized and anachronistic popular portrayals in the mass media. And the most recent contributor to professional conservatism has to do with the corporatization of architectural practice. As increasing numbers of (usually starting) architects find themselves working for other (more established) architects,[9] their budding creativity can be nipped as they are required to design in the style of their employer.

The conservatism of the architectural profession also derives from the social class to which architects belong. In the 1980s, most architecture students in the United States came from middle-income backgrounds (Mann, 5) and an astonishing two-thirds of all French architects came from families in the same or a related profession (Zeldin, 179). And those architecture students who are not already middle- or upper-middle-class generally become so via their professionalization, if not in terms of income, at least with regards to their "taste culture" (a term borrowed from Gans 1974). The resistance to treating the actual cause of the profession's troubles, then, might be attributed in part to a socialization and education which has not adequately prepared its members to discern it, as well as a fear that it would render architects obsolete.[10]

For those architects who do understand and acknowledge the constraints of architectural practice within a capitalist society, responses vary from attempting to capitalize on it as best they can (by garnering large commissions), to intervening in as socially responsible a way as possible within the constraints, practicing in a small capacity (with small commissions) or an alternative capacity (such as advocacy), retreating from architectural practice entirely and focusing on teaching and research, and abandoning architecture entirely. As the tasks, methods, clients, and goals of architects have been challenged and reconceived over the last few decades, they have variously responded by retreating from these changes (denial), adapting to them, or consciously opposing or resisting them. The historically elitist position of the architectural profession has made retreat the path of least resistance and the most often treaded,[11] with only a small minority choosing the more rugged route of opposition and resistance. Because of the inherent conservatism of the profession, those architects who embark upon their careers with a reformist agenda often end up conforming to the mainstream or being obstructed from practicing.

Rather than reform the profession, then, most architects aspire—or resign themselves—to joining or remaining among the hegemonic classes. This is not to imply that those drawn to the architectural profession tend to be politically conservative. On the contrary, it has been found that "architects have greater social concerns than the members of other established professions" (Blau 1991, 39).[12] But their political progressiveness and idealism confronts "occupational traditions and constraints [which] prevent architects from acting on these social concerns" (ibid.), a recipe for frustration and disillusionment among many members of the profession.

Architects, then, are hardly oblivious to the divergence between their own tastes and those of others. But rather than bridge the gap, they often respond to accusations of elitism by pleading apoliticism and by insisting they are artists first and if others do not like what they do, it is only because they do not understand it and pleasing others is not their primary goal. When their work is not appreciated, architects tend to respond with contempt for others' lack of taste and to call for educational programs to teach people "to see" or "to appreciate architecture," that is, to teach them the aesthetic values of the architect and to thereby increase demand for what architects supply. The French architectural critic François Chaslin, for instance, maintains that "a great distance exists in architecture between the tastes of the public and the efforts of the most gifted architects. Only a project of education and information will reduce this distance" (Chaslin, 32). But architects can pay lip service to "educating" others without fearing that the resulting consensus of taste would render them superfluous because, in actuality, their time and energy is otherwise spent and the few who do take steps in this direction only end up "educating" a select minority who choose to participate in such initiatives.

In sum, even though architects complain about the discrepancy between their own preferences and those of non-architects because it costs them jobs, endangers their profession, and makes it difficult to please others through their work, they contribute nonetheless to maintaining the distinctions between architecture and building and between their own perspectives and those of others in an effort to preserve their status as artists, their self-identity, and their livelihood. They distinguish themselves by carving out a niche which others acknowledge as necessary or at least desirable and protect this niche from encroachment by others. But in the end, architects become intent on preserving the same things on which they blame their troubles.

POSTMODERN URBANISM AS RESPONSE TO THE CRISIS

Architectural theory since the 1960s might be understood as a series of efforts to resolve the practical, artistic, and ethical dilemmas architects have been facing. One component of this theory is the claim to "humility" in reaction to the more authoritarian attitude characteristic of the modern architect. Supplanting the art-as-light attitude has been the art-as-mirror one. Robert Stern (1981, 4), for instance, asserts that the idea of the true artist standing in inspired isolation no longer abides and that architects believe once again that they should attempt to reflect society at least as much as transform it, if not more.

One arena in which this reconsideration of the architect's role is most apparent is that of housing. Rather than conceive of housing as a machine-for-living or a monument, the postmodernist city has been referring back to prewar housing typologies and attitudes toward housing, as articulated, for instance, by the early modernist architect Adolphe Loos who maintained:

The house should please everyone. It is that which distinguishes it from the work of art that is not obligated to please anyone. The work of art is the private affair of the artist. The house is not a private affair. The work of art is put into the world without anyone feeling a need for it. The house responds to a need. The artist is not responsible towards anyone. The architect is responsible toward everyone. The work of art tears people away from comfort. The house provides only comfort. The work of art is by its very essence revolutionary, the house conservative. The work of art thinks of the future, the house of the present. . . . But does that mean that the house is not a work of art? That architecture is not an art? Yes, that is so. There is only a small part of the work of the architect that belongs within the domain of Fine Arts: the tomb and the commemorative monument. All the rest, all that is useful, all that responds to a desire, should be removed from art. (1910; cited by Huet 1986, 12)

Along with lip service to humility, the architectural profession has since the early 1960s been more mindful of "contextual" design, sensitive to the site, local culture, and history. In reaction to the giganticism and impersonality of modern cities, architectural theory began calling for a return to the human-scale, diversity, and presumed "civic society" of pre-industrial settings. Seeking to correct the perceived deficiencies of the modern movement, this body of theory featured reactions to: universalism (in favor of regionalism and vernacular design); machine models (in favor of pre-industrial typologies and morphologies); the architect-as-divinely-inspired-genius working in isolation (in favor of collaboration with other architects, specialists in other areas, and local communities); and to the architect-as-savior (in favor of humility and apoliticism) (see Chapters 2 and 3).

The reaction to modernism, then, also betrayed an unease about the estrangement of architecture from city planning, which began around the turn of the century with the professionalization of planning and was exacerbated by modernist architecture and planning theory and the growing division of labor in society. As the architectural task grew more narrowly defined over the twentieth century to entail the design of individual buildings with little regard for their surroundings, the planning task became that of reconciling these piecemeal interventions largely for the purposes of facilitating circulation and protecting real-estate values. Initially intended as a holistic prescriptive task, planning had largely become a technical and curative one.[13] Rather than shape cities (physical planning) and implement social change (social planning), planners had largely become appendages of the state, of developers, and of architects, a role which led planner Marshall Kaplan to declare that "the impact of planning profession on the quality of life has been marginal at best and, at times, negative" (M. Kaplan 1973, v).[14]

Instead of a mutually beneficial symbiotic relationship, then, architects and planners assumed a dismissive or even antagonistic one as the two professions proceeded to develop parallel organizations, journals, and schools with little interaction between them and to defend their respective intellectual and professional turfs from incursion by the other. Rather than engage in productive collaborations, each grew to see the other as a deterrent to his or her progress. The antagonism between these two professions was symptomatic of development in a capitalist society, with architects representing the interests of individual clients and of unleashed free enterprise while planners represented the usually opposing interests of the larger community and the need to check growth.[15]

Expressing the dissatisfaction within both the architectural and the planning professions and the perceived need to achieve a rapprochement, the term "urban design" gained fluency in the late 1960s (Gosling and Maitland). According to Jonathan Barnett (1982, 12), urban design emerged as a branch of planning concerned with giving visual design direction to urban growth and conservation. Denise Scott Brown, an early advocate and practitioner of urban design, contends that "the essence of the urban design approach is that it concentrates more on relations between objects, more on linkages, contexts and in between places, than on the objects themselves" (Scott Brown 1990a, 19). Harvard University initiated a one-year Urban Design Professional Studio in 1960 in an effort to fill the "dangerous gap . . . which neither profession [architecture or planning] is at present being trained to fill" (Tyrwhitt 1966, 125). The Pratt Institute catalogue (1988) explains, "More specific than policy and more inclusive than the building program, the urban designer must interpret and resolve the aesthetic, social and economic forces which affect the building of cities." Alan Kreditor, former Dean of Planning at the University of Southern California, defines urban design thus: "If architecture is the combination of design with building technology and planning is the combination of city building with the social and management sciences, then perhaps urban design is formed out of the strategic overlap of the two fields" (Kreditor, 67). Edward Relph writes: "The planning equivalent of post-modernism is urban design, just as the planning equivalent of modernism was the institutionalized practice of planning by numbers" (Relph 1987, 229).

Around the same time that urban design was entering the Anglo-American idiom, so was the term "urbanism" in its romance-language sense: a holistic consideration of the built environment within physical, historical, and social contexts. Until then, urbanism was understood in the United States primarily as it had been coined by Louis Wirth in his seminal 1938 essay, to mean the way of life of city-dwellers. Although the romance-language meaning appeared occasionally in earlier works (such as Goodman 1956; Giurgola 1962;[16] Chermayeff and Alexander 1963; Scully 1969[17]), it did not appear widely until the late 1970s, probably owing to widely-read translations from Italian and French in which the term urbanism appears with some frequency, particularly Tafuri's *Architecture and Utopia: Design and Capitalist Development* (original 1973, English 1976, 133, 166).

In addition to indicating a globalization of dialogue about architecture and planning, the new concern with urban design and with urbanism also intimates dissatisfaction with the hermetic quality of design theory and the products it was yielding. To correct this, architects and planners on both sides of the Atlantic began replacing the authoritarian and rational models of modernism with efforts to design for and with people. Disappointing results, however, led many architects and planners to conclude that such efforts cast the architecture and planning nets too widely and that their respective tasks should more properly be restricted to physical planning. (See chapters 2 and 3.)

Largely purged of political and social intentions, the critique of modernism, like modernism before it, evolved to focus on formal aspects of the built environment. Indeed, good intentions largely fueled wide-ranging efforts to rectify problems of architectural theory and practice. But they largely failed to resolve the crisis in the architectural profession because they were treating the symptoms of the crisis rather than its etiology, which can be found in the climate that nourished the modern movement rather than in the modern movement itself. The persistent gloss of the larger context in which architects work (a holdover from modernism) continued to deprive these efforts of their potential for improving the built environment and for alleviating the crisis in the architectural profession.

The crisis began taking on some new dimensions as the profession increasingly felt the reverberations of new technologies driving the transition from industrial to corporate capitalism and from Fordist to more flexible forms of accumulation.[18] This transition has been recasting the architect's task as well as professional context (or, in Marxian terms, the mode of production as well as the social relations of production). In 1985, the chairman of the United States Co-ordinating Council for Computers in Construction predicted that four-fifths of the 80,000 practicing architects in the United States would be "dislocated" by the year 2000 (Pawley 1990, 6) because CAD will have automated the drawing process, product specification, and cost estimating. As building projects have grown more complex, tasks which initially fell to architects have been farmed out to the new professions of project managers, design consultants, and planning and building-control officers (Pawley 1990, 5). Since this intensified specialization discourages innovation and risk-taking, carbon copy buildings (which have the same consultants and the same structural and environmental systems) have become the norm. What is left to architects is "the power of specification," that is, the power to select contractors, components, and finishes. This role ensures that advertising is directed toward architects (in the way that pharmaceutical companies direct advertising toward physicians) and it throws them headlong into the society of consumption, as Buckminister Fuller had predicted (ibid.). Meanwhile, "the power of the architect over construction has shrunk to the literally superficial" (Pawley 1990, 10), or decoration. This is why the "signature building" has become so important.

At the same time, the profile of many architects' clients evolved to include increasing numbers of national and international investors and fewer small-scale local developers. The worldwide real-estate recession beginning in 1989, which eliminated smaller and weaker builders and favored the dominance of global capital, reinforced this trend. Keen to exploit the power of symbolism, corporate clients have commissioned "star" architects to design buildings which confer status and corporate recognition and which help to "sell" their corporate identity by providing a colorful package for it as a commercial artist would do for other products (Rybczynski 1989; Safdie 1988; C. W. Mills 1963b). Examples of "signature buildings" by "starchitects" include

Philip Johnson and John Burgee's AT&T building in New York City, Michael Graves's Humana Corporation in Louisville, Kentucky, and Kevin Roche's monumental corporate campuses for General Foods in the suburbs of New York City and for Bouyges construction enterprises in the Parisian suburbs.

The harnessing of architectural services for product recognition and status incited Paul Goldberger to report in the *New York Times* that this is "the age of the 'designer building,' not unlike designer sheets and designer jeans" (Goldberger 1988b) and to hail the arrival of a "cult of celebrity" (ibid.) surrounding certain architects. In the *Los Angeles Times*, Sam Hall Kaplan reported that "in Los Angeles these days we have the rich and famous buying designer houses and restaurants like they buy designer clothes, followed by a flock of photo-publicists and fawning writers" (S. H. Kaplan 1989). Sharon Zukin makes sense of this "emphasis on individualized products that can be identified with individual cultural producers" (Zukin 1988b, 438) by pointing out, "Similar competition among Hollywood film studios from the 1930s through the 1950s for audience loyalty to their products encouraged individual directors to make the 'signature film.' In architecture, as labor costs have increased and craft skills have atrophied, the burden of social differentiation has passed to the use of expensive materials and the ingenuity of the design itself. Not surprisingly, like Hollywood directors, architects assume and even become commercial properties" (ibid.).[19]

To adapt to these changing conditions, the AIA changed its code of ethics in 1978 to condone both development and advertising practices among architects. The profession adapted by mirroring its clients and growing more corporate. Like law, accounting, and advertising firms, architectural firms have been expanding on a global scale (Zukin 1988b, 435) to garner more clients. Some, such as Houston-based CRS, have even begun to sell shares of stock, becoming corporations for the production of buildings (Goldberger 1983, originally 1981).

This commercialization of architecture has elicited disdain, disappointment, and outright disgust. The sale of the AIA's monthly journal *Architecture* in August 1989 to the company that publishes *Hollywood Reporter* and other mass market magazines prompted Kaplan to remark that "the legitimate social concerns of architecture, and the good works of many architects to create a better, more habitable, attractive world, appear to be out of style. . . . Criticism," he said, "has given way to promotion" (S. H. Kaplan 1989). Michael Brill lamented that architecture "has become part of the distraction and entertainment industry," with "a fraudulently soothing and sentimental Bartles & Jaymes quality" (Brill). An unfortunate repercussion in architectural practice, according to Rybczynski, is "the apparent inability of contemporary architects to produce large numbers of unassuming but satisfying buildings to form the backdrop for the occasional important monument," because "everybody wants to be a star" (Rybczynski 1992, 51).

With the acceleration of global flows (of capital, labor, products, management styles, tourists, and ideas) over the last few decades, the architectural profession's need to stake out and protect its turf has become ever more urgent. As the building industry becomes increasingly regulated and as architectural commissions dwindle, architects worry that their task is growing limited to that of decorating a building whose form is determined by others and that their profession is only sustained by laws which demand recourse to an architect (Belmont 1980). As the time-honored competition with engineers has grown along with the more recent threat from large builders and developers, who have been increasingly usurping architects' tasks, many architects have reconceived their own role by working closely with developers or becoming developers themselves.

John Portman was instrumental in legitimizing the architect-as-developer role when the AIA's board of directors questioned him in 1968 about whether it was proper for him to be in development. He replied, "When the architect becomes the developer and is thus the client, does the potential for conflict of interest mean that he puts himself in the position of cheating himself?" (cited by Kennedy 1988). Since then, the AIA has been conducting large forums on architects-as-developers and a 1987 AIA survey reported that 20 percent of those responding said they were active in development, construction management, or joint ownership situations (ibid.).

While assuming the role of developer may resolve the dilemmas of individual practitioners, it does not resolve the crisis in the architectural profession. And among architects who have not become developers, the common scapegoating of developers for architects' frustrations is counterproductive since developers simply personify broader, underlying transformations in the political economy. Becoming developers and blaming developers only serves to sustain the gap and deflects social responsibilities. Instead, the profession must come to acknowledge the true sources of the crisis plaguing it and must contend with the pronounced resistance within the profession to change.

Rather than pursuing idealistic and transformative goals, however, many architects today are aspiring to become important players in the capitalist economy. They are adopting corporate models in their own practice, creating symbols of power for their corporate clients, and even expanding their repertoire to include linens, teakettles, silverware, tableware, shopping bags, and other merchandise, in a desperate attempt to establish a niche for a breed on the verge of extinction. Ultimately, the professed humility of architects is more likely to be an excuse, justification, or mask for complacency or for "selling out." It often appears that the potentially progressive rhetoric of pluralism is interpreted as aesthetic diversity while putative concerns with social responsibility, political correctness, and environmental sensitivity have become mere fads with little substance. Indeed, some of these means of coping with the crisis in the architectural profession further test the public's regard for architects' contribution to society, discourage recourse to architects, and exacerbate the rate of unemployment along with the personal frustration and disillusionment within the profession.

As Pawley contends, the architect's role today is "tragically diminished," "oscillating uneasily between envelopment by a burgeoning design profession and surrender to the reactionary forces of conservation and historicism" (Pawley 1990, 10). Pawley argues that "Architecture is obsolete in 1990" (Pawley 1990, 11), that it "has become a slow-moving, inefficient, ornamental target in a video game played by instantaneous information and technological change" (ibid.). Today, he says, "only the inertia of popular thinking and the politics of the construction industry allow [the architect] to escape the modified cry of the small boy: 'The Emperor is as expendable as a light bulb'" (Pawley 1990, 10). The retreat from confronting contemporary realities and the emphasis on decoration, Pawley contends, has resulted in the "conquest of theory by imagery" (Pawley 1990, 5). This "fall of ideology in architecture," he laments, has perhaps promulgated "the idea that there is no longer any need for expert judgement where the design of buildings is concerned" (Pawley 1990, 6). But, Pawley adds, this "dissolution of architecture in the Second Machine Age . . . is an almost biblical tale of a Fall from Grace, and as such is invariably seen as a warning rather than as a subject for further inquiry" (ibid.).

OPPORTUNITIES FOR THE ARCHITECTURAL PROFESSION

The Chinese word for crisis (*weiji*) is formed by two characters, the first meaning danger and the second opportunity, suggesting that inherent in all crises is the potential for positive transformation. Having outlined the contours of the crisis in the architectural profession, this chapter proceeds to explore some opportunities it might avail for resolving professional problems while improving the quality of the built environment.

While dissatisfaction with the built environment and within the architectural profession continues to grow, there are also signs of a renaissance. One of these is the growing public interest in architecture, as indicated by increased sales of books and magazines, the historically-unprecedented celebrity that certain works of architecture and certain architects are enjoying, more public debate (public hearings, lectures, conferences), the increased interest of other academic disciplines in architecture, and the growth in historic preservation, rehabilitation, and neighborhood associations. All these activities could be interpreted as grassroots indicators of a closing gap between what consumers want and what the market is providing.

Another indication of public interest is the increasing enrollment in design schools and the consequent swelling of the ranks of the profession. In the United States, the number of architects grew by 250 percent between 1960 and 1980 (Blau 1988) and from 61,500 to 74,000 between 1982 and 1987 (Goldberger 1988b), yielding a ratio of one architect per 3,000 members of the population. This growth occurred despite economic recessions that depressed construction and building activity, and greatly exceeded that of lawyers, physicians, or engineers during the same period (Blau 1988), even though a first-year architect would typically earn less than half of what a first-year lawyer or doctor would earn (Goldberger 1988b). In France, the growth was even more marked. The number of architects swelled from 12,000 in the early 1980s (Zeldin, 179) to 20,000 in 1986 (with an additional 10,000 architectural students)—almost doubling in a few years—yielding one architect per 2,000 citizens (Champenois 1986). This occurred despite the fact that construction in France declined by almost a half during this same period. While exacerbating the profession's crisis by intensified competition, the growing number of architects also suggests a growing interest and confidence in the services architects provide.

The enhanced public interest in architecture might be attributed to the heightened perception that our environment is threatened, in tandem with a recessionary economic climate contributing to a desire to protect what we have. It might also be accounted for by the re-ascendance of the visual image over the last half-century. Victor Hugo, in *Notre Dame de Paris*, described the waning power of architecture with the invention of the printing press and the growth of literacy from the fifteenth to the nineteenth century (see pages 28–29). Further advances in information technologies, however, along with increased access to these over the twentieth century, have elevated the power of the visual image once again over that of print. Although architecture is no longer the sole purveyor of these images, it certainly ranks among the most important of them. Some believe that this postmodern reconfiguration renders architects, with their unique combination of creative and technical skills, particularly well-attuned to the current post- (or hyper-) industrial scene and well-suited for designing its habitat, suggesting, for instance, that "The architect is the contemporary being incarnate, *homo-postmodernus*" (Crépu and Lenglart, 72).

In addition, there appears to be a growing weariness with the prevalent mercenary and complacent attitudes of the 1980s, along with a search for meaning and purpose beyond that offered by consumerism. Finally, some roadblocks obstructing large-scale planning have been removed, as frustration with planners' limited effectiveness has crested, and we have been witnessing a growth in large-scale plans (Battery Park City, Seaside, Playa Vista, Laguna West, and Civano), although these too face the constraints of building in a capitalist political economy.

This nexus of circumstances may provide a context that is more receptive to reform than the relatively affluent postwar period (until the early 1970s), which witnessed highly visible and strident calls for change yet stopped short of effecting deep and lasting transformations. Perhaps the more quiet desperation of the current period will ultimately leave deeper imprints on the social and physical landscapes.

But if these indicators are to pave the way toward resolving the crisis in the architectural profession, some changes in architectural training and practice must take place. No one would deny that our built environment stands improvement and that specially trained professionals could achieve this far better than others.[20] If architects are to be effective in assuming this task, however, they must first enhance their respectability among the public at large. Punitive measures requiring recourse to architects are not the answer. Nor is "educating the public" to appreciate what architects do. Rather, potential clients of all kinds need to make recourse to architects in the same way they would to doctors if they fell ill. They need to regard such recourse as a necessity rather than a luxury on the grounds that an architect can provide specialized skills and insight.

For architects to acquire greater respectability and more commissions, thereby easing the crisis in the profession and the sorry state of the contemporary built environment, changes must occur in the skills architects acquire and the attitudes they assume vis-à-vis their potential clients and constituency. These changes need to be implemented from the training stages through to practice, theory, and criticism. There are Luddites, such as the Krier brothers and Maurice Culot, who believe that architects should disavow machine technologies and become true craftsmen once again. Most, however, regard that perspective as unrealistic and a sure route to self-destruction, calling instead for forging new or modified roles for architects. Proposals for doing so range from the practical and immediate to the more idealistic and long-range.

To begin with what might be done now to improve the quality of the built environment and ensure the architect's role in shaping it, Cuff offers a number of concrete suggestions for reforming the studio, internships, continuing education, professional associations and journals, and architectural scholarships to ensure a closer reflection of actual situations (Cuff, 254–60). For architects to regain the public's trust and esteem, many assert the importance of engaging the public through writings and forums as well as through design (for example, C.W. Mills, Gutman, Cuff, and Fulton).

In order to accomplish these ends effectively, pleas for a more interdisciplinary approach to architecture are widespread. Architect and historian Bernard Huet, for instance, has said that if architecture is not to stagnate, "The participation of intellectuals is necessary. . . . Architects can not debate among themselves" (Huet 1985). The cultural anthropologist James Holston proposes that "architects and planners learn to work with social analysis and to appropriate the social effects of their projects in the processes of planning, without imposing a teleology that disembodies history or abandoning the goal of new social and aesthetic

possibilities" (Holston, 317–18).[21] Scott Brown also encourages architects to incorporate methods and findings from the social sciences, but
without the participation of social scientists. Drawing upon vast personal experience of negotiating among the disciplines, she tells architects the burden is upon them, saying: "My theory is that urban
sociologists will never know about things physical. They have hang-ups
about art. They think it is elitist. So architects will have to learn sociology, not the other way round. We at least get a verbal education in
school. They don't get a visual one. If there's going to be any meeting
of the disciplines, it will have to be achieved by us" (Scott Brown 1990a,
32).[22] The signing of a Declaration of Interdependence at the World
Architecture Congress in 1993 (Chicago) may indicate inroads in this
direction (ACSA News 1994).

The architectural studio, which survived the post-Beaux Arts transition, holds great potential for uniting theory and practice, the ideal and
the practical, learning and doing, gown and town, past and future. In
addition, the rise of urban design offers a legitimate and valuable forum
for expanding the discussion around architecture and for making it more
relevant, contextual, interdisciplinary, and socially responsible. The
fruitful collaboration between architects and planners which urban
design bespeaks would simultaneously contribute to resolving the concurrent crisis in the planning profession while harnessing the vast talent and capital which is wasted because of the antagonisms and turf
skirmishes which currently plague these professions.

Other solutions to the crisis in the architectural profession involve
deeper structural changes not only in architectural practice but also in
society at large. Rather than contribute to perpetuating the status quo,
this view holds that architecture should constitute a form of resistance to
the world capitalist system and its corresponding values. The approaches
that fall into this category—variously described as reflexive, humanistic,
critical, or radical—usually entail incorporating an awareness of and sensitivity to cultural diversity and social inequality, an acknowledgment of
architects' relationship to other groups of people, and a commitment to
practice architecture in a way that respects and preserves cultural diversity while contributing to diminish social inequalities.

Vincent Pecora, for instance, maintains that if architecture is to
become 'something other than an advertisement for itself," it "would

have to address the array of institutional apparatuses that, through their control of the built environment, help to maintain inequity in the present distributions of power and wealth" (Pecora, 47). He says that it is by "insisting on the irrelevancy of such relations [that] architecture finally succeeds in making itself irrelevant" (Pecora, 48). Frampton's "critical regionalism" aspires to benefit from new technologies ("universal techniques") while enhancing our rich and diverse cultural traditions (Frampton 1983a, 20) (see chapter 3). Clarke and Dutton (1986) speak of the importance of realizing a "counterhegemonic project," whereby architectural practice would assist in empowering oppressed peoples. Crawford (1991) similarly proposes that architects re-envision their clients in terms of specific groups, especially those whose needs are not being met by the marketplace. Architectural education, according to these approaches, should sensitize students to cultural diversity, social inequalities, power struggles, and forms of resistance. It should allow students to see themselves and their role as architects within the larger historical and sociological contexts, thereby enabling them to retain and/or develop social and environmental concerns and to responsibly forward these concerns in their capacities as architects and as citizens.

Jusuck Koh (1985) asserts that architects must heed the call of René Dubos to "think globally, act locally,"[23] unlike the modernists, who thought locally and acted globally. To do so, he says that architects need "to expand the conception of design beyond physical/structural/formal design to include policy/system/social/experiential design" and "to nurture pluralism and egalitarianism among the specializations within architecture and among related design disciplines" (Koh 1985, 12).[24] Koh maintains that architectural education should be broad and humanistic in order "to develop sound social perspectives and ethical orientation" (ibid.) and "to avoid the situation where excellent knowledge and skills are used for the wrong purposes" (Koh 1985, 16). He also recommends that architects develop an "evolutionary world view" which recognizes and designs for change and which understands "building and city not as a commodity, to be consumed and made obsolete, but as a habitat to be rehabilitated, improved and transmitted" (Koh 1985, 14).[25] In addition, Koh contends that architects must agree to work with businessmen, financiers, and developers because if they do not, they will only work for wealthy clients and the public sector, leaving many unserved.

Proponents of both immediate and long-term reform in the architectural profession aspire to a better environment as well as a more worthwhile and secure role for architects. They also share the conviction that training and practice must acknowledge the larger contexts of architecture. Some of them part ways, however, with regard to what a better environment looks like and beholds, and whether architecture should properly adapt to the world as it exists or somehow transform it. But these are questions to which there are no pat answers. Rather, they require decisions, which architects can responsibly make on a case-by-case basis if they are equipped with a general understanding of their historical role in society and in the political economy.

These immediate and long-term changes in training, practice, theory, and criticism must re-evaluate measures of success in the architectural profession. They must elevate goals such as contributing to environmental sustainability, preserving cultural traditions and historic environments while nurturing growth and change, and improving living standards for the greatest number, over goals defined in terms of prestige, power, and profits. Architectural history, theory, and criticism can assist in this task by evaluating built form according to these measures of success rather than by aesthetic criteria primarily. It can also assist by following the cue of Spiro Kostof, who understood architecture to encompass "all buildings, the standard and the fancy, and their arrangement into landscapes of form" and who believed that "the primary task of the architectural historian, behind all the sophisticated research and the erudition, is to recreate and convey the actual processes of designing, building, and using the manmade landscapes of the past" (Kostof 1987, ix). Although such commentary would address issues currently regarded as outside the purview of architectural critics and scholars, it would also be of interest to an audience beyond that of specialized journals, ultimately rendering it more relevant and more instrumental in improving architectural practice.

In sum, the response to the confusion about what architecture is and what the architect's task should be (incited by industrialization and the rise of a mass society) was a tendency toward essentialisms and universalisms as manifest in the ideology of modern urbanism. But rather than assist the profession in evolving with the times, this ideology further estranged it from other realms as it retreated into the pristine tenets of modern urbanism, the failure of which became evident with time. Then, efforts to overcome the flaws of modern urbanism, as manifest in postmodern urbanism, only achieved limited success and fell into some of the same traps because the reasons for modern urbanism's failure were not sufficiently understood. As the modernists denied contemporary change by retreating into essentialisms and universalisms, so postmodernists similarly denied it, this time by seeking inspiration from history or other "contexts." Both insisted upon architecture's separateness from (or transcendence beyond) other realms and other professions in an effort to preserve the architectural profession, but this insistence only further challenged the legitimacy of the profession.

Architects are accessories to this crime as well as victims; rather than reform architectural practice to better correspond with changing times, they tend to cling tenaciously to erstwhile self-definitions. But this fatuous adherence to outdated notions of the architect's role is part and parcel of the larger abdication from tackling the real problems of the profession.

Is the architectural profession moribund or has it simply been suffering some growing pains that will evolve into a more mature architectural theory and practice? As the growth of a mass society has proceeded to blur the distinction between high and popular culture, so the role of the architect has grown increasingly ambiguous. And political, economic, and social transformations on a global scale have recast the architectural profession and presented it with new challenges over the last few decades. But unlike chariot-makers and most other artisans, architects have not been rendered anachronistic with industrialization, or been sustained only through tourist dollars (like most existing artisanal work) or state subsidy (like bakers and winemakers in France). Despite threats from many fronts, the architectural profession has managed to persevere, and in some respects, even thrive. Although the unequivocal definition of architecture which prevailed when clients hailed exclusively from a small elite no longer pertains, the notion that architecture is a rather charmed subset within the larger category of building remains prevalent. Clearly, the profession is not losing popularity—even if it has been losing commissions—as demonstrated by significant increases in public interest and student enrollments.

Nonetheless, the reconciliation of architecture with a mass society has not been easy. There are signs on the horizon, however, of an architectural renaissance. If these signs are carefully heeded, the quality of the built environment will improve and the professional crisis will diminish. If not, the architectural profession will either persist in its largely elite (and uneasy) capacity or it will go the way of obsolete artisans. That will depend on whether we negotiate this pivotal moment by continuing to deny the source of the crisis in the practice of architecture today or by acknowledging it and making the necessary adjustments in architectural training and practice.

NOTES

1. Charles Jencks, Beverly Russell, and others mention an AIA Award, but Katharine Bristol maintains, "Pruitt-Igoe never won any kind of architectural prize" (Bristol, 168).

2. Jencks refers to the divergent loyalties dividing the architectural profession by the 1950s as "a credibility gap" (Jencks 1981).

3. These include Kevin Lynch's *The Image of the City* (1960); Jane Jacobs's *Death and Life of Great American Cities* (1961); Jean Gottmann's *Megalopolis* (1961); Lewis Mumford's *The City in History* (1961); Gordon Cullen's *The Concise Townscape* (1961); William Mitchell's *Sick Cities* (1963); Serge Chermayeff and Christopher Alexander's *Community and Privacy* (1963); Victor Gruen's *The Heart of our Cities: The Urban Crisis, Diagnosis, and Cure* (1964); Peter Blake's *God's Own Junkyard* (1964) and *Form Follows Fiasco* (1977); Murray Bookchin's *Crisis in our Cities* (1965); Robert Venturi's *Complexity and Contradiction in Architecture* (1966); Henri Lefebvre's *Le Droit à la Ville* (1967); Richard Sennett's *The Uses of Disorder* (1970); Robert Goodman's *After the Planners* (1971); Colin Rowe's "Collage City" (1975); Brent Brolin's *The Failure of Modern Architecture* (1976); Peter Blake's *Form follows Fiasco* (1977), and more.

4. The revolutionary modern movement "was a brilliantly successful strategy (though not planned as such) to keep architecture in the grip of Renaissance idealism just at the moment when the exhaustion of the tradition threatened to do it in" (Ackerman 1980, 16).

5. This theme has been developed by Rabinow (1989) and Boyer (1983).

6. In Ada Louise Huxtable's analysis, architects were not offering the product appropriate to the political economy and corresponding consumer tastes since their "objective was the ultimate house as a machine to live in, the building that would meet the twentieth century so well on its own terms that it could not be improved on—possessing a standardized, mass-produced, eternal utility and beauty, removed from transient fashions" (Huxtable 1981b, 102). But, she maintains, "This approach was wholly unsuited to the realities of twentieth-century production and marketing—to an economy that relied on moving goods and changing tastes. . . . This shifting consumer aesthetic took over taste and technology. Advertising superseded design. The modern architect, insisting on the one right and best way to design, was out of step and out of touch with his times" (ibid.). According to Paul Walker Clarke, the "mystifications [of modern architecture] were essential for an economy that was destroying in order to create. It was an economy which appropriated the practice of architecture and which alienated the very act of dwelling and called it housing [the product]. The architect was no longer designing for her or his class. The housing, factories, schools, 'public' libraries, warehouses, and other new building types were commissioned by the capitalist class, but not occupied by them, and certainly not occupied by architects. The subject of these objects was not the working classes, though indeed, they inhabited them. The subject was capitalism. . . . Objectified by a mode of production, the laboring masses were further objectified by an architectural philosophy which did not respect history, that rebelled against notions of class and thereby refused to recognize the continued relations of class. It

was a philosophy of universal norms, unconcerned with aspects of existing culture since its proposed architecture was the vanguard of a new 'emancipating' culture" (Clarke 1988, 5).

7.   Sociologically-speaking, these people would, for the most part, comprise the "new class" (Daniel Bell 1980; Gouldner, 83) which, according to Daniel Bell, marks an end to domination by the old moneyed class and represents an elite of a new kind of "cultural capital" (Bourdieu's term). The intellectual roots of the new class, Bell explains, can be found in the "adversary culture" (coined by Lionel Trilling in 1961), which was opposed to bourgeois conformity. Alvin Gouldner claims that this class is the most internationalist, universalist, and cosmopolitan of all social classes. Its members are highly educated, have the ability to work with ideas and abstract symbols, and spend much of their time engaged in leisure activities. Among this class, there is an increased participation of women in the political economy along with the postponing of marriage and childbearing, fewer children, dual-career couples with egalitarian division of household labor, and more one-person households.

8.   In similar fashion, a French architectural critic of the government-sponsored new towns built in the 1970s and 1980s commented, "the most interesting efforts are not those received most enthusiastically by the inhabitants" (Chaslin, 32).

9.   Currently in the United States, more architects work for other architects than for themselves (Cuff, 50).

10.   Clarke and Dutton observe that architects tend to ignore the social landscapes in which they build because it would complicate the design process and because they do not wish to upset the larger system which sustains them. They contend, "There is a tendency here to be intentionally naive, to be in a state of active ignorance that champions an undialectical view of the world and denies the realm of politics—characteristics which serve ultimately to buttress the status quo" (Clarke and Dutton, 5). Architects tend to accommodate themselves to the status quo rather than try to change it, according to Clarke and Dutton, because that is the path of least resistance and the surer means to protect their livelihood and status (Clarke and Dutton).

11.   Meanwhile, the civil service tradition of the planning profession has made it more inclined to accommodate itself to the changing political economy by, for instance, incorporating real-estate development programs and courses in public—private enterprise into planning curricula.

12.   See also Cuff (1991).

13.   The discussion here applies mainly to the United States. For a discussion of transformations in urban planning during this period focusing on Western Europe, see Albers (a German architect/planner) and Papageorgiou-Venetas (a Greek architect/planner) (1985).

14.   Prior to World War II, planners believed that they could "successfully look beyond the limitations of particular issues and concern [themselves] with larger questions, even . . . the good of the whole" (Fishman 1977 275). But like architects, their increasingly circumscribed role and need to work within the constraints of commercialism has limited their potential influence. Marc Weiss concedes that today, "Real estate speculation and development for profit, with political support and financial backing from government officials in pursuit of higher property values and

economic activity, is the engine that drives the metropolitan growth machine, not redistributive policies for economic equity or social justice" (Weiss, 4). With the 1970s recession, Peter Hall points out, planning was transmuting from "an orderly scheme of action to achieve stated objectives in the light of known constraints" (Hall 1988 240) to a developer-aligned growth-promotion undertaking which he calls "planning as property development" (ibid.). While the need for large-scale planning has grown and the means to execute it have improved (making it more viable), the need for planners to consistently compromise their visions has discouraged radical and utopian plans. Nonetheless, the planning profession has managed to offer a better life to millions (Hall). For instance, although the ability of planners to reach the poorest third of the population has been extremely limited, the percentage of substandard housing in the United States has decreased significantly over the last century while the percentage of homeownership has substantially increased (Weiss 1990).

15. See Terry Kahn (1990).

16. Urging Americans to adopt this term in 1962, Giurgola defined urbanism as an art and discipline "whose aim is an architectural synthesis of all those values which represent the urban aggregate in the broadest sense of the word.... Besides denoting the material act of planning," Giurgola maintained, urbanism "includes the entire complex of disciplines whose objective is the life of urban aggregates" (Giurgola, 104).

17. Although appearing in the title (possibly an editor's choice), the text of Vincent Scully's *American Architecture and Urbanism* (1969) does not use the word "urbanism" at all except for a reference to "French academic urbanism."

18. The 1970s crisis of the Fordist regime (due to heightened international competition) in the United States led to a transformation in the role of the state featuring a decline of regulatory and public-welfare obligations, privatization, growth of the third and fourth economic sectors, revival of craft specialty production, growth of the informal economy, decentralization, densification of central business districts in global cities, competition among second-tier cities, and the facilitation of capital mobility.

19. In his essay "Man in the Middle: The Designer," C. Wright Mills addresses this inevitability in mass culture. He describes the immense impact of what he calls the "cultural apparatus" encompassing "all those organizations and milieu in which artistic, intellectual and scientific work goes on" as well as "all the means by which such work is made available to small circles, wider publics, and to great masses" (C. W. Mills 1963b, 376). The fact that the cultural apparatus in the United States is "established commercially" and virtually dominates commercial culture, says Mills, "is the key to America's cultural scope, confusion, banalization, excitement, sterility" (C. W. Mills 1963b, 377).

20. In the more liberal economies, architects design only a small percentage of what gets built. In the United States, for instance, they only design approximately 10 percent of all projects given building permits.

21. Muschamp (1993b) makes a similar plea: "The problem with architecture in recent years has not been an overemphasis on art but an extreme disconnection between esthetics and sociology. Politicians are not the only people trapped by gridlock. Architects, too, have been caught in a stalemate between conflicting visions of public life. Architects, however, don't need the permission of governments to initiate

change. It is possible, even in a cynical time, to articulate ideals." Architecture, he continues, "operates in the realm of image and metaphor as well as that of matter. And to close the door on either realm is to trample the grass roots of architectural creativity."

22. In this spirit, a conference was convened at Harvard's Graduate School of Design in 1989 in response to the sense that "Contemporary design is seen as unrelated either to theoretical developments in other spheres of cultural production or to new conditions in politics and the economy" (Harvard GSD). At this conference, the architect Jorge Silvetti maintained that "the theory we have been practicing . . . has led us to an inability to recognize architecture as a social practice that has changed drastically and is positioned very differently than it was even twelve years ago . . . maybe it is time now to look outward and to see how those boundaries between architecture and other practices in society need to be redefined or staked out in a different way" (Silvetti, 124).

23. This is similar to E. F. Schumacher's call to think holistically, and act in a piecemeal fashion (Schumacher 1973).

24. Jusuck Koh calls for conceptualizing the built environment as a place (with concrete, experiential, and heterogeneous qualities) as opposed to a space (which is abstract, impersonal, and homogeneous) (Koh, 13). He says that we should have a "holistic view of building—people—place as one system" rather than that of "a building as an aesthetic object, a complete entity and closed system by itself" (Koh, 12), emphasizing the interdependency of beauty and economy, aesthetics and pragmatics.

25. To this end, Koh asks, "What would happen if architects conceptualized their designs as musical scores and as choreography open to creative interpretation by performances of users and builders" (Koh, 13)? According to this view, architecture "is not an object or end but a means to an end. . . . It must not sacrifice the basic sense of comfort, well-being, health, but must instead raise awareness of the role and value of supportive and inspiring environments. It must be open to and facilitate control, adjustment and change by the users and be responsive to change in physical and cultural environments" (Koh, 14). Koh adds, "Accepting the inevitability of change in use and users requires architects to forego their own egos and desires to imprint, and to place emphasis on processes of adaptation and adjustment rather than products" (ibid.).

8

RECONCEIVING THE CITY AND CULTURE

MAJOR AND WIDESPREAD CHANGES that began in the 1960s have wrought havoc on behavior and thinking as well as on the landscape, leading to what has been described as a "paradigm shift" (Kuhn)[1] and a "legitimacy crisis" (Habermas 1973). Like similar moments in history, such as the 1890s and the interwar period, this one has witnessed a search for meaning featuring a fascination with the past and calls for multidisciplinarity, multiculturalism, multivalence, and multilogue. During the current paradigm shift, notions about "city" and "culture" have been revised, as have the academic disciplines and professions devoted to them. This concluding chapter describes the reconceptualization that has taken place and dominant current metaphors. Explication of these terms historically and across disciplines may clear the way to more effectively discuss and engage both the city and culture.

METAPHORS FOR THE CITY AND CULTURE
From the 1750s to the 1880s (the first Industrial Revolution in Europe), the city and culture were widely conceived in terms of nature. Architects applied Laugier's model of the primitive hut while social philosophers regarded society as a natural organism. With the introduction of zoological classification (by Georges Cuvier) and the founding of a school of surgery in early nineteenth-century France, animal and bodily analogies for the city and culture became popular.

During the second Industrial Revolution—from the late nineteenth century to the interwar period—these organic metaphors persisted and were joined by the machine metaphor as expressed in Louis Sullivan's credo "Form follows function," Le Corbusier's aspiration to build "*machines à vivre,*" the City Functional movement in the US (1910s–), and the Athens Charter of 1933. Sometimes the machine was itself modeled after the organic, especially during the 1920s, as with Le Corbusier, for whom "the mechanical and biological analogies were almost interchangeable, the skeleton, organs and nervous system of the human body providing a complementary illustration to that of the chassis, engine and controls of the automobile, and the condition of the contemporary city alternating between that of a consumptive body or else like an engine which is seized" (Gosling and Maitland, 40). Although the machine metaphor was not new—E. P. Thompson (1967) points out that it had already appeared in the seventeenth century—it did not attain dominance until this period, which corresponds to the rise of heroic modernism, the various avant-gardes, taylorism, rationalism, and the rise of "experts" to study and guide change in the city and society: urban planners and social scientists.

Not incidentally, while functionalism was guiding the design of buildings and cities, so it was guiding social scientific thought. Functionalism reigned supreme among modern social scientists, who spoke of people in terms of their needs, as apparent in Bronislaw Malinowski and A. R. Radcliffe-Brown's functionalisms (1920s to 1950s) or Abraham Maslow's "hierarchy of needs." As architects were attacking the symbolic/ornamental architecture of the Academy, social anthropologists were attacking the historical particularists—whose work constituted a romantic rebellion against Enlightenment thought—for descending into triviality. Both were disparaging their predecessors for being preoccupied with meaningless detail.

Around the turn of the century, many social scientists directed their attention to the city, developing among other explanatory frameworks the notion of "human ecology" (the Chicago School), which viewed the city as an organism. Not unlike the European avant-garde movements, which sought to challenge the assumptions of bourgeois capitalist society with the hope of revolutionizing it through art, anthropology also challenged the status quo by familiarizing the exotic and thereby defamiliarizing the familiar.

Both modern architects and anthropologists, then, wished to distance themselves from the forms and norms of bourgeois life, and they did so

Abandonment and vandalism in New York City, 1980s

by establishing a clean slate through deliberate ahistoricism and by applying defamiliarizing and shock techniques. Seeking to be scientific in their work, architects and planners admired and emulated the engineer while social scientists modeled their research after that of natural scientists. From World War II to the 1960s, the machine metaphor grew even more embedded, almost fully eclipsing the organic one both in urban design and in the study of the city and culture. And just as the reactions to functionalist architecture continue to develop certain fragments of the functionalist doctrine today, so anthropology has never entirely discarded functionalist tenets, particularly the notion that behavior and thought follow (can be explained by) function. Both the machine and organic metaphors became bankrupt, however, as the post-industrial and information revolutions challenged traditional conceptions of the city and culture, which relied on geographic boundaries, political-economic circumscriptions, population densities and numbers, and a social consensus.[2]

The transition to a post-industrial global economy corresponded to many other changes. With the technological and economic transformations implied by de-industrialization and the growth of the third and fourth economic sectors, macroeconomic changes took place, contributing to a worldwide economic crisis, as did microeconomic ones, such as the introduction of credit and loan systems. In the nations of the Western world, the number of people earning their livelihoods from manufacturing declined (although the perception of decline surpassed the actual degree) while the service sector burgeoned and selective re-industrialization occurred in the highly technical sector. Sweatshops reappeared employing undocumented workers, a blatant reminder that the Third and First Worlds coexist side by side in the same locales. By the 1980s, labor unions (syndicalism) and collective bargaining had weakened considerably and there was increased polarization between high-pay/high-status jobs and low-pay/low-status ones. There was also a marked growth in unemployment and the informal sector. The result was a growing gap between the rich and the poor that characterized both late-industrial capitalist nations and the global political economy. Thomas Dutton observed that homeless people and stretch limousines seemed to be the two fastest growing items on the streets of New York City. He contended, "the magnified proliferation of the extremes, of wealth and poverty, of massive development and homelessness, can only be recognized as different aspects of the same process" (Dutton 1986, 23).

Along with these changes, we have also witnessed the growth of metropolitan regions, increased suburbanization and freeway construction, massive public-housing programs, the ghettoization of society along class and ethnic lines, gentrification, displacement, and homelessness. On the global level, we have seen increased concentration of capital in the form of diversified conglomerates (multinational and transnational corporations) and international banking; massive deficits and debts (within nations and Third World debts), largely because of the social costs of the dual market economy; and the rise of world cities.[3] Some of the pivotal global events and trends during this period include the war in Vietnam; the aerospace program; poor people's movements; the women's movement; Civil Rights movements; the rise of the radical right, fundamental religious revivals, neonationalist and neoregionalist movements; inflation; the fiscal crisis of the 1970s; a rise in terrorism and hate crimes; the accelerated movement of labor, capital, products, and ideas; the Green movement; the rise of Japan as an economic superpower; the unification of Germany; the decline of communist regimes; and the Persian Gulf War. These events and trends highlighted the crisis in the Western Enlightenment tradition and contributed to challenging it.

The transition from a culture of production to one of consumption in highly industrialized nations was related to these events and trends.

Along with the shift to a culture of consumption, related transformations in society and political economy included the commercialization
and commodification of architecture and architects; globalization of
national and transnational markets; and the breakdown of traditional
disciplinary boundaries, professional responsibilities, and dualities or
oppositions. These dualities and oppositions include: socialism and liberalism (C. W. Mills 1963a); the political left and right (Rosenau); the
public and the private (sectors, realms, domains, spheres, and space);
high and mass art and architecture; the city and the countryside; the
core and the periphery; and the First and Third Worlds. We have also
been witnessing a noticeable shift of attention from the centers to the
peripheries, from central cities to suburbs and rural areas, from global
cities (or "core" regions) to small towns and villages around the world
(the "periphery"), from the masculine-gendered modernity to a feminine
or un-gendered postmodernity (see B. K. Scott 1990; Jardine 1985), and
from the cultures of the dominant/mainstream/elite to the those of the
subaltern/oppressed/marginal/silenced.

All of these changes have conspired to further challenge traditional
conceptions of the city and culture. As William Sharpe and Leonard Wallock pointed out (1983), we experienced a "crisis of language" because
what we were naming changed. Efforts to recover a meaningful discourse
have featured more encompassing and usually less precise terms.

RECONCEIVING THE CITY

The distinctions between the city, suburbs, and countryside were rendered obsolete with advanced industrial capitalism, a development foreseen by a number of scholars and critics. Karl Marx, for instance,
observed in the *Grundrisse* (1858) the beginnings of "the urbanization of
the countryside." H. G. Wells predicted in 1900 that the industrial city
would become "post-urban" (Fishman 1987). After living in Los Angeles
in the 1910s and 1920s, Frank Lloyd Wright proposed planning for this
development rather than allowing it to happen haphazardly, with his project for Broadacres City (F. L. Wright 1932). During the interwar period,
members of the Regional Planning Association of America understood
the new scale of development and insisted upon the need for regional
planning. And Arthur Schlesinger asserted in 1940, "When the city
encroaches sufficiently on the country and the country on the city, there
will come an opportunity for the development of a type of civilization

such as the world has never known. The old hard-and-fast distinction between urban and rural will tend to disappear" (Schlesinger, 36).

With the tremendous growth of suburbs around central cities after the World War II, the juridical term *city* no longer corresponded to a significant entity and was replaced by the technical term SMSA (Standard Metropolitan Statistical Area), defined as a central city with at least 50,000 inhabitants and its surrounding communities which maintain a high degree of political and economic integration with the center. In 1968, the French geographer Jean Gottmann coined the term "megalopolis" to describe linkages of SMSAs in the United States. Melvin Webber called this the "non-place urban realm" (1964); Lewis Mumford called it the "anti-city" (1962); Kenneth Jackson called it the "centerless city" (K. Jackson 1985, 265–66); and Bennett Berger declared that we have been creating "an urban civilization without cities" (1960). Echoing H.G. Wells (above), Françoise Choay proposed the term "post-urban" to describe our current condition, saying, "This term would . . . permit us to let go of the imagery . . . of the large city of grand assemblages born of a time when technology and the economy demanded concentration" (Choay 1970, 1152). Other proposed ways of reconceiving the city (and the suburbs) since the 1960s include "collage city" (Rowe and Koetter), the "megaburb," the "technoburb" (Fishman 1987), "cyburbia" (Sorkin, Dewey), "exopolis" (Soja), the "new city" (Fishman 1992), and the "100-mile city" (Sudjic).

If the city is redefined, so the process of urban growth—or urbanization—and the lifestyle of city-dwellers—or urbanism—must also be redefined. Manuel Castells (1972) proposed that we define urbanization in global terms as the integration of regions into the world system and that we define urbanism as the culture of the world system. Immanuel Wallerstein (1974) similarly redefined urbanization as the growth and development of the world capitalist system and urbanism as the culture of this system. Eschewing the "traditional dichotomy of city and country," Loïc Julienne and Jean-Marie Mandon chose to speak of "an urbanity which touches all sectors of activity" (Julienne and Mandon). It is not, says Ingersoll, the city that is disappearing but the suburb (Ingersoll 1992, 5), as all becomes urban.

While defense largely motivated and justified dense settlements for centuries, new defense technologies (atomic energy) employed during World War II motivated and justified the dispersal of settlements. Along with the extended power of the state, mass media, and transnational corporations, the enclosed space of older cities was transformed into what Henri Lefebvre (1974) called "abstract space," where place became inconsequential, generalized, undifferentiated, indefinite, and undefined. Frederic Jameson asserted that the city has been displaced by a "new hyperspace," a "new world space of multinational capital," a kind of global space which is "bereft of spatial coordinates" (1984b). According to Dutton, cities have been "dramatically restructured to harbor new spatial and social relations of production in order to maximize the international mobility of capital to its highest profitability" (Dutton 1986, 22).

In the social sciences, the initial American notion of the city grew out of the work of the Chicago School, circa 1900–1930. Applying European social theory to the Chicago scene, these sociologists and anthropologists transposed theories about the transition from pre-industrial to industrial society (the shift from primary group and community solidarity to individual autonomy paradigm) onto the demographic movement from the countryside to the city then occurring in the United States. As distinct from Europe, where urbanization had been occurring for centuries, industrialization and urbanization occurred simultaneously in Chicago and other American cities and thus appeared as synonymous and indissociable processes (Arensberg). The Chicago School, then, confused urbanization (migration to cities or the spread of urban form and function) with industrialization (the increase in the number of people engaged in industry), a confusion which continued to plague American urban and social theory through Robert Redfield's attempt to devise a folk–urban continuum (1947), up until the present.

The assumptions of this school of "human ecology" began to be challenged after World War II when massive suburbanization could not be explained by Ernest Burgess's theory of graduated concentric zones (1925), and as "ways of life" in cities no longer conformed to Louis Wirth's description in "Urbanism as a Way of Life" (1938). Herbert Gans revised Wirth's thesis in "Urbanism and Suburbanism as Ways of Life" (1962; in Gans 1968), explaining that the rise of metropolitan regions in the United States revealed the inadequacy of the rural/urban distinction posited by Wirth. Rather, one's "way of life," Gans said, has less to do with whether one lives in the city, the suburbs, or the countryside, than with such factors as social class, life-cycle stages, and rates of social mobility, unless people are not free to make choices (ibid.).

As regards defining the city, a consensus among urban social scientists no longer prevailed. Since the 1960s, they have tended to define cities in a deliberately vague way, as settings in which certain characteristics appear together but need not all occur in every case.[4] Likewise, urban historians as well as architectural historians, theorists, and critics have also been loathe to define the city. It is not surprising, then, that urban designers—architects and planners—have been struggling with the question of how to define the canvas upon which they labor.[5]

RECONCEIVING CULTURE

As actual and perceptual changes called for redefining the container (the city), so they called for redefining its contents, or culture. In place of the traditional notion of culture as a bounded entity whose members share common "templates" (cognitive maps of beliefs and behaviors), world systems theory, along with the interpretive, humanistic, and symbolic brands of anthropology, reconceived culture as something which is more fluid and permeable, having the capacity to both absorb and transform long-term historical and cross-cultural influences. In contrast to the human ecology and functionalist paradigms which dominated anthropology until the 1960s, this less monolithic understanding of culture engendered a widely spread sentiment that we can not reduce culture to its functions, but must understand it on its own terms. This sentiment led anthropologists away from scientific analysis, dissection, and explanation and toward the uncovering or interpreting of meanings.[6] If culture was a language, according to this approach, the language would not be only for communicating, for getting one's message across (its function); it would also be for poetry and word games. The emphasis would be on phonemics, or meanings, rather than on phonetics. Religion, for instance, would not be understood as functioning to unite people, or to instruct. Rather, it would be understood as an expression of feeling. The emphasis would be on the "native's point of view" (the emic), not the outsider's view (the etic), and the anthropologist's contribution would be regarded merely as one outsider's interpretation rather than a definitive account of the culture being observed.

The turn to structural linguistics and semiology in architecture and planning theory in the 1960s was in part influenced by the structuralism of the humanities and social sciences as initiated by anthropologists, particularly Claude Lévi-Strauss. Structuralism "presented culture as a system of codes, genres, and conventions which produce identifiable meanings and values. Relentlessly demystifying texts and ideas, structuralism made the cultural system itself the object of intense study" (Watts, 628). By the mid-1960s, however, it was regarded as too insular, and was joined by more contextual and critical approaches including poststructuralism (see chapter 6).

Rather than envision themselves as white-jacketed scientists, anthropologists began to question "the effort to create a formal vocabulary of analysis purged of all subjective reference" and the claim to moral neutrality and the Olympian view, the " 'God's truth' idea" (Geertz 1980a, 178). James Clifford described part of the motivation for this trend, saying, "Anthropology no longer speaks with automatic authority for others defined as unable to speak for themselves" (Clifford, 10). Suggesting the absence of foundations, grand explanatory frameworks (what the French call *grands récits*), or "meta-narratives" (see chapters 4 and 6), the anthropologist Clifford Geertz recounted an Indian story of a conversation between an Indian and an Englishman. When the Indian maintained that the world rests on a platform that rests on the back of an elephant which rests on the back of a turtle, the Englishman asked what that turtle rests on and the Indian replied, "Another turtle." "And that turtle?" the Englishman asked. "After that," said the Indian, "it is turtles all the way down" (Geertz 1973, 28–9). This abandonment of the belief in and search for objective truths led some anthropologists (such as George Marcus and Michael Fischer) to contend that the culture concept itself had become "post-paradigmatic," that it had somehow transcended paradigms. Meanwhile, the abandonment of the positivistic empirical base upon which anthropology stood reconfigured it for many as a humanistic study rather than a social science.

Pauline Marie Rosenau distinguishes this postmodernist study of society from its modern precursors, saying that the moderns "seek to isolate elements, specify relationships, and formulate a synthesis" (Rosenau, 8) while the postmoderns "offer indeterminacy rather than determinism, diversity rather than unity, difference rather than synthesis, complexity rather than simplification. They look to the unique rather than to the general, to intertextual relations rather than causality, and to the unrepeatable rather than the re-occurring, the habitual, or the routine. Within a postmodern perspective social science becomes a more subjective and humble enterprise as truth gives way to tentativeness. Confidence in emotion replaces efforts at impartial observation. Relativism is preferred to objectivity, fragmentation to totalization. Attempts to apply the model of natural science inquiry in the social sciences are rejected because post-modernists consider such methods to be part of the larger techno-scientific corrupting cultural imperative, originating in the West but spreading out to encompass the planet" (Rosenau, 9). Postmodern social scientists, Rosenau attests, criticize the excesses and abuses of modernity, but try to avoid substituting an alternative "meta-narrative."

As the social sciences evolved, so the traditional disciplines of history and anthropology underwent a rapprochement. In anthropology (which might be defined as the study of human diversity and inequalities throughout space and time), there was a crisis of the ethnographic "object." This confusion (Who is the other and who are we?) signaled a crisis of representation and of the discipline as a whole, leading anthropologists to investigate questions of representation and history. Meanwhile, dissatisfaction among historians with their customary claim to objectivity and with the discipline's emphasis on elites led them to stress narrative and subjective histories of non-elites.[7]

Not only did the methods of anthropologists and historians begin to converge, then, so did their fields of study. As anthropologists largely shifted their focus from "traditional" cultures or "simple" societies to elites ("studying up"), "complex" societies, their own culture and subcultures (particularly if regarded as somehow marginal), and themselves; historians shifted from the study of the most famous and powerful to those who have been neglected by the historical record, particularly ethnic groups other than the White Anglo-Saxon Protestant one (so-called minorities), women, and the poor. Both disciplines began paying more attention to the margins and to silence (to those without voices or with voices not previously recognized), not simply to the norm and the most visible or documented groups.[8] As an antidote to the determinism of earlier paradigms, social scientists and historians began opting for the plural—cultures, subcultures, histories—(for example, Geertz 1980a; Rollwagen)—over the singular. At the same time, postmodern culture generally affirmed and celebrated pluralism, understood as social diversity.

STUDYING THE CITY AND CULTURE

As urban design theory underwent a shift from models to the less prescriptive type, parallel epistemological shifts took place in the study of culture and history. As urban designers employed the figure-ground drawing to highlight the relationship between built and open space and to encourage sensitivity to the design context, social and humanistic studies similarly questioned representation as scholars began paying attention to what was not there (written, said, present) as well as what was there. As urban design devalued the architectural object in favor of contextualism, functionalism in favor of conveying meanings, the architect-as-inspired-genius in favor of humility and collaboration, and the architect-as-social-engineer in favor of being responsive to prospective users, so the social sciences and humanities jettisoned "pure" or objective studies for subjective ones, explanation in favor of interpretation, the scholar as expert in favor of the scholar as mere explorer and perpetual student, and strictly controlled variables in favor of transactive methods and multidisciplinarity.[9]

While the machine metaphor largely corresponded to a notion that the city and culture were discrete entities, the prevalent attitude in architecture, planning, the social sciences, and history since the 1960s regarded the city and culture as inextricably intertwined and mutually influential. They regarded both as impure and each a rich source of inspiration for the other. So as urban designers and culture theorists gradually abandoned the pursuit of pure objects and knowledge through carefully controlled scientific methods, they grew to favor complex solutions through a wide array of methods borrowed from other fields. In brief, exclusivity was largely replaced by inclusivity, quantitative methods by qualitative ones.

Recalling the interdisciplinary nature of the Industrial Revolution as scholars pondered the "social question," the post-industrial revolution also witnessed an impatience with disciplinary boundaries,[10] seeing them as obstacles rather than convenient landmarks in better understanding and contributing to the world around us.[11] Caroline Mills describes this temper by saying that the "expanding postmodern culture [stresses] the merging of separate realms, the search for design processes and solutions which are humanistic and expressive, open to dialogue and negotiation" (C. Mills 1986, 2). As a result, interdisciplinary approaches to the study of the city and culture have surfaced on the interstices of traditional disciplines, falling within the trend described by Geertz as the "blurring of genres" (Geertz 1980a).[12] These include urban studies, urban sociology (e.g., Gans; Gutman), urban anthropology (e.g., O. Lewis; Rapoport; Hannerz), a certain sub-genre of urban history (e.g., Beeman; Ebner; Hershberg; Warner), proxemics (E. T. Hall), ekistics (Doxiadis), environmental studies (e.g., McHarg), and environmental psychology (e.g., Proshansky). We have also seen a renewed interest since around 1970 in geopolitical theory, in the social aspects of spatiality, and in the aesthetics of place (Harvey 1989, 284) (e.g., Soja; Gregory and Urry).

Reflecting the loss of faith in progress and in technocratic solutions, these new formulations tend to supplant the effort to discover "laws" and to guide change with other methods such as Geertz's "thick description" and Michel Foucault's "archaeology of knowledge," both strategies which vindicate original thinking unfettered by traditional disciplinary boundaries. Without certainties and positive means for discovering them, human subjectivity regains a place in both the study of culture and the design task. Rather than derive knowledge exclusively or at all from "scientific" means, it would be accessed through transactive and qualitative means.

The work of Michel Foucault documented this shift while also contributing to it. Leaving its mark on virtually every field of study since the 1970s, Foucault's influence on urban design theory centered mainly on his ideas about the relationship between space, power, and knowledge. Taking Jeremy Bentham's 1787 "panopticon" plan for institutional buildings (especially the prison) as "the paradigmatic example of the interworkings of space, power, and knowledge in a disciplinary society" (Wright and Rabinow 1982), Foucault contended that "space is where discourses about power and knowledge are transformed into actual relations of power" (ibid.). For Foucault, "architecture and its concomitant theory never constitute an isolated field to be analyzed in minute detail; they are only of interest when one looks to see how they mesh with economics, politics, or institutions" (ibid.). He argued: "I think it is somewhat arbitrary to try to dissociate the effective practice of freedom by people, the practice of social relations, and the spatial distributions in which they find themselves. If they are separated, they become impossible to understand. Each can only be understood through the other. . . . Nothing is fundamental. That is what is interesting in the analysis of society. . . . There are only reciprocal relations, and the perpetual gaps between intentions in relation to one another. . . . What is interesting is always interconnection, not the primacy of this over that, which never has any meaning" (Rabinow 1982b, 20).

The challenge posed to the scientific pursuit has rendered the method and theory implied by "ethnography" increasingly relevant to a variety of scholarly and professional undertakings. Traditionally a tool of cultural anthropologists, ethnography entails the close study of a group of people particularly through immersion (involving prolonged participant-observation, language acquisition, and unstructured interviewing) in order to understand the "native's point of view." Stephen Tyler asserts that ethnography "is the discourse of the post-modern world, for the world that made science, and that science made, has disappeared, and scientific thought is now an archaic mode of consciousness" (Tyler, 123).[13] George Marcus interprets this "move toward the ethnographic in American academic political economy [as] related to a widely perceived decline of the post-World War II international order in which America has held a hegemonic position and to an undermining of the American form of the welfare state itself" (G. Marcus, 167). According to Marcus, this transition (as seen from the American perspective) has been "reflected intellectually in a widespread retreat from theoretically centralized and organized fields of knowledge" (ibid.) and has incited "a spirit of experimentation that aims to explore ways to evoke and represent diversity in social life to convey the richness of experience, to probe the meaning of details of everyday life, to remember symbols and associations long forgotten" (ibid.).

Urban designers have sought to apply ethnography in their work.[14] Sanjoy Mazumdar explains the ten aspects of architectural ethnography:

> First, the primary emphasis is on taking genuine interest in, learning about, and understanding the culture of the group, and what culture members see as important. Second, personal contact with the culture members and their place, through site visits, is essential. Third, one needs to observe and note all observables, such as the people, their clothes, their interactions and behavior, the buildings, and the products of their common efforts and enterprise. . . . Fourth, it is important to ask questions, especially those based on the observations. The questions should address the relationships between the culture and the physical environment. It helps to be open and unrestricted about the questions, as it is possible that these relationships may appear in unusual places. Fifth, for asking questions it is necessary to identify knowledgeable and forthcoming informants. Sixth, it is important to study the culture's buildings and their use of them, why they build them the way they do, and what they mean to them. . . .

Seventh, it may also require going farther afield from buildings to learn about all aspects of life that may lead to a better understanding of their culture, and their relationships with the physical environment ... Eighth, since the researcher will have personal experiences of the field and site, these too can be used as data. Ninth, questions need to be asked regarding the meaning, nature, and use of the specific facility to be designed. Tenth, the field data needs to be recorded so that one can reexamine and analyze it (Mazumdar 1991, 123).

Another architect who has applied anthropological method to design is Lucien Kroll. According to Kroll, architects should adopt an "ethnological attitude" (Kroll 1984c and 1985c). "It is a process—not a procedure—[that] receives and transmits, not wanting to master everything, but to allow some things to remain obscure, apparently irrational," Kroll has contended, "It is not rational, but it is reasonable. It promises, then, a much better understanding of a reality that is fluid, moving, and unknowable. To allow things to happen themselves is much more efficacious than to prescribe everything" (Kroll 1984c). In adopting the ethnological attitude, Kroll has enlisted the ethnographic method for several projects in Belgium and France with varying results (see Ellin 1994).

NEW METAPHORS: TEXT AND COLLAGE

The hyper-inclusive and noncommittal ways of approaching the city and culture since the 1960s are responses to the broadbased challenge posed to rationalism that eschews the notions that knowledge can be pigeonholed and that experts can dispense authoritative knowledge. But this refusal to define the city and culture in an exacting way also renders them elusive. This elusivity in turn contributes to provoking our curiosity and to inciting urban and cultural research in search of new approaches to discussing and engaging the city and culture.

From inside the eye of the post-industrial tornado, we may seem to have transcended paradigms, grand explanatory narratives, models, and metaphors. But living without these would be like living without language, culture, and ideology. With the benefit of hindsight, future generations will be able to understand the present in a way which we, its participants, can not. Presently, in the midst of this "mutation" (Jameson 1984b), its outlines appear hazy but may be discerned nonetheless. From our admittedly disadvantaged viewpoint, it appears that the predominant metaphors for the city and culture have become the *text* and the *collage*.

Regarding the city and culture as confluences of meanings rather than functions, urban designers and cultural anthropologists have turned to literary criticism in an effort to interpret the city and culture as literary critics do a text. Also contributing to this turn has been the increasing perception that the contributions of these "experts" are subjective interpretations (or fictions) rather than definitive solutions or analyses. The obsession with the text metaphor for the city and culture is revealed in the extensive use of terms such as discourse, legibility, narrative, the vernacular, and interpretive communities, as well as in the growing interest in "reading and writing" architecture, the city, and culture.

After seeking insight from literary theory of the 1950s and 1960s—structuralism, semiology, and linguistics—some urban designers and cultural anthropologists began turning to deconstructionism, which began to appear in the late sixties. Inspired mainly by the work of Jacques Derrida (from his reading of Heidegger), deconstructionism challenges the modernist presupposition that the signifier and signified are tightly related, suggesting instead that "signifiers always become signifieds for other signifiers, and vice versa" (Barthes 1973). This assertion that there is no "final signified," only "infinite metaphorical chains" (ibid.), challenged the modernist presuppositions that form can follow function and that purity can be achieved, since we live in an impure world. 15 Instead, deconstructionism views the text (and by extension, individual lives, whole cultures, buildings, and cities) as a series of intersecting texts drawn from past experience. Influenced by Derrida, Roland Barthes defined "*texte*" in the *Encyclopédie Universalis* as derived from the Latin "*textum*," meaning "a thing woven" or a tapestry. Barthes contended that "there is always language before the text and around it" (Barthes 1973, 1015; cited by Sammarcelli).

Challenging the purity of a text, deconstructionism views "collage/montage as the primary form of postmodern discourse" (Harvey 1989, 51). The application of collage is intended to require the audience to participate in the production of meaning while minimizing the authority of the author, who is to some extent under the power of the created object, which takes on a life of its own. 16 As Derrida maintains, the fragments offered up by the producer require a "double reading": "that of the fragment perceived in relation to its text of origin [and] that of the fragment as incorporated into a new whole, a different totality" (Derrida; cited by Harvey 1989, 51).

A related concept of literary criticism is that of intertextuality, also referred to as trans-textuality. Reacting to the resolute autonomy of modern literature and literary criticism, intertextuality acknowledges that the reading or writing of a text is always affected by other texts and life experiences; it presupposes that "Reading is always re-reading" ("*Lire c'est toujours relire*," Sammarcelli, 59). The notion of intertextuality is often attributed to Julia Kristeva, who wrote in *Semiotike* (1969) that "every text is constructed as a mosaic of quotations, every text is absorption and transformation of another text" (845, cited by Sammarcelli). A variation on intertextuality is "transfiction," which denudes literary processes, demasking "narrative conventions and changing them into 'counter-conventions' in order to break the illusion of reality" (Sammarcelli, 70). One kind of transfiction is "metafiction," which presents the theme of the non-interpretability of the world. Mas'ud Zavarzadeh describes this: "Through an extravagant over-totalization and mock interpretation of the human condition, the metafictionist accentuates the arbitrariness of uniting the elements of a disjunctive universe into a significant whole. His over-totalizing approaches a parody of the ordered, causal, and realistically performed interpretation of the fictive novelist. By substituting parody of interpretation for straight interpretation, the metafictionist demonstrates the confusing multiplicity of reality and thus the naïveté involved in attempting to reach a total synthesis of life within narrative. [Over-totalization,] consequently, creates a work at the zero degree of interpretation" (1976, 39–40; cited by Sammarcelli).

The novels of John Barth offer examples of both intertextuality and transfiction. Two characters in *Chimera*, for instance, "speculated endlessly on such questions as whether a story might imaginably be framed from inside, as it were, so that the usual relation between container and contained would be reversed and paradoxically reversible" (Barth 1972, 32). And an oft-repeated declaration by characters in Barth's *Tidewater Tales* is, "The key to the treasure may be the treasure itself" (Barth 1986), suggesting that words and language may themselves be the treasures, rather than what is done with them. Such rumination about whether characters in a story might create the story, rather than the authors, parallels the interest among some architects and planners in enabling inhabitants to create their habitats and among some anthropologists in "auto-ethnography" or in assembling (or "editing") compositions written by the people they are studying. In literature, urban design, and anthropology, this approach reflects upon the absence of the author, or at least the apparent absence of the author, and it entertains the possibility of people shaping their own destinies.

The text and collage metaphors have been central to the reconception of culture. Geertz, for instance, asserted that the world is constituted symbolically, that people organize the various aspects of their lives into a coherent assemblage through the medium of culture or of ideology (Geertz 1964). Similarly, the anthropologists Claude Lévi-Strauss and Barbara Myerhoff described culture as a *bricolage*. As anthropologists came to value interpretation over analysis, they increasingly modeled their work after literary criticism rather than science and their *modus operandi* became that of "reading, interpreting, translating, and writing" culture (Geertz 1980b). Geertz asserted: "Arguments, melodies, formulas, maps, and pictures are not idealities to be stared at but texts to be read; so are rituals, palaces, technologies, and social formations" (Geertz 1980b, 135). Like the literary critic, he contended, the anthropologist should seek structures of significance and describe these "thickly" (1973). This suggestion served as a point of departure for the influential collection *Writing Culture* (Clifford and Marcus, eds), which discusses culture as though it were a narrative or, in the less restricted sense of text, as anything which represents. One of the contributors, Vincent Crapanzano, explained that the anthropologist "presents languages, cultures, and societies in all their opacity, their foreignness, their meaninglessness; then like the magician, the *hermeneut*, Hermes himself, he clarifies the opaque, renders the foreign familiar, and gives meaning to the meaningless. He decodes the message. He interprets" (Crapanzano 1986, 51). Such cultural representation, or "cultural critique," does not assume authority (like its modern precursors), but instead assumes contingency and contestability.[17]

As the culture concept evolved, so too did the concept of community and of the city. According to Warriner and Conviser, the pre-industrial conception of community posited a cosmological order, the industrial conception posited an instrumental and rational order, and the postmodern conception posits personal constructions of order. Indeed, the sociologist Gerald Suttles (1972) asserted that community is socially constructed and is done so differently by different people.[18] In similar fashion, the notion of a monolithic "city" was supplanted by the notion that the city has multiple meanings, for it is perceived differently by each person, influenced largely by Kevin Lynch's *The Image of the City*

(1960).[19] The urban historian Sam Bass Warner—inspired by Lynch and by Geertz—contended that we must speak of "multiple urban images" (Warner, 384).[20] The firm Narrative Architecture Today (NATO) explained that "narrative" refers to many possible stories, not a single one.[21] Turning his gaze to urbanism, Barthes maintained that "the city is a discourse and this discourse is truly a language" (Barthes 1975, 92; cited by Harvey 1989, 67). And more recently, in *The City of Collective Memory*, Christine Boyer attempts to read the city as a "text" (1994, 19–21).

As the city was being reconceived as text and collage, the task of the urban designer shifted accordingly. There was an emphasis, for instance, on creating legible cities and a sense of place (see chapter 3), in reaction to the "illegibility" of much postwar urban development. As Allan Jacobs and Donald Appleyard contended, "A city should present itself as a readable story, in an engaging and, if necessary, provocative way, for people are indifferent to the obvious, overwhelmed by complexity" (Jacobs and Appleyard, 116). Boyer has pointed out that "the postmodern aesthetic claims to return to narrative forms, searching for an architectural language that communicates with the public, that manipulates simple combinations and patterns that are part of our collective recall or memory" (Boyer 1990). In architecture and urban design, these concerns are often articulated in terms of con*text*uality, the text remaining central. Indeed, as our environments grow increasingly hyperreal, one critic maintained, people generally "must now exchange their role as 'users' and become 'readers' " (Bergum, 131).[22]

Derrida's notion of double reading finds analogues in urban design theory, where it is broken down as the architect's perception on the one hand and the perception of non-architects on the other, or alternatively, as the historical source and the new context. Some articulations of this include Robert Venturi's (1966) inclusivist "both/and" approach, which plies a pluralistic and ironic language of architecture; Charles Jencks's "double coding" (Jencks 1977, see chapter 3); Robert Stern's "doubles of post-modern" (1981), and Kenneth Frampton's "critical regionalism."

The French architectural historian Robert Delevoy recommended that Barthes's *S/Z* (1970), which was based on the short story "Sarrasine" by Balzac, "become the handbook of architects and those who teach architecture" (Delevoy, 19). For Delevoy its "method of creation and criticism presents singular analogies with the approaches we are seeking to develop in architecture" (ibid.). *S/Z*, Delevoy contended, "is

based on an absolutely new reading of an old text, on a cutting, a fragmentation, a dissociation, an explosion and a regrouping of the
exploded parts which gives rise to new, attractive and overwhelming
texts" (Delevoy, 18). In applying this to architecture, Delevoy called for
a use of quotation which is not eclectic but "strongly controlled" and
"capable of giving expression to different codes so as to confer its historical legitimacy on a practice that has suddenly become unusual"
(Delevoy, 19). This is what the neorationalists were doing, along with
the American contextualists and neotraditionalists.

In a subverted fashion, this is also what some neomodern or deconstructivist work has been doing, such as Bernard Tschumi's follies at the
Parc de la Villette in Paris as well as its "thematic garden" (Chaslin, 227)
for which Derrida teamed up with Peter Eisenman to create "Chora l
Works" by deconstructing the chora in Plato's *Timeaus* (Derrida and
Eisenman). Eisenman has proposed "architecture as writing" and "architecture as fiction," not a "simulation of history, reason, or reality" but "a
representation of itself, of its own values and internal experience" (1984).

The French architect Antoine Grumbach regards the city as a collective collage—or a "theatre of memory"—and the architect's task as
enhancing this collage rather than detracting from it (Grumbach 1978,
15). He likewise sees the architectural historian's task as that of examining how new buildings relate to what existed before and what stands
around them now. Grumbach contends, "The history of architecture—
or rather the histories that have been written on architecture until
now—are the strange product of a collective myopia. There is a kind of
morality throughout these books, which is always looking for the purity,
the origin, of the work" (ibid.). He suggests that "architecture might be
rewritten from an impure angle: the Louvre would then become the Lou-
vres, Versaille, the Versailles—each would be the sum of all the memories of the place in the same way that a cathedral is only the product of
a long series of accumulations. . . . The evolution of architecture
towards the conception of the city as an impure object is part of this
enterprise: the city as a collage" (ibid.).[23]

The notion of the "collage city" (Rowe)—or the city as montage,
assemblage, bricolage, or pastiche—has largely replaced that of the
functional city of modernism. Boyer maintains, "The city of distinctive
mono-zoning gives way to undirected hetero-zoning, just as mono-pro-
grammatic buildings themselves give way to hetero-programmatic

buildings. Work 'here,' play 'there,' and live 'elsewhere,' gives way to a 'work-play,' 'live-work' and 'play-live' heterotopic urban fabric" (Boyer 1990, 127).[24] This city is "not a *cité industriel* or a City Beautiful but a city-montage. Not an Osaka nor a Washington DC but a Los Angeles" (ibid.). For architects and planners, this city-montage is no longer modeled after nature or the machine, but after cities of the past, what Anthony Vidler has described as "the third typology" (Vidler 1978, see chapter 2). In regional planning, the emphasis on plurality and collage has been manifest in proposals for many centers, or pluricentrality, diverging from the traditional model of a single central city. Examples include the growth plans for the Paris and Los Angeles regions.

As culture has been conceived as text and collage, then, so has its container, the city. In architecture, urban design, the social sciences, and the humanities, the text and collage metaphors apply historical and cultural quotation. These new metaphors are different from their predecessors in that they are less dogmatic, more synthetic, and more self-conscious. They acknowledge the role of the author/creator as an integral part of the work, as opposed to the modernist stance of art for art's sake, evincing what Walter Benjamin described as an "aura." The assembler of the collage or text is not submerged by it, but is nonetheless more humble than the modern artist as the role of the reader or observer in interpreting the work accrues. This attitude condones self-consciousness as well as self-criticism and it nurtures reflexivity on the part of both author and audience. It also emphasizes the social context of the work and the nature of the work as artifice or spectacle. The collages are regarded as three-dimensional—space, time, and point of view[25]—implying that one's perspective on the city or on culture depends on one's place within it.

Urban, architectural, and cultural theory since the 1960s is less idealistic than that which preceded it. Rather than subscribing to a utopian vision, seeking the truth or ultimate solutions, it is more humble, pragmatic, and cynical. It is also less passionate, politically and otherwise. It acknowledges the blurring of high art/culture and pop art/culture, champions cultural pluralism, and subscribes to a more inclusive anything-goes mentality. Postmodernism has thus been regarded by sociologists and architectural historians alike as bearing certain similarities with the Baroque period (B. Turner 1990; Belmont 1987), one of these being that both periods experienced a crisis of modernity, the first during the seventeenth century, the second during the twentieth. According to Bryan

Turner, "the Baroque fascination with allegory, with *trompe l'oeil* creations, with mechanical devices and constructions, with artificial ruins, with melancholy, and with metaphor anticipated the postmodern fascination with texts about texts, with stories inside narratives, with simulations—in a word, with the socially constructed textuality of reality" (B. Turner, 9). The Baroque also mixed the high and low cultures of the time.

The revamped role of urban designers and social scientists has featured a shift in focus, a retreat from a position of knowing and acting upon the city. From the architect's and planner's standpoint, this shift has brought increased sensitivity to the physical and social contexts in which they build and increased collaboration with other specialists and prospective users alike. From the perspective of the architectural and urban historian, this shift has broadened the definition of what constitutes architecture and of how it should be judged (for example, Kostof). As urban designers shifted from an emphasis on universal solutions to local ones, anthropologists made a similar shift from the exotic to one's own back yard. At the same time, anthropologists largely exchanged the nomothetic approach to the study of culture, which seeks cross-cultural universals and enjoyed prominence along with functionalism (1920s to 1950s), for the idiographic approach, which focuses on more detailed aspects of single cultures and was popular among the historical particularists (of the early twentieth century).

Although these shifts have been motivated by a desire to avoid accusations of authoritarianism, colonialism, imperialism, and elitism, they have also contributed to deflecting the concern for improving the world, leaving behind a concern for enhancing one's personal form of expression and career advancement. In anthropology, this tendency has been manifest in "reflexive ethnography," "auto" ethnography (Marcus and Fischer), or "I-witnessing" (Geertz 1988), in which the ethnographer chronicles his or her own experience alongside the traditional ethnography and sometimes at the expense of those putatively being studied. The anthropologist David Schneider pokes fun at this trend in relating a story about a long conversation between a postmodern anthropologist and an informant, pursuant upon which the informant remarks: "Okay, enough about you, now let's talk about me" (cited by Newton, 3). James Clifford points out that this kind of "extreme self-consciousness certainly has its dangers—of irony, of elitism, of solipsism, of putting the whole world in quotation marks" (Clifford, 25). Todd Gitlin contends

that this tendency in postmodern culture at large to regard "'the individual' as a sentimental attachment, a fiction to be enclosed within quotation
marks" means that "'The individual' has decomposed, as 'reality' has dissolved; nothing lives but 'discourses,' 'texts,' 'language games,' 'images,'
'simulations' referring to other 'discourses,' 'texts,' etc." (Gitlin 1988, 35).

In urban design, this tendency to "navel-gaze" is manifest in the preoccupation with formal considerations, money-making, and personal
notoriety rather than serving the unserved or even the prospective
users. This attitude is apparent in the inclusivist approaches, which suggest a desire to have it both ways (populist/elitist, market-oriented and
pragmatically-driven/artist) along with a reluctance to demonstrate
strong convictions which will inevitably displease some. Jencks's double
coding, for instance, could be understood as deeply cynical because it
does not even attempt to establish a meeting ground.

The less fortunate outcomes of this attitude are relativism to a
pathological degree and self-aggrandizement. For if there can be no
meta-narratives, if the chain of signifiers is endless, if "it is turtles all
the way down," then we have no basis on which to stand, no common
language with which to communicate. And the task of the social scientist, historian, writer, artist, or urban designer simply becomes the collection and assembling of elements in what Foucault has called the
museum of knowledge. Or it becomes an intensely personal pursuit.
Either way, the task is that of creating fictions since nothing else is possible. And the void allowed by this back seat or *arrière-garde* position is
filled by the marketplace.[26] While aspiring toward political correctness,
then, this reaction to the hubris of the modern project also signals a resignation, a reluctance to be engaged and to make a difference, ultimately
contributing to the perpetuation of unsatisfactory circumstances. More
positively, the celebration of pluralism can also translate into a concern
for representing and communicating with other peoples, and into liberation from oppressive pasts and hierarchies.

CONCLUSION: BEYOND IRONY AND ARTIFICE

This is only the second time in history that we are approaching a millennium and, not unlike the first time,[27] we are entertaining thoughts about
eschatology (the study of last things) and apocalypse. The historical
moment through which we are passing has been variously described as:
the end of ideology (Bell 1960); the end of history (Fukuyama 1989;

1992); the end of philosophy (for example, Rorty, Toulmin, Wittgenstein); the end(s) of ethnography (Clough 1992); the end of art (Arthur Danto); the death of man (Foucault); the death of history (Chakrabarty); the death of the subject and the self (Baudrillard); the death of the Author (Paul de Man); the age of post-ideology (*Los Angeles Times* March 27, 1992); the death of post-modern (Farrelly); the post–Cold War period (implying the end of a bi-polar global antagonism and the rise of multi-antagonisms); post-humanism (Hal Foster); the end of the modern age (Lukacs 1992); the end of the classical; the end of the end; the end of the beginning; the ends of value (all Eisenman 1984); the end of American history (Noble); the end of work (Rifkin); the end of modernity (Baudrillard 1980;[28] Bhabha); the end of taboos; the end of affluence; the end of intelligent writing; the end of Christendom; the end of British politics; the end of comedy; the end of sex; the end of libraries; the end of law; the end of art theory; the end of beauty; the end of conversation; the end of organized capitalism; the end of desire (all cited by C. Murphy 1992, 79); the end of cities (Blake 1982); the end of suburbia (Ingersoll 1992); the disappearing suburb (Ingersoll 1992); and the end of public space (Sorkin). While some of these declarations are clearly despairing and some hopeful, others simply mark a departure, the destination of which is as yet uncertain.

The changes that have incited such eschatological and apocalyptic meditations have also recast the city and culture while eliciting "crises" in the fields devoted to studying and engaging them. In both urban design and the social sciences, functionalist theories have lost legitimacy, in part because things no longer seemed to be functioning and in part because the rational concern with "how" (which predominated during the first half of the twentieth century) was being usurped by the more romantic concern with "why."[29] As the millennium approaches, both urban design theory and the study of society are harking back to their pre-modern humanistic traditions, with implications for the roles of the designer and the social scientist and for their respective methods and goals.

Although the built environment is more resilient to change than the cultures it contains, the changes implied by post-industrialism nonetheless have a vast impact on the shape of the landscape and the ideals and intentions of urban designers. Over the past century, specialization in the urban design professions has accelerated along with mass production. But as the number of middlepersons between client and user has grown, so, it appears, has user dissatisfaction. The divergence between that which urban designers champion and what non-urban designers prefer is evident, even blatant at times, and has been responsible for a number of disasters in urban design worldwide, notably just after World War II with the rapid building for large numbers.

Critiques of modern urbanism abounded. Modern urbanists were accused of being too utopian and unrealistic as well as too megalomaniac and authoritarian in their desire to change the world through changing the physical landscape according to their own visions. Witnessing the aesthetic monotony of what was being built in the 1950s and 1960s as well as the social correlates—places lacking in "soul" and character, social segregation, displacement, homelessness, decline of central cities and quality public space, privatization, rootlessness, fear, and paranoia—critics of modern urbanism countered the search for order with a search for diversity and disorder. A romantic rebellion ensued, as a "counterculture" emerged which emphatically did not wish to live like or live in machines. Cynicism prevailed along with the sentiments that no solutions exist and that history is not a linear movement toward perfection.

The loss of legitimacy of the machine as a model for planners and architects coincided, not incidentally, with a loss of faith in the inherent beneficence of technology subsequent to its use for destructive purposes during World War II and to the crisis offset by the Western world's dependence on oil in the late 1960s. It also coincided with the decline of machine-based industries, both in absolute number and status, as well as a general disillusionment apparent in and magnified by riots, social movements, and demonstrations surrounding issues of social inequality: racial, ethnic, gender and age-based discrimination as well as the more global neoimperialisms and neocolonialisms. All of these shattered the once unified idealistic modern vision.

A brake on building in the 1970s (due to the fiscal crisis) provided an occasion for reflecting upon what had gone wrong and how to go about changing it. Emanating both from within the design professions and without, from different perspectives and for different audiences, the critiques of modern urbanism maintained that urban design should be more contextual (physically and socially), that functional zoning regulations should be abandoned, that more power should be granted to local communities and less to planning commissions (or other State planning agencies), and that we should return to many of the features of pre-industrial cities. So planners and architects began, paradoxically, to plan for spontaneity and diversity, to design buildings and cities which would be complex and contradictory, and to look to the past for inspiration. The renewed interest in the past coincided with an interest in "preserving" it, and efforts to "reorganize" regions so as to diminish the negative effects of urban sprawl. These occurred alongside a resistance toward large-scale planning (unless approved design guidelines that allow for variety accompanied the plan). Although transportation, communication, and building technologies are increasingly sophisticated, postmodern urbanism tends to resist extensive use of them—in reaction to the perceived over-reliance of modern urbanism upon them—and sometimes even calls for a return to pre-industrial building methods, especially for housing.

Superficially, then, we have come full circle. This time, however, the pre-industrial-looking landscapes (some of which are more convincing than others) are the product of hyper-rational efforts. As such, postmodern urbanism might be perceived as dishonest or pretentious for trying to be something it is not. In addition, its complicity with the political economy in which it is embedded often renders its intents unrealizable, or in the interests of capital rather than the larger good. As a result, many contextual intentions are stymied and, even when realized, are judged unsuccessful by users and designers alike. When successful, though, these efforts can result in environments that harmonize with the physical and social contexts and which people appreciate for their nonintrusive quality and formal interest.

Although the lessons of modern urbanism have yet to be fully assimilated and postmodern urban design theory is inherently flawed (as described in chapter 5), it nonetheless offers certain correctives to its predecessor and has generated some built environments that are widely recognized as superior to those which issued from the tenets of modern urbanism. Most important is the renewed attention to fulfilling non-functional needs and tastes, as manifest in building on a human scale; reintroducing ornament, color, and whimsy; developing a mix of uses in one project; valuing public spaces of many kinds; and valuing experimentation with new typologies, morphologies, and modes of architectural production including various kinds of user participation, computer-aided design, and serial production techniques. Some of this experimentation has undeniably enhanced the lives of its users as well as the shape of the landscape.

The reconceptualizations of the city and of culture over the last few decades are inscribed within the larger challenge to the modern canon in contemporary Western society. This broadbased challenge is reflected in legitimacy crises in our basic assumptions, ways of knowing, and practice, and it is expressed in the millennial meditations described above. While all indications suggest a threshold, what lies on the other side remains unclear. At its worst, the extreme relativism and disengagement that may result from a distrust of master narratives and expertise can eliminate any possibility for communication, ethics, and democratic practice. With regards to cultural forms of expression, it can detract from any emancipatory and educational possibilities. The result can be an ultra-subjective alienating sense that there is no longer a "real," and a corresponding obsession with artifice[30] which allows for easy manipulation by the deft imagery of advertising and other forms of persuasion. In some respects, then, the efforts among urban designers to remedy the growing sense of fragmentation by drawing from the past and from mass imagery merely play into the hands of this process, ultimately intensifying rather than combating the prevailing sense of insecurity.

At its best, however, the wide-ranging challenge to the positivism and paternalism of the modern canon may clear the way for a new sensibility in which elitisms (in both Culture and culture) are supplanted by a celebration or incorporation of difference. Already manifest in certain social transformations and cultural forms of expression, particularly those that express a respect for diversity and for nature, this new sensibility can be sustained only if our responses to insecurity and fragmentation in our daily lives go beyond irony and an obsession with artifice. For this to transpire in urban design, architects and planners must truly heed their own call for contextualism through a more sophisticated understanding of their place in history, of cultural differences, and of the larger political economy in which they currently work. This will liberate them from the fashions and fascisms of the day and enable them to draw most richly from their creative wells to best suit each specific design task. The current reconceptions of the city and culture in thought and practice harbor the potential for both the worst and the best. We must attend to offsetting the former by nurturing the latter.

NOTES

1. In *The Structure of Scientific Revolutions,* Thomas Kuhn describes periods when scientists share a common framework, which are punctuated by moments when the received theories and methods can no longer address the problems that scientists choose to study. At these moments, a crisis is acknowledged and a scientific revolution occurs as researchers seek a new paradigm to address these new problems. This new paradigm does not necessarily build on the previous one (contrary to what a positivist paradigm would suggest) and can even be antithetical to it. Kuhn's thesis, then, was anti-positivistic.

2. In urban design, the discrediting of these analogies was expressed by Christopher Alexander's "A City is Not a Tree" (1965).

3. Edward Soja succinctly describes this transformation: "The dynamics of late-capitalism over the last 30 years can be generally characterized by the following: (1) an increasing concentration of capital in the form of diversified conglomerates facilitated by the global mobility of capital; (2) de-industrialization marked by industry shifts, plant closures, and capital flight to those regions of less-unionized and cheap labor; (3) selective re-industrialization in primarily high-tech sectors; (4) a sharper polarization of labor between high pay/high skill and low pay/low skill workers (let alone the unemployed) which further burdens the state to meet its welfare and social service obligations in this time of unprecedented government deficits, massive Third World debt, and general economic stagnation. If these dynamics can be considered as the effects, the causes are the reorganization of capitalism on a world scale, manifested in a changing international division of labor, modifications in the role of the state, accelerated regional economic shifts within countries, and widespread changes in the urbanization process, employment patterns, and the internal structure of cities" (Soja).

4. Eames and Goode described three kinds of urban anthropology. One uses the city as setting; the second describes life in modern society anywhere, not necessarily in cities; and the third focuses on the city as an institution, examining its formal attributes (architecture and urban design, settlement zones, and demography) and functional attributes (economic, political, educational, and recreational activity). Although neglecting to define what constitutes a city, they regard this third category as the "core of urban anthropology." In Conrad Arensberg's view (1968), the subfield of Applied Anthropology emerged during the Second World War in order to study the relationship between "natives" and "moderns." In the 1960s, he said, this traditional/modern paradigm was abandoned in favor of a rural/urban one and Applied Anthropology was rechristened Urban Anthropology.

5. Since decentralization has contributed to this confusion, it is also not surprising that postmodern urbanism features a renewed interest in suburban design and the individual house, an interest which had waned during the early decades of the twentieth century. Jérome Bindé asks: "Is it a coincidence that just as we talk so much about postmodernism there has never been such an affirmed suburban growth" (Bindé)?

6. Clifford Geertz reported a "refiguration of social theory" (Geertz 1973, 29) as challenges were "being mounted to some of the central assumptions of mainstream social science" (Geertz 1980a, 178). Instead of the traditional goal of social science "to find out the dynamics of collective life and alter them in desired directions" (ibid.), Geertz said that explanation was coming to be "regarded as a matter of connecting action to its senses rather than behavior to its determinants" (ibid.).

7. Influenced by the French *Annales* tradition, this trend in the United States was largely instigated by Natalie Zemon Davis, Robert Darnton (both at Princeton), and Carlo Ginzburg (at UCLA).

8. These efforts were carrying out what Foucault described as the "principle of reversal," which seeks to rescue what has been traditionally repressed and stifled in Western discourse.

9. In a parallel move found in literary criticism, the New Historicists (1980s) declared that texts should not be regarded as the New Criticism (1930s to 1960s) or deconstruction (1960s–) contended, as isolated non-referential works, but within their historical and social contexts, conceding that objectivity is not only unobtainable but even undesirable. Instead, the New Historicism, exemplified by the work of Stephen Greenblatt, insists upon examining art works within their historical, political, economic, and behavioral contexts (McConnell 1992, 59).

10. In French, this is often described as a *décloisonnement*, literally an unpartitioning. In this context, it is referring to the breaking down of barriers or boundaries among fields of knowledge and action.

11. Jonas (1979) points to parallels with the early period of industrialization, saying that both eras feature urban decline and anti-city movements; a desire to control urban sprawl; changing relations between the city and its surroundings and the search for a new kind of urban unit challenging traditional notions of city, countryside, and suburb; a reorganization of social groups; and experiments with new political practices such as participation and advocacy.

12. Marcus contends, "Goals of organizing scholarly practice in such diverse fields as history, the social sciences, literature, art, and architecture have given way to fragmentation . . .." (Marcus 1986, 167).

13. Tyler continues: "In the totalizing rhetoric of its mythology, science purported to be its own justification and sought to control and autonomize its discourse. Yet its only justification was proof, for which there could be no justification within its own discourse, and the more it controlled its discourse by subjecting it to the criterion of proof, the more uncontrollable its discourse became. Its own activity constantly fragmented the unity of knowledge it sought to project" (Tyler, 123). As among architects and planners, the label "postmodern" is considered pejorative by most anthropologists. Aside from Tyler, who champions the postmodern, most others shun the label and insist that they are continuing in the modern tradition (Pool).

14. There are precursors to this recent trend in urban design, particularly Patrick Geddes's work. Geddes sought to understand the Indian communities, for which he proposed urban designs from 1914 to 1924, and was opposed to the imposition of Western planning practices such as Edward Lutyens's design for New Delhi. He also employed public participation at both the input and implementation stages. Geddes wrote: "the planner who is anything of a geographer and anthropologist . . . sees the peoples of different climates and environments as adapted through past ages to these. Thus he comes to their ways, their habits, their customs, their institutions, their laws, their morals, their manners, with the ordinary naturalistic attitude of observant and interpretive interest, and not that of superiority" (in Town Planning towards *City Development: A Report to the Durbar of Indore* 1918; cited by Goodfriend). He contended that "our quest cannot be attained without participation in the active life of citizenship . . . to have shared the environment and conditions of the people . . . to have sympathised

with their difficulties and their pleasures, and not merely with those of the cultured or the governing classes" (in *Cities in Evolution*, 1949 version; cited by Goodfriend).

15. The *New York Times* journalist Richard Bernstein derides deconstructionism as "the doctrine of the indeterminacy of the text" (Bernstein 1988) and Barbara Johnson (a former student of Paul de Man and teacher of French and Comparative Literature at Harvard) has said that "Deconstruction's focus on the way language works makes it sound like a denial of what both the left and the right hold dear. . . . To the right it sounds like a denial of meaning and value. To the left it sounds like a denial of the possibility of action and political opposition" (cited by Bernstein 1988). Paul de Man was largely responsible for developing deconstructionism in the United States at Yale University. A number of critics suggest that de Man invented a theory providing justification for political disengagement when he learned the terrible implications of his earlier Nazi beliefs (ibid.).

16. Although this reliance on collage resembles that of modern writers and designers on assemblage, the intentions and results usually differ. According to the philosopher John McDermott, "Assemblage is historically rooted in futurism, with its concern for a 'completely renovated sensitiveness,' and in dada, which, in the words of Tristan Tzara, held that art would be created by 'materials noble or looked down upon, verbal clichés or clichés of old magazines, bromides, publicity slogans, refuse, etc.—these incongruous elements are transformed into an unexpected, homogenous cohesion as soon as they take place in a newly created ensemble.' In assemblage the context is the source of meaning. The materials shed their prior meanings and regather along a different, even drastically different, line of intelligibility. Nothing belongs anywhere until it is present. And with every new entry to the assemblage, all the other entries are reconstructed in their meanings. One of the intriguing factors here is that the masters of assemblage are very young children, for they are the least dominated by definitions of materials and, in the pejorative sense, by 'proper' space, color, and texture relationships" (McDermott). Postmodern collage reverses the meaning of assemblage because its pieces are not usually intended to "shed their prior meanings," but to evoke their original contexts in order to generate a sense of cultural continuity and character, all elements of romanticism. Indeed, the masters of postmodern collage could not be young children since it requires a certain learned sophistication.

17. An example of applying the text metaphor to understanding our own culture is offered by Hal Foster, who calls for a "critique of origins, not a return to them" (Foster 1983, xii) and says that deconstructionism can accomplish such a "postmodernism of resistance" (ibid.). It would entail, he explains, a critical reading that begins with discourse but moves beyond this to critique the larger system that sustains and is sustained by the discourse.

18. Martin Pawley has maintained, "In our addiction to antiquated terms like 'community' we display an inappropriateness of vocabulary that prevents us from understanding what is happening before our very eyes" (Pawley 1973, 11). For Pawley, "The community unit is not the city, the suburb, the neighbourhood, the block or the drive, it is the private connection with a worldwide credit and supply service, the freemasonry of the private owner" (Pawley 1973, 25).

19. "Perhaps," said Lynch, "there is a series of public images [of any given city], each held by some significant number of citizens. Such group images are necessary if an individual is to operate successfully within his environment and to cooperate with his fellows" (Lynch 1960, 41).

20. Warner suggests that "as our empirical research becomes more thorough, . . . we will confront the fact that the modern city is, and has been for a long time, a place of multiple ideologies, and therefore it goes by many names and is seen through many pictures" (Warner, 394).

21. A member of NATO, Nigel Coates (of Branson Coates Architecture, London), said that the advertising image strongly penetrates his work. He exclaimed, "I'm not looking for absolute signs, I'm looking for volatile signs, signs that are as fleeting as those that we see in advertising or on the street, or in the nightclub; these sorts of signs are much more a part of our communication and media world: the architecture of messages, thoughts, ideas. And I think [these] have a place in architecture" (Coates, 2).

22. According to Huyssen, "The problem with postmodernism is that it relegates history to the dustbin of an obsolete *episteme*, arguing gleefully that history does not exist except as text, i.e., as historiography" (Huyssen, 172).

23. In his own work, Grumbach has revalorized the work of Haussmann's engineer of public spaces, Adolphe Alphand, and has directed studies on historic preservation and on generating urban fabrics.

24. Replacing the "use-value" strategy of functional zoning and the "object-value" strategy of landmark planning is the city based on "the structural law of value" (Boyer 1990, 127).

25. This recalls Foucault's archaeology of knowledge.

26. Terry Eagleton asserts that "There is, perhaps, a degree of consensus that the typical postmodernist artefact is playful, self-ironizing and even schizoid; and that it reacts to the austere autonomy of high modernism by impudently embracing the language of commerce and the commodity. Its stance towards cultural tradition is one of irreverent pastiche, and its contrived depthlessness undermines all metaphysical solemnities, sometimes by a brutal aesthetics of squalor and shock" (1987; cited by Harvey 1989, 7–8).

27. Cullen Murphy contends that "Century after century the 90s no sooner heave into view than the pamphleteer and street-corner orators whip a goodly portion of the populace into a fearful frenzy" (C. Murphy, 81). As the year 1000 approached, for instance, the historian Henri Focillon observed that Europe was afflicted with "an ill-defined fear" (cited by C. Murphy, 81).

28. According to Baudrillard, modernity was an "aesthetic of rupture," of the "destruction of traditional forms," and of the authority and legitimacy of previous models of fashion, sexuality, and social behavior. But because of this, modernity lost "little by little all its substantial value, all moral and philosophical ideology of progress which sustained it at the beginning, and [became] an aesthetic of change and for change . . . ultimately, becoming purely and simply fashion, which means the end of modernity" (Baudrillard 1980).

29. As Ley contends, during the 1960s there occurred "A philosophical reorientation . . . in the social sciences, in planning and architecture, and in urban politics, as a critical ideology concerned with the reconstitution of meaning, with a respect for human subjectivity and the private realms of everyday life" (Ley 1987, 43) replaced a more instrumental orientation.

30. Vincent Crapanzano asserts: "Ironically, demonically, the denial of the possibility of a 'real' mimetic account, of any master narrative, proclaimed by the relentless signals of artifice does in fact announce an overarching narrative of—a consuming obsession with—artifice" (Crapanzano 1991, 431). As Deleuze and Guattari wrote in *Anti-Oedipus*, "the real is not impossible; it is simply more and more artificial" (1983, 34).

APPENDIX A

THE PENDULAR SWING

HISTORIANS OFTEN CONCEPTUALIZE the succession of ideas as a pendular swing, a cycle, or a spiral whereby a particular spirit of the time is replaced—either gradually or abruptly by another one, which is in turn transplanted by the first and so on.[1] In an effort to track trends in urban design theory, David Ley[2] counterposes two ideologies which have run intermittently through Western culture over the past two hundred years: the expressive and instrumental dimensions. Ley explains: "Exemplified by Camillo Sitte, the expressive dimension represents a romantic theme treasuring the subjective, the interpersonal and the aesthetic. Exemplified in Otto Wagner, the instrumental dimension is associated with the world-view of modernism: functional, technological, and sharing the purposive–rational values of bourgeois society" (Ley 1987, 41) including the belief in a "universal logic" wherein industrial urban society has no authentic culture left to preserve. He adds: "Expressivism and instrumentalism are not free-floating spirits but the ideologies of discrete social groups who emerge in particular places at particular times when, according to the extent of their prominence, they may become significant cultural architects, moulding a repertoire of symbols and forms, including the built environment" (Ley 1987, 40). Françoise Choay (1965) discerns a similar pendular swing moving from culturalism to progressivism and back. And referring to architectural history specifically, Wojciech G.

Lesnikowski (1982) applies the terms romanticism and rationalism, adopted in the following discussion.

We might understand the history of urban design theory as that of a continual search for the most harmonious balance between control and freedom, a search for the order which liberates rather than oppresses. Each generation reacts to deficiencies in its own social and physical landscapes, so the search swings back and forth like a pendulum from rationalism to romanticism and back to rationalism. To speak of rationalism and romanticism as two clearly distinguished and opposing camps is merely a heuristic device. In actuality, these are two ideal poles of a continuum along which design ideas fall, each containing elements of both romanticism and rationalism. Neither tendency is ever extinguished entirely[3] even when one of them takes precedence, and the perpetual tension between them generates a constant source of creativity. The shift discussed in this book is not, of course, the first time that sentiment has moved from the rational to the romantic pole. And in more recent years (especially since the mid-1980s), we have been witnessing reactions to the perceived inadequacies and excesses of postmodern urban design, reactions which bear features of rationalism. This Appendix presents a brief and selective intellectual history of the pendular swing in the West, emphasizing the persistence of romanticism during predominantly rational periods, focusing on, but not exclusive to, urban design theory.

Stephen Toulmin describes a shift on the part of the educated oligarchy in Christian Europe from a pluralistic attitude regarding ethics and morality to a dogmatic one that invoked "tradition" as a means of securing and perpetuating their social position. Since the Western Church was a transnational institution, he explains, "Moral issues had pluralism built in from the start" and "In the years before the Reformation, moral and general theology were open for discussion in the Provinces of the Church, on a collegial basis" (Toulmin, 136).[4] But around 1700, Toulmin says, the "scaffolding of Modernity was used to rationalize respectable moral and social doctrines (ibid.) and it paradoxically employed the rhetoric of "traditional values" as an instrument of conservatism. For Toulmin, this "move from 16th-century humanism to 17th-century exact science was a swing from the practical, Aristotelian agenda, to a Platonist agenda, aimed at theoretical answers" (Toulmin, 192).[5] One component of this shift was the substitution of logic and geometry for rhetoric and narrative.[6]

Andreas Huyssen locates the origins of this polar opposition in the debates between Ancients and Moderns, beginning in the seventeenth century with Herder and Schlegel (Huyssen, 172). In all of these battles, he says, the Moderns have upheld the need to pass through modernity so that "the lost unity of life and art could be reconstructed on a higher level" (ibid.), whereas the Ancients seek to achieve this unity by harking back to the past. Alan Colquhoun locates the origins of this opposition in the late eighteenth century, saying, "With the rise of the historicist outlook in the late eighteenth century . . . , what was 'rational' and therefore 'natural' in classical thought became increasingly dubious. In the subsequent Marxian development of this new attitude, what was 'rational' was seen as ideology—opinion and not science. Beauty, which had been underwritten, as it were, by absolute reason, was now seen as contingent, subjective, and relative. But at the same time, in reaction to this skeptical relativism, a new idealism emerged, which attributed to beauty a transcendental status. Idealism and historical relativism were two sides of the same coin" (Colquhoun, 103–05). According to Colquhoun, "We are still in this debate. . . . Modernism tended to take a historicist and relativist view of architecture and to regard the city as an epiphenomenon of social functions, resulting in a certain kind of urban space. But postmodern developments tend to disengage urban space from its dependence on functions, and to see it as an autonomous formal system" (ibid.).

Harvey distinguishes two urbanistic reactions to the anxiety generated by what he calls the "time-space compression" of modernism. One was rational and universalistic: a return to the Enlightenment project (for example, late-nineteenth-century Otto Wagner, early-twentieth-century Le Corbusier, Gropius, and Mies van der Rohe). "This kind of reaction," Harvey writes, "which many were later to dub as exclusively modernist, typically entailed a whole set of accoutrements. Despising history, it sought entirely new cultural forms that broke with the past and solely spoke the language of the new. Holding that form followed function and that spatial rationality should be imposed on the external world in order to maximize individual liberty and welfare, it took efficiency and function (and hence the image of the metropolis as a well-oiled machine) as its central motif. It had a deep concern for purity of language, no matter whether it was in architecture, music, or literature" (Harvey 1989, 270–71).

The other reaction was the romantic and particularistic one with its emphasis on self-identity. Epitomized by the work of Camillo Sitte, Harvey says, "This kind of reaction looks much more strongly to the identification of place, the building and signalling of its unique qualities in an increasingly homogeneous but fragmented world. . . . Architects like Louis Sullivan in Chicago and Gaudemar in Paris . . . searched for new and local vernacular styles that could satisfy the new functional needs but also celebrate the distinctive qualities of the places they occupied. The identity of place was reaffirmed in the midst of the growing abstractions of space" (Harvey 1989, 271–72). This romantic reaction, Harvey contends, is concerned with the spatialization of time (Being) rather than the annihilation of space by time (Becoming) (Harvey 1989). While the annihilation of space through time was occurring at a rapid pace, this reaction assured that "geopolitics and the aestheticization of politics underwent a strong revival" (Harvey 1989, 273).

This was evident, Harvey points out, in the writings of Nietzsche (1844–1900) and Heidegger (1889–1976). In Nietzsche's *The Will to Power* (English version, 1924), he declared that European culture "has been moving as toward a catastrophe, with a tortured tension that is growing from decade to decade: restlessly, violently, headlong, like a river that wants to reach the end, that no longer reflects, that is afraid to reflect" (cited by Harvey 1989, 273). With the dissolution of old traditions and the collapse of space through mass transport and communications, Nietzsche believed that people must become "supermen," "very strong and protean," with the "will to power," that is to attempt a "revolution of all values" in a quest for a new morality. Heidegger, Harvey writes, "was evidently disturbed by the bland universalisms of technology, the collapse of spatial distinctiveness and identity, and the seemingly uncontrolled acceleration of temporal processes. . . . His search for permanence (the philosophy of Being) connects with a place-bound sense of geopolitics and destiny that was both revolutionary (in the sense of forward-looking) and intensely nationalistic. From a metaphysical point of view this entailed rooting himself in classical values (particularly those of pre-Socratic Greek civilization), thereby highlighting a parallel orientation towards classicism in Nazi rhetoric in general and in architecture in particular. . . . Reactionary modernism of the Nazi sort simultaneously emphasized the power of myth (of blood and soil, of race and fatherland, of destiny and place) while mobilizing all the accoutrements of social progress towards a project of sublime national achievement. The application of this particular aesthetic sense to politics altered the course of history with a vengeance" (Harvey 1989, 209).

The morality ascribed to power and to "supermen," Harvey suggests, "lay at the heart of the new science of geopolitics . . . Friedrich Ratzel in Germany, Camille Vallaux in France, Halford Mackinder in Britain, and Admiral Mahan in the United States all recognized the significance of command over space as a fundamental source of military, economic, and political power" (Harvey 1989, 274–75). Each privileged their national interest and thus vindicated the right of their people to defend their own space and "if survival, necessity, or moral certitudes impelled it, to expand in the name of 'manifest destiny' (USA), the 'white man's burden' (Britain), the *mission civilisatrice'* (France) or the need for *'Lebensraum'* (Germany)" (Harvey 1989, 275).

Describing the urban planning reactions to the anxiety generated by modernism, Peter Calthorpe writes: "The two trends in planning at the turn of the century, the romantic and classic traditions, were locked in a false confrontation. The classic tradition was represented by the academic school, enshrined by the *Ecole des Beaux Arts* in Paris (where Garnier was trained), and manifested by Georges-Eugene Haussmann's rehabilitation of large sections of Paris at the mid-nineteenth century, Otto Wagner's proposals for Vienna, and even work in Bath, England. This work used axes, symmetry, uniformity, and classical forms to create monumental urban spaces. The counterpoint was provided by Ruskin, Morris, and Camillo Sitte, advocating the gothic vernacular as a set of design principles. . . . Unwin, for the garden cities, welded the two traditions by employing the grand axial forms of the Beaux Arts school for the public sections of the town, and the intimate, curving, and site-specific qualities of the romantic tradition in the residential areas. Garnier transcended these planning styles to generate a new formal tradition: modern planning and architecture" (Calthorpe 1986, 203). According to Calthorpe, that which distinguishes modernism from both the romantic and classic traditions is the emphasis on function over form and the "formal shift from buildings as edges to buildings as objects" (Calthorpe 1986) without concern for defining public space.

Nonetheless, historicism and contextualism continued to play an important role in modern urbanism, a role that is usually downplayed. Huyssen points out, for instance, that modernism generally featured "the mixing of codes, the appropriation of regional traditions, and the uses of symbolic dimensions other than the machine" (Huyssen, 187) and that it contained "some of the starkest critiques of modernization" (Huyssen, 186). Modernism included the "historical avant-garde," defined by Peter Burger as a reaction to the early modernist autonomy aesthetic and notions of high culture as manifest in expressionism, dada, constructivism, futurism, the prolecult, and surrealism (Huyssen, vii–viii). As Frampton recounts, "The mid-19th century . . . saw the historical avant-garde assume an adversary stance towards both industrial process and Neoclassical form. This is the first concerted reaction on the part of 'tradition' to the process of modernization as the Gothic Revival and the Arts-and-Crafts movements take up a categorically negative attitude towards both utilitarianism and the division of labor" (Frampton 1983a, 18). But colonialism and exploitation continued nonetheless, says Frampton, and by the end of the century, "the avant-gardist Art Nouveau takes refuge in the compensatory thesis of 'art for art's sake,' retreating to nostalgic or phantasmagoric dream-worlds" (ibid.). Then, the progressive avant-garde of futurism proposed a critique of the *ancien régime* and gave rise to the purism, neoplasticism and constructivism of the 1920s wherein the radical avant-garde identified itself with modernization, an identification soon challenged by the Spanish Civil War and the rise of the Third Reich.[7]

Modernism, then, was not entirely ahistorical. As Toulmin points out, evoking "tradition" was a very modern thing to do. According to Jean Baudrillard (1980), modernity opposes the canonical form of tradition but has its own tradition, that of the new.[8] In culture and social mores, he says, it translates into an "exaltation of profound subjectivity, of passion, of singularity, of authenticity, of the ephemeral and the unseizable, by the breaking down of rules and the irruption of the personality" (Baudrillard, 1980), a "tradition" curiously sounding much like romanticism.

With regards to architecture and urbanism, Graham Shane contends that a concern with history and context remained a vital tradition as a subculture within modernism (Shane, 77), pointing especially to the work of the Amsterdam School between the wars and the teachings of Sir Reginald Blomfield and A. E. Richardson in Great Britain which influenced the RIBA Committee's Plan for the Reconstruction of London in 1945. Shane argues that the members of CIAM maintained a contextual/historical approach, with Sigfried Giedion, for instance, lecturing on the history of the agora, forum, and piazza at CIAM 8 in 1945.

Then, Team X emerged in 1950 (including Alison and Peter Smithson, Georges Candilis, Jacob Bakema, Aldo van Eyck, Shadrach Woods, Giancarlo de Carlo, et al.) with a different attitude toward history. Aldo van Eyck wrote in his journal *Forum* (1967) about the importance of remembering the past, saying that architects "tend to sever the past from the future with the result that the present is rendered emotionally inaccessible, without temporal dimension" (cited by Frampton 1985, 300). But, he said, the "past, present and future must be active in the mind's interior as a continuum" or "the artifacts we make will be without temporal depth or associative perspective." He claimed to dislike both the "sentimental antiquarian attitude toward the past" and the "sentimental technocratic one toward the future," both of which "are founded on a static, clockwork, notion of time." He thus called for architects to start "with the past for a change and discover the unchanging condition of man" (ibid.). The members of Team X borrowed from the past and the vernacular, but translated these into modern terms to avoid direct imitation, pastiche, or phoniness. Foreshadowing the concerns of the townscape movement, these disaffected CIAM proponents aspired to give people a sense of rootedness and identity by, for instance, establishing "significant road hierarchies" and inducing "human associations" by using the traditional units of the city, town, village, and homestead as starting points. Nonetheless, Team X never really challenged the functionalist paradigm.[9]

Emilio Ambasz writes in the catalogue to an exhibition entitled "Precursors of Postmodernism," that "As the anti-historical mist dissolves, we are beginning to perceive that there were architectural enclaves in time and space which have actively fought to preserve their roots. Whether it was due to a deep intellectual understanding of architecture as an historical continuum, or whether it was . . . the result of an overwhelming longing for metaphysical images dwelling in para-historical domains [as the exhibition suggests] is not the smallest question raised by this remarkable body of work" (Ambasz).

Anthony Vidler reminds us that modern architecture was suffused with a "latent neoclassicism . . . born of the need to justify the new in the face of the old. The classical world once again acted as a 'primal past' wherein the utopia of the present might find its nostalgic roots" (Vidler

1978, 30). This neoclassicism was also apparent in the literature of this period. T. S. Eliot's epic poem *The Wasteland* (1922), for instance, evokes the barrenness and anguish of modern life through allusions to seventeenth-century metaphysical poets, Dante, Jacobean drama, and French symbolists. And Thomas Mann's (1875–1955) *Doctor Faustus* (1947), which was written in the United States after fleeing Hitler's Germany, emphasizes a return, in this case to Johann Faust, the sixteenth-century German doctor who, according to legend, sold his soul to the devil (Mephistopheles) in exchange for youth, knowledge, and magical power.

In the political realm, the Vichy regime (1940–45) had simultaneously championed technocracy and the use of traditionalist and ruralist propaganda while the Third Reich was similarly promoting indigenous architecture. In art, the modern artistic movements–such as dada, surrealism, and later Pop–betrayed a nostalgic component as artists drew from outdated consumer products (such as old catalogues) and time-worn clichés, sometimes collaging these. For instance, the Campbell's soup can immortalized by Andy Warhol was originally designed circa 1900. The idea of the "city as a spectacle," another supposedly postmodern characteristic, was also present in modern art, such as in Picasso's *Landscape with Posters* (1912) and in Fernand Léger's *The City* (1919). In the social sciences, a concern with history also persisted throughout the first half of the twentieth century, although vastly overshadowed by the infatuation with the functionalisms of Malinowski and Radcliffe-Brown. This unbroken historicist thread highlights postmodernism's continuation of modernism despite its rhetoric of rupture (see chapter 4).

The anxiety generated by what Harvey describes as the time-space compression of postmodernism once again incited both universalist and localist reactions analogous to those of modernism. As Lesnikowski observed, "The dialogue between classicizing tendencies and individual outlooks (which in the nineteenth century stood for romanticism) is rising again" (Lesnikowski 1982, 310). And just as strands of historicism, contextualism, and romanticism persisted throughout the era of modern urbanism, so have the tendencies toward ahistoricism and decontextualism persisted since the 1960s by urban designers described as practicing late (new or neo) modernism or functionalism. While reconstituting elements of the original modernist and functionalist doctrines, these practitioners may diverge from them by adding the dimension of meaning (Rowe; Jencks). The American architects who came to be known as "The Five" (Eisenman, Graves, Gwathmey, Hejduk, and Meier 1975), for instance, sought to discover a source of pure architectural forms as the French structuralists sought to discover a fundamental order of language, behavior, and thought. Practitioners of deconstructivism similarly harken back to certain elements of the modernist and functionalist doctrines. But at the same time, modernism's geopolitical reaction continues into postmodernism as evidenced by Lyotard's "local determinisms," Stanley Fish's "interpretive communities," Frampton's "regional resistances," and Foucault's "heterotopias," all of which posit places in which "otherness" can flourish free from the leveling impact of global processes.

Not only do modernism and postmodernism both contain a universalizing rationality on the one hand and a more romantic and particularistic emphasis on locality on the other, these two reactions have often been contained within the same school of thought or within the same individual,[10] Le Corbusier and Léon Krier being prime examples. Other similarities between Le Corbusier and Léon Krier include the belief that architecture and planning alone can change society (although their aesthetic ideals diverge) and a commitment to bringing about this change through their work (Dutton 1986; Jameson 1985).

Harvey intimates that it is in fact the coincidence of these apparently contradictory impulses that characterizes modernity and postmodernity and distinguishes them from pre-modernity. According to this view, the rational and romantic responses to the anxieties generated by modernity and postmodernity are two sides of a coin, not unlike the two sides of Marshall McLuhan's formulation: global village and tribalization (Harvey 1989; Toulmin 1990). Although the global village (universalism) side predominated during modernism, the natives grew restless and, during the 1960s, the tribal side (localism) became more prevalent. But neither fire is ever extinguished; in fact, each one provides kindling for the other since each defines itself in opposition to the other.

The motor of the pendular swing, according to Harvey, is capitalism. Comparing features generally attributed to postmodernism with those attributed to modernism, he observes that we might "dissolve the categories of both modernism and postmodernism into a complex of oppositions expressive of the cultural contradictions of capitalism. We then get to see the categories of both modernism and postmodernism as static reifications imposed upon the fluid interpenetration of dynamic oppositions. Within this matrix of internal relations, there is never one fixed configuration, but a swaying back and forth between centralization and decentralization, between authority and deconstruction, between hierarchy and anarchy, between permanence and flexibility . . . .The sharp categorical distinction between modernism and postmodernism disappears, to be replaced by an examination of the flux of internal relations within capitalism as a whole" (Harvey 1989, 340–41). Harvey also contends that "the tension between the mystifications, fetishisms, and mythological constructions of the older order, and the penchant for revolutionizing our conceptions of the world has to be appreciated as central to intellectual, artistic, and scientific life" (Harvey 1989, 110).

Nonetheless, interpretations of the modern condition generally privilege the universalizing reaction while interpretations of the postmodern condition tend to emphasize the localist reaction. Why do contemporaries as well as historians of the modern and postmodern periods tend to understand them as diametrically opposed? Harvey suggests that since the marketing of tradition tends to accentuate—rather than attenuate—people's sense of ephemerality, it can increase their "need to discover or manufacture some kind of eternal truth that might lie therein" (Harvey 1989, 292). We consume these understandings of our times just as we do commodities produced in factories and if they are going to sell, as their producers wish them to, they must appeal to the largest common denominator. In order to do so, they must be "new and improved," better than what had been previously offered, and relatively simple to assemble and use. But they must not be too durable and foolproof or the producers will lack a market for subsequent products and the consumers will sense frustration in being subjected too long to the same product and in being deprived of the opportunity to consume something "new."[11]

NOTES

1. Arnold Toynbee in his *A Study of History* (1947) and other works is well-known for his pendular theory of history. A more recent example is Stephen Toulmin's history of philosophy which, he explains, has "displayed a sequence of pendulum swings between two rival agendas. . . . Theoretically minded Platonists speculate freely, framing broad generalizations about human knowledge, practical-minded Aristotelians hesitate to claim universality in advance of actual experience" (Toulmin, 192).

2 . Ley is drawing from the formulation of Bernice Martin in *A Sociology of Contemporary Cultural Change* (1981).

3. For recent discussion of how contemporary architectural and urban design themes were present in modernism, see Gwendolyn Wright (1994) on the interwar period and Ockman (1993) for the postwar period.

4. Toulmin says that "Throughout the Middle Ages and Renaissance, clerics and educated laymen understood that problems in social ethics (or 'values') are not resolved by appeal to any single and universal 'tradition'. In serious situations, multiple considerations and coexisting traditions need to be weighed against one another" (Toulmin, 135). He contends that "people lived happily with an Aristotelian idea of 'prudence', in which it was not just needless but foolish to impose a single code of moral rules—a code that ignored the crucial difference between abstract problems in a theory like geometry, and concrete problems of moral practice" (Toulmin, 136).

5. Toulmin contends, "The dream of 17th-century philosophy and science was Plato's demand for episteme, or theoretical grasp; the facts of 20th-century science and philosophy rest on Aristotle's phronesis, or practical wisdom" (Toulmin, 192).

6. Robert A. Levine describes a similar shift with the ascetic Puritanism of the eighteenth century, which, he says, promoted an aseptic use of language as "The ideal of sincerity came to replace a courtly ideal of grace and charm with a call for plain and direct speaking." A cross-cultural analogue can be found among the Ilonglot, who, as described by Michelle Rosaldo (1973), make a distinction between "straight" and "crooked" speech, the latter relying on tropes and metaphors. While straight speech is used by people in positions of power to convey their authority or by people who feel powerless to change things, the potential of crooked speech to convey multiple meanings is used both to negotiate differences and for enjoyment and aesthetic pleasure.

7. For more on the avant-gardes, see Burger (1981) and Wodiczko (1987, 33–34).

8. See Harold Rosenberg's *The Tradition of the New*.

9. On Team X, see Robbins; Smithson (ed.); Frampton (1985); and Jencks (1973).

10. Harvey says that it would be wrong to consider universalism and particularism as separate from one another, for they are "two currents of sensibility that flowed along side by side, often within the same person" (Harvey 1989, 275).

11. Personal communication, 1990.

APPENDIX B

TIMELINE OF POSTMODERN URBANISM

THIS TIMELINE FOCUSES on contributions to urban design theory, primarily writings. It also includes conferences, exhibitions, buildings, and master plans that have had a significant impact upon theory.

1943

Eliel Saarinen, *The City: Its Growth, Its Decay, Its Future*

1945

Lewis Mumford, "Introduction" to Ebenezer Howard's *Garden Cities of Tomorrow*

Camillo Sitte's *Der Städtebau* (1889), translated into English as *The Art of Building Cities* (French translation 1902, Russian translation 1925, Spanish translation 1926)

Henry S. Churchill, *The City is the People* (reissued 1962)

Gaston Bardet, *L'urbanisme*

CIAM 8: Sigfried Giedion lectures on the history of the agora, forum, and piazza

1947

Paul and Percival Goodman, Communitas: *Means of Livelihood and Ways of Life*

Henri Lefebvre *Critique de la vie quotidienne*
(English translation, *Critique of Everyday Life*, 1991)

1948

Sigfried Giedion, *Mechanization Takes Command: A Contribution to Anonymous History*

1949

Joseph Hudnut, *Architecture and the Spirit of Man*
He applies the term "postmodern" to architecture.

Garrett Eckbo, *Landscape for Living*
He calls for more public control over land use in order to protect both countryside and city and to achieve greater social equity.

Steen Eiler Rasmussen, *Towns and Buildings Described in Drawings and Words* (Original Danish edition; English translation, 1951)

1950

Joseph Rykwert, *The Idea of a Town* (reissued 1988)

James Gibson, *The Perception of the Visual World*
His "ground theory of perceptual space" suggests that space cannot be perceived without a background.

CIAM 9: Team X emerged.

1950s

Social planners at University of Pennsylvania (see D. Scott Brown 1990a)

Townscape movement emerges in Great Britain, led by the *Architectural Review.*

1951

Clarence Stein, *New Towns for America*

1952

Lewis Mumford, "The Ideal Form of the Moden City"

Jaqueline Tyrwhitt, José Luis Sert, and E. N. Rogers (eds), *The Heart of the City: Toward the Humanization of Urban Life*

1953

Frederick Gibbard, *Town Design* (architecture textbook, reissued in many later editions).

Ivan Chtcheglov, "Formulary for a New Urbanism"
A critique of functionalist urbanism and a call for "symbolic urbanism" to allay alienation and ennui (Member of Lettrists International).

1955

Guy Debord, "Introduction to a Critique of Urban Geography"
Description of the Lettrists International's project to create an integrated urban environment without boundaries between public and private, work, and leisure (an *urbanisme unitaire*) by undertaking an investigation into the effects of the environment on emotions and behavior (*psychogeographie*).

Disneyland in Anaheim, California, opens

1956

CIAM X in Dubrovnik
The last International Congress of Modern Architecture.

1957

Editors of Fortune Magazine, *The Exploding Metropolis: A Study of the Assault on Urbanism and How Our Cities Can Resist It*
Contributors include Jane Jacobs and William H. Whyte, who coined the phrase "urban sprawl."

Ferdinand Toennies, *Community and Society*
English translation of *Gemeinschaft and Gesellschaft*, 1887; trans. by Charles Loomis and John McKinney

American Institute of Architects's Committee on Urban Design is re-established; members include Edmund Bacon, Frederick Bigger, Henry Churchill, Robert Geddes, Albert Mayer, and Clarence Stein. Committee commissions 12 articles published in the *AIA Journal*, 1962-1965 (see Spreiregen).

Situationiste Internationale and journal of same name are established (Guy Debord, Ivan Chtcheglov, and about 70 other participants lasting until 1962). This group opposes the alienation of the modern city and society as epitomized by the "spectacle," and seeks to create authentic collective and personal experiences by instigating "situations" through such methods as *détournement* and the *dérive*.

1958

C. Wright Mills, *Design and Human Problems*

1959

S. Muratori, *Studi per una operante storia urbana di Venezia*
(An early typological study)

Edward T. Hall, *The Silent Language*

Steen Eiler Rasmussen, *Experiencing Architecture*

Paul Zucker, *Town and Square from the Agora to the Village Green*

Death of Frank Lloyd Wright (1867–1959)

1960

Kevin Lynch, *The Image of the City*

Reyner Banham, *Theory and Design in the First Machine Age*
He argued that "early modernism's engagement with technical and
industrial issues was confined to the realm of the symbolic and
aesthetic."

Gideon Sjoberg, *The Preindustrial City: Past and Present*

1960s

Environmental psychology established in the curriculum at City
University of New York and Unviersity of California, Berkeley
(see Proshansky, Montgomery).

Contraspazio founded, an Italian neorationalist journal edited by
Enzo Bonfati and Massimo Scolari.

1961

Jane Jacobs, *The Death and Life of Great American Cities*

Gordon Cullen, *The Concise Townscape*

Lewis Mumford, *The City in History*

Jean Gottmann, *Megalopolis*

Nicolas Habraken, *Supports: An Alternative to Mass Housing*
(original edition; English edition, 1972)

Oscar Newman, *New Frontiers in Architecture*

John F. Kennedy's administration introduces legislation to combat
urban sprawl by conserving open space.

1962

Lewis Mumford "The Case against Modern Architecture" and "The
Future of the City, Parts I and II," in *Architectural Record*

Robert Venturi, *Complexity and Contradiction in Architecture*
(not published until 1966)

Alison Smithson, ed., "Team X Primer," *Architectural Design*
(Published as a book in 1968)

E. A. Gutkind, *The Twilight of Cities*

Kevin Lynch, *Site Planning*

Rachel Carson, *Silent Spring*

Jürgen Habermas, *Habilitationsschrift, Strukturandel der Öffentlichkeit*
(French edition: *L'espace public,* 1978; English edition: *The Structural Transformation of the Public Sphere,* 1989)

Herbert Gans, *The Urban Villagers*

"The Architect and the City" seminar at Cranbrook Academy of Art, Michigan; sponsored by the AIA and the Association of Collegiate Schools of Architecture (ACSA); participants include J. B. Jackson, Ian McHarg, Victor Gruen, Romaldo Giurgola, and Jacqueline Tyrwhitt.

1963

Serge Chermayeff and Christopher Alexander, *Community and Privacy: Towards a New Architecture of Humanism*

Lawrence Halprin, *Cities*

Christian Norberg-Schulz, *Intentions in Architecture*
He calls for "cultural symbolism" in architecture.

Leonardo Benevolo, *The Origins of Modern Town Planning*

Constantinos A. Doxiadis, *Architecture in Transition*

Ada Louise Huxtable becomes full-time architecture critic for the *New York Times,* the first for any American newspaper. Other newspapers follow suit.

1964

Christopher Alexander, *Notes on the Synthesis of Form*

D. Appleyard, K. Lynch, and J. R. Myer, *The View from the Road*

Victor Gruen, *The Heart of Our Cities: The Urban Crisis: Diagnosis and Cure*

Peter Blake, *God's Own Junkyard*

Bernard Rudofsky, *Architecture without Architects*
(accompanies exhibition at Museum of Modern Art, New York City)

Melvin Webber, "The Urban Place and Non-Place Urban Realm"

1965

Christopher Alexander, "A City is not a Tree"
He attacks hierarchical thinking about space.

George C. Collins and Christiane C. Collins, *Camillo Sitte and Birth of Modern City Planning.*

Murray Bookchin, *Crisis in our Cities*

Scientific American Editors, *Cities*
Contributors include Kingsley Davis, Gideon Sjoberg, Hans Blumenfeld, Lloyd Rodwin, Charles Abrams, John Dyckman, Nathan Glazer, and Kevin Lynch.

Françoise Choay, ed., *L'urbanisme: Utopies et réalités*

Paul D. Spreiregen, *1965 Urban Design: The Architecture of Towns and Cities*

Death of Le Corbusier (1887–1965)

1966

Robert Venturi, *Complexity and Contradiction in Architecture.* Introduction by Vincent Scully

Carlo Aymonino, *Il significato della città*

Vittorio Gregotti, *Il territorio dell' architettura*

Aldo Rossi, *L'architettura della città*
(English edition: *Architecture of the City*, 1982)

Pierre Lavedan, *Histoire de l'Urbanisme*, 3 volumes (*Antiquity, Renaissance, Contemporary City*, 1952–1966)

1967

Jacques Derrida, *L'écriture et la difference*; *De la grammatologie*

Robert Auzelle, *Encyclopédie de l'urbanisme*

Marcel Poëte, *Introduction à l'urbanisme*

Henri Lefebvre, *Le droit à la ville*

Edmund Bacon, *Design of Cities* (appearing simultaneously in French: *D'Athènes à Brasilia: Une histoire de l'urbanisme*)

Wolf Von Eckardt, *A Place to Live: The Crisis of the Cities*. Foreword by August Heckscher

H. Wentworth Eldredge, ed., *Taming Megalopolis*
Contributors include Christopher Tunnard, Melvin Webber, Gideon Sjoberg, Robert Wood, Lyndon B. Johnson, John Dyckman, Edmund Bacon, Jean Gottmann, William H. Whyte, Charles Abrams, Ian McHarg, Jane Jacobs, Edward Banfield, Harvey Perloff, John Reps, Herbert Gans, Lloyd Rodwin, and Jack Fisher.

Guy Debord, *Society of the Spectacle*

Moshe Safdie's Habitat 67, in Montreal, Canada

François Spoerry's new town of Port-Grimaud opens in Southern France.

1968

Henri Lefebvre, *La vie quotidienne dans le monde moderne*
(English edition: *Everyday Life and the Modern World*, 1971)

Lewis Mumford, *The Urban Prospect*

Herbert Gans, *People and Plans: Essays on Urban Problems and Solutions*

Sibyl Moholy-Nagy, *Matrix of Man: An Illustrated History of Urban Environments*

Robert Venturi, "A Bill Ding," and "Board Involving Movies, Relics, and Space," in *Architectural Forum*

Whole Earth Catalogue is founded by Stewart Brand, a celebration of design as a way of life, dedicated to Buckminister Fuller.

May 8: Strike at the ENSBA (École Nationale Supérieure des Beaux-Arts) in France, founded in 1671 and the model for architectural education around the world. The strike is mounted by the SNESUP (Syndicat National de L'Enseignement Supérieur) and the UNEF (Union Nationale des Étudiants de France). Strikers request that the ENSBA be closed and the Ordre des Architectes terminated. On August 20, Minister of Culture André Malraux announces the closing of the ENSBA and the creation of UPAs (Unités Pédagogiques d'Architecture).

1969

Charles Jencks and George Baird, eds., *Meaning in Architecture*

Vincent Scully, *American Architecture and Urbanism*
(revised edition, 1988)

Robert Stern, *New Directions in American Architecture*
(revised edition, 1977)

Maxwell Fry, *Art in a Machine Age: A Critique of Contemporary Life Through the Medium of Architecture*
(4 lectures at the Royal Academy, London, 1968)

Michel Foucault, *L'archéologie du savoir*

Philippe Boudon, *Pessac de Le Corbusier*
(English edition: *Lived-In Architecture*, 1972)

Hassan Fathy, *Gourna: A Tale of Two Villages*, published in Cairo by the Ministry of Culture
(Early version: *Gourna New Town in Egypt*, 1947; English edition: *Architecture for the Poor*, 1973)

Lawrence Halprin, The *RSVP Cycles: Creative Processes in the Human Environment*

Ian McHarg, *Design with Nature*

Bernard Rudofsky, *Streets for People: A Primer for Americans*

Edward T. Hall, *Hidden Dimension*

Amos Rapoport, *House Form and Culture*

Robert Sommer, *Personal Space: The Behavioral Basis of Design*

Environmental Design Research Association (EDRA) founded in the United States and first national conference.

Lucien Kroll's Medical School faculty in Louvain-la-Neuve, Belgium

Death of Walter Gropius (1883–1969) and Ludwig Mies van der Rohe (1886–1969)

1970

Henri Lefebvre, *La révolution urbaine*

Richard Sennett, *The Uses of Disorder: Personal Identity and City Life*

Moshe Safdie, *Beyond Habitat*

Buckminister Fuller, *Utopia or Oblivion: The Prospects for Humanity*

Ulrich Conrads, ed., *Programs and Manifestos on Twentieth-Century Architecture*

Paolo Soleri begins building Arcosanti near Phoenix, Arizona, realizing his concept of Arcology, which synthesizes architecture and ecology.

1970s

University of La Cambre in Brussels, the place of a great deal of discussion and activity about urban design

International Design Centre in Berlin, the site for architectural symposia organized by Heinrich Klotz

1971

Robert Goodman, *After the Planners*

Kenneth Frampton, "America 1960–1970: Notes on Urban Image and Theory," *Casabella*

Tom Schumacher, "Contextualism," *Casabella*

1972

Institute for Architecture and Urban Studies, New York City, is founded; disbanded in 1984. Cofounders include Peter Eisenman, Kenneth Frampton, and Mario Gandelsonas, joined by Anthony Vidler in 1977.

Charles Jencks and Nathan Silver, *Adhocism: The Case for Improvisation*

Robert Venturi, Denise Scott Brown, and Steven Izenour, *Learning from Las Vegas* (reprinted 1977)

Kevin Lynch, *What Time is this Place?*

Alexander Tzonis, *Towards a Non-Oppressive Environment*

Oscar Newman, *Defensible Space: People and Design in the Violent City*

Henri Lefebvre, *La pensée marxiste de la ville*

Manuel Castells, *La question urbaine*
(English edition: *The Urban Question*, 1977)

Pruitt-Igoe housing projects in St. Louis are demolished by dynamite; designed by Minoru Yamasaki, 1951; construction completed, 1956.

Pietro Belluschi is awarded the AIA Gold Medal.

1973

Oppositions, journal of the Institute for Architecture and Urban Studies, founded; folded when the group disbanded in 1984.

Douglas Lee, "Requiem for Large-Scale Planning Models," *Journal of the American Institute of Planners*

E. F. Schumacher, *Small is Beautiful*

County Coucil of Essex, *A Design Guide for Residential Areas*

Manfredo Tafuri, *Projetto et Utopia*
(English edition: Architecture and Utopia, 1976)

Andreas Faludi, ed., *A Reader in Planning Theory*

Umberto Eco, *Travels in Hyperreality*
(English translation, 1986)

Triennale in Venice is organized by Aldo Rossi, "Rational Architecture," presenting "past and present masters of rationalism," including Rossi, Scolari, Bonicalzi, Bonfati, and others.

1974

Vincent Scully, *The Shingle Style Today or the Historian's Revenge*

Murray Bookchin, *The Limits of the City*

Henri Lefebvre, *La production de l'espace*
(English edition: *The Production of Space*, 1991)

Robert Sommer, *Tight Spaces: Hard Architecture and How to Humanize It*

Walter C. Kidney, *The Architecture of Choice: Eclecticism in America, 1880–1930*
He emphasizes the virtues of historic and eclectic styles prior to modernism.

The Triennale of Milan codifies the notion of an autonomous architecture (September).

Getty Museum opened, Malibu, California; the building re-creates a first-century Roman villa, designed by Langdon and Wilson, Norman Neuerburg, and Stephen Garrett, primarily for the display of Greek and Roman antiquities.

Ralph Erskine's Byker Wall in Newcastle-upon-Tyne, England.

1974–1978

Architectural competitions (selected) recalling the traditional city:

1974: Les Côteaux du Val-Maubuée at Marne-la-Vallée, France
1976: The Townhouse competition for Jouy-le-Moutier, France
1978: The Apartment House competition for Cergy-St. Christophe, France
1978: The IBA competition for the reconstruction of West Berlin

1975

Christopher Alexander, *The Oregon Experiment*

Alexander Tzonis and Liane Lefaivre, "In the Name of the People," *Forum*

The first English translation of Rossi's work, in *Oppositions*

Rob Krier, *Stadtraum*
(English edition: *Urban Space*, 1979)

Jean Castex, Jean-Charles Depaule, and Philippe Panerai, *De l'îlot à la Barre: Contribution à la definition de l'architecture urbaine* (reprinted 1977)

Colin Rowe, "Collage City" in *Architectural Review*

Alastair Service, ed., *Edwardian Architecture and Its Origins.*
On virtues of pre-modern architecture

Jonathan L. Freedman, *Crowding and Behavior*
He refutes Hall and Sommer.

A larger version of the 1973 Venice exhibition opens in London.

1976

Kevin Lynch, *Managing the Sense of a Region*

Edward Relph, *Place and Placelessness*

Brent Brolin, *The Failure of Modern Architecture*

Edward T. Hall, *Beyond Culture*

Richard Sennett, *The Fall of Public Man*

Sally Woodbridge, ed., *Bay Area Houses*
On virtues of a regional vernacular style

John Summerson, *The Architecture of Victorian London*
On virtues of pre-modern architecture

"Signs of Life: Symbols in the American City"
Exhibition at Renwick Gallery, Smithsonian Institution, Washington D.C. Catalogue by Denise Scott Brown and Steven Izenour.

Perez and Associates' / Charles Moore's Piazza d'Italia in New Orleans

1977

Percival Goodman, *The Double E*

Christopher Alexander, *A Pattern Language: Towns, Buildings, Construction*

Charles Jencks, *The Language of Postmodern Architecture*
(reprinted 1981, 1984, 1991)

Peter Blake, *Form follows Fiasco: Why Modern Architecture Hasn't Worked*
He systematically challenges each of modernism's "sacred cows."

Bernard Rudofsky, *The Prodigious Builders* (sequel to 1964 book)

Kent Bloomer and Charles Moore, *Body, Memory and Architecture*

P. L. Cervellati, R. Scannavini, and C. de Angelis, *La nuova cultura delle città*
(French edition: *La nouvelle culture urbaine*, 1981)

"Postmodernism," *Architectural Design* 47 no.4.
Contributors include Charles Moore, Paul Goldberger, Geoffrey Broadbent, Charles Jencks, and Robert Stern.

"Beyond the Modern Movement," conference at Harvard University
Panelists include Stanford Anderson, Peter Eisenman, John Hejduk, Léon Krier, Donlyn Lyndon, Cesar Pelli, Robert Stern, and Stanley Tigerman. (Published 1980, below)

1978

Colin Rowe and Fred Koetter, *Collage City*

Charles Jencks, *What is Postmodernism?*
(reprinted 1986)

Rem Koolhaas, *Delirious New York*
A "retroactive manifesto" celebrating the anonymous and accidental aspects of urbanism in Manhattan; calls for a revival of "Manhattanism" and its "fictional conclusion."

Architecture rationelle: Témoignages en faveur de la reconstruction de la ville européenne. Rational Architecture 1978 (Testimonies in favor of the reconstruction of the European city)
Originally compiled for 1975 London exhibition by Léon Krier, with articles by Delevoy, Vidler, L. Krier, Scolari, and Huet.

Robert W. Burchell and George Sternlieb, eds., *Planning Theory in the 1980s*

"The Structural Crisis of the 1970s and Beyond: The Need for a New Planning Theory," conference is convened at Virginia Polytechnic Institute and State University, May (see H. Goldstein and S. Rosenberry, eds)

"Roma Interotta," Michael Graves invites 12 architects including Rowe, Stirling, and Krier to redesign segments of the Nolli map of Rome using "collage."

"La Reconstruction de la ville européenne," conference convened in Brussels, November 16–17.

Philip Johnson and John Burgee's AT&T (now Sony) Building is announced; built 1981-82. *New York Times* critic Paul Goldberger proclaims it the first monument of the postmodern movement, March 31. This is probably the first time most people outside the urban design professions hear about postmodern architecture.

Major exhibition on nineteenth-century Beaux-Arts buildings at the Museum of Modern Art in New York City, curated by Arthur Drexler

1979

Christopher Alexander, *The Timeless Way of Building*

Christian Norberg-Schulz, *Genius Loci: Towards a Phenomenology of Architecture*

Paul de Man, *Allegories of Reading*

International conference and theoretical competition is sponsored by the French Union of Architects on filling the space left by the destruction of Victor Baltard's Marché des Halles, Paris.

Philip Johnson is featured on the cover of *Time* magazine (January).

Philip Johnson awarded the first Pritzker Prize.
Modeled after the Nobel Prizes, the Pritzker Prize is established by the Hyatt Foundation to honor living architects who have "produced consistent and significant contributions to humanity and the built environment through the art of architecture."

1980

Kenneth Frampton, *Modern Architecture: A Critical History*
(reprinted 1985)

Brent Brolin, *Architecture in Context*

David Watkin, *The Rise of Architectural Theory*.
On rise of early nineteenth-century romanticism

Alexander Tzonis, *The Predicaments of Architecture: Narcissism and Humanism in Contemporary Architecture*

Charles Jencks, ed., *Post-Modern Classicism: The New Synthesis*

Léon Krier, "Manifesto: The Reconstruction of the European City or Anti-Industrial Resistance as a Global Project," *Counterprojects*

First volume of *Harvard Architectural Review*
Editorial: "Beyond the Modern Movement"; articles by Robert Stern and Charles Moore

Venice Biennale inaugurates its first international architectural exhibition; Paolo Portoghesi, director. Theme: "The Presence of the Past: The End of Prohibition," featuring 22 three-story townhouse façades lining a mock street named Strada Novissima (July).

The first Paris Biennale on Architecture; Jean Nouvel, director. Theme: "Urbanité: Savoir faire la ville et savoir vivre en ville"

Luis Barragán awarded the Pritzker Prize.

1981

Kevin Lynch, *A Theory of Good City Form*

Bernard Huet, *Anachroniques d'architecture*

Tom Wolfe, *From Bauhaus to our House*

Robert Stern and John Montague Massengale, eds., *The Anglo-American Suburb*

Robert Stern, ed., special issue of *Architecture and Urbanism*, "American Architecture: After Modernism"
Contributors included Michael Sorkin and Suzanne Stephens

Aldo van Eyck's Annual Discourse to the Royal Institute of British Architects on "Rats, Posts and other Pests"

Alexander Tzonis and Liane Lefaivre, "The Grid and the Pathway" They coin the term *critical regionalism*

Ada Louise Huxtable, "The Troubled State of Modern Architecture" and "Is Modern Architecture Dead?" in *Architectural Record*

Moshe Safdie, "Private Jokes in Public Places" in *Atlantic Monthly* and *Inland Architect*

Festival d'Automne in France. Theme: "Architectures en France, Modernité Postmodernité," presenting the previous ten years of French architecture and condemning the architecture of the "grands ensembles" (housing projects)

Strada Novissima exhibition opens in Paris at the Salpetrière, titled "La présence de l'histoire"

France's President Mitterand presents his plan for a universal exposition in Paris in 1989 to celebrate the bicentennial of the French Revolution. Jean Nouvel wins the competition and a team is assembled, including Vittorio Gregotti, Renzo Piano, Ionel Schein, and Antoine Grumbach. This project is aborted in 1983, due mainly to opposition from then Mayor Chirac

France's President Mitterand initiates his program of political decentralization as well as the architectural program of the Grands Projets

Seaside, Florida is initiated; Andres Duany and Elizabeth Plater-Zyberk, master planners; Robert Davis, developer

Village Homes in Davis, California; Michael Corbett, developer

Death of Robert Moses (1888–1981)

James Stirling is awarded the Pritzker Prize

1982

Rossi, *Architecture of the City* (English edition)

Rossi, *A Scientific Autobiography.* Postscript by Vincent Scully (English edition)

Paolo Portoghesi, *After Modern Architecture*
Foreword by Vincent Scully

Alberto Pérez-Gómez, *Architecture and the Crisis of Modern Science*

Charles Jencks, ed., *Free-Style Classicism*

"Naissance et renaissance de la cité," theme of *Urbanisme* no. 90-1.

"La modernité, un projet inachévé" (Modernity, An Unfinished Project)
Exhibition at ENSBA, Paris

Paris Biennale, "La modernité ou l'esprit du temps" (Modernity or the
Spirit of the Times), presenting designs of about thirty architects
under the age of 40

"Precursors of Post-Modernism, Milan 1920s–30s," exhibition by
The Architectural League, New York City

Strada Novissima exhibition opened in San Francisco as "The Presence
of the Past."

Michael Graves's Portland Public Service Building opens.

National Center for Scientific Research (CNRS), France, begins
considering the inclusion of a new research group to examine the
relationship between social and physical landscapes; group established
1985: "Architecture, Urbanistique et Société."

Kevin Roche awarded the Pritzker Prize

1983

Paolo Portoghesi, *Postmodern: The Architecture of Postindustrial Society*

Christine Boyer, *Dreaming the Rational City: The Myth of American
City Planning*

Paul Goldberger, *On the Rise: Architecture and Design in a Post Modern Age*

Lucien Kroll, *Composants: Faut-il industrialiser l'architecture?*
(English edition: *An Architecture of Complexity*, 1987)

E. T. Hall, *The Dance of Life: The Other Dimension of Time*

Kenneth Frampton, "Towards a Critical Regionalism" and "Prospects for a Critical Regionalism"

Ada Louise Huxtable, "After Modern Architecture" and "Rebuilding Architecture," *New York Review of Books*

France's President Mitterand establishes the program Banlieues 89, at the behest of Roland Castro and Michel Cantal-Dupart, who become its leaders. The goal is to improve the suburbs around France's large cities. Many exhibitions and publications devoted to this effort follow.

Bernard Tschumi is named chief architect for the Parc de la Villette in Paris. He proposed an open grid of "follies" as a framework for future transformations.

I. M. Pei awarded the Pritzker Prize.

1984

Dolores Hayden, *Redesigning the American Dream*

Rob Krier, *Elements of Architecture*

David Gosling and Barry Maitland, *Urbanism (an Architectural Design Profile)* and *Concepts of Urban Design*

Pier Luigi Cervellati, *La citta post-industriale*

Fredric Jameson, "Postmodernism, or the Cultural Logic of Late Capitalism," *New Left Review*

Richard Meier awarded the Pritzker Prize and commissioned to design the Getty Center in Los Angeles.

1985

Vittorio Magnago Lampugnani, *Architecture and City Planning in the Twentieth Century*

Mike Davis, "Urban Renaissance and the Spirit of Postmodernism," *New Left Review*

Heinrich Klotz curates exhibition, "Die Revision der Moderne, Postmodern Architecture 1960–1985," Frankfurt; writes *Moderne und*

Postmoderne: Architekture der Gegenwart 1960–1980; edits *Postmodern Visions: Drawings, Paintings, and Models by Contemporary Architects*

Exhibition of Léon Krier's drawings at Museum of Modern Art, New York City

Michael Graves's proposed addition to Whitney Museum of American Art, is accused of trashing the original modernist building.

Hans Hollein awarded the Pritzker Prize.

1980s–1992

EuroDisney in the French new town of Marne-la-Vallée begins construction. Architects include Antoine Predock, Frank Gehry, Robert Stern, Michael Graves (Americans), and Antoine Grumbach (French). Opens April 12, 1992. The American Disney Corporation also began hiring "starchitects," including Arata Isozaki, Robert Stern, and Michael Graves.

1986

Michael Dennis, *Court and Garden: From the French Hôtel to the City of Modern Architecture*

George R. Collins and Christiane Crasemann Collins, *Camillo Sitte: The Birth of Modern City Planning* (revised edition of original 1965)

Sim Van der Ryn and Peter Calthorpe, eds., *Sustainable Communities*

Roger Trancik, *Finding Lost Space: Theories of Urban Design*

Jonathan Barnett, *The Elusive City*

Donald Miller, ed., *The Lewis Mumford Reader*

Stanford Anderson, ed., *On Streets*
Contributors include A. Vidler, J. Rykwert, T. Schumacher, D. Agrest, G. Levitas, R. Gutman, and K. Frampton.

Alexander Tzonis and Liane Lefaivre, *Classical Architecture: The Poetics of Order*

Michael Dear, "Postmodern Planning," *Environment and Planning*

"La reconstruction de la ville et le concept de l'identique," symposium at the French Institute of Architecture, Paris. Participants include M. Culot, B. Huet, R. Krier, and R. Schoonbrodt (March 13).

Gottfried Boehm awarded the Pritzker Prize.

1987

Charles Jencks, *Post-Modernism: The New Classicism in Art and Architecture*

Christopher Alexander, *A New Theory of Urban Design*

John Friedmann, *Planning in the Public Domain: From Action to Knowledge*

Jeremy Dixon, *Post-Modernism and Discontinuity* (Architectural Design Profile no.65)

Allan Jacobs and Donald Appleyard, "Toward an Urban Design Manifesto," *Journal of American Planning Association*

Retrospective on postmodernism at the IBM Gallery, New York City

Kenzo Tange awarded the Pritzker Prize.

1988

William H. Whyte, *City: Rediscovering the Center*

Heinrich Klotz, *The History of Postmodern Architecture* (Translation of 1984 original)

Robert A.M. Stern and Raymond Gastil, *Modern Classicism*

Clive Aslet et al., eds., *The New Classicism in Architecture and Urbanism* (Architectural Design Profile no.71)

"Deconstructivist Architecture," exhibition at the Museum of Modern Art, New York City. Curated by Philip Johnson 50 years after curating the "Modern Architecture" exhibition (with H. R. Hitchcock); features designs of Peter Eisenman, Coop Himmelblau, Zaha Hadid, Frank Gehry, Daniel Libeskind, Bernard Tschumi, and Rem Koolhaas.

Gordon Bunshaft and Oscar Niemeyer awarded Pritzker Prizes.

1989

James Holston, *The Modernist City: An Anthropological Critique of Brasilia*

His Royal Highness The Prince of Wales, *A Vision of Britain: A Personal View of Architecture*

Werner Hegemann and Elbert Peets, *The American Vitruvius: An Architect's Handbook of Civic Art.* Preface by Léon Krier (Revised edition; originally published, 1922)

Doug Kelbaugh, ed., *The Pedestrian Pocket Book: A New Suburban Strategy*

Alan Colquhoun, *Modernity and the Classical Tradition: Architectural Essays 1980–1987*

"Postmodern Urbanism," *Design Book Review* no. 17

AIA's monthly journal *Architecture* sold to BPI Communications, which publishes *Hollywood Reporter* and other mass market magazines (April).

Exhibition on suburbia at the downtown Whitney Museum, New York City

Runcorn, Great Britain, new town decides to demolish 1,300 houses designed by Stirling and MacGowan with colored plastic facades (1970–77); Stirling attributes the decision to Prince Charles's influence, but the town claims they are too expensive to maintain (April).

Joseph Esherick awarded the AIA Gold Medal.

Frank Gehry awarded the Pritzker Prize.

1990

Andreas Papadakis, ed., "Postmodernism on Trial," *A.D. Profile* no. 88

Martin Pawley, *Theory and Design in the Second Machine Age*

Denise Scott Brown, *Urban Concepts*

Richard Sennett, *The Conscience of the Eye: The Design and Social Life of Cities*

Dennis Crow, ed., *Philosophical Streets: New Approaches to Urbanism*

David Kolb, *Postmodern Sophistications: Philosophy, Architecture, and Tradition*

Andreas Papadakis and Harriet Watson, eds., *New Classicism: Omnibus Volume*. Foreword by Léon Krier

Tridib Banerjee and Michael Southworth, eds., *City Sense and City Design: Writings of Kevin Lynch*

Amos Rapoport, *History and Precedent in Environmental Design*

Jacques Lucan, ed., *Rem Koolhaas–OMA*. Koolhaas reflects on the oppressive nature of architecture and raises the possibility of a "post-architectural modernity" by focussing on the program or "event" rather than the built form.

E. Fay Jones awarded the AIA Gold Medal.

Aldo Rossi awarded the Pritzker Prize.

1991

Alex Krieger and William Lennertz, eds., *Andres Duany and Elizabeth Plater-Zyberk: Towns and Town-Making Principles*. Afterword by Léon Krier

Charles Jencks, *Post-Modern Triumphs in London*

Diane Ghirardo, ed., *Out of Site: A Social Criticism of Architecture*

Aldo Rossi, *Architecture, 1981–1991*

Michael Dear, "The Premature Demise of Postmodern Urbanism"

Aldo Rossi's project for the South Bronx Academy of Art commissioned by Tim Rollins and the K.O.S. (Kids of Survival) (December).

Nexus Kashii new town built on reclaimed land in Fukuoka, Japan; master-planned by Arata Isozaki (inspired by IBA model) with perimeter housing designed by Osamu Ishiyama, Steven Holl, Rem Koolhaas, Mark Mack, Christian de Portzamparc, and Oscar Tusquets; landscaping by Martha Schwartz.

Robert Venturi awarded the Pritzker Prize.

1992

Richard Ecomomakis, ed., *Leon Krier: Architecture and Urban Design, 1967-92.* Introduction by Demetri Porphyrios; essay by David Watkin

Charles Jencks, ed., *The Post-Modern Reader*

Benjamin Thompson awarded the AIA Gold Medal.

Alvaro Siza awarded the Pritzker Prize.

1993

The Exploding Metropolis (reprint; original published, 1957)

Peter Calthorpe, *The Next American Metropolis*

Charles Jencks, *Heteropolis*

Joan Ockman with Edward Eigen, eds., *Architecture Culture, 1943–68: A Documentary Anthology*

Magali Sarfatti Larson, *Behind the Postmodern Façade: Architectural Change in Late 20th Century America*

First Congress for the New Urbanism, Alexandria, Virginia (October)

"Search for Substance: Critical Reflections on Architecture in the 1980s," conference at University of California, San Diego, seeks "to distinguish between transient fashion and more lasting substance." Participants include Peter Buchanan, François Chaslin, William Curtis, and Luis Fernandez-Galiano (January).

Signing of a Declaration of Interdependence at the World Architecture Congress, Chicago, Illinois

Architectural Digest sold to Condé Nast publications (February).

Kevin Roche awarded the AIA Gold Medal (January).

Fumihiko Maki awarded the Pritzker Prize.

1994

Peter Katz, *The New Urbanism*

M. Christine Boyer, *The City of Collective Memory*

Richard Sennett, *Flesh and Stone: The Body and the City in Western Civilization*

Michael Sorkin, *Exquisite Corpse: Writing on Buildings*

Alan Balfour, ed., *Cities of Artificial Excavation: The Work of Peter Eisenman, 1978–1988*

"Urban Revisions: Current Projects for the Public Realm," exhibition at Museum of Contemporary Art, Los Angeles, California (May–June)

"OMA at MoMA: Rem Koolhaas and the Place of Public Architecture," exhibition at Museum of Modern Art, New York City

Norman Foster awarded the AIA Gold Medal.

Christian de Portzamparc awarded the Pritzker Prize.

1995

Charles Jencks, *The Architecture of the Jumping Universe: A Polemic; How Complexity Science is Changing Architecture and Culture*

Tadao Ando awarded the Pritzker Prize.

1996

Diane Ghirardo, *Architecture After Modernism*

Stephen Willats, *Between Buildings and People*

Iain Borden, ed., *Strangely Familiar: Narratives of Architecture in the City*

Kate Nesbitt, ed., *Theorizing a New Agenda for Architecture: An Anthology of Architectural Theory 1965-95*

Rem Koolhaas, *S,M,L,XL*
XL plans and projects include EuraLille, Melun-Senart, La Defense, Point City/South City, Yokohama, and Universal City.

Lee Mitgang and Ernest Boyer, *Building Community: A New Future for Architecture Education and Practice,* commonly referred to as the "Boyer Report." Commissioned in 1993 by the AIA, the American Institute of Architecture Students, the Association of Collegiate Schools of Architecture, the National Council of Architectural Registration Boards, Inc., and the National Architectural Accrediting Board, Inc.

Michael Spens, ed., *The Recovery of the Modern: Architectural Review 1980-1995*

Rafael Moneo awarded the Pritzker Prize.

1997

Charles Jencks and Karl Kropf, eds., *Theories and Manifestoes of Contemporary Architecture*

Edward Blakely and Mary Gail Snyder, *Fortress America*

Nan Ellin, ed., *Architecture of Fear*

Steven Harris and Deborah Berke, eds., *Architecture of the Everyday*

Gulsum Bydar Nalbantoglu and Wong Chong Thai, eds., *Postcolonial Space(s)*

Peter Noever et al., *Architecture in Transition : Between Deconstruction and New Modernism*

Thomas L. Doremus, *Classical Styles in Modern Architecture: From the Colonnade to Disjunctured Space*

Charlene Spretnak, *The Resurgence of the Real: Body, Nature, and Place in a Hypermodern World*

Civano, new town outside of Tucson, Arizona, planned by Community Design Associates, Duany Plater-Zyberk & Company, and Elizabeth Moule & Stephanos Polyzoides. New Urbanism integrates designing for sustainability.

Getty Center opens, designed by Richard Meier, located on a 110-acre hilltop site in Los Angeles; built at a cost of $1 billion.

Sverre Fehn awarded the Pritzker Prize.

1998

Congress for the New Urbanism, Denver, Colorado, "Cities in Context" Focuses on integrating environmentalism with the New Urbanism and on urban infill (April–May).

"Modern Architecture: An Incomplete Project," ACSA Regional Meeting, University of Tennessee (October)

Guggenheim Museum, Bilbao, Spain, opens; designed by Frank Gehry.

First major commissions in the United States awarded to foreign designers:

> Rem Koolhaas, to revitalize Illinois Institute of Technology (finalists include Peter Eisenman, Zaha Hadid, Helmut Jahn, and Kazuyo Sejma)

> Yoshio Taniguchi, to expand Museum of Modern Art, New York City (finalists include Bernard Tschumi and Herzog and de Meuron)

> Zaha Hadid, to design Contemporary Arts Center, Cincinnati (finalists include Tschumi and Daniel Libeskind)

Renzo Piano awarded the Pritzker Prize.

REFERENCES

Ackerman, James S. 1980. The History of Design and the Design of History. *VIA*. 4: 12–18. MIT and University of Pennsylvania.

——. 1987. Why Classicism? (Observations on Post-Modern Architecture). *Harvard Architectural Review*. 5: 78–79.

ACSA News. 1992. Prince Charles Forms Architecture School. Reprinted from *The New York Times*, February 13, 1992. Washington, DC: American Collegiate Schools of Architecture.

——. 1994. ACSA/AIA Teachers' Seminar. 23 (9), May.

Adorno, Theodor and Max Horkheimer. 1946. *Dialectic of Enlightenment*. English translation by John Cumming, 1991. New York: Continuum.

Albers, Gerd and Alexander Papageorgiou-Venetas. 1985. Town Planning 1945–1980: An Attempt Toward a Synoptic View. *Ekistics*. 311 (March/April): 116–30.

Alexander, Christopher. 1964. *Notes on the Synthesis of Form*. Cambridge, MA: MIT.

——. 1965. A City is Not a Tree. *Architectural Forum*. April: 58–62 and May: 58–61 Reprinted, 1966, *Design Magazine*, 206: 46–55. French translation, 1967, Une ville n'est pas un arbre, *Architecture Mouvement Continuité*.

——. 1975. *The Oregon Experiment*. New York: Oxford University. French edition, 1976, *Une expérience d'urbanisme démocratique*.

——. 1977. *A Pattern Language: Towns, Buildings, Construction*. New York: Oxford University.

——. 1979. *The Timeless Way of Building*. New York: Oxford University.

——. 1985. *The Production of Houses*. With Howard David and Julia Martinze. New York: Oxford University.

——. 1987. *A New Theory of Urban Design*. New York: Oxford University.

Allen, Edward, ed. 1974. *The Responsive House*. Cambridge, MA: MIT.

Ambasz, Emilio. 1982. Preface to Precursors of PostModernism, Milan 1920s–30s. Exhibition catalogue.

Amendola, Giandomenico. 1989. Postmodern Architects' People. R. Ellis and D. Cuff, eds., *Architects' People*, 239–59.

Amsden, Jon. 1979. Historians and the Spatial Imagination. *Radical History Review*. 21: 11–30.

Anderson, Benedict. 1983. *Imagined Communities: Reflections on the Origin and Spread of Nationalism*. New York: Verso.

Anderson, Martin. 1964. *The Federal Bulldozer: A Critical Analysis of Urban Renewal 1949–1962*. Cambridge, MA: MIT.

Anderson, Stanford. 1966. Architecture and Tradition. Marcus Whiffen, ed., *The History, Theory, and Criticism of Architecture*. Cambridge, MA: MIT.

——. 1975. Old Lamps for New. *Architectural Review*. November.

———. 1991. People in the Physical Environment: The Urban Ecology of Streets. S. Anderson, ed., *On Streets.* Cambridge, MA: MIT, 1–12.

Anderson, Stanford, ed. 1991 [1986]. *On Streets.* Cambridge, MA: MIT.

Angus, Ian. 1989. Circumscribing Postmodern Culture. Ian Angus and Sut Jhally, eds., *Cultural Politics in Contemporary America*, 96–110.

Angus, Ian and Sut Jhally, eds. 1989. *Cultural Politics in Contemporary America.* London: Routledge, 1–17.

Appelbaum, Richard P. 1978. Planning as Technique: Some Consequences of the Rational-Comprehensive Model. Harvey Goldstein and Sara Rosenberry, eds., *The Structural Crisis of the 1970s and Beyond: The Need for a New Planning Theory*, 148–67.

Appleyard, Donald. 1969. City Designers and the Pluralistic City. Lloyd Rodwin, ed., *Planning Urban Growth and Regional Development.* Cambridge, MA: MIT.

Appleyard, Donald, ed. 1979. *The Conservation of European Cities.* Cambridge, MA: MIT.

Appleyard, D., K. Lynch, and J. R. Myer. 1964. *The View from the Road.* Cambridge, MA: MIT.

Architectural Design Profile. 1989. Prince Charles and the Architectural Debate. London and New York: St Martin's.

Ardener, Shirley, ed. 1981. *Women and Space: Ground Rules and Social Maps.* Oxford: Berg.

Arendt, Hannah. 1958 [1973]. *The Human Condition.* Chicago: University of Chicago.

Arensberg, Conrad. 1968. The Urban in Crosscultural Perspective. E. Eddy, ed., *Urban Anthropology.* Athens, GA.

Aslet, Clive, Demetri Porphyrios, Charles Jencks, et al. 1988. The New Classicism in Architecture and Urbanism. *Architectural Design Profile.* London and New York: St. Martin's.

Attoe, Wayne and Donn Logan. 1989. *American Urban Architecture: Catalysts in the Design of Cities.* University of California.

Audirac, Ivonne and Anne H. Shermyen. 1994. An Evaluation of Neotraditional Design's Social Prescription: Postmodern Placebo or Remedy for Suburban Malaise? *Journal of Planning Education and Research.* 13 (3): 161–73.

Auzelle, Robert. 1967. *Encyclopédie de l'urbanisme.* Paris: Presses universitaires de France.

Aymonino, Carlo. 1966. *Il significato della città.* Bari: Laterza.

Bacon, Edmund. 1967. *Design of Cities.* New York: Viking.

Banerjee, Tridib and Michael Southworth, eds. 1990. *City Sense and City Desig: Writings and Projects of Kevin Lynch.* Cambridge: MIT.

Banham, Reyner. 1960. *Theory and Design in the First Machine Age.* London: Architectural Press.

Barbe, Bernard and Alain Duclent. 1986. *Le vécu de l'architecture. La Noiserai (H. Ciriani), Les Arcades du Lac (R. Bofill), 135 rue de l'Ourcq, Paris 19e (Levy, Maison-Haute, Coutine).* Paris: Plan Construction.

Bardet, Gaston. 1945. *L'urbanisme*. Paris: Presses universitaires de France.

Barnett, Jonathan. 1982. *An Introduction to Urban Design*. New York: Harper & Row.

———. 1986. *The Elusive City: Five Centuries of Design, Ambition, and Miscalculation*. New York: Harper & Row.

Barre, François. 1985. Banlieue et monumentalité. Round table discussion in Esprit.

Barth, John. 1972. *Chimera*. New York: Random House.

———. 1980. The Literature of Replenishment: Postmodernist Fiction. *The Atlantic*. January: 65–71.

———. 1986. *Tidewater Tales*. New York: Putnam.

Barthes, Roland. 1970. *S/Z*. Paris: Editions du Seuil.

———. 1973. Semiology and Urbanism. *VIA*. 2: 155–57.

———. 1975. *The Pleasure of the Text*. Translated by Richard Miller. New York: Hill & Wang.

Bartone, Carl. 1991. Environmental Challenge in Third World Cities. *Journal of the American Planning Association*. 57(4): 411–15.

Bateson, Mary Catherine. 1990. *Composing a Life*. Plume.

Baudrillard, Jean. 1975. Mirror of Production. St Louis: Telos Press.

———. 1980. La fin de la modernité ou l'ère de la simulation. *Encyclopédie Universalis*. Reprinted in *Biennale de Paris*, 1982, 28–33.

———. 1981. *For a Critique of the Political Economy of the Sign*. Translated by C. Levin. St. Louis, MO: Telos. Chapter 10, Design and Environment, 185–203.

——— 1983a. The Ecstasy of Communication. Hal Foster, ed. *The Anti-Aesthetic*. Seattle: Bay Press, 126–34.

———. 1983b. *Simulations*. New York: Semiotext(e).

Bauer, Gérard. 1978. Ordre et diversité. *Macadam*. October 15–31.

———. 1981. Le charme plutôt que l'ordre. *Créé*. 184 (September).

———. 1982. Des villes loin des cités. les grandes opérations péri-urbaines d'aménagement concerte aux États-Unis. IFA, ed., *Paysage Pavillonnaire*. Paris: Institut Français d'Architecture, 57–74.

Bauer, Gérard and J.-M. Roux. 1975. *La rurbanisation ou la ville éparpillée*. Paris: Collection Espacements, Seuil.

Bauer, Gérard, J.-M. Roux, and V. Renaud. 1979. *Un urbanisme pour les maisons*. Paris: Inédit. No. 1018.

Bauer, Gérard, Gildas Baudez, and Jean-Michel Roux. 1980. *Banlieues de charme ou l'art des quartiers-jardins*. Paris: Pandora.

Bauman, Zygmunt. 1983. Industrialism, Consumerism, and Power. *Theory, Culture and Society*. 1(3): 32–43.

Bell, Daniel. 1960. *The End of Ideology*. New York: The Free Press.

———. 1976. *The Cultural Contradictions of Capitalism*. New York: Basic Books.

———. 1980. *The Winding Passage*. New York: Basic Books.

Bell, Daniel. 1992. The Cultural Wars: American Intellectual Life, 1965–1992. *Wilson Quarterly.* Summer: 74–107.

Bell, David. 1988. Reflection. *Journal of Architectural Education.* 41(3): 2–3.

Belmont, Joseph. 1980. *Les architectes et l'industrialisation.* Paris: Centre d'Études et de Recherche Architecturale.

———. 1987. *Modernes et postmodernes.* Paris: Moniteur.

———. 1989a. *De l'architecture à la ville.* Paris: Moniteur.

———. 1989b. *Villes du passé, villes du futur.* Paris: Moniteur.

Benevolo, Leonardo. 1960. *History of Modern Architecture: 1890–1930.* Cambridge, MA: MIT.

———. 1982 [1963]. *The Origins of Modern Town Planning.* Translated by Judith Landry. Cambridge, MA: MIT.

Benjamin, Walter. 1969. The Work of Art in the Age of Mechanical Reproduction. *Illumination.* New York: Schoeken Books, 217–51.

Benzel, Katherine. 1997. *The Room in Context: Design Without Boundaries.* NY: McGraw-Hill.

Bergdoll, Barry. 1989. Pioneers of Postmodern Design. *Design Book Review.* 17: 67–8.

Berger, Bennett. 1960. *Working-Class Suburb: A Study of Auto Workers in Suburbia.* University of California.

Berger, John. 1972. *Ways of Seeing.* London: BBC, and Harmondsworth: Penguin.

Bergum, Christian. 1990. Urban Form and Urban Representation. Dennis Crow, ed., *Philosophical Streets.* Washington DC: Maisonneuve Press, 113–32.

Berke, Deborah. 1982. Rob Krier and the utopian Tradition in Housing. Kenneth Frampton and D. Berke, eds., *Rob Krier: Urban Projects 1968–1982.* New York: Institute for Architecture and Urban Studies. Catalogue no. 5: 10–13.

Berman, Marshall. 1982. *All that is Solid Melts into Air.* Harmondsworth: Penguin.

Bernstein, Richard. 1988. Critics Attempt to Interpret a Colleague's Disturbing Past: The de Man Affair. *New York Times.* July 17.

———. 1990. Academic Left Finds the Far Reaches of Postmodernism. *New York Times.* April 8.

Best, Steven and Douglas Kellner. 1991. *Postmodern Theory: Critical Interrogations.* New York: Guilford Press.

Betsky, Aaron. 1993. All Roads Lead Downtown: The Emerald City Plans its Future. *LA Weekly.* November 12–18: 17–19.

Bhabha, Homi. 1992. Race and the Humanities: The 'Ends' of Modernity? *Public Culture.* 4(2): 81–88.

Bindé, Jérome. 1982. Le pavillon des aliénés ou le fantôme du privé. IFA, ed., *Paysage pavillonnaire.* Paris: Institut Français de l'Architecture, 34–48.

Biriotti, Roger, with Pierre Lefevre and Marc Benlevi. 1980. *Habiter l'Hautil.* Cergy-Pontoise: Etablissement Public d'Aménagement, April.

———. 1986. Interviewed by author. Paris, Jouy-le-Moutier.

Blake, Peter. 1964. *God's Own Junkyard*. New York: Holt Reinhart Winston.

———. 1977. *Form follows Fiasco: Why Modern Architecture Hasn't Worked*. Boston: Little, Brown.

———. 1982. The End of Cities. Lisa Taylor, ed., *Cities: The Forces that Shape Them*. New York: Rizzoli.

Blau, Judith R. 1984. *Architects and Firms: A Sociological Perspective on Architectural Practice*. Cambridge, MA: MIT.

———. 1988. Where Architects Work: A Change Analysis 1970–1980. Paul L. Knox, ed., *The Design Professions and the Built Environment*. New York: Nichols, 12–46.

———. 1991. The Context and Content of Collaboration: Architecture and Sociology. *Journal of Architectural Education*. November: 36–40.

Bletter, Rosemarie. 1985. The Meaning of the Beaux-Arts Plan. Paper at the American Center in Paris.

Bloomer, K. C. and Charles Moore. 1977. *Body, Memory and Architecture*. New Haven, CT: Yale University Press.

Boddy, Trevor. 1992. Underground and Overhead: Building the Analogous City. Michael Sorkin, ed., *Variations on a Theme Park*. New York: Hill & Wang, 123–53.

———. 1993. Review of *Architecture in Europe since 1968: Memory and Invention*, by Alexander Tzonis and Liane Lefaivre (New York: Rizzoli, 1992). Design Book Review. 29/30: 93–98.

Bohígas, Oriol. 1991. Barcelona 1992. *The New City: Foundations*. University of Miami School of Architecture. Fall: 119–23.

Bonnin, Philippe, ed. 1985. *Habitats Autogérés: MHGA*. Paris: Syros, Collection Anarchitecture.

Bookchin, Murray. 1974. *The Limits of the City*. New York: Harper & Row.

Boorstin, Daniel. 1973. *The Americans: The Democratic Experience*. New York: Vintage.

Borden, Iain, ed. 1996. *Strangely Familiar: Narratives of Architecture in the City*. London: Routledge.

Boudon, François and Monique Mosser. 1983. Le dialogue architecte-historien. *Artpress*. Hors série no. 2 (June–August): 28–9.

Boudon, Philippe. 1967a. Editorials. *Architecture Mouvement Continuité*. 1 (November) and 2 (December).

———. 1967b. Structure, espace et architecture. *Architecture Mouvement Continuité*. 1: 16–23.

———. 1969. *Pessac de Le Corbusier*. Paris: Dunod.

———. 1979. *Lived-In Architecture: Le Corbusier's Pessac Revisited*. Cambridge, MA: MIT. Translation of 1969 original.

———. 1985. *Pessac de Le Corbusier* (reissued with Preface by H. Lefebvre). Paris: Dunod.

———. 1985. *Pessac II, Le Corbusier 1969–1985*. With L. Bony, P. Deshayes, J.-F. Dhuys, M. Emery, L. Kroll, B. Lassus, R. Quincerot, A. Sarfati. Paris: Dunod.

Bourdieu, Pierre. 1984 [1979]. *Distinction: A Social Critique of the Judgement of Taste*. Translated by Richard Nice. Cambridge, MA: Harvard.

Boyer, M. Christine. 1978. Planning the City of Capital: II. Harvey Goldstein and Sara Rosenberry, eds., *The Structural Crisis of the 1970's and Beyond: The Need for a New Planning Theory*, 44–61.

——. 1983. *Dreaming the Rational City: The Myth of American City Planning*. Cambridge, MA: MIT.

——. 1988. The Return of Aesthetics to City Planning. Society. 25 (4): 49–56. Reprinted in Dennis Crow, ed., *Philosophical Streets*, 1990, 93–112.

——. 1990. *Erected Against the City*. Center. 6: 36–43.

——. 1994. *The City of Collective Memory*. Cambridge, MA: MIT.

Boyle, Bernard Michael. 1977. Architectural Practice in America, 1865–1965—Ideal and Reality. Spiro Kostof, ed., *The Architect*, 309–344.

Bressi, Todd W. 1992. The Neo-traditional Revolution. *Utne Reader*. May/June: 101–04. Originally published in *Metropolis*.

Brière, Claude. 1982. Le retour à la ville. *Le Monde*. November 28.

Brill, Michael. 1989. The Architect and Society. *Architecture*. July.

Bristol, Katharine. 1991. The Pruitt-Igoe Myth. *Journal of Architectural Education*. May: 163–71.

Broadbent, Geoffrey, Richard Bunt, and Charles Jencks, eds. 1980. *Signs, Symbols, and Architecture*. New York: Wiley.

Brolin, Brent. 1976. *The Failure of Modern Architecture*. New York: Van Nostrand Reinhold.

——. 1980. *Architecture in Context*. New York: Van Nostrand Reinhold.

Brown, Patricia Leigh. 1990. Disney Deco. *New York Times Magazine*. April 8: 18–24, 42–43, 48.

——. 1997. The New 'God Forbid' Room. *New York Times*. September 25: B1, B8.

Burchell, Robert W, and James W. Hughes. 1978. Planning Theory in the 1980s—A Search for Future Directions. Robert W. Burchell and George Sternlieb, eds., *Planning Theory in the 1980s*, xv–xxiii.

Burchell, Robert W. and George Sternlieb, eds. 1978. *Planning Theory in the 1980s*. New Brunswick: Rutgers University.

Burger, Peter. 1981. Avant-garde and Contemporary Aesthetics: A Reply to Jurgen Habermas. *New German Critique*. 22 (Winter): 19–22.

Burgess, Ernest W. 1925. The Growth of the City: An Introduction to a Research Project. Robert E. Park and E. W. Burgess, eds., *The City*. University of Chicago, 47–62.

Burlen, Katherine, Jean Castex, et al. 1977. Revised 1980. *Lecture d'une ville: Versailles*. Paris: CORDA.

Byrne, David. 1986. *True Stories*. Harmondsworth: Penguin.

Byrum, Oliver E. 1992. Edge Cities: A Pragmatic Perspective. *Journal of the American Planning Association*. Summer: 395–96.

Cahnman, Werner. 1964. Max Weber and the Methodological Controversy in the Social Sciences. W. Cahnman and Alvin Boskoff , eds., *Society and History*. Glencoe: Free Press, 103–27.

Callahan, Daniel, ed. 1966. *The Secular City Debate.* New York: Macmillan.

Callinicos, Alex. 1990. *Against Postmodernism.* New York: St Martin's.

Calthorpe, Peter. 1986. The Urban Context and A Short History of Twentieth Century New Towns. Sim Van der Ryn and Peter Calthorpe, eds., *Sustainable Communities,* 1–33, 189–234.

———. 1989. Introduction and Pedestrian Pockets: New Strategies for Suburban Growth. Doug Kelbaugh, ed., T*he Pedestrian Pocket Book: A New Suburban Design Strategy,* 3–20.

———. 1993. *The Next American Metropolis.* Princeton Architectural Press.

Calthorpe, Peter, William A. Isley, and Doug Kelbaugh. 1989. Pedestrian Pockets. Anne Vernez Moudon, ed., *Master–Planned Communities,* 69–72.

Calvino, Italo. 1974. *Invisible Cities.* Translated by William Weaver. New York: Harcout Brace.

Canter, David. 1977. *The Psychology of Place.* New York: St Martin's.

Carson, Rachel. 1962. *Silent Spring.* Boston: Houghton Mifflin.

Carter, Thomas. 1989. Review of *Common Places,* Dell Upton and J.M. Vlach, eds. *Journal of the Society for Architectural Historians.* 48(2): 202.

Case, F. Duncan. 1986. Putting Science into Practice: A Problem of Pedagogical Folklore. J. William Carswell and David G. Saile, eds., *Built Form and Culture Research.* Conference Proceedings, 9–10.

Castells, Manuel. 1980. *The Urban Question: A Marxist Approach.* Cambridge, MA: MIT. Translated by Alan Sheridan from original French edition, 1972, *La Question Urbaine.*

———. 1983. *The City and the Grassroots: A Cross-Cultural Theory of Urban Social Movements.* University of California.

Castex, Jean, J.-C. Depaule and P. Panerai. 1975a. *Principes d'analyse urbaine.* ADROS-CORDA.

———. 1975b. D*e l'îlôt à la barre: Contribution à la définition de l'architecture urbaine.* ADROS-CORDA.

———. 1977. *Formes urbaines: De l'îlôt à la barre.* Paris: Dunod. Revised edition of 1975b.

———. 1980. *Éléments d'analyse urbaine.* Brussels: AAM. Revised edition of 1975a.

Castro, Roland. 1978. Le système Beaux-Arts avant 1968. *Architecture Mouvement Continuité.* 45 (May).

———. 1984. Interviewed by Le Dantec. *Enfin, l'architecture?* Paris: Autrement, 154–58.

Centre de Création Industrielle and Institut Français d'Architecture. 1981. *Architectures en France, Modernité-Postmodernité.* Paris: Centre de Création Industrielle.

Cervellati, Pier Luigi. 1984. *La citt´ post-industriale.* Bologna: Il Mulino.

Cervellati, Pier Luigi, R. Scannavini, and C. De Angelis. 1981 [1977]. *La nouvelle culture urbaine: Boulogne face à son patrimoine.* Translated from original Italian edition by E. Tempia and A. Petita. Paris: Seuil.

Chakrabarty, Dipesh. 1992. The Death of History? Historical Consciousness and the Culture of Late Capitalism. *Public Culture.* 4 (2): 47–66.

Chamboredon, Jean-Claude. 1985. Nouvelles formes de l'opposition ville-campagne. Georges Duby, ed., *Histoire de la France Urbaine*, 5, 557–67.

Champenois, Michelle. 1979. La Galaxie Culot. *Macadam*. September 5–October 15: 4–5.

———. 1986. Les semeurs de villes. *Le Monde Aujourd'hui*. March 16–17: VI.

Charles, Eleanor. 1986. Living Over the Store: An Old Tradition Revives as Builders and Buyers Recognize its Advantages. *New York Times*. September 7: Real Estate, 48–9.

Chaslin, François. 1985. *Les Paris de Mitterand*. Paris: Gallimard.

Chermayeff, Serge and Christopher Alexander. 1963. *Community and Privacy: Toward a New Architecture of Humanism*. New York: Doubleday. French edition, 1972.

Choay, Françoise. 1965. *L'urbanisme: utopies et réalités: une anthologie*. Paris: Seuil.

———. 1969a. *Le jeu et la règle*. Paris: Seuil, Espacements series.

———. 1969b. *The Modern City: Planning in the 19th Century*. New York: Braziller.

———. 1970. L'histoire et la méthode en urbanisme. *Annales ESC*.

———. 1985. Production de la ville, esthétique urbaine et architecture. Georges Duby, ed., *Histoire de la France Urbaine*. 5: 233–80.

Chtcheglov, Ivan. 1995. Formulary for a New Urbanism. *Situationiste Internationale Anthology*, 1–4. Translated from original 1953 edition.

Churchill, Henry S. 1962 [1945]. *The City is the People*. New York: W.W. Norton.

Clarke, Paul Walker. 1989. The Economic Currency of Architectural Aesthetics: Modernism and Postmodernism in the Urbanism of Capitalism. M. Diani and C. Ingraham, eds., *Restructuring Architectural Theory*.

———. 1991. Critical Pedagogy and the Architectural Concept of Context. *Back to Life*. Washington DC: American Collegiate Schools of Architecture, 287–92.

Clarke, Paul Walker and Thomas A. Dutton. 1986. Notes toward a Critical Theory of Architecture. *The Discipline of Architecture: Inquiry through Design*. Proceedings of the 73rd ACSA Meetings, Washington DC.

Clifford, James. 1986. Introduction: Partial Truths. J. Clifford and G. E. Marcus, eds., *Writing Culture*, 1–26.

Clifford, James and George E. Marcus. 1986. *Writing Culture: The Poetics and Politics of Ethnography*. University of California.

Clough, Patricia Ticineto. 1992. *The End(s) of Ethnography*. Newbury Park: Sage.

Coates, Nigel. 1990. Interviewed by Brian Hatton. *Newsline*. New York: Columbia University, April: 2.

Cohen, Jean-Louis. 1982. L'union sacrée: technocrates et architectes modernes à l'assaut de la banlieue parisienne. *Les Cahiers de la Recherche Architecturale*. 9: 6–26.

———. 1984. La coupure entre architectes et intellectuels, ou les enseignements de l'italophilie. Monique Eleb-Vidal, B. Haumont, et al., eds., *Extenso*. 1: entire issue.

Cohen, Stuart. 1974. Physical Context/Cultural Context: Including it All. *Oppositions*. 2: 1–22.

Cohen, Stuart. 1985. On Adding On. *Thresholds: The Journal of Architecture*. University of Illinois, 3: 75–91.

Collins, Clare. 1994. Home Alarm Systems Cost Billions a Year: Are they Worth It?, How to Choose a Residential Security System, and Hiring Private Security Guards to Cut Neighborhood Crime. *New York Times*, August 18.

Collins, George R. and Christiane Crasemann Collins. 1965. *Camillo Sitte and the Birth of Modern City Planning*. NY: Random House.

——. 1986. *Camillo Sitte: The Birth of Modern City Planning*. New York: Rizzoli.

Collins, Peter. 1965. *Changing Ideals in Modern Architecture 1750–1950*. Montreal: McGill-Queens University.

Colomina, Beatriz, ed. 1992. *Sexuality and Space*. New York: Princeton Architectural Press.

Colquhoun, Alan. 1985. On Modern and Post-Modern Space. Joan Ockman, ed., *Architecture, Criticism, Ideology*. New York: Princeton Architectural Press, 103–17.

Comité de grève. 1968. Motion du 15 mai. *Architecture Mouvement Continuité*, Spécial Mai 1968, July.

Conan, Michel. 1982. Le déplacement et la question de l'identité régionale. IFA, ed., *Paysage pavillonnaire*, Paris: Institut Français de l'Architecture, 16–25.

Connor, Steven. 1989. *Postmodernist Culture*. Oxford: Blackwell.

Conrads, Ulrich, ed. 1970. *Programs and Manifestos on Twentieth-Century Architecture*. Translated by Michael Bullock. Cambridge: MIT.

Cooke, Philip. 1988. Modernity, Postmodernity, and the City. *Theory, Culture, and Society*, 5, 475–92.

——. 1990. *Back to the Future: Modernity, Postmodernity and Locality*. London: Unwin Hyman.

Cooper, Clare. 1975. *Easter Hill Village*. New York: Free Press (Macmillian).

Corbett, Michael. 1981. *A Better Place to Live: New Designs for Tomorrow's Communities*. Ammaus, PA: Rodale Press.

Corrigan, Philip and Derek Sayer. 1985. *The Great Arch: State Formation as Cultural Revolution*. Oxford: Blackwell.

Corwin, Miles. 1992. Buildings that Say "Back Off." *Los Angeles Times*. June 9.

County Council of Essex. 1973. *A Design Guide for Residential Areas*. Essex: County Council. Original edition translated into French, 1981, *Créé* 184 (September): 91–96.

Cox, Harvey. 1965. *The Secular City*. New York: Macmillan.

Crapanzano, Vincent. 1986. Hermes' Dilemma: The Masking of Subversion in Ethnographic Description. J. Clifford and G. E. Marcus, eds., *Writing Culture*, 51–76.

——. 1991. The Postmodern Crisis: Discourse, Parody, Memory. *Cultural Anthropology*. 6(4): 431–46.

Crawford, Margaret. 1991. Can Architects be Socially Responsible? Diane Ghirardo, ed., *Out of Site*, 27–45.

Crépu, Michel and Denis Langlart. 1985. La république des architectes. *Esprit.* 198 (December).

Crépu, Michel, Denis Langlart, and Agnès Vince. 1985. Réveil de l'architecture? *Esprit.* 198 (December).

Crimp, Douglas. 1987. Art in the 80s: The Myth of Autonomy. *PRECIS.* Columbia University, 6: 83–91.

Crook, J. Mordaunt. 1987. *The Dilemma of Style: Architectural Ideas from the Picturesque to the Post-Modern.* University of Chicago.

Crow, Dennis, ed. 1990. *Philosophic Streets: New Approaches to Urbanism.* Washington DC: Maisonneuve.

Crow, Timothy. 1991. *Crime Prevention through Environmental Design.* London: Butterworth-Heinemann.

Cruickshank, Dan. 1991. Interview with Léon Krier. *Newsline.* Columbia University, April, 2.

Cuff, Dana. 1991. *Architecture: The Story of Practice.* Cambridge, MA: MIT.

Cullen, Gordon. 1961. *The Concise Townscape.* New York: Reinhold.

Culot, Maurice. 1977. Portrait de François Spoerry. *Archives d'Architecture Moderne.* 12 (November).

———. 1979. Expositions: Dessins pour la reconstruction de la ville; Art et Culture. *Macadam.* September 5–October 15.

———. 1983. Avec l'aide de Dieu. *Art Press.* Hors série no. 2: 52–3.

Daniel, Heidi. 1989. Oxon Hill, MD.: $1 Billion Town on the Potomac. *New York Times,* March 19.

Davidoff, Paul. 1965. Advocacy and Pluralism in Planning. *Journal of the American Institute of Planners.* November. Reprinted in Andreas Faludi, ed., *A Reader in Planning Theory,* 1973. Oxford: Pergamon Press, 277–96.

Davis, Doug. 1987. Late Postmodern: The End of Style. *Art in America.* June: 15–23.

Davis, Mike. 1985. Urban Renaissance and the Spirit of Postmodernism. *New Left Review.* 151 (May–June).

———. 1990. *City of Quartz: Excavating the Future in Los Angeles.* New York: Verso.

———. 1991. The Infinite Game: Redeveloping Downtown L.A. Diane Ghirardo, ed., *Out of Site,* 77–113.

———. 1994. Cannibal City: Los Angeles and the Destruction of Nature. Elizabeth A. T. Smith, comp., *Urban Revisions: Current Projects for the Public Realm,* 39–57.

Dear, Michael. 1986. Postmodern Planning. *Environment and Planning, D: Society and Space.* 4(3): 367–84.

———. 1988. The Postmodern Challenge: Reconstructing Human Geography. *Transactions.* Institute of British Geographers. 13: 262–74.

———. 1989. Privatization and the Rhetoric of Planning Practice. *Environment and Planning, D.* 7(4): 449–62.

———. 1991. The Premature Demise of Postmodern Urbanism. *Cultural Anthropology.* 6(4): 538–52.

Debord, Guy. 1970. Society of the Spectacle. *Detroit: A Black and Red translation,* unauthorized. Also in *Radical America,* 4 (5). Translated from original 1967 French edition.

———. 1995. Introduction to a Critique of Urban Geography. *Situationiste Internationale Anthology.* Translated from 1955 original.

Deleuze, Gilles and Félix Guattari. 1983. *Anti-Oedipus.* Minneapolis: University of Minnesota Press.

Delevoy, Robert, ed. 1978. *Rational Architecture/Rationelle 1978: The Reconstruction of the European City.* Brussels, 15–21.

Delsohn, Gary. 1989. The First Pedestrian Pocket. *Planning.* December, 20–2.

De Man, Paul. 1967a. *L'écriture et la différence.* Paris: Seuil. English translation, *Writing and Difference,* 1978.

———. 1967b. *De la grammatologie.* Paris: Minuit. English translation, *Of Grammatology,* 1976.

———. 1970. *Allegories of Reading.* New Haven: Yale University.

Dennis, Michael. 1986. *Court and Garden: From the French Hôtel to the City of Modern Architecture.* Cambridge, MA: MIT.

Derrida, Jacques. 1988. Interview. BMO4, City University of New York Graduate Center.

Derrida, Jacques and Peter Eisenman. 1997. *Choral Works.* NY: Monacelli. Edited by Jeffry Kipnis and Thomas Leeser.

Design Book Review. 1989. Postmodern Urbanism 17 (Winter).

———. 1992. Gender and Design. 25 (Summer).

Dethier, Jean, ed. 1980. Special supplement to *h: la revue de l'habitat social.* 50 (March): 69–84.

Devillers, Christian and Bernard Huet. 1981. *Le Creusot.* Preface by Louis Bergeron. Seyssel: Champ Vallon.

———. 1986. Le Sublime et le Quotidien. *Architecture Mouvement Continuité.* 14 (December): 102–09.

Dewey, Fred. 1994. Cyburbia: L.A. as the New Frontier, or Grave? *LA Forum on Architecture and Urban Design Newsletter.* May: 1, 7.

Diani, Marco and Catherine Ingraham, eds. 1989. *Restructuring Architectural Theory.* Evanston, IL: Northwestern University. Originally published as Introduction to *Threshold,* 1988, 4 (Spring): 1–8.

Dillon, David. 1989. Las Colinas Revisited. *Planning.* December, 6–11.

Doxiadis, Constantinos. 1963. *Architecture in Transition.* NY: Oxford University.

———. 1968. *Ekistics: An Introduction to the Science of Human Settlements.* New York: Oxford University.

———. 1960. *The Death of Our Cities.* Athens: Doxiadis Associates.

Duany, Andres. 1992. Toward the New Urbanism. Speech at the Million Dollar Theatre, Los Angeles. June.

Duany, Andres and Elizabeth Plater-Zyberk. 1992. The Second Coming of the American Small Town. *Wilson Quarterly.* Winter: 19–48.

Duby, Georges, ed. 1985. *Histoire de la France urbaine,* 5. Directed by Marcel Roncayolo.

Dutton, Thomas. 1986. Toward an Architectural Praxis of Cultural Production: Beyond Leon Krier. J. William Carswell and David Saile, eds. *Purposes in Built Form and Culture Research.* Proceedings of Conference on Built Forms and Culture Research at the University of Kansas, 21–6.

———. 1988. Cities, Cultures, and Resistance: Beyond Leon Krier and the Postmodern Condition. *Journal of Architectural Education.* Fall.

Dutton, Thomas and Bradford Grant. 1991. Campus Design and Critical Pedagogy. *Academe.* 77 (4): 37–43.

Dyckman, John W. 1962. The European Motherland of American Urban Romanticism. *Journal of the American Institute of Planners.* 28: 277–81.

Eagleton, Terry. 1987. Awakening from Modernity. *Times Literary Supplement.* February 20.

Eames, Edwin and Judith Goode. 1977. *Anthropology of the City.* New York: Prentice-Hall.

Ebner, Michael H. 1981. Urban History: Retrospect and Prospect. *Journal of American History.* 61 (June): 69–84.

Eckbo, Garrett. 1949. *Landscape for Living.* New York: Architectural Record.

Eco, Umberto. 1973. Function and Sign: Semiotics of Architecture. *VIA 2: Structures Implicit and Explicit.* Graduate School of Fine Arts, University of Pennsylvania, 136–45.

———. 1984. Postmodernism, Irony, the Enjoyable. *Postscript to the Name of the Rose.* New York: Harcourt Brace Jovanovich.

———. 1986 [1973]. *Travels in Hyperreality.* New York: Harcourt Brace Jovanovich.

Ecomomakis, Richard, ed. 1992. *Leon Krier: Architecture and Urban Design,* 1967–1992. Introduction by Demetri Porphyrios. Essay by David Watkin. London: Academy Editions.

Editorial. 1990. Facades, Reversed. *New York Times.* August 19.

Eickelman, Dale. 1985. *Knowledge and Power in Morocco.* Princeton University Press.

Eisenman, Peter. 1984. The End of the Classical: The End of the End, the End of the Beginning. *Perspecta: The Yale Architectural Journal.* Volume 21.

———. 1992. Visions' Unfolding: Architecture in the Age of Electronic Media. *Domus.* No.734 (January).

Eisenman, Peter and Leon Krier. 1989. My Ideology is Better than Yours. *Architectural Design Profile: Reconstruction-Deconstruction:* 6–19.

Eisenman, Peter, Michael Graves, Charles Gwathmey, John Hejduk, and Richard Meier. 1975. *Five Architects.* New York: Oxford University.

Eisenman, Peter and Robert Stern, eds. 1974. White and Gray. *Architecture and Urbanism.* 52: 3–180.

Eliot, T. S. 1932. Tradition and the Individual Talent. *Selected Essays, 1917–32*. New York: Harcourt & Brace.

Ellin, Nan. 1986. Urban Design: Cergy-St Christophe. Paper presented to the Columbia Atelier, Paris.

———. 1994. In Search of a Usable Past: Urban Design in a French New Town. Ph.D. dissertation, Columbia University.

———. 1995a. Battery Park City. *Encyclopedia of New York City*. New Haven: Yale University.

———. 1995b. Carroll Gardens. *Encyclopedia of New York City*. New Haven: Yale University.

———. 1997. Shelter from the Storm or Form Follows Fear and Vice Versa. *Architecture of Fear*. New York: Princeton Architectural Press, 13–45.

Ellin, Nan, ed. 1997. *Architecture of Fear*. New York: Princeton Architectural Press.

Ellis, Charlotte. 1986. Function follows Form: Housing. *Architectural Review*. 1078 (December): 63–72.

Ellis, Russell and Dana Cuff, eds. 1989. *Architects' People*. New York: Oxford.

Emery, Marc. 1979. Du village à la ville. *Architecture d'Aujourd'hui*: 203.

———. 1986. Preface. *Paris Architecture Moderne Guide, 1977–86*. Paris: L'Equerre.

Evenson, Norma. 1979. *Paris: A Century of Change, 1878–1978*. New Haven: Yale University Press.

Fachard, Sabine, ed. DATE. *Architectures Capitales: Paris 1979–1989*. Paris: Electa Moniteur.

Faludi, Andreas, ed. 1973. *A Reader in Planning Theory*. Oxford: Pergamon.

Farelly, E. M. 1986. The New Spirit. Letter to the Editor. *Architectural Review*. August; December.

Fathy, Hassan. 1973. *Architecture for the Poor*. University of Chicago. Original edition, 1969, *Gourna: A Tale of Two Villages*, Cairo: Egypt: Ministry of Culture.

Fatosme, Jean. 1981. Le plaisir plutôt que la théorie. *Créé*. 184 (September).

Fernandez-Galiano, Luis. 1989. Bofill Superstar. *Design Book Review*. 17: 59–60.

Festival d'Automne à Paris. 1980. *La présence de l'histoire: l'après modernité*. Paris: L'Equerre. Translated by L. Revelli Beaumont from the Italian edition. *Le Bienalle di Venezia*. 1980. Electra.

———. 1982. *La modernité: un projet inachevé*. Paris: L'Equerre. Articles by J.-P. Chimot, K. Frampton, J.-C. Garcías, J. Habermas, P. Chemetov.

Filler, Martin. 1981. Architect for a Pluralist Age. *Art in America*: 69.

Finotti, John. 1988. Portman in the Suburbs: The $1.2 Billion Northpark. *New York Times*. May 15: Real Estate, 16–17.

Fishman, Robert. 1977. *Urban Utopias in the Twentieth Century*. New York: Basic Books.

———. 1980. The Anti-Planners: The Contemporary Revolt against Planning and its Significance for Planning History. Gordon E. Cherry, ed., *Shaping an Urban World*, 243–52.

———. 1987. *Bourgeois Utopias.* New York: Basic Books, 103–33.

———. 1988. The Postwar American Suburb: A New Form, a New City. D. Schaeffer, ed., *Two Centuries of American Planning.*

———. 1992. America's New City: Megalopolis Unbound. *The Best of the Wilson Quarterly*: 9–25.

Fitch, James Marston. 1963. The Profession of Architecture. Kenneth S. Lynn, ed., *The Professions in America.* Boston: Beacon, 231–41.

Fleming, Ronald Lee. 1993. Letter to the Editor. *Harper's Magazine.*

Flusty, Steven. 1994. Building Paranoia: The Proliferation of Interdictory Space and the Erosion of Spatial Justice. Los Angeles Forum for Architecture and Urban Design.

Fogelson, Richard E. 1986. *Planning the Capitalist City: The Colonial Era to the 1920s.* Princeton University Press.

Fortier, Bruno. 1975. *La politique de l'espace parisien à la fin de l'ancien régime.* CORDA.

———. 1980. L'invention de la maison. *Architecture Mouvement Continuité.* 51 (March): 29–35.

Fortune Magazine Editors. 1957. *The Exploding Metropolis: A Study of the Assault on Urbanism and how our Cities can Resist It.* Garden City, New York: Doubleday. 1993 reprint, Foreword by Sam Bass Warner, University of California Press.

Foster, Hal. 1985. *Recodings: Art, Spectacle, Cultural Politics.* Seattle: Bay Press.

———. 1990. Architecture, Development, Memory. K. Michael Hays and Carol Burns, eds., *Thinking the Present: Recent American Architecture*, 110–22.

Foster, Hal, ed. 1983. *The Anti-Aesthetic.* Seattle: Bay Press.

———. 1987. *Discussions in Contemporary Culture.* New York: Dia Art Foundation.

Foucault, Michel. 1969. *L'archéologie du savoir.* Paris: Gallimard.

———. 1980. *The History of Sexuality.* Vol. 1. New York: Vintage.

Frampton, Kenneth. 1971. America 1960–1970: Notes on Urban Image and Theory. *Casabella.* 359–60(xxv): 24–38.

———. 1972. Criticism. Museum of Modern Art, ed., *Five Architects: Eisenman, Graves, Gwathmey, Hejduk, Meier.* New York: Oxford University.

———. 1975. Des vicissitudes de l'idéologie. *Architecture d'Aujourd'hui.* 177 (January–February): 62–5.

———. 1983a. Towards a Critical Regionalism: Six Points for an Architecture of Resistance. Hal Foster, ed., *The Anti-Aesthetic*, 16–30.

———. 1983b. Prospects for Critical Regionalism. *Perspecta.* 20: 147–62.

———. 1985 [1980]. *Modern Architecture: A Critical History.* London: Thames and Hudson.

———. 1991. Reflections on the Autonomy of Architecture: A Critique of Contemporary Production. Diane Ghirardo, ed., *Out of Site*, 17–26.

Frampton, K. and Deborah Berke. 1982. *Rob Krier: Urban Projects 1968–1982.* New York: IAUS Catalogue no. 5.

Francescato, Guido. 1992. Type and the Possibility of an Architectural Scholarship. Unpublished manuscript.

Franck, Karen and Sherry Ahrentzen, eds. 1989. *New Households, New Housing*. New York: Van Nostrand Reinhold.

Freedman, Jonathan L. 1975. *Crowding and Behavior*. NY: Viking.

Friedman, Yona. 1968. Toward a Coherent System of Planning. *Architects' Year Book*. XII. London: Elek Books.

——. 1975. *Toward a Scientific Architecture*. Translated by Cynthia Lang. Cambridge, MA: MIT.

Friedmann, John. 1987. *Planning in the Public Domain: From Knowledge to Action*. Princeton University Press.

Fukuyama, Francis. 1989. The End of History? *The National Interest*. Summer.

——. 1992. *The End of History and the Last Man*. New York: Free Press.

Fuller, Buckminister. 1970. *Utopia or Oblivion: The Prospects for Humanity*. London: Penguin.

Fulton, William. 1991. *Guide to California Planning*. Point Arena, CA: Solano Press.

——. 1993. Playa Vista is Ambitious Try at Neo-Village. California Neotraditional Plans, Projects. *Los Angeles Times*. August 29: K1, K6.

Gablik, Suzi. 1992. *Reenchantment of Art*. New York: Thames & Hudson.

Galbraith, John Kenneth. 1973. *Economics and the Public Purpose*. Boston: Houghton Mifflin.

Gandelsonas, Mario. 1972. On Reading Architecture. *Progressive Architecture*. 53: 69–85. Reprinted in G. Broadbent, ed., Signs, Symbols, and Architecture, 1980, 243–73.

——. 1975. Neo-Functionalism. *Oppositions 5*. Summer.

Gans, Herbert. 1962. *The Urban Villagers*. Glencoe: Free Press.

——. 1967. *The Levittowners*. New York: Vintage.

——. 1968. *People and Plans: Essays on Urban Problems and Solutions*. New York: Basic. Includes 1962 essay, Urbanism and Suburbanism as Ways of Life: A Re-evaluation of Definitions, 34–52.

——. 1974. *Popular Culture and High Culture: An Analysis and Evaluation of Taste*. New York: Basic Books.

Garbarine, Rachelle. 1986. Montclair Renewal Plan in Homestretch. *New York Times*. September 28: R10.

——. 1988. An Urban Center Rises in the Suburbs. *New York Times*. June 12.

Garcías, Jean-Claude and Martin Meade. 1986. Politics of Paris. *Architectural Review*.

Garcías, Jean-Claude, J.-J. Treuttel, and Jérome Treuttel. 1980. XIe Session du PAN: Temps, Franges, Terres, Ramparts. *Architecture Mouvement Continuité*. 51 (March): 7–8.

Garreau, Joel. 1991. *Edge City: Life on the New Frontier*. New York: Doubleday.

Geertz, Clifford. 1964. Ideology as a Cultural System Reprinted. *The Interpretation of Culture*, 1973, 193–233.

Geertz, Clifford. 1973. Thick Description: Toward an Interpretive Theory of Culture. *The Interpretation of Culture*, 3–32.

———. 1980a. Blurred Genres: The Refiguration of Social Thought. *The American Scholar.* 49 (2): 165–79.

———. 1980b. *Negara: The Theatre State in Nineteenth-Century Bali.* Princeton University.

———. 1988. *Works and Lives: The Anthropologist as Author.* Stanford University.

Ghirardo, Diane, ed. 1991. *Out of Site: A Social Criticism of Architecture.* Seattle: Bay Press. Introduction, 9–16.

———. 1992. Review essay. *Journal for the Society of Architectural Historians.* December: 443–47.

———. 1996. *Architecture After Modernism.* New York: Thames & Hudson.

Gibberd, Frederick. 1959. *Town Design.* Third edition. New York: Praeger.

Gibson, James. 1950. The Perception of the Visual World. Boston: Houghton & Mifflin.

Giddens, Anthony. 1981. Modernism and Postmodernism. *New German Critique.* 22 (Winter): 15–18.

Giedion, Sigfried. 1941. *Space, Time, and Architecture: The Growth of a New Tradition.* Cambridge, MA: Harvard. Charles Eliot Norton Lectures, 1938–39.

———. 1948. *Mechanization Takes Command: A Contribution to Anonymous History.* New York: Oxford University.

Giovanni, Joseph. 1986. The 'New' Madison Avenue. *New York Times.* June 26.

———. 1988. Breaking All the Rules. *New York Times Magazine.* June 12: 40–3, 126, 130.

Girardot, Jean-Paul. 1978a. Les Figures: Cergy-Pontoise. Unpublished manuscript, February.

———. 1978b. Paris discrèt: Le guide des villas parisiennes. *Les Cahiers de la Recherche Architecturale.* 3. Special issue, November. Paris: Centre d'Études et de Recherche Architecturales.

———. 1981. Les règles de jeu. Créé. 184, September: 102–07. With Michel Routin.

———. 1986. Interviewed by author. Paris. February 5.

Gitlin, Todd. 1988. Hip-Deep in Post-modernism. *New York Times Book Review.* November 6: 1, 35–6.

———. 1989. Postmodernism: Roots and Politics. Ian Angus and Sut Jhally, eds., *Cultural Politics in Contemporary America*, 347–60.

Giurgola, Romaldo. 1966. Architecture in Change. Marcus Whiffen, ed., *The Architect and the City*, 103–20.

Gleye, Paul Henry. 1983. The Breath of History. PhD dissertation, UCLA.

Goldberger, Paul. 1983. *On the Rise: Architecture and Design in a Postmodern Age.* New York Times Books.

———. 1985. An Architect to Pull Paris Together. *New York Times.* May 27.

———. 1988a. 80s Design: Wallowing in Opulence and Luxury. *New York Times.* November 13.

Goldberger, Paul. 1988b. What's at Stake is Control over the Building Process? *New York Times.* May 15.

——. 1988c. Theories as the Building Blocks for a New Style. *New York Times.* June 26: 29, 37.

——. 1989a. Crossing the Threshold from Medieval to Modern. *New York Times Home Design.* April 9.

——. 1989b. Can Architects Serve the Public Good? *New York Times.* June 25.

——. 1989c. On a Desolate Beach in Queens, a Point of Departure. *New York Times.* July 23: H29.

——. 1989d. The Quest for Comfort: Architecture Eases into the '90s. *New York Times.* October 15.

——. 1990a. A More Perfect Union. *New York Times Magazine.* April 22: 41–5.

——. 1990b. Aldo Rossi: Sentiment for the Unsentimental. *New York Times.* April 22.

——. 1990c. Four Walls and a Door. *New York Times Home Design.* October 14: 40, 66–7.

——. 1991. Robert Venturi, Gentle Subverter of Modernism. *New York Times.* April 14.

——. 1993. A Remembrance of Visions Pure and Elegant. *New York Times.* January 3: H29.

Goldstein, Harvey A. and Sara A. Rosenberry, eds. 1978. The Structural Crisis of the 1970s and Beyond: The Need for a New Planning Theory, The Proceedings of the Conference on Planning Theory. Virginia Polytechnic Institute and State University. May.

Good Housekeeping. 1988a. Advertisement. *New York Times Magazine.* October 9.

——. 1989. Advertisement. *New York Times.* May 15.

——. 1990. Advertisment. *New York Times Magazine.* June 17.

Goode, Terrance. 1992. Typological Theory in the United States: The Consumption of Architectural 'Authenticity.' *Journal of Architectural Education.* 46(1): 2–13.

Goodfriend, Douglas. 1979. Nagar Yoga: The Culturally Informed Town Planning of Patrick Geddes in India 1914–1924. *Human Organization.* 38: 343–55.

Goodman, Paul. 1956. *Growing Up Absurd.* New York: Random House.

Goodman, Paul and Percival Goodman. 1960 [1947]. *Communitas: Means of Livelihood and Ways of Life.* New York: Knopf and Random House.

Goodman, Percival. 1984. Lecture at Avery Hall. Columbia University. [On precursors of postmodernism.]

——. 1977. *The Double E. Garden City,* NY: Doubleday Anchor.

Goodman, Robert. 1971. *After the Planners.* New York: Simon & Schuster.

Gordon, Larry. 1993. The Slow Dawn of an Oasis. *Los Angeles Times.* August 15.

Gordon, Mitchell. 1963. *Sick Cities.* New York: Macmillan.

Gordon, Richard E., Katherine K. Gordon, and Max Gunther. 1960. *The Split-Level Trap.* New York: Dell.

Gorman, Tom. 1992. Looking for "Our Town." *Los Angles Times.* April 23.

Gosling, David. 1984. Definitions of Urban Design. *Architectural Design Profile.* 54 (1/2): 16–24.

Gosling, David and Barry Maitland. 1984. *Concepts of Urban Design.* New York: St Martin's.

Gottmann, Jean. 1961. *Megalopolis.* New York: The Twentieth Century Fund.

Gouldner, Alvin W. 1979. *The Future of Intellectuals and the Rise of the New Class.* New York: Oxford.

Goulet, Patrice. 1981a. Interview with Clive Harris. *Créé.* 184 (September): 95–6.

———. 1981b. Interview with Edouard de Penguilly. *Créé.* 184 (September): 73–80.

———. 1985. Le nouveau monde: la lévure et les épices. *Architecture d'Aujourd'hui.* 242 (December): 2–3.

Grassi, Giorgio. 1967. *La construzione logica dell'architettura.* Padova: Marsilio.

Gregory, Derek and John Urry, eds. 1985. *Social Relations and Spatial Structures.* New York: St Martin's.

Gregotti, Vittorio. 1966. *Il territorio dell'architettura.* Milano: Feltrinelli.

Griffin, D.R. 1992. The Reenchantment of Science. (Excerpt from *The Reenchantment of Science: Postmodern Proposals,* 1988, SUNY.) Creativity and Postmodern Religion. (Excerpt from *God and Religion in the Postmodern World,* 1989, SUNY.) Charles Jencks, ed., *The Postmodern Reader,* 354–82.

Griffin, David Ray, ed. 1988. *Spirituality and Society: Postmodern Visions.* Albany: SUNY.

Groat, Linda and David Canter. 1979. Does Post-Modernism Communicate? *Progressive Architecture.* 12: 84–87.

Gruen, Victor. 1964. *The Heart of Our Cities: The Urban Crisis: Diagnosis and Cure.* New York: Simon & Schuster.

Grumbach, Antoine. 1976. Les promenades de Paris. *Architecture d'Aujourd'hui.* 185: May–June.

———. 1978. The Theatre of Memory. *Architectural Design Profile.* 48: 8–9.

———. 1981. L'art de compléter les villes. *Architectures en France, Modernité-Postmodernité.* Paris: CCI.

———. 1982. Reconcilier la maison individuelle et la ville. IFA, ed., *Paysage pavillonnaire.* Paris: Institut Français de l'Architecture, 83–6.

Guiheux, Jean. 1989. *Europan.* Paris: Plan Construction.

Guillaume, Jacques. 1977. *The Idea of Architecture-Language: A Critical Inquiry.*

Gulgonen and Laisney. 1977. *Morphologie urbaine et typologie architecturale.* Paris: CORDA.

Gunts, Edward. 1988a. Deconstructivism: An Architecture of Instability. *Baltimore Sun.* July 3: Section J, 1, 3.

———. 1988b. Creating a $350 Million City "Neighborhood." *Baltimore Sun.* November 13: Section D, 1, 15.

———. 1988c. Designing a Neighborhood. *Baltimore Sun.* DATE? Section C, 14–15.

Guterson, David. 1992. No Place like Home. *Harper's Magazine.* November: 55–64.

Gutiérrez, Ramón. 1994. Toward an Appropriate Modernity. *Design Book Review.* 32/33: 98.

Gutkind, E. A. 1962. *The Twilight of Cities.* New York: Free Press.

Gutman, Robert. 1972a. *People and Buildings.* New York: Basic Books.

——. 1972b [1966]. The Questions Architects Ask. *People and Buildings,* 337–69.

——. 1988. *Architectural Practice: A Critical View.* NewYork: Princeton Architectural Press.

——. 1989. Human Nature in Architectural Theory: The Example of Louis Kahn. R. Ellis and D. Cuff, eds., *Architects' People,* 105–29.

——. 1985. *The Design of American Housing: A Reappraisal of the Architect's Role.* New York: Publishing Center for Cultural Resources.

Guyon, Lionel. 1990. *Architecture et publicité.* Liège: Madraga.

Habermas, Jürgen. 1970. *Toward a Rational Society.* Boston: Beacon Press.

——. 1975 [1973]. *Legitimation Crisis.* Boston: Beacon Press.

——. 1981. Modernity versus Postmodernity. *New German Critique.* 22 (Winter): 2–14.

——. 1982. L'autre tradition. *Modernité: Un projet inachevé, Festival d'Automne à Paris.* Translated by Gerard Raulet. Paris: Moniteur, 22–31.

——. 1991. The Public Sphere. Chandra Mukerji and Michael Schudson, eds. *Rethinking Popular Culture,* 398–404.

——. 1983 [1981]. Modernity-An Incomplete Project. Hal Foster, ed. *The Anti-Aesthetic,* 3–15.

——. 1986. The New Obscurity. *Philosophy and Social Criticism.* 2(2): 2–18. Translated by Phillip Jacobs.

——. 1987. *Lectures on the Philosophical Discourse of Modernity.* Cambridge, MA: MIT.

——. 1989a. *The Structural Transformation of the Public Sphere: An Enquiry into a Category of Bourgeois Society.* Translated by Thomas Burger. Cambridge, MA: MIT. Original German edition, 1962; French edition, 1978, *L'espace public, Paris, Payot.*

——. 1989b. Modern and Postmodern Architecture. *The New Conservatism: Cultural Criticism and the Historians' Debate.* Translated by Shierry Webe Nicholsen. Cambridge, MA: MIT.

Habraken, Nicolas J. 1972. *Supports: An Alternative to Mass Housing.* London: Architectural Press. Original Dutch edition, 1961, translated by B. Valkenburg.

Hall, Edward T. 1959. *The Silent Language.* New York: Doubleday.

——. 1968. Human Needs and Inhuman Cities. *Ekistics.* 27(160).

——. 1969. *Hidden Dimension.* New York: Doubleday.

——. 1976. *Beyond Culture.* New York: Doubleday.

——. 1983. *The Dance of Life: The Other Dimension of Time.* New York: Doubleday.

Hall, Peter. 1988. *Cities of Tomorrow.* Oxford: Basil Blackwell.

Halprin, Lawrence. 1963. *Cities.* New York: Reinhold Publishing.

——. 1969. *The RSVP Cycles: Creative Processes in the Human Environment.* New York: Braziller.

Hannerz, Ulf. 1980. *Exploring the City: Inquiries Toward an Urban Anthropology.* New York: Columbia University.

Harries, Karsten. 1982. Building and the Terror of Time. *Perspecta: The Yale Architectural Journal.* 19: 59–69.

Harries, Paul, Alan Lipman, and Stephen Purden. 1988. Meaning in Architecture: Post-Modernism, Hustling and the Big Sell. David Canter and David Stea, eds. *Ethnoscapes.* Vol. 1: 188–99.

Harris, Steven, and Deborah Berke, eds. 1997. *The Architecture of the Everyday.* New York: Princeton Architectural Press.

Hartman, Chester W. 1978. Social Planning and the Political Planner. Robert W. Burchell and George Sternlieb, eds. *Planning Theory in the 1980s.* New Brunswick: Rutgers University Press, 73–82.

Harvard Architectural Review. 1980. Editorial. Beyond the Modern Movement. 1, Spring: 4–7.

Harvard Graduate School of Design. 1986. *GSD News.* Special Issue. Fall.

——. 1989. Conference announcement. Thinking the Present: The Last Twelve Years of American Architecture. April 8 9.

Harvey, David. 1973. *Social Justice and the City.* Baltimore: Johns Hopkins University.

——. 1985a. *Consciousness and the Urban Experience: Studies in the History and Theory of Capitalist Urbanization.* Baltimore: Johns Hopkins University.

——. 1985b. *The Urbanization of Capital: Studies in the History and Theory of Capitalist Urbanization.* Baltimore: Johns Hopkins University.

——. 1989. *The Condition of Postmodernity.* Oxford: Blackwell.

Hassan, Ihab. 1975. *Paracriticisms: Seven Speculations of the Times.* Urbana, IL: University of Illinois.

——. 1985. The Culture of Postmodernism. *Theory, Culture, and Society.* 2(3): 119–32.

——. 1987. *The Postmodern Turn: Essays in Postmodern Theory and Culture.* Columbus: Ohio State University. Excerpt in Jencks, 1992.

Hayden, Dolores. 1976. *Seven American Utopias: The Architecture of Communitarian Socialism,* 1790–1975. Cambridge, MA: MIT.

——. 1980a. *The Grand "Domestic" Revolution: Feminism, Socialism, and the American Home,* 1870–1930. Cambridge, MA: MIT.

——. 1980b. What would a Nonsexist City be Like? Speculations on Housing, Urban Design, and Human Work. *Women and the American City. Signs.* Special Issue. Catherine Stimpson, ed. Spring: 167–84.

——. 1984. *Redesigning the American Dream: The Future of Housing, Work, and Family Life.* New York: W.W. Norton.

Hays, K. Michael and Carol Burns, eds. 1990. *Thinking the Present: Recent American Architecture.* Princeton Architectural Press. Proceedings, Harvard Graduate School of Design conference, April 8–9, 1989.

Hebdige, Dick. 1987. The Impossible Object: Toward a Sociology of the Sublime. *New Formations.* 1(1).

Hegemann, Werner and Elbert Peets. 1989 [1922]. *The American Vitruvius: An Architect's Handbook of Civic Art.* Edited by Alan Plattus. Preface by Léon Krier. New York: Princeton Architectural Press.

Heresies. 1981. Making Room: Women and Architecture. 11(3).

Hershberg, Theodore. 1978. The New Urban History: Toward an Interdisciplinary History of the City. *Journal of Urban History.* 5(1), November: 3–40.

Hester, Randolph. 1985. Subconscious Landscapes of the Heart. *Places.* 2(3): 10–22.

Hewison, R. 1987. *The Heritage Industry.* London: Methuen.

Hines, Thomas. 1985. Windows into their Work: Architects as Writers. *New York Times Book Review.* September 8.

His Royal Highness the Prince of Wales (Prince Charles). 1988. Untitled article. *GSD News* (Harvard Graduate School of Design). Special Issue. Fall: 5.

———. 1989. *A Vision of Britain: A Personal View of Architecture.* Garden City, NY. Doubleday.

Hobsbawm, Eric. 1983. Inventing Traditions. Mass-Producing Traditions: Europe, 1870–1914. E. Hobsbawm and Terence Ranger, eds. *The Invention of Tradition.* New York: Cambridge University Press, 1–14, 263–308.

Hoge, Warren. 1998. In Stone, a Prince's Vision of Britain. *New York Times.* June 11: B1, B6.

Holl, Steven. 1991. Edge of a City. *The New City: Foundations.* University of Miami School of Architecture. Fall: 132–36.

———. 1998. http://www.walrus.com/~sha/loca_foc.htm.

Holston, James. 1989. *The Modernist City: An Anthropological Critique of Brasilia.* Chicago: University of Chicago.

Hough, Michael. 1991. *Out of Place: Restoring Identity to the Regional Landscape.* New Haven: Yale University.

Howard, Ebenezer. 1898. *To-morrow: A Peaceful Path to Real Reform.* London: S. Sonnennschein.

———. 1902. *Garden Cities of To-morrow.* London: S. Sonnennschein.

Hudnut, Joseph. 1949. *Architecture and the Spirit of Man.* Cambridge, MA: Harvard University.

Huertas, Claude. 1982. Marne-la-Vallé, Val Maubuée. *Architecture d'Aujourd'hui.* 220 (April): 40–41.

Huet, Bernard. 1975. Requiem pour un Ordre. *Architecture d'Aujourd'hui.* 181 (September–October).

———. 1978. Petit manifeste. *Retional Architecture,* 54.

———. 1981. *Anachroniques d'Architecture.* Brussels: AAM.

———. 1985. Apprendre aux architectes la modestie. *Esprit.*

———. 1986. L'architecture contre la ville. *Architecture Mouvement Continuité.* 14 (December): 10–13.

Hummel, J. Brandt. 1989. Mashpee, Mass.: English Theme for Community. *New York Times.* June 11: R21.

Humphrey, Caroline. 1988. No Place like Home in Anthropology: The Neglect of Architecture. *Anthropology Today.* 4(1), February.

Hunziker, Christian. 1976. Portrait de Lucien Kroll. *Architecture d'Aujourd'hui,* 183.

Hutcheon, Linda. 1992. Theorising the Postmodern. Charles Jencks, ed. *The Postmodern Reader,* 76–93. Excerpted from *A Poetics of Postmodernism, History, Theory, Fiction.* London: Routledge, 1988.

Hutchinson, Maxwell. 1989. *The Prince of Wales: Right or Wrong? An Architect Replies.* London: Faber and Faber.

Huxtable, Ada Louise. 1981a. The Troubled State of Modern Architecture. *Architectural Record.* 169 (January): 72–79.

———. 1981b. Is Modern Architecture Dead? *Architectural Record.* 169 (October): 100–05.

———. 1983a. After Modern Architecture. *New York Review of Books.* December 8: 29–35.

———. 1983b. Rebuilding Architecture. *New York Review of Books.* December 22: 55–61.

———. 1992. Inventing American Reality. *New York Review of Books.* December 3: 24–9.

Huyssen, Andress. 1986. *After the Great Divide: Modernism, Mass Culture, Postmodernism.* Bloomington, IN: Indiana University Press.

Hyatt Foundation. 1995. *Media Kit Announcing the 1995 Pritzker Architecture Prize Laureate.* Los Angeles: The Hyatt Foundation.

IFA (Institut Français d'Architecture), ed. 1982. *Paysage pavillonnaire.* Paris: IFA.

Ingersoll, Richard. 1989a. People without Housing and Cities without People. Postmodern Urbanism: Forward into the Past. *Design Book Review.* 17 (Winter): 21–25.

———. 1989b. Review of The American Vitruvius. *Design Book Review.* 17 (Winter): 23.

———. 1989c. Interview with Colin Rowe. *Design Book Review.* 17 (Winter): 11–14.

———. 1992. The Disappearing Suburb. *Design Book Review.* 26 (Fall): 5–8. (Inludes review of Peter Rowe's *Making a Middle Landscape,* Andre Corboz's *Looking for a City in America,* and Deyan Sudjic's *The 100 Mile City.*)

Iniguez, Manuel. 1989. The City and Classical Tradition. *Architectural Design: Reconstruction-Deconstruction,* 88–91.

Jackson, John Brinkerhof. 1970. *Landscapes: Selected Writings of J. B. Jackson.* Edited by Ervin H. Zube. University of Massachusetts.

———. 1977. *Changing Rural Landscapes.* Edited by Ervin H. Zube and Margaret J. Zube. University of Massachusetts.

———. 1980. *The Necessity for Ruins and Other Topics.* University of Massachusetts.

Jackson, Kenneth T. 1985. *Crabgrass Frontier: The Suburbanization of the United States.* New York: Oxford University.

Jacobs, Allan and Donald Appleyard. 1987. Toward an Urban Design Manifesto. *Journal of the American Planning Association.* 53(1): 112–20.

Jacobs, Jane. 1957. Downtown is for People. Fortune Magazine, eds. *The Exploding Metropolis*, 140–68.

——. 1961. *The Death and Life of Great American Cities: The Failure of Town Planning*. New York: Vintage.

Jameson, Fredric. 1983. Postmodernism and Consumer Society. Hal Foster, ed. *The Anti-Aesthetic*. Seattle: Bay Press, 111–25.

——. 1984a. The Politics of Theory: Ideological Positions in the Post-modernism Debate. *New German Critique*. 33: 53–65. Reprinted 1987, P. Rabinow and William Sullivan, eds., *Interpretive Social Science*, University of California Press, 351–64.

——. 1984b. Postmodernism, or the Cultural Logic of Late Capitalism. *New Left Review*. 146, July–August: 52–92. Revised and expanded edition of 1983.

——. 1985. Architecture and the Critique of Ideology. Joan Ockman, ed. *Architecture, Criticism, Ideology*. New York: Princeton Architectural Press, 51–87.

——. 1988. Cognitive Mapping. Nelson and Grossberg, eds. *Marxism and the Interpretation of Culture*. Urbana, IL: University of Illinois.

Jardine, Alice. 1985. *Gynesis: Configurations of Women and Modernity*. Ithaca: Cornell University Press.

Jarzombek, Mark. 1989. Post-Modernist Historicism: The Historian's Dilemma. M. Diani and C. Ingraham, eds. *Restructuring Architectural Theory*, 86–98.

Jay, Paul. 1989. Critical Historicism and the Discipline of Architecture. M. Diani and C. Ingraham, eds. *Restructuring Architectural Theory*, 26–34.

Jencks, Charles. 1973. *Modern Movements in Architecture*. New York: Anchor/Doubleday.

——. 1977. *The Language of Post-Modern Architecture*. New York: Rizzoli. Reprinted 1981, 1984, 1991.

——. 1978. *What is Postmodernism?* New York: St Martin's. Reprinted 1986.

——. 1981. Vers un éclectisme radical. Portoghesi, compiler. *La présence de l'histoire*, 47–55.

——. 1983. Post-Modern Architecture: The True Inheritor of Modernism. *RIBA Transactions*. 2: 26–41.

——. 1985. *Towards a Symbolic Architecture: The Thematic House*. New York: Rizzoli.

——. 1987. *Post-Modernism: The New Classicism in Art and Architecture*. London: Academy Editions.

——. 1988. Postmodernist Classicism versus Narrative and De-construction in Architecture. Debate with James Wines at the New School for Social Research. February 25.

——. 1990. *The New Moderns: From Late- to Neo-Modernism*. New York: Rizzoli.

——. 1991. *Post-Modern Triumphs in London*. London: Academy Editions.

——. 1992. The Post-Modern Agenda (Excerpt of Jencks, 1987). The Post-Avant Garde (Originally published, *Art and Design*, 3, 1987). Jencks, ed. *The Postmodern Reader*, 10–39, 215–24.

——. 1993. *Heteropolis: The Riots and the Strange Beauty of Hetero-Architecture*. London: Academy Editions.

Jencks, Charles. 1995. *The Architecture of the Jumping Universe: A Polemic: How Complexity Science is Changing Architecture and Culture.* London Academy Editions.

Jencks, Charles, ed. 1980. Post-Modern Classicism: The New Synthesis. Introduction to *Architectural Design Profile*, 4–17. NY: St. Martin's.

——. 1982. Free-Style Classicism. *Architectural Design Profile.* NY: St. Martin's.

——. 1992. *The Postmodern Reader.* London: Academy Editions.

Jencks, Charles and George Baird, eds. 1969. *Meaning in Architecture.* London: Barrie & Rockliff, Cresset Press.

Jencks, Charles and Nathan Silver. 1972. *Adhocism.* New York: Doubleday.

Jonas, S. 1979. Du quartier au voisinage. *Architecture d'Aujourd'hui.* 203 (June).

Julienne, Loic and Jean-Marie Mandon. 1985. From Mass Housing to Other Dwellings. *Architecture d'Aujourd'hui.* 239, June. English abstract.

Kagi, Edmond. 1989. Master-planned Community Developments versus Traditional Neighborhood Development. Anne Vernez Moudon, ed. *Master-Planned Communities*, 63–67.

Kahn, Andrea. 1989. Shifting Geographies. *Design Book Review.* 17: 48–49.

Kahn, Terry D. 1990. Architecture vs. Planning: Collision, Collaboration and the Design of American Cities. *Center.* 6: 46–53.

Kaplan, Marshall. 1973. *Urban Planning in the 1960s: A Design for Irrelevancy.* Cambridge, MA: MIT.

Kaplan, Sam Hall. 1989. Is Architecture becoming the Latest Merchandising Fad? *Los Angeles Times.* August 6.

Kasinitz, Philip. 1988. The Gentrification of "Boerum Hill": Neighborhood Change and Conflicts over Definitions. *Qualitative Sociology.* 4 (3): 163–82.

Katz, Peter. 1994. *The New Urbanism.* New York: McGraw-Hill.

Kaufmann Emil. 1929 [1991]. *De Ledoux à Le Corbusier.* Paris: Demi-Cercle.

——. 1966. *Architecture in the Age of Reason.* Hamden, CT: Archon Books.

Kelbaugh, Doug, ed. 1989. Preface. *The Pedestrian Pocket Book: A New Suburban Strategy.* New York: Princeton Architectural Press.

Kennedy, Shawn G. 1988. Architects now Double as Developers. *New York Times.* February 7.

Kidney, Walter C. 1974. *The Architecture of Choice: Eclecticism in America, 1880–1930.* New York: Braziller.

Kimball, Roger. 1988. *The Death and Resurrection of Postmodern Architecture.* New Criterion. June: 21–31.

King, Anthony. 1990. Architecture, Capital and the Globalization of Culture. Mike Featherstone, ed. *Global Culture.* London: Sage, 397–411.

Kingwell, Mark. 1998. Fast Forward: Our High-Speed Chase to Nowhere. *Harper's.* May: 37–48.

Kipnis, Jeffrey. 1993. Towards a New Architecture: Folding. *Architectural Design.* 63 (3–4).

Kirshenblatt-Gimblett, Barbara. 1983. The Future of Folklore Studies in America: The Urban Frontier. *Folklore Forum.* 16(2): 175–234.

Klapp, Orin. 1991. *Inflation of Symbols: Loss of Values in American Culture.* New Jersey: Transaction Press.

Kleinfield, N. R. 1987. Creating Shangri-La on the Hudson. *New York Times.* January 4: F4.

Klotz, Heinrich. 1981. Combats et polémiques. Portoghesi, director. *La présence de l'histoire,* 56–58.

———. 1988 [1984]. *The History of Postmodern Architecture.* Translated by Radka Donnell. Cambridge, MA: MIT. (Excerpted in Jencks, 1992, 234–47.)

Klotz, Heinrich, ed. 1985. *Postmodern Visions: Drawings, Paintings, and Models by Contemporary Architects.* New York: Abbeville. Translation of Revision der Moderne.

Knox, Paul L. 1988. The Design Professions and the Built Environment in a Postmodern Epoch. Paul Knox, ed. *The Design Professions and the Built Environment,* 1–11.

———. 1984. Symbolism, Styles and Settings: The Built Environment and the Imperatives of Urbanized Capitalism. *Architecture et Comportement.* 2: 107–22.

Knox, Paul L., ed. 1988. *The Design Professions and the Built Environment.* New York: Nichols.

———. 1993. *The Restless Urban Landscape.* Englewood Cliffs, NJ: Prentice-Hall.

Koh, Jusuck. 1985. Success Strategies for Architects through Cultural Changes Leading into the Post-Industrial Age: An American Perspective. Stephan Klein, Richard Wener, and Sheila Lehman, eds. *Environmental Change/Social Change.* Proceedings of the 16th Annual Conference of the Environmental Design Research Association, 10–21.

Kolb, David. 1990. *Postmodern Sophistications: Philosophy, Architecture, and Tradition.* University of Chicago.

Koolhaas, Rem. 1978. *Delirious New York: A Retroactive Manifesto for Manhattan.* New York: Oxford University. Reprint, 1994, New York: Monacelli.

———. 1996. *S, M, L, XL.* New York: Monacelli.

Kopp, Anatole. 1982. Contribution to a Never-Ceasing Debate: "Modern Architecture" Progress or Regression. *Carré Bleu,* 3. (Originally presented at the Royal College of Arts, London, February 4, 1982, conference, The Modern Movement: A Death Danse of Principles.)

Kostof, Spiro. 1985. *A History of Architecture.* New York: Oxford University.

———. 1987. *America by Design.* New York: Oxford University.

Kostof, Spiro, ed. 1977. *The Architect.* New York: Oxford University.

Kramer, Jane. 1988. Letter from Europe. *New Yorker.* April 25: 74–82.

Kreditor, Alan. 1990. Urban Design: A Victim of American Academic Tastes. *Center.* 6: 64–71.

Krieger, Alex. 1991. Since (and Before) Seaside. A. Krieger and William Lennertz, eds. *Andres Duany and Elizabeth Plater-Zyberk: Towns and Town-Making Principles.* New York: Rizzoli, 9–16.

Krier, Léon. 1978a. The Consumption of Culture. *Oppositions.* 14 (Fall): 59.

———. 1978b. The Reconstruction of the European City. R. Delevoy, ed. *Rational Architecture,* 38–42.

———. 1980. Manifesto: The Reconstruction of the European City or Anti-Industrial Resistance as a Global Project. Krier and Culot, eds. *Counterprojects.* Brussels: AAM.

———. 1981. Forward Comrades, We Must Go Back. *Oppositions.* 24 (Spring).

———. 1982. The New Traditional Town: Two Plans by Léon Krier for Bremen and Berlin-Tegel. Lotus. 36: 101–07.

———. 1983. *Atlantis.* New York: Princeton Architectural Press.

———. 1984. Critique of the Megastructural City. Critique of Industrialization. Demetri Porphyrios, ed. Léon Krier: Houses, Palaces, Cities. *Architectural Design Profile.* 54 (7/8).

———. 1986. The Completion of Washington DC. *Washington, Paris, Toulouse, Nîmes.* Brussels: Archives de l'Architecture Moderne.

———. 1987. Tradition-Modernity-Modernism: Some Necessary Explanations. *Architectural Design Profile.* 65.

———. 1989. Master Plan for Poundbury Development in Dorchester. Architectural Design Profile. 79: 46–55.

———. 1991. Afterward. Krieger and Lennertz, eds. *Andres Duany and Elizabeth Plater-Zyberk.* New York: Rizzoli, 117–19.

Krier, Léon and Maurice Culot. 1980. Pourrir dans les tranchées? Non merci. *Architecture Mouvement Continuité.* 52–53 (June–September): 22–23.

Krier, Léon and Maurice Culot, eds. 1980. *Counterprojets.* Brussels: AAM.

Krier, Léon and Peter Eisenman. 1989. My Ideology is Better than Yours. *Architectural Design. Reconstruction/Deconstruction,* 6–19.

Krier, Léon and L. O. Larson. 1986. *Albert Speer: Architecture 1932–1942.* Brussels: AAM.

Krier, Rob. 1979. *Urban Space.* Translated by C. Czechowski and G. Black. New York: Rizzoli. Foreword by Colin Rowe. Original edition, *Stadtraum,* 1975.

———. 1986. La reconstruction de la ville et le concept de l'identique. Lecture, Institut Français d'Architecture. March 13.

———. 1989. Elements of Architecture. *Architectural Design Profile.* 49. London: Academy Editions.

Kristeva, Julia. 1969. *Semiotiké.* Paris: Seuil.

Kroll, Lucien. 1977a. Conference, Les nouvelles pratiques des architectes. Pierre Lefevre, organizer. CERA. January 11. *Architecture.* 402, April.

———. 1977b. Cergy-Pontoise: Ilôt des Jouannes. *Techniques et Architecture,* 316.

———. 1979. Réflexion sur concours de Cergy-St Christophe. *Créé,* 169–71.

———. 1980a. Concours de Bernalment, Belgique. Soixante ans d'industrialisation. *Techniques et Architecture.* 327: 134–39, 73–74.

———. 1980b. Architecture and bureaucracy. Byron Mikellides, ed. *Architecture for people.*

Lucien, Kroll. 1980c. Doctrines et incertitudes. Special issue. *Cahiers de la Recherche Architecturale.* 6–7: 68–9.

———. 1981a. Participations. CCI, ed. *Architectures en France, Modernité-Postmodernité.* Paris: CCI, 74–82.

———. 1981d. Our Friends the Rationalists. *Architectural Design.* 51(12): 91.

———. 1982a. Entrer dans la ronde. *Créé,* 184.

———. 1983a. *Composants: Faut-il industrialiser l'architecture?* Brussels: SOCERAMA.

———. 1983b. Pour une démilitarisation de l'acte de bâtir. *Art Press.* Hors série 2, June–August: 18–9.

———. 1984a. UCL Zone Sociales. Richard Hatch, ed. *The Scope of Social Architecture,* 166–81.

———. 1984b. Les Vignes Blanches, Cergy-Pontoise. David Gosling and Barry Maitland, eds. Urbanism. *Architectural Design Profile.* 51: 26–35.

———. 1984c. Comment intervenir sans empêcher l'autre de construire? J.-P. LeDantec, ed. *Enfin, l'architecture?* Paris: Autrement, 132–41.

———. 1985a. Faire ou laisser se faire. Philippe Boudon, Pessac de Le Corbusier. *Pessac II.* Paris: Dunod, 190–91.

———. 1985b. La répétition est un crime. *Architecture d'Aujourd'hui.* 239 (June).

———. 1985c. LaRoche-Clermault. Unpublished manuscript. July, 5 pages.

———. 1986a. Letter to Bernard Kohn. Kohn and Saget, eds. *Experimentations: Réflexion sur une pratique.*

———. 1986b. Interview with author. Brussels.

———. 1987. *An Architecture of Complexity.* Translation of *Composants* by Peter Blumdell Jones. Boston: MIT.

Kruger, Barbara. 1990. What's High, What's Low–and Who Cares? *New York Times.* September 9: H43.

Kuhn, Thomas. 1970 [1962]. *The Structure of Scientific Revolutions.* 2nd edition. University of Chicago.

Kuspit, Donald. 1993. *The Cult of the Avant-Garde Artist.* New York: Cambridge University.

LAING (Los Angeles Independent Newspaper Group). 1994. Study Pinpoints New Trail Opportunities in the L.A. Area. *Los Angeles Independent Newspaper.* November 2: A, B1, B2, C.

Lambert, Nicolas, 1980, La revue nouvelle. Jean Dethier, ed. Special supplement. *h: la revue de l'habitat social.* 50, March: 69–84. Originally published November 1979.

Lampugnani, Vittorio Magnago. 1985. *Architecture and City Planning in the Twentieth Century.* NY: Van Nostrand Reinhold. Translation of *Architektur und Stadtebau des 20.*

———. 1991. The City of Tolerance: Notes on Present Day Urban Design. *The New City: Foundations.* University of Miami School of Architecture. Fall: 107–18.

Langdon, Philip. 1988. A Good Place to Live. *Atlantic Monthly.* March: 39–60.

Lapham, Lewis. 1988. Politics nouveau. *Harper's.* December: 13.

Larson, Magali Sarfatti. 1983. Emblem and Exception: The Historical Definition of the Architect's Professional Role. Blau, La Gory and Pipkin, eds. *Professionals and Urban Form*, 49–86.

———. 1993. *Behind the Postmodern Façade: Architectural Change in Late Twentieth-Century America.* University of California.

Lash, Scott. 1990a. Postmodernism as Humanism: Urban Space and Social Theory. Bryan Turner, ed. *Theories of Modernity and Postmodernity*, 62–74.

———. 1990b. *Sociology of Postmodernism.* New York: Routledge.

Lavedan, Pierre. 1952–1966. *Histoire de l'Urbanisme.* 3 volumes. Paris: H.Laurens.

Lears, Jackson. 1981. *No Place of Grace: Antimodernism and the Transformation of American Culture 1880–1920.* New York: Pantheon.

Le Dantec, J.-P. 1984. *Enfin l'architecture?* Paris: Autrement.

Lee, Douglas. 1973. Requiem for Large-Scale Planning Models. *Journal of the American Institute of Planners.* 39: 117–42.

Lefaivre, Liane. 1989. Dirty Realism in European Architecture Today: Making the Stone Stony. *Design Book Review.* 17, Winter: 17–20.

Lefebvre, Henri. 1947. *Critique de la vie quotidienne, I: Introduction.* Paris: Grasset. Second edition, 1958.

———. 1966. Preface. H. Raymond, N. Haumont, et al, eds. *L'habitat pavillonnaire*, 3–24.

———. 1967. *Le droit à la ville.* Paris: Anthropos.

———. 1968. *La vie quotidienne dans le monde moderne.* Paris: Gallimard.

———. 1970. *La révolution urbaine.* Paris: Gallimard.

———. 1971. *Everyday Life in the Modern World.* Harmondsworth: Penguin. (Translation of 1968 edition by Sacha Rabinovitch.)

———. 1972. *La pensée marxiste et la ville.* Paris/Tournai: Casterman.

———. 1974. *La production de l'espace.* Paris: Anthropos.

———. 1981. *Critique of Everyday Life.* Translation by John Moore of 1947 edition. London: Verso.

———. 1991. *The Production of Space.* Translation by Donald Nicholson-Smith of 1974 edition. Oxford: Blackwell.

Lefevre, Gabrielle. 1980. La cité. Jean Dethier, ed. Special supplement. *h: la revue de l'habitat social.* 50 (March): 69–84. Originally published October 22, 1979.

Lefevre, Pierre. 1979. L'architecture et l'architecte. P. Bonnin, ed. *Habitats Autogérés: MHGA.* Paris: Editions Alternatives, 121–32.

———. 1984. *Associer l'usager dès la conception de son logement.* Paris: Crédit Foncier.

———. 1985, 1986. Interview with author. Jouy-le-Moutier.

Lefevre, Pierre and Pierre Clément, eds. 1967. *Regards sur l'architecture et l'urbanisme.* Paris.

Leinberger, Christopher B. and Charles Lockwood.1986. How Business is Reshaping America. *Atlantic Monthly.* October: 43–52.

Lennertz, W. 1991. Town-Making Fundamentals. A. Krieger and W. Lennertz, eds. *Andres Duany and Elizabeth Plater-Zyberk*. New York: Rizzoli, 21–24.

Lesnikowski, Wojciech G. 1982. *Rationalism and Romanticism in Architecture*. New York: McGraw-Hill.

———. 1988. Letter from France. *Inland Architect*. September–October: 73–77.

———. 1990. *The New French Architecture*. New York: Rizzoli.

Lewis, Oscar. 1951. *Life in a Mexican Village*. Urbana, IL: University of Illinois.

Ley, David. 1980. Liberal Ideology and the Postindustrial City. *Annals of the Association of American Geographers*. 70(2), June: 238–58.

———. 1987. Styles of the Times: Liberal and Neo-conservative Landscapes in Inner Vancouver, 1968–86. *Journal of Historical Geography*. 13(1): 40–56.

Ley, David and Caroline Mills. 1993. Can There Be a Postmodernism of Resistance in the Urban Landscape? Paul L. Knox, ed. *The Restless Urban Landscape*. New York: Prentice-Hall, 255–78.

Lofland, Lyn. 1980. The "Thereness" of Women: A Selective Review of Urban Sociology. Marci Millman and R. M. Kanter, eds. *Another Voice: Feminist Perspectives on Social Life and Social Science*. New York: Anchor.

Logan, John R. and Todd Swanstrom, eds. 1990. *Beyond the City Limits: Urban Policy and Economic Restructuring in Comparative Perspective*. Philadelphia: Temple University.

Lowe, Donald. 1982. *History of Bourgeois Perception*. University of Chicago.

Lowenthal, David. 1986. *The Past is a Foreign Country*. New York: Cambridge University

Lucan, Jacques. 1978a. To Build Nevertheless. *Architectural Design Profiles*. 15.

———. 1978b. La forme et la répétition. *Architecture Mouvement Continuité*. 47: 49–52.

———. 1980a. Propriété privée - Défense d'entrer. *Architecture Mouvement Continuité*. 51, March.

———. 1980b. Inquiétudes [on 1980 Venice Biennale]. *Architecture Mouvement Continuité*. 52–53 (June–September).

———. 1985. Logement social: 1950–1980. Supplement. *Bulletin d'Informations Architecturales*. Institut Français de l'Architecture. 95 (May). With Odile Seyler and Marie-Hélène Contal.

———. 1986. 1950–1980: 30 ans d'architecture française. Special issue. *Architecture Mouvement Continuité*. 11, April.

———. 1989. *France Architecture 1965–1988*. Paris: Electa Moniteur.

Lucan, Jacques, ed. 1991. *Rem Koolhaas-OMA*. (Translated from original 1991 French edition. New York: Princeton Architectural Press.

Lukacs, John. 1992. *The End of the Twentieth Century and the End of the Modern Age*. New York: Ticknor & Fields.

Lynch, Kevin. 1960. *Image of the City*. Cambridge, MA: MIT.

———. 1962. *Site Planning*. Cambridge, MA: MIT.

———. 1972. *What Time is This Place?* Cambridge, MA: MIT.

———. 1976. *Managing the Sense of a Region.* Cambridge, MA: MIT.

———. 1981. *A Theory of Good City Form.* Cambridge, MA: MIT. Revised edition, 1984, Good City Form.

Lynn, Greg. 1993. Architectural Curvilineariy: The Folded, the Pliant and the Supple. *Folding in Architecture, Architectural Design.* 63 (3–4).

Lyotard, Jean-François. 1985. *The Postmodern Condition: A Report on Knowledge.* University of Minneapolis.

Maitino, Hilda and Arnaud Sompairac. 1986. Formes urbaines et habitat social. *120 réalisations expérimentales du Plan Construction et Habitat (1978–1984).* Paris: Plan Construction.

Maitland, Barry. 1984. The Uses of History. *Architectural Design.* 54 (January–February): 4–7.

Mangin, David. 1985. L'architecture urbaine dans l'impasse. *Architecture d'Aujourd'hui.* 240 (September).

Mann, Dennis Alan. 1985. Between Traditionalism and Modernism: Approaches to a Vernacular Architecture. *Journal of Architectural Education.* 39 (2): 10–16.

Mann, Thomas. 1948. *Doctor Faustus.* Translated by H. T. Lowe-Porter. New York: Knopf.

March, Lionel. 1967. Homes Beyond the Fringe. *RIBA Journal.* August.

Marcus, Clare Cooper. 1986. *Housing as if People Mattered.* Berkeley: University of California. With Wendy Sarkissian and Sheena Wilson.

Marcus, George E. 1986. Contemporary Problems of Ethnography in the Modern World System. J. Clifford and G. E. Marcus, eds. *Writing Culture,* 165–94.

Marcus, George E. and Michael M. J. Fischer. 1986. *Anthropology as Cultural Critique: An Experimental Moment in the Human Sciences.* University of Chicago.

Marcuse, Herbert. 1964. *One-Dimensional Man.* New York: Beacon.

Marcuse, Peter. 1995. Not Chaos, but Walls: Postmodernism and the Partitioned City. Watson and Gison, eds. *Postmodern Cities and Spaces.* London: Blackwell, 243–53.

Marx, Karl. 1973 [1858]. *Grundrisse: Foundations of the Critique of Political Economy.* New York: Vintage.

———. 1987 [1852]. *The Eighteenth Brumaire of Louis Bonaparte.* New York: International Publishers. Excerpted in *Basic Writings on Politics and Philosophy: Marx and Engels,* 1959, 318–49.

Maxwell, Robert. 1977. Architecture, Language, and Process. Tafuri, Culot, and Krier. *Architectural Design Profile.* 3 (March).

Mayo, James M. 1994. Book Review of *Critical Theory, Public Policy, and Planning Practice:* Toward a Critical Pragmatism by John Forester. *Journal of Planning Education and Research.* 13(3): 229–30.

Mazumdar, Sanjoy. 1991. Design in Multicultural Societies: Programming for Culture, Life and Diversity. *American Collegiate Schools of Architecture Proceedings.* 122–5.

McCamant, Kathryn and Charles Durrett. 1988. *Cohousing: A Contemporary Approach to Housing Ourselves.* Ten Speed Press.

Mazziotti, Donald F. 1971. *Advocacy Planning: Toward the Development of Theory and Strategy*. Monticello, IL: Council of Planning Librarians.

McCarthy, Thomas. 1985. Reflections on Rationalization in the Theory of Communicative Action. Richard Bernstein, ed. *Habermas and Modernity*. Cambridge, MA: MIT, 176–91.

McConnell, Frank D. 1992. Will Deconstruction be the Death of Literature? *The Best of the Wilson Quarterly*, 52–61.

McDermott, John. 1976. Deprivation and Celebration. *The Culture of Experience*, 83–98.

McHarg, Ian. 1966. The Ecology of the City: A Plea for Environmental Consciousness of the City's Physiological and Psychological Impacts. *The Architect and the City*, 53–66.

———. 1969. *Design with Nature*. Natural History Press.

McLeod, Mary. 1983. Meaning in Architecture Reconsidered. Conference proceedings. Reprinted in *Reader for Contemporary Architecture Theory and Criticism*. New York. Columbia University, 187–200.

———. 1984. Review of Aldo Rossi's *Architecture of the City*. Design Book Review. 3 (Winter): 49–55.

———. 1985. Introduction. J. Ockman, ed. *Architecture, Criticism, Ideology*, 7–11.

———. 1986. Paper presented at Reid Hall, Paris.

McLuhan, Marshall. 1967. *The Media is the Massage*. London: Bantam Books.

McMillan, Penelope. 1992. Keepers of the Gates. *Los Angeles Times*. February 2.

———. 1993. Judge Disallows Gates Blocking Public Streets. *Los Angeles Times*. January 23.

Melonio, François. 1981. *Les dents creusés*. Paris: *Créé*, 184.

Mestrovic, Stjepan Gabriel. 1991. *The Coming Fin de Siècle: An Application of Durkheim's Sociology to Modernity and Postmodernity*. New York: Routledge.

Meyrowitz, Joshua. 1985. *No Sense of Place*. New York: Oxford University.

Miller, Donald, ed. 1986. *The Lewis Mumford Reader*. New York: Pantheon.

Miller, Wallis. 1993. IBA's "Models for a City": Housing and the Image of Cold-War Berlin. *Journal of Architectural Education*. 46 (4).

Mills, C. Wright. 1958. The Man in the Middle: The Designer. *Industrial Design*. November. Reprinted in *Power, Politics and People: The Collected Essays of C. Wright Mills*, New York: Ballantine, 374–86.

———. 1963. *Culture and Politics. Power, Politics and People: The Collected Essays of C. Wright Mills*. New York: Ballantine, 236–59. (Published in *The Listener*, 1959.)

Mills, Caroline. 1986. Landscape and Lifestyle: The Production and Consumption of Images in the Revitalized Inner City. Unpublished manuscript.

Minar, David W. and Scott Greer, eds. 1969. *The Concept of Community*. New York: Aldine.

Mitchell, Gordon. 1963. *Sick Cities*. New York: Macmillan.

Mitchell, John L. 1992. Not Defensive about Look of his Malls. *Los Angeles Times*. June 18.

Mitgang, Lee and Ernest L. Boyer. 1996. *Building Community: A New Future for Architecture Education and Practice.*

Mohney, David. 1991. Interview with Andres Duany. D. Mohney and K. Easterling, eds. *Seaside*, 62–73.

Mohney, David and Keller Easterling, eds. 1991. *Seaside: Making a Town in America.* New York: Princeton Architectural Press.

Moholy-Nagy, Sibyl. 1968. *Matrix of Man: An Illustrated History of Urban Environment.* NY: Praeger.

Moley, C. 1979. *L'innovation architecturale dans la production du logement social.* Paris: Plan Construction.

Moneo, Rafael. 1976. Aldo Rossi: The Idea of Architecture and the Modena Cemetery. *Oppositions.* 5: 1–21.

———. 1978. On Typology. *Oppositions.* 13: 36–45.

Montes, Fernando. 1978. Le Corbusier and the École des Beaux-Arts. *Architectural Design Profile.* 48 (8–9).

Montgomery, Roger. 1966. Comment on Fear and House-as-Haven in the Lower Class [by Lee Rainwater]. *Journal of the American Institute of Planners.* 31: 31–37.

Moravia, Alberto. 1987. The Terrorist Aesthetic. *Harper's.* June: 37–44.

Moudon, Anne Vernez, ed. 1989. Master-Planned Communities: Shaping Exurbs in the 1990s. Proceedings of conference. University of Washington. October 20–21.

Moulin, Raymonde. 1969. L'architecte, l'urbanisme et la société: Avons-nous encore besoin d'architectes? Special issue. *Esprit.* 10 (October).

Moulin, Raymonde, Françoise Dubost, Alain Gras, Jacques Lautman, Jean-Pierre Martinon, Dominique Schnapper. 1973. *Les architectes: Métamorphose d'une profession libérale.* Paris: Calman-Levy.

Mumford, Lewis. 1924. *Sticks and Stones: A Study of American Architecture and Civilization.* New York: Norton.

———. 1926. *The Golden Day: A Study of American Experience and Culture.* New York: Boni & Liverlight.

———. 1945. Introduction. Ebenezer Howard. *Garden Cities of Tomorrow.* Cambridge, MA: MIT, 29–40.

———. 1952. The Ideal Form of the Modern City. Talbot Hamlin, ed. *Form and Functions of Twentieth Century Architecture.*

———. 1961. *The City in History.* New York: Harcourt Brace Jovanovich.

———. 1962. The Case against "Modern Architecture." The Future of the City, Parts I and II. *Architectural Record.* 131 and 132.

———. 1968. *The Urban Prospect.* New York: Harcourt Brace Jovanovich.

———. 1970. *The Pentagon of Power.* New York: Harcourt Brace Jovanovich.

Muratori, S. 1959. *Studi per una operante storia urbana di Venezia.* Rome: Istituto Poligrafico dello Stato.

Murphy, Brian. 1988. Quoted. *New York Times.* December 15.

Murphy, Cullen. 1992. The Way the World Ends. *The Best of the Wilson Quarterly,* 78–82.

Muschamp, Herbert. 1991. Creativity in Design as an Urban Survival Skill. *New York Times.* December 15: H36.

——. 1993a. Thinking about Tomorrow and How to Build It. *New York Times.* January 10: Section 2, 1, 32.

——. 1993b. Fear, Hope and the Changing of the Guard. *New York Times.* November 14: H37.

——. 1994a. Two for the Roads: A Vision of Urban Design. *New York Times.* February 13: H1, H33.

——. 1994b. Architecture as Social Action, and Vice Versa. *New York Times.* February 27: H40.

——. 1994c. Queens West: Why Not Something Great? *New York Times.* May 22: H36.

Myerhoff, Barbara. 1979. *Number our Days.* New York: Simon & Schuster.

Naizot, Guy. 1985. Banlieue et monumentalité. Round table discussion. *Esprit.*

Nalbantoglu, Gulsum Baydar and Wong chong Thai, eds. 1997. *Postcolonial Space(s).* New York: Princeton Architectural Press.

Nesbitt, Kate, ed. 1996. *Theorizing a New Agenda for Architecture. An Anthology of Architectural Theory 1965–95.* New York: Princeton Architectural Press.

Nesbit, Lois. 1990. Arquitectonica: Flamboyant Modernism. *Newsline.* Columbia University. April: 3.

Newman, Oscar. 1961. *New Frontiers in Architecture: CIAM '59 in Otterlo.* New York: Universe Books.

——. 1972. *Defensible Space: People and Design in the Violent City.* New York: Macmillan.

——. 1982. *Community of Interest.* New York: Doubleday.

Newton, Esther. 1993. My Best Informant's Dress: The Erotic Equation in Fieldwork. *Cultural Anthropology.* 8 (1): 3–23.

Nilsen, Richard. 1998. Sincerity Defeating Irony. *Arizona Republic.* March 8: H1, H3.

Nisbet, Robert A. 1953. *The Quest for Community.* New York: Oxford University. Reprinted in 1962, Community and Power.

Noble, David N. 1985. *The End of American History.* University of Minnesota.

Norberg-Schulz, Christian. 1964. *Intentions in Architecture.* Oslo: Universitetsforlaget.

——. 1969. Meaning in Architecture. Jencks and Baird, eds. *Meaning in Architecture,* 215–29.

——. 1971. *Existence, Space and Architecture.* London: Studio Vista.

——. 1984 [1979]. *Genius Loci: Towards a Phenomenology of Architecture.* New York: Rizzoli.

——. 1981. Vers une architecture authentique. Portoghesi, director. *La présence de l'histoire,* 36–46.

Nouvel, Jean, compiler. 1980a. *Biennale de Paris.* Paris: Academy Editions.

Nouvel, Jean. 1980b. 1980: L'avenir de l'architecture n'est plus architecturale. *Les Cahiers de la Recherche Architecturale*. 6–7, October.

——, compiler. La modernité: critères et repères. *1982: La modernité ou l'esprit du temps*. Paris: L'Equerre, 20.

Noviant, Patrice. 1978. Projets de formes urbaines. *Architecture Mouvement Continuité*. 47: 3–25.

——. 1980. French Tendances. *Architecture Mouvement Continuité*. 52–53 (June–September).

Ockman, Joan. 1988. Resurrecting the Avant-Garde: The History and Program of Oppositions. *Revisions: Papers on Architectural Theory and Criticism*. 11. New York: Princeton Architectural Press, 181–99.

Ockman, Joan with Edward Eigen, ed. 1993. *Architecture Culture 1943–1968*. New York: Rizzoli.

Olsen, Donald J. 1983. The City as a Work of Art. Fraser and Sutcliffe, eds. *The Pursuit of Urban History*.

——. 1986. *The City as a Work of Art: London, Paris, Vienna*. New Haven: Yale University.

Orr, David W. 1992. The Problem of Sustainability. *Ecological Literacy: Education and the Transition to a Postmodern World*. Albany: State University of New York.

Oser, Alan S. 1986. Creating an Urban Neighborhood. *New York Times*. November 16: R6, 20.

——. 1988a. Bronx to get a Big Town-House Complex. *New York Times*. June 12, Section 10: 1, 20.

——. 1988b. Oceanfront Site Terms Challenge Builders. *New York Times*. November 20.

——. 1990. Introducing a New Style in Tract Housing. *New York Times*. April 29.

Overbye, Dennis. 1997. The Cosmos According to Darwin. *New York Times Magazine*. July 17: 24–7.

Owens, Mitchell. 1994. Saving Neighborhoods One Gate at a Time. *New York Times*. August 25.

Packard, Vance. 1972. *A Nation of Strangers*. New York: Pocket Books.

Papadakis, Andreas, ed. 1990. Postmodernism on Trial. *Architectural Design Profile*. 88.

Papadakis, Andreas and Harriet Watson, eds. 1990. *New Classicism: Omnibus Volume*. Foreword by Leon Krier. NY: Rizzoli.

Pareles, Jon. 1989. Whose Song is it Anyway? New York Times. August 27.

——. 1991. When Country Music Moves to the Suburbs. *New York Times*.

Partridge, Ernest. 1985. Are We Ready for an Ecological Morality? Martin Wachs, ed. *Ethics in Planning*. New Brunswick, NJ: Rutgers University Press, 318–34.

Pawley, Martin. 1973. *The Private Future*. London: Pan Books.

——. 1990. *Theory and Design in the Second Machine Age*. Oxford: Blackwell.

Peattie, Lisa R. 1978. Politics, Planning, and Categories Bridging the Gap. Robert W. Burchell and George Sternlieb, eds. *Planning Theory in the 1980s*. New Brunswick: Rutgers University Press, 83–94.

Pecora, Vincent. 1991. Towers of Babel. Diane Ghirardo, ed. *Out of Site*, 46–76.

Pérez-Gómez, Alberto. 1983. *Architecture and the Crisis of Modern Science*. Cambridge, MA: MIT.

Peterson, Iver. 1991. Planned Communities are Multiplying. *New York Times*. April 21: Section 10, 1, 11.

Pevsner, Nicolas. 1961. *The Return of Historicism*. London: Royal Institute of British Architects.

Pietila, Antero. 1994. Street Barriers that Work-in Carefully Defined Circumstances. *Baltimore Sun*.

Plattus, Alan. 1989. Review of The History of Postmodern Architecture by H. Klotz. *Design Book Review*. 17, Winter: 68–70.

Poëte, Marcel. 1967. *Introduction à l'urbanisme*. Paris: Anthropos.

Pool, Robert. 1991. Postmodern Ethnography? *Critique of Anthropology*. 11 (4): 309–32.

Pope, Albert. 1989. The Profession, the Academy, and the Social Contract. *Design Book Review*. 17: 83–84.

Popenoe, David. 1984. *Public Pleasure, Private Plight*. New Jersey: Transaction.

Port Cergy. 1988. Advertisement.

Port Liberté Partners. 1986. Advertisement. *New York Times*. September 28: R13.

Portoghesi, Paolo. 1981 [1980]. La fin des "interdits." La présence de l'histoire: L'après modernisme. *Festival d'automne*. Paris, 23–8.

———. 1982. *After Modern Architecture*. Translated by Meg Shore. New York: Rizzoli.

———. 1983. *Postmodern: The Architecture of Postindustrial Society*. New York: Rizzoli. Revised and updated from original 1982 edition.

Portzamparc, Christian de. 1985. Interviewed by Jean-Claude Eslin and D. Langlart. *Esprit*. December.

Poyner, B. 1983. *Design Against Crime: Beyond Defensible Space*. London: Butterworth-Heinemann.

Pratt Institute School of Architecture. 1988. Catalogue for the Graduate Program. New York.

Proshansky, Harold. 1990. The Pursuit of Understanding: An Intellectual History. Irwin Altman and Kathleen Christensen, eds. *Environment and Behavior Studies*. New York: Plenum.

Querrien, Gwendael. 1985. Logement social 1950–1980. *Bulletin d'Informations Architecturales*. Supplement. 95 (May).

Queysanne, Bruno. 1988. Die Macht der Traume-Mai 1968–Mai 1988. *Archithese*, 4.

Rabinow, Paul. 1982a. Ordonnance, Discipline, Regulation: Some Reflections on Urbanism. *Humanities in Society*. 5 (3–4): 267–78.

———. 1982b. Interview with Michel Foucault. Skyline. March: 18–20.

———. 1989. *French Modern*. University of Chicago.

Radin, Max. 1934. Tradition. Encyclopedia of the Social Sciences.

Rapoport, Amos. 1969. *House Form and Culture.* Englewood Cliffs, NJ: Prentice-Hall.

———. 1981. Vernacular Design and the Cultural Determinants of Form. Anthony D. King, ed. *Buildings and Society.* London: Routledge and Kegan Paul.

———. 1982. *The Meaning of the Built Environment.* Beverly Hills: Sage.

Rasmussen, Steen Eiler. 1951. *Towns and Buildings Described in Drawings and Words.* Cambridge, MA: MIT. Original Danish edition, 1949.

———. 1959. *Experiencing Architecture.* Translated from Danish by Eve Wendt. Cambridge, MA: MIT.

Raymond, Henri. 1980. Architectes et pavillons. *Architecture Mouvement Continuité.* 51 (March): 70–72.

———. 1984. *L'architecture, les aventures spatiales de la raison.* Paris: CCI.

Raymond, Henri, Nicole Haumont, M. G. Raymond, and A. Haumont. 1966. *L'habitat pavillonnaire.* 3rd edition. Paris: Centre de Recherche d'Urbanisme.

Redfield, Robert. 1947. The Folk Society. *American Journal of Sociology.* 41: 293–308.

Relph, Edward. 1976. *Place and Placelessness.* London: Pion.

———. 1987. *The Modern Urban Landscape.* Baltimore: Johns Hopkins University.

Rensbarger, Fran. 1990. An "Old" Downtown Now Taking Shape. *New York Times.* November 11.

Riboud, Jacques. 1968. Un mode d'urbanisme nouveau. *Urbanisme.* 106: 35–42.

———. 1981. *La ville heureuse: Doctrine et expériments de création urbaine.* Paris: Moniteur.

Richards, Jonathan. 1994. *Façadism.* London: Routledge.

Riesman, David, Nathan Glazer, and Reuel Denney. 1950. *The Lonely Crowd.* New Haven: Yale University.

Rifkin, Jeremy. 1995. *The End of Work: The Decline of the Global Work Force and the Dawn of the Post-Market Era.* New York: G.P. Putnam's Sons.

Riley, Robert B. 1992. Review of Out of Place by Michael Hough. *Design Book Review.* 24: 55–57.

Roach, Catherine. 1996. Loving Your Mother: On the Woman-Nature Relation. Karen J. Warren, ed. *Ecological Feminist Philosophies.* Bloomington: Indiana University, 52–65.

Robbins, David, ed. 1990. *The Independent Group: Postwar Britain and the Aesthetics of Plenty.* Cambridge, MA: MIT.

Roberts, Marion. 1991. *Living in a Man-Made World: Gender Assumptions in Modern Housing Design.* London: Routledge.

Robertson, Roland. 1990. After Nostalgia? Wilful Nostalgia and the Phases of Globalization. Bryan Turner, ed. *Theories of Modernity and Postmodernity,* 45–61.

Robinson, Sidney K. 1989. The Picturesque: Sinister Dishevelment. M. Diani and C. Ingraham, eds. *Restructuring Architectural Theory,* 74–79.

Rodier, François. 1981. Le type plutôt que le modèle. *Créé,* 184.

Rollwagen, Jack. 1980. New Directions in Urban Anthropology: Building an Ethnography and an Ethnology of the World System. Gmelch and Zenner, eds. *Urban Life*. New York: St Martin's, 370–82.

Rosaldo, Michelle. 1973. I Have Nothing to Hide: The Language of Ilongot Oratory. *Language in Society*. 2: 193–223.

Rosaldo, Renato. 1989. *Culture and Truth: The Remaking of Social Analysis*. Boston: Beacon.

Rose, Margaret. 1992. Defining the Postmodern. C. Jencks, ed. The Postmodern Reader, 119–36. Excerpted from Rose, *The Postmodern and the Post-industrial: A Critical Analysis*. New York: Cambridge University, 1991.

Rosenau, Pauline Marie. 1992. *Post-Modernism and the Social Sciences: Insights, Inroads, and Intrusions*. Princeton University Press.

Rosenberg, Harold. 1959. *The Tradition of the New*. New York: Horizon.

Rossi, Aldo. 1973. Rational Architecture. Catalogue for the Triennale of Architecture in Venice. Reprinted in *Oppositions*, 1975.

———. 1982 [1966]. *Architecture of the City*. Translated by Diane Ghirardo and Joan Ockman. Cambridge, MA: MIT. Introduction by Peter Eisenman.

———. 1982 [1968]. *A Scientific Autobiography*. Translated by Lawrence Venuti. Cambridge, MA: MIT. Postscript by Vincent Scully.

Rossi, Aldo, Josef Paul Kleihues, and Giorgio Grassi. 1991. Berlin Tomorrow: Potsdamer and Leipziker Platz. *The New City. Foundations*. Fall: 1, 124–31.

Roszak, Theodore. 1972. *Where the Wasteland Ends: Politics and Transcendence in Postindustrial Society*. New York: Doubleday.

Rowe, Colin. 1972. Introduction. Museum of Modern Art, ed. *Five Architects*. New York: Oxford University.

———. 1975. Collage City. *Architectural Review*. August: 65–91.

———. 1985. Address to the 1985 American Collegiate Schools of Architecture Annual Meeting in Vancouver. *Journal of Architectural Education*. Fall.

———. 1989. Interview with Colin Rowe. *Design Book Review*. 17 (Winter): 11–14.

Rowe, Colin and Fred Koetter. 1978. *Collage City*. Cambridge, MA: MIT.

Rubenstein, James. 1978. *The French New Towns*. Baltimore: Johns Hopkins University.

Rudofsky, Bernard. 1964. *Architecture without Architects: An Introduction to Non-Pedigreed Architecture*. New York: MoMA.

———. 1969. *Streets for People: A Primer for Americans*. Garden City, NY: Doubleday.

———. 1977. *The Prodigious Builders*. London: Secker & Warburg.

Russell, Beverly. 1989. *Architecture and Design 1970–1990: New Ideas in America*. New York: Harry N. Abrams.

Ryan, Karen-Lee, ed. 1993. *Trails for the Twenty-First Century*. Washington, DC: Island Press.

Ryan, Karen-Lee and Julie A. Winterich, eds. 1993. *Secrets of Successful Rail Trails*. Washington DC: Rails-to-Trails Conservancy.

Rybczynski, Witold. 1989. Architects Must Listen to the Melody. *New York Times.* September 24.

——. 1992. The Art of Building, or the Building of Art? *Wilson Quarterly.* Autumn: 46–57.

Rykwert, Joseph. 1988 [1950]. *The Idea of a Town.* Cambridge, MA: MIT.

Saarinen, Eliel. 1943. *The City: Its Growth, Its Decay, Its Future.* New York: Reinhold Publishing Company.

Saarinen, Esa. 1993. Not the Last Word. *ANY (Architecture New York).* 3 (Nov/Dec): 70.

Saegart, Susan. 1982. Toward the Androgynous City. Gary Gappert and Richard Knight, eds. *Cities in the 21st Century. Urban Affairs Annual Review.* 23: chapter 11.

Safdie, Moshe. 1970. *Beyond Habitat.* Cambridge, MA: MIT.

——. 1981. Private Jokes in Public Places. *Atlantic Monthly.* Reprinted in *Inland Architect.* 25 (9): 20–27.

——. 1988. Skyscrapers Shouldn't Look Down on Humanity. *New York Times Magazine.* May 29.

Said, Edward. 1978. *Orientalism.* New York: Pantheon.

Sammarcelli, Françoise. 1983. L'intertextualité chez John Barth. *Théorie, Littérature, Enseignement.* 3, December: 58–80.

Sandercock, Leonie and Ann Forsyth. 1992. A Gender Agenda: New Directions for Planning Theory. *Journal of the American Planning Association.* 58 (1): 49–59.

Sarfati, Alain. 1979. Entretien: L'architecture comme oeuvre ouverte. *Urbi.* 1, September: cxxxi–cxli.

Schlesinger, Arthur. 1970 [1940]. A Panoramic View: The City in American History. Paul Kramer and Frederick L. Holborn, eds. *The City in American Life,* 13–36.

Schumacher, E. F. 1973. *Small is Beautiful.* New York: Harper & Row.

Schumacher, Tom. 1971. *Contextualism.* Casabella, 359–60, 78–86.

Schuman, Tony. 1988. Professionalization and the Social Goals of Architects: A History of the Federation of Architects, Engineers, Chemists and Technicians. Paul Knox, ed. *The Design Professions and the Built Environment,* 12–41.

——. 1987. Participation, Empowerment, and Urbanism: Design and Politics in the Revitalization of French Social Housing. *Journal of Architectural and Planning Research.* 4 (4): 349–59.

Schwarting, Jon Michael. 1985. In Reference to Habermas. J. Ockman, ed. *Architecture Criticism Ideology,* 94–100.

Schwartz, Barry. 1980. The Suburban Landscape: New Variations on an Old Theme. *Contemporary Sociology.* 9 (5): 640–50.

Schwarzer, Mitchell. 1998. Ghostwards: The Flight of Capital from History. *Thresholds.* 16 (Spring): 10–19.

Scientific American Editors. 1965. *Cities.* New York: Knopf.

Scott, Bonnie Kime, ed. 1990. *The Gender of Modernism: A Critical Anthology.* Indiana University Press.

Scott, Geoffrey. 1974 [1914]. *The Architecture of Humanism.* New York: W.W.Norton.

Scott, Mel. 1969. *American City Planning since 1890.* University of California.

Scott Brown, Denise. 1976. *Signs of Life: Symbols in the American City.* New York: Aperture. With Steven Izenour.

———. 1990a. *Urban Concepts: Rise and Fall of Community Architecture.* New York: St Martin's.

———. 1990b. Participant in "Discussion. K. Michael Hays and Carol Burns, eds. *Thinking the Present,* 123–34.

———. 1991. The Public Realm. Lecture. The Urban Center, New York City. February 21.

Scully, Vincent. 1961. *Modern Architecture.* New York: George Braziller.

———. 1966. Preface. *Complexity and Contradiction in Architecture.* Robert Venturi. New York: Museum of Modern Art.

———. 1974. *The Shingle Style Today or The Historian's Revenge.* New York: George Braziller.

———. 1981. L'architecture en mutation: pourquoi? Portoghesi, compiler. *La présence de l'histoire,* 29–35.

———. 1988 [1969]. *American Architecture and Urbanism.* New York: Henry Holt.

Seager, Joni. 1993. *Earth Follies: Coming to Feminist Terms with the Global Environmental Crisis.* New York: Routledge.

Seligman, Adam B. 1990. Towards a Reinterpretation of Modernity in an Age of Postmodernity. Bryan Turner, ed. *Theories of Modernity and Postmodernity,* 117–35.

Sennett, Richard. 1970. *The Uses of Disorder: Personal Identity and City Life.* New York: Random House.

———. 1974. *The Fall of Public Man. On the Social Psychology of Capitalism.* New York: Random House.

———. 1990. *The Conscience of the Eye: The Design and Social Life of Cities.* New York: Knopf.

———. 1994a. The Powers of the Eye. *Urban Revisions: Current Projects for the Public.*

———. 1994b. *Flesh and Stone: The Body and the City in Western Civilization.* New York: W.W. Norton.

Service, Alastair, ed. 1975. *Edwardian Architecture and Its Origins.* London: Architectural Press.

Shane, Graham. 1976. Contextualism. *Architectural Design.* November: 46.

Sharpe, William and Leonard Wallock. 1987. From "Great Town" to "Nonplace Urban Realm": Reading the Modern City. Sharpe and Wallock, eds. *Visions of the Modern City.* Baltimore: Johns Hopkins University, 1–39.

———. 1992. The Edge of a New Frontier? *Journal of the American Planning Association.* Summer: 393–95.

———. 1994. Bold New City or Built-Up Burb: Redefining Contemporary Suburbia. *American Quarterly.* March: 46.

Shweder, Richard A. 1984. Anthropology's Romantic Rebellion against the Enlightenment, or There's More to Thinking than Reason and Evidence. R. Shweder and Robert Levine, eds. *Culture Theory.* New York: Cambridge University, 27–66.

Silvetti, Jorge. 1990. Discussion. K. Michael Hays and Carol Burns, eds. *Thinking the Present,* 123–34.

Simmel, Georg. 1969 [1902–03]. The Metropolis and Mental Life. Richard Sennett, ed. *Classic Essays on the Culture of Cities,* 19–30

Simmons, Melody. 1992. Turnstiles will Curb Visitors to High-Rises. *Baltimore Sun.* October 23.

Sitte, Camillo. 1889. *Der Städtebau.* Translated, 1945. *The Art of Building Cities.* New York: Reinhold.

Sjoberg, Gideon. 1960. *The Preindustrial City: Past and Present.* New York: Free Press.

Slater, Philip E. 1970. *The Pursuit of Loneliness: American Culture at the Breaking Point.* Boston: Beacon.

Slesin, Suzanne. 1993. Character Counts. *New York Times Magazine.* April 4.

Smith, C. Ray. 1977. *Supermannerism: New Attitudes in Post-Modern Architecture.* New York: E. P. Dutton.

Smith, Elizabeth A. T., compiler. 1994. *Urban Revisions. Urban Revisions: Current Projects for the Public Realm.* Cambridge, MA: MIT, 3–15.

Smith, Sam. 1992. Communal Living, 90s Style. *Utne Reader.* May/June: 96 Excerpted from *Progressive Review,* November 1990.

Smithson, Alison, ed. 1968. *Team 10 Primer.* Cambridge, MA: MIT. Originally published in *Architectural Design,* December 1962.

Soja, Edward. 1989. *Postmodern Geographies: The Reassertion of Space in Critical Social Theory.* New York: Verso.

Solomon, Daniel. 1989. Fixing Suburbia. Doug Kelbaugh, ed. *The Pedestrian Pocket Book.* New York: Princeton Architectural Press, 21–33.

Sommer, Robert. 1969. *Personal Space: The Behavioral Basis of Design.* Englewood Cliffs, NJ: Prentice-Hall.

———. 1974. *Tight Spaces: Hard Architecture and How to Humanize It.* Englewood Cliffs, NJ: Prentice-Hall.

Sorkin, Michael, ed. 1992. *Variations on a Theme Park: The New American City and the End of Public Space.* New York: Hill and Wang.

Spain, Daphne. 1992. *Gendered Spaces.* University of North Carolina.

Speer, Albert. 1970. *Architectural Megalomania. Inside the Third Reich.* Translated by Richard and Clara Winston. New York: Macmillan.

Spens, Mi chael, ed. 1996. *The Recovery of the Modern: Architectural Review 1980–1995.* Boston: Butterworth Architecture.

Spirn, Anne. 1984. *Granite Garden: Urban Nature and Human Design.* New York: Basic Books.

Spreiregen, Paul D. 1965. *Urban Design: The Architecture of Towns and Cities.* New York: McGraw-Hill.

Spretnak, Charlene. 1991. *States of Grace: The Recovery of Meaning in the Postmodern Age*. New York: HarperCollins.

Stein, Clarence. 1951. *New Towns for America*. Liverpool: Liverpool Press.

Stein, Maurice. 1960. *The Eclipse of Community: An Interpretation of American Studies*. New York: Harper.

Steiner, Wendy. 1991. Calling for a Return to Sanity in Architecture. *New York Times*. May 19.

Stephens, Mitchell. 1994. The Theologian of Talk. *Los Angeles Times Magazine*. October 23: 26–44.

Stern, Robert A. M. 1977 [1969]. *New Directions in American Architecture*. New York: George Braziller.

———. 1981. The Doubles of Post-Modern. *Harvard Architectural Review*. 1 (Spring): 75–87.

———. 1986. *Pride of Place: Building the American Dream*. New York: Houghton Mifflin.

Stern, Robert A.M., ed. 1981. American Architecture: After Modernism. Special issue. *Architecture & Urbanism*. 3 (March).

Stern, Robert and John Montague Massengale, eds. 1981: The Anglo-American Suburb. *Architectural Design Profile*. 50 (10/11).

Stewart, Kathleen. 1988. Nostalgia-A Polemic. *Cultural Anthropology*. 3 (3): 227–41.

Sudjic, Deyan. 1991. *The 100-Mile City*. New York: André Deutsch.

Summerson, John. 1976. *The Architecture of Victorian London*. Charlottesville: University Press of Virginia.

Suttles, Gerald D. 1972. *The Social Construction of Community*. University of Chicago.

Sutton, Sharon E. 1991. Creating a Safe Space in which to Grow. *Architecture: Back to Life*. Washington DC: American Collegiate Schools of Architecture, 293–99.

Tafuri, Manfredo. 1976 [1973]. *Architecture and Utopia: Design and Capitalist Development*. Cambridge, MA: MIT.

———. 1980 [1976]. *Theories and History of Architecture*. New York: Harper & Row.

———. 1979. The Historical Project. *Oppositions*. 17.

———. 1987. *The Sphere and the Labyrinth: Avant-Gardes and Architecture from Piranesi to the 1970s*. Cambridge, MA: MIT.

Taylor, Mark C. 1989. Deadlines Approaching Architecture. M. Diani and C. Ingraham, eds. *Restructuring Architectural Theory*, 18–25.

Tempia, Emilio. 1977. Le dossier sur le concours. *Cahiers de l'IAURIF*. 47 (October).

———. 1982. *Pour une architecture urbaine*. Paris: Moniteur.

Thomas, John L. 1990. The Uses of Catastrophism: Lewis Mumford, Vernon

L. Parrington, Van Wyck Brooks, and the End of American Regionalism. *American Quarterly*. 42 (2), June: 223–51.

Thompson, E. P. 1967. Time, Work-Discipline, and Industrial Capitalism. *Past and Present*. 38: 56–97.

Toennies, Ferdinand. 1957. *Community and Society. Translation of Gemeinschaft & Gesellschaft.* 1887. Charles Loomis and John McKinney. East Lansing: Michigan State University.

Toulmin, Stephen. 1990. *Cosmopolis: The Hidden Agenda of Modernity.* New York: Free Press.

Trachtenberg, Marvin and Isabelle Hyman. 1986. *Architecture: From Prehistory to Post-Modernism.* NJ: Prentice-Hall/Abrams.

Trancik, Roger. 1986. *Finding Lost Space: Theories of Urban Design.* New York: Van Nostrand Reinhold.

Trucco, Terry. 1989. Two New Fronts in Charles's Architecture War. *New York Times.* September 9.

Tsing, Anna Lowenhaupt. 1992. *In the Realm of the Diamond Queen.* Princeton University.

Turner, Bryan S., ed. 1990. *Periodization and Politics in the Postmodern. Theories of Modernity and Postmodernity.* London: Sage, 1–13.

Turner, John. 1976. *Housing by People.* London: Marion Boyars.

Turner, John and Robert Fichter, eds. 1972. *Freedom to Build.* New York: Macmillan.

Tyler, Stephen A. 1986. Post-Modern Ethnography: From Document of the Occult to Occult Document. J. Clifford and G. E. Marcus, eds. *Writing Culture,* 122–40.

Tyrwhitt, Jaqueline. 1966. Education for Urban Design. Marcus Whiffen, ed. *The Architect and the City.* Cambridge, MA: MIT, 121–38.

Tyrwhitt, Jaqueline, J. L. Sert and E. N. Rogers, eds. 1952. *The Heart of the City: Towards the Humanization of Urban Life.* New York: Pellegrini & Cudahy.

Tzonis, Alexander. 1972. *Towards a Non-Oppressive Environment.* New York: George Braziller.

——. 1979. Architecture as a Social Science. Harvard University Faculty Paper Series, Department of Architecture.

Tzonis, Alexander and Liane Lefaivre. 1975. In the Name of the People. *Forum.* 3.

——. 1978. The Populist Movement in Architecture. Harvard University Faculty Paper Series, Department of Architecture. Translated by author from original Dutch edition, 1976.

——. 1980a. The Narcissistic Phase in Architecture. *Harvard Architectural Review,* 1, Spring: 53–61.

——. 1980b. Narcissism and Humanism in Contemporary Architecture. *Carré Bleu.* 4.

——. 1980c. *The Predicament of Architecture: Narcissism and Humanism in Contemporary Architecture.* Cambridge: Harvard GSD.

——. 1981. The Grid and the Pathway: An Introduction to the Work of Dimitris and Susana Antonakakis. *Architecture in Greece.* Athens, 15.

——. 1984. Commentary on UCL Zone Sociale. Richard Hatch, ed. *The Scope of Social Architecture,* 182–5.

——. 1986. *Classical Architecture: The Poetics of Order.* Cambridge, MA: MIT.

Underwood, Grahame. 1984. *The Security of Buildings.* London: Butterworth-Heinemann.

Upton, Dell. 1990. A Landscape Approach to Architectural History. Paper. Society of Architectural Historians conference. May.

Urbanisme. 1982. Naissance et renaissance de la cité. 190–91. See Jean Gohier, La campagne européenne pour la renaissance de la cité; A. Papageorgiou-Venetas, Tendances de la morphologie urbaine; and, Pierre Joly, Inventer la ville européenne.

Van der Ryn, Sim and Peter Calthorpe, eds., 1986, *Sustainable Communities*, San Francisco: Sierra Club Books.

Van Eyck, Aldo. 1962. Contributions. A. Smithson, ed. *Team 10 Primer.*

——. 1981. Rats, Posts, and Other Pests. Annual Discourse to the Royal Institute of British Architects. *RIBA Journal.* 88 (4): 47–50.

Ventre, Francis T. 1988. Myth and Paradox in the Building Industry. Paul Knox, ed. *The Design Professions and the Built Environment,* 147–74.

Venturi, Robert. 1966. *Complexity and Contradiction in Architecture.* New York: Museum of Modern Art.

——. 1968. A Bill Ding. Board involving Movies, Relics, and Space. *Architectural Forum.* April: 74–76.

——. 1983. Excerpt from *Complexity and Contradiction in Architecture.* Leland Roth, ed. American Builds. New York: Harper & Row, 619–35.

Venturi, Robert and Denise Scott Brown. 1980. Interview. *Harvard Architectural Review.* 1 (Spring).

Venturi, Robert, Denise Scott Brown, and Steven Izenour. 1977 [1972]. *Learning from Las Vegas.* Cambridge, MA: MIT.

Vergani, G., P. Shinoda, and D. Kesler. 1987. The Culture of Fragments. *PRECIS 6,* The Journal of the Columbia University Graduate School of Architecture Planning and Preservation.

Vidler, Anthony. 1978. The Third Typology. Delevoy, ed. *Rational Architecture,* 28–32.

——. 1991. The Scenes of the Street: Transformations in Ideal and Reality, 1750–1871. S. Anderson, ed. *On Streets,* 29–112.

——. 1992. *The Architectural Uncanny.* Cambridge, MA: MIT.

Viorst, Judith. 1986. *Necessary Losses.* New York: Ballantine.

Von Eckhardt, Wolf. 1967. *A Place to Live: The Crisis of the Cities.* Foreword by August Heckscher. New York: Dell.

Wallerstein, Immanuel. 1974. *The Modern Wold System: Capitalist Agriculture and the Origins of the European World-Economy in the 16th-century.* New York: Academic Press.

Walzer, Michael. 1986. Pleasure and Costs of Urbanity. *Dissent.* Fall: 470–75.

Warner, Sam Bass. 1983. The Management of Multiple Urban Images. *The Pursuit of Urban History.*

Warriner, Ken and Richard Conviser. 1986. Postmodernism and Community. J. William Carswell and David Saile, eds. *Purposes in Built Form and Culture Research,* 127–30.

Watkin, David. 1980. *The Rise of Architectural History.* London.

Watts, Steven. 1991. The Idiocy of American Studies: Poststructuralism, Language, and Politics in the Age of Self-Fulfillment. *American Quarterly.* 43 (4), December: 625–60.

Watson, Sophie and Katherine Gibson, eds. 1995. *Postmodern Cities and Spaces.* London: Blackwell.

Webber, Melvin. 1963. Order in Diversity, Community without Propinquity. L. Wingo Jr., ed. Cities and Space. *The Future Use of Urban Land.* Baltimore: Johns Hopkins University.

———. 1964. *The Urban Place and Non-Place Urban Realm. Explorations into Urban Structure.* Philadelphia: University of Pennsylvania.

Weisman, Leslie Kanes. 1992. *Discrimination by Design: A Feminist Critique of the Man-Made Environment.* Urbana: University of Illinois.

Weiss, Marc. 1990. Developing and Financing the "Garden Metropolis": Urban Planning and Housing Policy in the Twentieth Century. The Working Paper Series.

Wekerle, Gerda R. 1980. Women in the Urban Environment. Women and the American City. Special issue. *Signs.* Spring: 185–211.

Wekerle, Gerda, Rebecca Peterson, and David Morley. 1980. *New Space for Women.* Boulder, CO: Westview Press.

Wheelis, Allen. 1958. *The Quest for Identity.* New York: W. W. Norton.

Whiffen, Marcus, ed. 1966. *The Architect and the City.* Cambridge, MA: MIT. Papers delivered at the American Institute of Architects-Association of Collegiate Schools of Architecture seminar, 1962.

White, Dana. 1988. Frederick Law Olmsted, Placemaker. D. Schaeffer, ed. *Two Centuries of American Planning.* Baltimore: Johns Hopkins University Press.

White, Garrett. 1988. SCI-Arc. *L.A. Style.* September: 168–74, 264.

Whyte, William H. 1957. Urban Sprawl. *Fortune Magazine,* ed. *The Exploding Metropolis,* Garden City, NY: Doubleday Anchor, 115–39.

———. 1988. *City: Rediscovering the Center.* New York: Doubleday.

Williams, Sarah. 1985. More is More. (On Robert Stern.) *Art News.* January: 11–13.

Wines, James. 1988a. Postmodernist Classicism versus Narrative and De-construction in Architecture. Debate with Charles Jencks. New School for Social Research. February 25.

———. 1988b. *De-architecture.* New York: Rizzoli.

Wirth, Louis. 1938. Urbanism as a Way of Life. Albert J. Reiss, ed. *On Cities and Social Life.* University of Chicago.

Wise, Michael Z. 1994. Creating a New Architectural Vocabulary for a Democratic Berlin. *Los Angeles Times.* May 1: M2.

Wiseman, Carter. 1986. Case Study in Changing Urban Priorities. *Architectural Record. 5* (2), February: 81–83.

Wodiczko, Krzysztof. 1987. Strategies of Public Address. Hal Foster, ed., *Discussions in Contemporary Culture,* 1, 41–45.

Wolfe, Tom. 1980. Introduction. *VIA.* MIT and University of Pennsylvania. 4: 1–5.

———. 1981. *From Bauhaus to Our House.* New York: Farrar Strauss Giroux.

Woodbridge, Sally, ed. 1976. *Bay Area Houses.* New York: Oxford University.

Wright, Frank Lloyd. 1932. *The Disappearing City*. New York: W.F. Payson.

———. 1983 [1901]. The Art and Craft of the Machine. Leland Roth, ed. *America Builds*. New York: Harper & Row, 364–76.

Wright, Gwendolyn. 1981. *Building the Dream*. Cambridge, MA: MIT.

———. 1988. Urban Spaces and Cultural Settings. Zeynep Celik and Diane Favro, eds. *Journal of Architectural Education*. 4 (1/3): 10–14.

———. 1990. At Home and Abroad: French Colonial Planning in the Early Twentieth Century. Seminar on the City. Columbia University. March 13.

———. 1991. *The Politics of Design in French Colonial Urbanism*. University of Chicago.

———. 1994. Inventions and Interventions: American Urban Design in the Twentieth Century. Elizabeth A. T. Smith, compiler. *Urban Revisions: Current Projects for the Public Realm*. Cambridge, MA: MIT, 27–37.

Wright, Gwendolyn and Paul Rabinow. 1982. A Discussion of the Work of Michel Foucault. *Skyline*. March: 14–5.

Zavarzadeh, Mas'ud. 1976. *The Mythopoeic Reality: The Postwar American Nonfiction Novel*. Urbana: University of Illinois.

——— and Donald Morton. 1991. *Theory (Post) Modernity Opposition: An "Other" Introduction to Literary and Cultural Theory*. Washington DC: Maisonneuve Press.

Zeldin, Theodore. 1983. *The French*. New York: Random House.

Zucker, Paul. 1959. *Town and Square from the Agora to the Village Green*. NY: Columbia.

Zukin, Sharon. 1980. A Decade of the New Urban Sociology. *Theory and Society*. 9: 575–601.

——— 1982. *Loft Living: Culture and Capital in Urban Change*. Baltimore: Johns Hopkins University

———. 1988a. *Loft Living*. 2nd edition. London: Radius/Hutchinson.

———. 1988b. The Postmodern Debate over Urban Form. *Theory, Culture and Society*. 5: 431–46.

———. 1991. *Landscapes of Power: From Detroit to Disney World*. University of California.

Zwingle, Erla. 1991. Docklands London's New Frontier. *National Geographic*. July: 31–59.

INDEX

Abrams, Charles, 314, 315
Ackerman, James, 263n
Adorno, Theodor, 136, 146, 152n, 206, 217
advanced industrial capitalism, *see* postindustrialism
advocacy architecture and planning, 60, 65–6; *see also* community design
Agrest, Diana, 119n, 328
Ahwahnee Principles, The, 99
Alexander, Christopher, 62–3, 64, 66, 102, 172, 179, 196–7n, 211–12, 241, 244–5, 263n, 293n, 313, 314, 319, 321, 322, 328
Ambasz, Emilio, 230n, 303
Amendola, Giandomenico, 196n
American Institute of Planners conference, 65
American Institute of Architects (AIA), 65, 110, 204n, 252, 253–4, 329, 333
Anderson, Benedict, 149n
Anderson, Stanford, 119n, 321, 327
Ando, Tadao, 87, 332
Angélil, Marc and Sarah Graham, 192
Angus, Ian, 149n, 226n
Annales School, 80, 293n
anthropology, 268–69, 273–6, 278–80, 293n; *see also* social science, reconceiving culture
anti-planning, 6
Anzaldua, Gloria, 6
Appelbaum, Richard, 220, 230n
Appleyard, Donald, 62, 65, 166, 172, 197n, 245, 284, 313, 328
Archigram, 63, 115n
architectural exhibitions, 52–5
architectural publications, 163, 242,

architectural publications (continued), 253, 255
architectural training/education, 14–5, 238, 250
Arcosanti, *see* Paolo Soleri
AREA (Atelier de Recherche et Études d'Aménagement), 44, 47, 57n, 58n
Arendt, Hannah, 147–48n
Arensberg, Conrad, 273, 293n
Argan, G. C., 23
Arquitectonica, 121n, 242–3
Aslet, Clive, 329
Athens Charter, 22, 188, 203n, 210, 228n, 268; *see also* modern architecture, modern urbanism
Auzelle, Robert, 315
avant-garde, 146, 302, 307n
Aymonino, Carlo, 27, 314

Bacon, Edmund, 311, 315
Baird, George, 76, 316
Balfour, Alan, 332
Balmori, Diana, 191
Baltard, Victor, 46, 322
Baltimore, 103, 123n, 165
Banerjee, Tridib and Michael Southworth, 330
Banfield, Edward, 315
Banham, Reyner, 183, 195n, 312
Banlieues '89, 190, 326
Bardet, Gaston, 308,
Barnett, Jonathan, 249–50, 327
Baroque, 37, 57–8n, 286
Barragan, Luis, 323
Barre, François, 190–1, 204n
Barth, John, 141, 156, 282
Barthes, Roland, 148n, 210, 221, 226n,

Barthes, R. (continued), 238, 281, 283, 284
Bateson, Gregory, 12n
Bateson, Mary Catherine, 7
Battery Park City, 97–8, 121–22n, 159
Battle of the Marolle, 32
Baudrillard, Jean, 21n, 128–29, 136, 141, 148n, 184, 206, 238, 288, 289, 296n, 302
Bauhaus, 33, 150n, 209
Bauman, Zygmunt, 151n
Bell, David, 198–99n, 200n
Bell, Daniel, 14, 207, 226n, 264n, 288
Belluschi, Pietro, 318
Belmont, Joseph, 37, 194n, 253
Benevolo, Leonardo, 313
Benjamin, Walter, 149n, 286
Bergdoll, Barry, 184
Berger, John, 130, 160n
Berger, Bennett, 271–2
Bergum, Christian, 284
Berke, Deborah, 9–10, 194n, 333
Berman, Marshall, 214
Bernstein, Richard, 295n
Best, Steven and Douglas Kellner, 231n, 232n, 233n,
Beyer Blinder Belle, 98, 103
Bhabha, Homi, 289
Bindé, Jérome, 167, 293n
Biriotti, Roger, 49, 158
Blake, Peter, 263n, 289, 314, 321
Blakely, Edward and M.G. Snyder, 333
Blau, Judith, 255–6
Bletter, Rosemarie, 175
Bloomer, Kent, 164, 321
Blumenfeld, Hans, 314
Boddy, Trevor, 27, 164–65
Boehm, Gottfried, 328
Bofill, Ricardo, 38–9, 46–7, 52, 87, 98, 158, 174
Bohígas, Oriol, 87, 191, 204n
Bonfati,Enzo, 312, 319
Bookchin, Murray, 12n, 67, 263n, 314, 319

Borden, Iain, 332
border, 4–5, 6–7
borderlands, 6
Botta, Mario, 57n, 87
Boudon, Philippe, 47, 316
Bourdieu, Pierre, 136, 238, 264n
Bouyges headquarters, 102, 252
Boyer, Christine, 131, 134, 138, 151n, 160, 164, 167, 185, 198n, 232n, 263n, 283, 284, 285, 296n, 325, 332
Boyer Report, 7, 333
Brand, Stewart, 315
Brasilia, 224
Brill, Michael, 253
Bristol, Katherine, 263n
Broadbent, Geoffrey, 321
Brolin, Brent, 263n, 320, 323
Brown, Patricia Leigh, 184
Buchanan, Peter, 331
Bunshaft, Gordon, 329
Burchell, Robert W. and George Sternlieb, 322
Burgee, John, *see* Philip Johnson
Burger, Peter, 307n
Burgess, Ernest, 273
Burnham, Daniel, 81
Byrne, David, 240
Byrum, Oliver, 107

Callinicos, Alex, 231n
Calthorpe, Peter, 96–7, 121n, 197n, 229n, 301, 327, 331
Calvino, Italo, 222
Canary Wharf, 100
Cantal-Dupart, Michel, 326
Canter, David, 233n, 244
Carnegie Foundation, *see* Boyer Report.
Carpenter, Ben, 106
Carson, Rachel, 67, 313
Castells, Manuel, 157, 173, 196n, 197–98n, 224, 272, 318
Castex, Jean, 42, 320
Castro, Roland, 42, 43, 57n, 326

Cervellati, P.L, R. Scannavini, and C.
de Angelis, 36, 331, 326
Champenois, Michele, 31, 256
chaos, 7–8
Chaslin, François, 247, 285, 331
Chemetov, Paul, 44, 47, 50, 54
Chermayeff, Serge, 62–3, 172, 196–7n,
241, 244–45, 263n, 313
Chicago School, 268, 272–73
Chirac, Jacques, 47, 324
Choay, François, 177, 272, 297, 314
Chtcheglov, Ivan, 310–11
Churchill, Henry, 308, 311
Citicorp Tower, 92
citizen participation, *see* community
design
Citywalk, 168, 169
Civano, 99, 333, 257
Clarke, Paul Walker, 161, 182–83, 187,
200n, 201n, 202–3n, 245, 259, 263n,
264n
Clifford, James, 274, 283, 287
Coates, Nigel, 296n
Cohen, Jean-Louis, 78
Cohen, Stuart, 61
cohousing, 40, 47, 66, 116n
collage, 3, 48, 78, 79, 111, 127, 137,
138, 183, 282, 285, 286, 295n, 322
Collins, George and Christiane C.
Collins, 115n, 314, 327
Colquhoun, Alan, 194n, 299, 329
Columbia University, 237
Columbia new town, 119n
community architecture, *see* community design
community design, 40–1, 48–9, 65–6,
180, 193, 233n
community participation, *see* community design
Connor, Steven, 152–53n, 175–76,
198n
Conrads, Ulrich, 317
conservation, *see* historic preservation,
environmentalism, sustainability

contextualism, 16, 183, 185, 187, 248
Contraspazio, 27, 312
Cooke, Philip, 201n
Coop Himmelblau, 329
Cooper, Alexander, 97, 98, 122n
Corbett, Michael, 66, 324
corporate capitalism, *see* postindustri-
alism, flexible accumulation
cosmological natural selection, 8
Country Club Plaza, 105
Cowan, Stuart, 3
Cox, Harvey, 14, 66
Crapanzano, Vincent, 283, 296n
Crawford, Margaret, 10, 174, 181, 259
Crepu, Michel and Denis Lenglart,
256
Crime Prevention Through Environ-
mental Design (CPTED), 89
Crimp, Douglas, 136, 138, 231n
critical regionalism, 8, 86–7, 200n,
259, 284, 324, *see also* Kenneth
Frampton
Crow, Dennis, 330
CRS, 253
Cuff, Dana, 244–45, 257–58, 264n
Cullen, Gordon, 61, 263n, 312
Culot, Maurice, 30–4 *passim*, 57n, 257,
328
cultural modernism, 209
cultural theory/studies, 3, 6
culture, reconceiving, 273–76,
277–283 passim
Curtis, William, 331
cyburbia, 195n, 272

Daniels, Steven, 114n, 177
Davis, Doug, 160, 173, 175
Davis, Kingsley, 314
Davis, Mike, 92, 120n, 169, 327
Davis, Robert S., 94, 324
de Jouvenal, Bertrand, 150n
de Portzamparc, Christian, 43, 52, 54,
58n, 331, 332
de Man, Paul, 288, 295n, 322

Dear, Michael, 328, 330

Debord, Guy, 310, 311, 315

deconstructionism, 15, 24, 281, 295n, 329; *see also* Jacques Derrida and Paul de Man

deconstructivism, 196n, 213–14, 227n, 231n, 284–85, 305

defamiliarization, 112, 138, 269

Deleuze, Gilles and Felix Guattari, 5, 47, 139, 296n

Delevoy, Robert, 24, 28, 31, 56n, 284, 322

Dennis, Michael, 327,

Depaule, Jean-Charles, 42, 320

Derrida, Jacques, 24, 47, 206, 208, 221, 281, 284, 285, 315

Dethier, Jean, 32–3

Dewey, Fred, 195n, 272

Disney, 165, 174, 184, 203n, 310, 327

Dixon, Jeremy, 328

Docklands, 100

Doremus, Thomas, 333

double coding, 108, 140, 160, 222, 233n, 284, 288

Doxiadis, Constantinos, 14, 277, 313

DPZ, *see* Andres Duany, Elizabeth Plater–Zyberk

Drexler, Arthur, 322

Duany, Andres, 94–5, 99, 121n, 131, 324, 330, 333

Dunbar, Melville, 99

Dutton, Thomas, 157, 187, 200n, 201n, 259, 264n, 269–70, 272, 305

Dyckman, John, 114n, 156–57, 314, 315

Eagleton, Terry, 145, 296n

Eames, Charles and Ray, 12n

Eames, Edwin and Judith Goode, 293n

Eckbo, Garrett, 116n, 309

Eckstut, Stan, 97, 98, 122n

Eco, Umberto, 47, 163, 177, 231n

ecofeminism, 68, 208, 223, 226–27n,

ecofeminism (continued), *see also* ecological postmodernism

École National Supérieure des Beaux-Arts, 54, 210, 234, 237, 301, 316, 325

ecological planning, *see* environmentalism

ecological postmodernism, 223, 227n, *see also* ecofeminism

ecology, 3–4, 6

Economokis, Richard, 331

edge, focus on the, 4–5, 6–7, 190–91, 204n

edge cities, 106–7, 171, 183, 204n

Eigen, Edward, 331

Eikelman, Dale, 175

Einstein, Albert, 8

Eisenman, Peter, 5, 76, 77, 181, 285, 289, 305, 318, 321, 329, 332, 334

Eisner, Michael, 184

Eldredge, H. Wentworth, 315

Eliot, T. S., 75, 304

Engels, Freidrich, 68

Enlightenment project, the, 15, 16, 21n, 25, 125, 137, 147n, 155, 205–33, 270

Enterprise Zones, 84–5

environmental psychology, 67, 277, 312, 317

environmentalism, 8, 67–8, 176, 189, 208, 259–60, 223, 332, *see also* ecofeminism

Erskine, Ralph, 66, 319

Esherick, Joseph, 329

Essex new town, 99, 200, 318

ethnography and ethnology, 278, 280

façadism, 165–66

Faludi, Andreas, 318

Farelly, E.M., 198n

Fathy, Hassan, 74, 316

fear, 62, 125, 129, 144, 167–77, 201n

Fehn, Sverre, 333

feminism, 67–71, 118n, 208 *see also* ecofeminism

Fernandez-Galiano, Luis, 331
Ferris, Roger, 104
festival marketplace, 84, 165, 183
Festival of Autumn, Festival d'Automne, 54
Fiddler on the Roof, 129–30
Fiedler, Leslie, 145
Filler, Martin, 112
Fish, Stanley, 222, 305
Fishman, Robert, 264, 271, 273
Fischer, Michael, 275, 287
Fisher, Jack, 315
Fiszer, Stanislas, 44
Fleming, Ronald Lee, 99
Flusty, Steven, 92–3, 120n, 170
fold, 5–6
Ford, Henry, 209, 238, 239
Fortier, Bruno, 42
Foster, Hal, 190, 200n, 242, 289, 295n
Foster, Norman, 332
Foucault, Michel, 42, 135, 151n, 170, 200–1n, 206, 221, 222, 230n, 277–78, 288, 294n, 296n, 305, 316
Frampton, Kenneth, 25, 53, 76, 77, 86–7, 118n, 119n, 174, 184, 200n, 202n, 216, 222–23, 237, 259, 289, 302, 303, 305, 307n, 317, 318, 326, 328
French urban design and regional planning, 38–55, 175, 198n, 256, 319, 323, 324
Francescato, Guido, 160
Freedman, Jonathan, 320
Friedman, Yona, 63
Friedmann, John, 220, 223, 328
Fry, Maxwell, 316
Fukuyama, Francis, 215, 288
Fukuoka, 331
Fuller, Buckminster, 12, 63, 123n, 251, 315, 317
Fulton, William, 258
functionalism in social sciences, 19, 20, 268–69, 286
functionalism, critique of, *see* modern architecture and urbanism, critique of
Fussell, Paul, 141

Gablik, Suzi, 12n
Galbraith, Kenneth, 68, 150n
Gandelsonas, Mario, 25, 76, 177, 318
Gans, Herbert, 66, 82, 179, 191, 246, 273, 277, 313, 315
Garnier, Tony, 210, 229n
Garreau, Joel, 106, 107
Gastil, Raymond, 328
gated communities, 88–93, 167–68
Geddes, Patrick, 65, 72, 210, 294–95n
Geddes, Robert, 311
Geertz, Clifford, 274, 275, 276, 277, 282–83, 287, 293n
Gehry, Frank, 327, 329, 334
General Foods, 102, 252
gentrification, 45–6, 82–4, 183, 270
Getty Museum/Center, 109, 319, 326, 333
Ghirardo, Diane, 56n, 330, 332
Gibbard, Frederick, 310
Gibson, James, 309
Giedion, Sigfried, 303, 308, 309
Girardot, Jean-Paul, 48–51
Gitlin, Todd, 126, 138–39, 140, 141, 142, 151n, 153n, 287
Giurgola, Romaldo, 265n, 313
Glazer, Nathan, 314
Gleye, Paul Henry, 82, 187
globalization, 13, 124, 222, 250, 253, 269
Goldberger, Paul, 26, 54, 77, 81, 119n, 158, 199n, 231n, 252, 255, 256, 321, 322, 325
Goldstein, H. and S. Rosenberry, 322
Good Housekeeping, 132–33
Goodman, Paul, 61, 114–15n, 309
Goodman, Percival, 201n, 309, 321
Goodman, Robert, 63, 263n, 317
Gosling, David and Barry Maitland, 200n, 249, 268, 326

Gottmann, Jean, 14, 263n, 271, 312, 315

Gouldner, Alvin, 264n

Graff, Gerald, 214

Grands Projets, 50, 324

Grassi, Giorgio, 27

Graves, Michael, 77, 252, 305, 322, 325, 327

Greenblatt, Stephen, 294n

Gregotti, Vittorio, 27, 160, 314, 324

Griffin, David, 139, 221, 231n

Groat, Linda, 233n

Gropius, Walter, 83, 299, 317

Gruen, Victor, 14, 263n, 313, 314

Grumbach, Antoine, 42, 52, 285, 296n, 324

Guiheux, Alain, 178, 199n, 228n

Guillaume, Jacques, 198n

Gutierrez, Ramon, 219

Gutkind, E. A., 14, 313

Gutman, Robert, 248, 258, 277, 328

Haagen, Alexander, 90

Habermas, Jürgen, 54–5, 63, 115n, 125, 130, 150n, 171, 207–8, 221, 224, 226n, 233n, 313

Habraken, Nikolaas, 41, 312

Hadid, Zaha, 329, 334

Hahn, Tom, 9, 12n

Hall, Edward T., 244, 277, 311, 316, 320, 326

Hall, Peter, 176, 181, 265n

Halprin, Lawrence, 84, 90, 313, 316

Hamburger, Bernard, 44, 47

Hannerz, Ulf, 277

Hanson, Brian, 102

Harbison, Robert, 162

Harries, Karsten, 198n

Harris, Steven, 9–10, 333

Harvard University, 250, 266n, 321

Harvey, David, 111, 128, 130, 136, 137, 141, 149n, 150n, 151n, 165, 166–67, 183, 188, 195n, 196n, 203–4n, 209, 214, 215, 217, 226n,

Harvey, David (continued), 229n, 232n, 277, 281, 299, 300–1, 304–6 *passim*, 307n

Hassan, Ihab, 152n

Haussmann, Baron Georges Eugene, 45, 296n, 301

Hayden, Dolores, 69, 117n, 326

Hebdige, Dick, 233n

Hecksher, August, 112, 315

Hegemann, Werner and Elbert Peets, 329

Heidegger, Martin, 215, 300

Hejduk, John, 77, 305, 321

heritage industry, *see* historic preservation

heroic modernism, 209, 268

Hertzenberger, Herman, 41

Herzog and de Meuron, 334

Hester, Randy, 65–6

heterotopia, 111, 198n, 206, 222

Hewison, R., 129, 149n

high modernism, *see* universal modernism

Hines, Thomas, 81

His Royal Highness Prince of Wales, 57n, 100–2, 197n, 329

historic preservation, 45–6, 81–3, 93, 99, 150n, 161, 167, 176

Hitchcock, H.R., 329

Hobsbawm, Eric, 130, 149–50n

Hoch, Charles, 230n

Holl, Steven, 5, 8–9, 191, 331

Hollein, Hans, 327

Holston, James, 159, 176, 182, 194n, 203n, 224, 228n, 231n, 258, 329

homesteading, 72

Horkheimer, Max, 206

Howard, Ebenezer, 210, 308

Hudnut, Joseph, 108, 309

Huertas, Claude, 194n

Huet, Bernard, 31, 42, 52, 58n, 229n, 258, 322, 323, 328

Hugo, Victor, 28–9, 256

human ecology, 268, 272–3

Hutcheon, Linda, 152n
Hutchinson, Maxwell, 101–2
Huxtable, Ada Louise, 156, 173, 178,
    199n, 204n, 242, 263n, 313, 324, 326
Huyssen, Andreas, 21n, 114n, 139,
    146, 152n, 153n, 215, 227n, 233n,
    296n, 299, 302
hyperreality, 128, 163, 166, 183, 184,
    220

IBA competition, 35, 57n, 319
Illich, Ivan, 12n, 65
imagineering, 161
Imperatore, Arthur, 98
Ingersoll, Richard, 157–8, 194n, 203n,
    272, 289
Iñiguez, Manuel, 38–40
Institute for Architecture and Urban
    Studies, 26, 76, 119n, 318
interior design, 85–6
International Style, *see* modern archi-
    tecture
intertextuality (or trans–textuality),
    281
invention of tradition, of history, of
    the past, 13, 83, 93–4, 130, 149n,
    161, 163, 166, 189, 194n
irony, 18, 139–42, 160, 195n
Ishiyama, Osamu, 331
Isozaki, Arata, 327, 331
Izenour, Steven, *see* Venturi, Scott
    Brown and Izenour

Jackson, John Brinkerhof, 73–4, 204n,
    238, 313
Jackson, Kenneth, 271
Jacobs, Allan, 166, 172, 197n, 245,
    263n, 284, 328
Jacobs, Jane, 14, 61, 62, 64, 82, 115n,
    150n, 156, 172, 179, 311, 312, 315
Jahn, Helmut, 334
Jameson, Fredric, 136, 145–446, 147n,
    151n, 217, 218, 232n, 272, 280, 305,
    326

Janss Court building, 104, 105
Japanese Metabolists, 63
Jarzombek, Mark, 183, 196n, 201n
Jencks, Charles, 6, 7, 57n, 76, 80,
    108–9, 112, 119n, 123n, 139, 140,
    160, 196n, 221, 222, 233n, 263n,
    284, 288, 304, 307n, 316, 318, 321,
    323, 325, 328, 330, 331, 332, 333
Johnson, Barbara, 295n
Johnson Fain and Pereira Associates,
    192, 204n
Johnson, Lyndon B., 315
Johnson, Philip, 47, 80, 98, 110, 119n,
    171, 252, 322, 329,
Jonas, S., 294n
Jones, E. Fay, 330
Jouy-le-Moutier, 44
Julienne, Loic and Jean-Marie Man-
    don, 272

Kahn, Louis, 216
Kahn, Terry, 265n
Kaplan, Marshall, 249
Kaplan McLaughlin Diaz, 103, 104
Kaplan, Sam Hall, 252, 253
Kasinitz, Phil, 82–3
Katz, Peter, 332
Kelbaugh, Doug, 197n, 329
Kennedy, John F., 312
Kidney, Walter, 319
Kingwell, Mark, 2
Kipnis, Jeffrey, 5
Kirshenblatt-Gimblett, Barbara, 187,
    203n
kitsch, 153n, 166, 196n
Klapp, Orin, 152n
Klotz, Heinrich, 110, 194–5n, 196n,
    317, 327, 328
Koestler, Arthur, 8
Koetter, Fred, 272, 321
Koh, Jusuck, 259–60, 266n
Kolb, David, 330
Koning Eisenberg Architects, 192
Koolhaas, Rem, 191, 321, 329, 330,

Koolhaas, Rem (continued), 331, 332, 333, 334
Kopp, Anatole, 163, 233n
Kostof, Spiro, 260, 287
Kreditor, Alan, 250
Krieger, Alex, 191–2, 330
Krier, Léon, 28–32, 52, 57n, 94–5, 157, 160, 174–5, 191, 257, 305, 321–22, 323, 327, 329, 330, 331
Krier, Rob, 31, 57n, 160, 257, 320, 326, 328
Kristeva, Julia, 226n, 281
Kroll, Lucien, 40, 48, 50, 55, 58a, 279–80, 317, 326
Kropf, Karl, 333
Kruger, Barbara, 144
Kuhn, Thomas, 293n
Kuspit, Donald, 127

La Cambre, 31, 32, 33, 317
Laisney, François, 42
Lampugnani, V. M., 326
Lang, Jack, 45
Langdon & Wilson, 319
Lapham, Lewis, 127
Larson, Magali Sarfatti, 331
Las Colinas, 106–7
Lash, Scott, 166, 196n
late-industrial capitalism, *see* postindustrialism, flexible accumulation
Laugier, Marc-Antoine, 23
Lavedan, Pierre, 314
Lears, Jackson, 230n
Le Corbusier, 25, 28, 34, 83, 210, 211, 216, 229n, 268, 299, 305, 314
Le Dantec, Jean, 42, 43
Lee, Douglas, 63, 318
Lefaivre, Liane, 22, 26, 86, 173, 178, 181, 200n, 324, 328
Lefebvre, Henri, 10, 16, 43, 238, 263n, 272, 309, 315, 317, 318, 319, 320
Leger, Fernand, 304
legitimacy crisis, 218, 267, 291
Legoretta, Ricardo, 121n

Leibman Melting Partnership, 120n, 122n
Lennertz, William, 330
Leopold, Aldo, 12n
Lesnikowski, Wojciech, 47, 111, 114n, 160, 178, 202n, 204n, 232n, 297–°°98, 304
Lesser, Alexander, 56n
Levine, Robert, 307n
Lévi-Strauss, Claude, 24, 79, 274, 282
Levitas, Gloria, 328
Levitt, Abraham,235, 238–39
Lewis, David, 66
Ley, David, 16, 155, 166, 179–80, 188, 203–4n, 296n, 297
Libeskind, Daniel, 5, 329, 334
literary criticism, 280–84, 294n
loft-living, 83–4, 162
Logan, J.R. and Todd Swanstrom, 223
Loi Malraux, 45–6
Loos, Adolphe, 38, 226n, 248
Lucan, Jacques, 114n, 159, 194n, 216, 330
Lynch, Kevin, 48, 61, 62, 63, 65, 204n, 263n, 283, 295n, 312, 313, 314, 318, 320, 323, 330
Lyndon, Donlyn, 321
Lynn, Greg, 5–6
Lyotard, Jean-François, 114n, 206, 222, 226n, 305

Mack, Mark, 331
Mackay, David, 204n
Maki, Fumihiko, 332
Malinowski, Bronislaw, 268, 304
Malraux, André, 145, 316
Mangin, David, 25–6, 159, 187, 194n
Mann, Dennis Alan, 245
Mann, Thomas, 304
March, Lionel, 212
Marché des Halles, 46–7, 322
Marcus, George, 275, 278–9, 283, 287, 294n

Marcuse, Herbert, 19
Marcuse, Peter, 12n
Martin, Bernice, 307n
Marx, Karl, 129, 149n, 167, 191, 271
Maslow, Abraham, 268
master-planned communities, 87–8, 163
Mayo, James, 230n
Mazumdar, Sanjoy, 279
McDermott, John, 295n
McHarg, Ian, 12n, 67, 179, 204n, 238, 277, 313, 315, 316
McLeod, Mary, 76, 160, 211
McLuhan, Marshall, 126, 305
megalopolis, 271
Meier, Richard, 77, 119n, 305, 326, 333
Mestrovic, Stjepan, 137, 166, 196n, 214–5, 226n, 231n
meta-narratives, 19, 275, 288, 292
Meyrowitz, Joshua, 14
Mies van der Rohe, Ludwig, 75, 80, 210, 216, 299, 317
Mills, Caroline, 166, 188, 203–4n, 277
Mills, C. Wright, 135–6, 147n, 149n, 217, 241, 252, 258, 265n, 270, 311
Miller, Donald, 327
Mitchell, William, 263n
Mitterand, François, 50, 324, 326
modern architecture and urbanism (urban design), and critique of, 15, 16, 22–3, 24, 182, 224–25, 233n, 289–91, 324, 334
Modern Movement, *see* modern architecture and urbanism
Modern project, the, *see* the Enlightenment project
Moholy-Nagy, Sibyl, 315
Moneo, Rafael, 160, 333
Montès, Fernando, 31, 44, 54,
Montgomery, Roger, 245, 312
monumentality, 26, 38, 41, 111
Moore, Charles, 57n, 63–4, 66, 77, 80–1, 115n, 116n, 121n, 161, 320,
Moore, Charles (continued), 321, 323

Moravia, Alberto, 147n
morphology, 23, 25, 29, 42
Morrish, William and Catherine Brown, 192–93, 204n
Moses, Robert, 324
Moule & Polyzoides, 121n, 122–23n, 333
Movement for the Reconstruction of the European City, 27–31 *passim*, 194n
multiculturalism, 19, 23, 175
Mumford, Lewis, 63, 72–3, 263n, 271, 308, 310, 312, 315, 327
Muratori, Saverio, 27, 311
Murphy, Brian, 91–2, 162
Murphy, Cullen, 289, 296n
Muschamp, Herbert, 21n, 25, 81, 159, 187, 192, 265–66n
music, 134
Myer, J.R., 313
Myerhoff, Barbara, 141, 282

Nairn, Ian, 61, 82
Naizot, Guy, 240
Nalbantoglu, G.B. and W.C. Thai, 333
National Environmental Policy Act, 116n
neighborhood associations, 89
neoclassicism, 37–40, 109, 173–75, 198n, 301, 304, 322
neorationalism, 23–36, 216
neotraditional urbanism, 93–105
Nesbit, Lois, 243
Nesbitt, Kate, 332
New Historicism, 294n
new regionalism, 74, 118n
New Urbanism, The, 93–105, 331, 333, 334
New York Neo-Rationalist School or "The Five," 77, 305
Newman, Charles, 127
Newman, Oscar, 63, 89, 312, 318
Nichols, Jesse Clyde, 105
Niemeyer, Oscar, 182, 329
Nietzsche, F. W., 142, 221, 232n, 300

Nilsen, Richard, 12n
NIMBYism, 131, 176
Noever, Peter, 333
Norberg-Schulz, Christian, 64, 67, 76, 313, 322
nostalgia, 13, 19, 24, 26, 29, 106, 109, 124, 126, 134, 147n, 157, 159, 162, 167, 189
Nouvel, Jean, 54, 55, 323, 324
Noviant, Patrice, 166, 176

Ockman, Joan, 230–1n, 307n, 331
Olmsted, Frederick Law, 63, 115n, 204n
Olsen, Donald, 191
open architecture, 40–1
Oppositions, 26, 76–7, 78, 119n, 318

Packard, Vance, 14, 21n
Pancreacíh, Georges, 47
Panerai, Philippe, 42, 320
panopticon, 90, 170–71, 278
Papadakis, Andreas, 330
paradigm shift, 267, 293n
Pareles, Jon, 134
Parent, Claude, 183
Paris Biennale, 54–5, 323, 325
Park Labrea, 90–1
participatory architecture, *see* community design
Pawley, Martin, 14, 125–27, 131–2, 148n, 183–4, 195n, 196n, 202n, 251–52, 254–55, 295n, 330
Pecora, Vincent, 259
Pedestrian Pocket, 94, 96, 121n, 197n
Pei, I. M., 326
Pelli, Cesar, 321
Perez and Associates and Charles Moore, *see* Piazza d'Italia
Pérez-Gómez, Alberto, 325
peripheries, *see* edge, border
Perloff, Harvey, 315
Peterson, Steven, 47–8
Piano, Renzo, 324, 334

Piazza d'Italia, 161, 320
Picasso, Pablo, 304
picturesque, the, 61, 114n, 176–77
Planned-Unit Developments, 87–8
planner, the role and profession of the, 108, 115–16n, 119n, 210, 211–13, 220, 225, 249–51, 264–65n, 268–69, 287
Plater-Zyberk, Elizabeth, 94–5, 99, 121n, 131, 324, 330, 333
Plattus, Alan, 114n, 215–6
Playa Vista, 95, 121n
Poëte, Marcel, 315
political correctness, 19, 130, 254, 288
Pope, Albert, 200
Popenoe, David, 131
Popova-Kerbel, Maria V., 105
Porphyrios, Demetri, 331
Port Liberté, 98
Portman, John, 93, 120n, 121n, 123n, 253–4
Portoghesi, Paolo, 27, 52–3, 56n, 200n, 201n, 323, 325
post-occupancy studies, 66
postindustrialism, 201–2n, 203n, 206, 211, 217–18, 229n, 251, 257, 265n, 269–71, 293n
postmodern architecture and urban design, 1, 14, 60, 86–7, 107–13, 159–60, 179, 182, 185–9, 212, 216, 291, 309, 321, 322, 329
postmodern social science, 273–76, 277–79, 282–83, 286–88, 293n
postmodernism, def., 108, 123n, 147n
poststructuralism, 15, 143, 206, 226n
Poundbury, 101
Predock, Antoine, 327
Prince Charles, *see* His Royal Highness Prince of Wales
Pritzker Prize, 74, 322–34 *passim*
Proshansky, Harold, 116n, 277, 312
proxemics, *see* Edward T. Hall
Pruitt-Igoe housing projects, 203n, 234, 263n, 318

Quatremère de Quincy, 23, 26, 40

Rabinow, Paul, 175, 201n, 263n, 278
Radcliffe–Brown, A. R., 268, 304
Radin, Max, 149n
Rails-to-Trails Conservancy, 192
Rapoport, Amos, 277, 316, 330
Rasmussen, Steen Eiler, 309, 311
Reagan, Ronald, 127, 175
Redfield, Robert, 273
Regional/Urban Design Assistance
    Teams, 65
Reichen, Bernard, 16
Relph, Edward, 14, 120n, 187, 198n,
    211, 231–32n, 250, 320
Reps, John, 315
Reston new town, 98, 119n
restoration, rehabilitation, *see* historic
    preservation, gentrification
Riboud, Jacques, 44, 58n–59n
Richards, J. M., 61
Ricoeur, Paul, 219
Ritchie, Ian, 12n
Roach, Catherine, 3
Robertson, Roland, 147n, 215
Roche, Kevin, 102, 252, 325, 332
Rodwin, Lloyd, 314, 315
Rollwagen, Jack, 276
Roma Interotta, 35, 322
romanticism, 13–9, 209, 297–98, 300,
    301, 304
Rosaldo, Michelle, 307n
Rosaldo, Renato, 6
Rosenau, Pauline Marie, 139, 227–8n,
    270, 275
Rosenberg, Harold, 307a
Rossi, Aldo, 24–7, 53, 56n, 160, 191,
    314, 319, 325, 330
Rotondi, Michael, 204n
Rouse, James, 84, 119n
Rowe, Colin, 77–8, 157–58, 194n,
    263n, 272, 285, 304, 320, 321, 322
Rudofsky, Bernard, 73, 314, 316, 321
Rudolph, Paul, 237

Russell, Beverly, 263n
Rybczynski, W., 252, 253
Rykwert, Joseph, 203n, 229n, 309, 328

Saarinen, Eliel, 309
Saarinen, Esa, 221, 232n
Safdie, Moshe, 73, 252, 315, 317, 324
Said, Edward, 137
Sammarcelli, Francoise, 281–2
Sarfati, Alain, 44, 47, 54
Sartre, Jean-Paul, 196n
Schein, Ionel, 324
Schlesinger, Arthur, 191, 271
Schnaidt, Claude, 22
Schneider, David, 287
Schoonbrodt, Rene, 32, 328
Schumacher, E. F., 12n, 67, 211, 266n
Schumacher, Tom, 79, 210, 317, 328
Schwartz, Martha, 331
Schwarzer, Mitchell, 4
science fiction, cyberpunk literature,
    135, 221
Scolari, Massimo, 312, 319, 322
Scott, Bonnie Kime, 271
Scott Brown, Denise, 74–5, 184, 202n,
    250, 258, 309, 318, 320, 330
Scully, Vincent, 76, 85, 119n, 265n,
    314, 316, 319, 325
Seaside, 94–5, 101, 324
security, *see* fear
Sejma, Kazuyo, 334
semiology, 177–8
Sennett, Richard, 14, 63, 125, 148n,
    150n, 190, 197n, 263n, 317, 320,
    330, 332
Sert, José Luis, 210, 310
Service, Alastair, 320
Shane, Grahame, 302
Sharp, Thomas, 176
Sharpe, William and Leonard Wal-
    lock, 271
Sherman, Cindy, 128
shopping mall, 168, 196n
Situationists, 10, 311

Shweder, Richard, 21n
Silver, Nathan, 76, 318
Silvetti, Jorge, 266n
Simmel, Georg, 2, 144, 232n
simulacra, simulacrum, 128, 130,
    147n, 148n, 164, 195n
Sitte, Camillo, 35, 115n, 297, 300, 301,
    308
Siza, Alvaro, 331
Sjoberg, Gideon, 312, 314, 315
Skidmore, Owings & Merrill, 100
Slovic, David, 66
Smithson, Alison and Peter Smithson,
    303, 307n, 313
Smolin, Lee, 8
Soja, Edward, 272, 277, 293n
Soleri, Paolo, 67, 317
Solomon, Daniel, 163
Sommer, Robert, 316, 319, 320
Sorkin, Michael, 195n, 272, 289, 324,
    332
Speer, Albert, 35
Spens, Michael, 333
Spoerry, François, 30, 44, 98, 315
Spreiregen, Paul, 314
Spretnak, Charlene, 143, 208, 221,
    225 7n
Stein, Achva Benzinberg, 193
Stein, Clarence, 14, 310, 311
Stein, Gertrude, 126
Stein, Joseph, 129–30
Stephens, Suzanne, 324
Stern, Robert, 77, 80, 102–3, 109–10,
    156, 160, 176, 184, 201n, 248, 284,
    316, 321, 323, 324, 327, 328
Stevens, Wallace, 140
Stewart, Kathleen, 126
Stirling, James, 35, 19, 322, 324, 329
structural linguistics, structuralism,
    24, 77, 148–49n, 177–78, 226n, 274,
    305
Stubbins, Hugh, 92
suburbanization, 15, 19, 87, 235–36,
    323, 329

Sudjic, Deyan, 272
Sullivan, Louis, 210, 268, 300
Summerson, John, 320
sustainability, 8, 67, 72, 116n, 189,
    204n, 260
Suttles, Gerald, 14, 283
Sutton, Sharon, 150n
Swaback, Vernon, 12n

Tafuri, Manfredo, 26, 27, 217, 218,
    229n, 232n, 250
Tamiguchi, Yoshio, 334
Tange, Kenzo, 328
Taylor, Charles, 7
Taylor, Mark, 152n
Team X, 26, 41, 119n, 303, 307n, 309,
    313
television, 125–7, 128, 131, 132–33,
    144, 148n, 150n
Tempia, Emilio, 179, 200n
Tendanza, La, 25, 57n
Terry, Quinlan, 57n, 160
Tessenow, Heinrich, 34–5
theme parks, 90, 161, 165
Thompson, Benjamin, 84, 331
Thompson, E. P., 268
Tigerman, Stanley, 321
Todd, John, 12n
Toennies, Ferdinand, 34–5
Tolstoy, Leo, 140
Toulmin, Stephen, 145, 153n, 217,
    298, 302, 305, 307n
townscape movement, 61–4, 309
Toynbee, Arnold, 307n
Traditional Neighborhood Develop-
    ment, 94–5, 197n; *see also* Andres
    Duany, Elizabeth Plater–
    Zyberk, and New Urbanism
Trancik, Roger, 327
transfiction, 281
Transit-Oriented Developments, 96
Trilling, Lionel, 264n
Tschumi, Bernard, 50, 285, 326, 329,
    334

Tsing, Anna Lowenhaupt, 6
Tunnard, Christopher, 315
Turner, John, 65, 66, 181
Tusquets, Oscar, 331
Two Rodeo Drive, 103, 104
Tyler, Stephen, 278, 294n
typology, type, 23, 25, 42, 160
Tyrwhitt, Jaqueline, 14, 250, 310, 313
Tzara, Tristan, 295n
Tzonis, Alexander, 26, 76, 86, 173,
    178, 181, 318, 320, 323, 324, 328

universal modernism, 211, 232n
urban architecture, 36, 41–5, 179–80,
    194n, 319
urban design, defined, 249–50
urban designer, the role and profes-
    sion of, 107–8, 154–56, 180–83,
    208–9, 212–13, 225, 258, 260–61,
    276, 279, 284–85, 286–92
urban social theory 66; *see also*
    Chicago School, Lefebvre, Castells,
    Harvey
Urban Renewal, 234–5
urbanism, 250, 272

van Eyck, Aldo, 303, 324
Van Tilburg, Johannes, 104
Van der Ryn, Sim, 3, 327
Vasconi, Claude, 47
Venice Biennale of 1980, 52, 54, 224
Venice Triennale of 1973, 27, 319
Venturi, Scott Brown & Izenour, 74–5,
    184, 202n
Venturi, Robert, 55, 74–6, 77, 156,
    160, 184, 202n, 218, 263n, 284, 313,
    314, 315, 318, 331
vernacular design, 16, 72–4, 118n, 300
Vichy regime, 16
Vidler, Anthony, 28–9, 56–7n, 76,
    152n, 204n, 210–11, 229n, 285,
    303–4, 318, 322, 328
Viollet-le-Duc, Eugene-Emanuel, 216

Viorst, Judith, 147n
Von Eckardt, Wolf, 315

Wagner, Otto, 279, 299, 301
Wallerstein, Immanuel, 272
Walt Disney Company, *see* Disney
Warhol, Andy, 304
Warner, Sam Bass, 283, 296n
Warriner, Ken and Richard Conviser, 283
Watkin, David, 323, 331
Watson, Harriet, 330
Watts, Steven, 143
Weaver, Robert, 65
Webber, Melvin, 271, 314, 315
Weber, Max, 12n
Weiss, Marc, 264–65n
Wekerle, Gerda, 71
Wells, H. G., 271, 272
Whitehead, Alfred North, 8
Whyte, William H., 310, 315, 328
Wilford, Michael, 108
Willats, Stephen, 332
Wines, James, 12n
Wirth, Louis, 128, 250, 273
Wodiczko, Krzysztof, 307n
Wolfe, Tom, 22, 177, 195n, 231n, 323
Wood, Robert, 315
Woodbridge, Sally, 320
Wright, Frank Lloyd, 65, 67, 83,
    229n, 271, 311
Wright, Gwendolyn, 71, 175,
    199–200n, 230n, 278, 307n

Yale University, 237, 295n
Yamasaki, Minoru, 318; *see also*
    Pruitt–Igoe housing projects
Yaro, Robert, 94

Zavarzadeh, Mas'ud, 282
Zeldin, Theodore, 256
zoning, 27, 64, 111
Zucker, Paul, 311
Zukin, Sharon, 83–4, 162, 195n, 214, 252